A Celebration of Poets

South
Grades 7-9
Fall 2008

creativeCOMMUNICATION
A CELEBRATION OF TODAY'S WRITERS

A Celebration of Poets
South
Grades 7-9
Fall 2008

AN ANTHOLOGY COMPILED BY CREATIVE COMMUNICATION, INC.

Published by:

creativeCOMMUNICATION
A CELEBRATION OF TODAY'S WRITERS

1488 NORTH 200 WEST • LOGAN, UTAH 84341
TEL. 435-713-4411 • WWW.POETICPOWER.COM

All rights reserved. No part of this book may be reproduced or transmitted in any form or by any means, electronic or mechanical without written permission of the author and publisher.

Copyright © 2009 by Creative Communication, Inc.
Printed in the United States of America

ISBN: 978-1-60050-227-9

FOREWORD

When Charles Dickens wrote, "It was the best of times, it was the worst of times," he was describing a period of history that occurred over one hundred years ago. Dickens' words could easily describe many periods of history. They seem to be especially applicable today. If you listen to the media, we have much to fear: terrorism, crime, the economy. These are all messages that bombard us through newspapers, radio and television. However, in reading the poems inside this anthology, these student writers reflect a much different world. These poets reflect their world in a fresh voice. This book is not filled with pessimism and fear. Instead, they provide an optimistic hope. The "best of times" is still with us.

We hope you enjoy this book as much as we enjoyed reading each poem. There were thousands of poets who entered our writing contest and were not chosen to be published. I congratulate all the poets who entered. They each took the time to share a bit of themselves with us. This book is dedicated to them and to those that helped inspire and guide their words.

Thomas Worthen, Ph.D.
Editor
Creative Communication

WRITING CONTESTS!

Enter our next POETRY contest!

Enter our next ESSAY contest!

Why should I enter?
Win prizes and get published! Each year thousands of dollars in prizes are awarded in each region and tens of thousands of dollars in prizes are awarded throughout North America. The top writers in each division receive a monetary award and a free book that includes their published poem or essay. Entries of merit are also selected to be published in our anthology.

Who may enter?
There are four divisions in the poetry contest. The poetry divisions are grades K-3, 4-6, 7-9, and 10-12. There are three divisions in the essay contest. The essay divisions are grades 3-6, 7-9, and 10-12.

What is needed to enter the contest?
To enter the poetry contest send in one original poem, 21 lines or less. To enter the essay contest send in one original essay, 250 words or less, on any topic. Each entry must include the student's name, grade, address, city, state, and zip code, and the student's school name and school address. Students who include their teacher's name may help their teacher qualify for a free copy of the anthology. Contest changes and updates are listed at www.poeticpower.com.

How do I enter?

Enter a poem online at:
www.poeticpower.com

or

Mail your poem to:
Poetry Contest
1488 North 200 West
Logan, UT 84341

Enter an essay online at:
www.studentessaycontest.com

or

Mail your essay to:
Essay Contest
1488 North 200 West
Logan, UT 84341

When is the deadline?
Poetry contest deadlines are August 18th, December 3rd, and April 14th. Essay contest deadlines are July 15th, October 15th, and February 17th. You can enter each contest, however, send only one poem or essay for each contest deadline.

Are there benefits for my school?
Yes. We award $15,000 each year in grants to help with Language Arts programs. Schools qualify to apply for a grant by having a large number of entries of which over fifty percent are accepted for publication. This typically tends to be about 15 accepted entries.

Are there benefits for my teacher?
Yes. Teachers with five or more students accepted to be published receive a free anthology that includes their students' writing.

For more information please go to our website at **www.poeticpower.com**, email us at editor@poeticpower.com or call 435-713-4411.

TABLE OF CONTENTS

POETIC ACHIEVEMENT HONOR SCHOOLS 1

LANGUAGE ARTS GRANT RECIPIENTS 5

GRADES 7-8-9 9
    TOP POEMS 10
    HIGH MERIT POEMS 20

INDEX 201

STATES INCLUDED IN THIS EDITION:

ALABAMA
GEORGIA
LOUISIANA
MISSISSIPPI
NORTH CAROLINA
SOUTH CAROLINA

Fall 2008 Poetic Achievement Honor Schools

* Teachers who had fifteen or more poets accepted to be published

The following schools are recognized as receiving a "Poetic Achievement Award." This award is given to schools who have a large number of entries of which over fifty percent are accepted for publication. With hundreds of schools entering our contest, only a small percent of these schools are honored with this award. The purpose of this award is to recognize schools with excellent Language Arts programs. This award qualifies these schools to receive a complimentary copy of this anthology. In addition, these schools are eligible to apply for a Creative Communication Language Arts Grant. Grants of two hundred and fifty dollars each are awarded to further develop writing in our schools.

Albemarle School
  Elizabeth City, NC
    Mrs. C. Mann*

Alexandria Middle Magnet School
  Alexandria, LA
    Stacy Gunter*
    Mrs. Parmely

Appling County Middle School
  Baxley, GA
    Melanie Clark*
    Sue Hayes*
    Suzanne Herrington*
    Pamela P. Johnson*

Ardrey Kell High School
  Charlotte, NC
    Polly Paulson*

Armstrong Middle School
  Starkville, MS
    Miki Christy*

Atlanta Academy
  Roswell, GA
    Josephine Slater*

Bishop Noland Episcopal Day School
  Lake Charles, LA
    Beverly Kelley*

Carolina International School
  Harrisburg, NC
    Lorraine Belachew*

Cathedral School
  Raleigh, NC
    Diane Lee*

Challenger High School
  Hickory, NC
    Paul Bonham*

Chapin Middle School
  Chapin, SC
    Shannon Allonier*
    Martina D. Fox

Dillard Drive Middle School
  Raleigh, NC
    Mrs. C. Duerr*

East Millbrook Magnet Middle School
Raleigh, NC
    Kathryn Lapinski*

Fannin County Middle School
Blue Ridge, GA
    Anona Hemming*

Fayette Middle School
Fayetteville, GA
    Dr. Franklin
    Mrs. Gillette
    Laurie Gividen
    Kristen Rutland
    Ms. Tallman
    Juliana Wright

First Flight Middle School
Kill Devil Hills, NC
    Jill Morris*
    Colleen Vaughan

Haynes Academy for Advanced Studies
Metairie, LA
    Teresa Bennett
    Cheryl Bordelon
    Sandra DeMers*
    Janet C. Gubler
    Faye Haley*
    Judy Kase
    Juliet Kellam*
    Wendi Majeau
    Leslie Straight*

Hubert Middle School
Savannah, GA
    Dr. Wanda Denise Dixon*

L E Gable Middle School
Roebuck, SC
    Janet Bittner
    Wanda Forrest*
    Cassie Hampton*
    Dawn Williams

Lake Castle Private School
Slidell, LA
    Christine Monnin*

Lake Middle School
Lake, MS
    Lisa Johnson*

Laurin Welborn Middle School
High Point, NC
    Tully Ritchie*

Leesville Road High School
Raleigh, NC
    Carlie Bowman*
    Eric Broer
    Carol Brown

Leesville Road Middle School
Raleigh, NC
    Vickie Newland*

Leonville Elementary School
Leonville, LA
    Lisa Abshire
    Barbara Jesclard*

Marion High School
Marion, AL
    Ida Longmire*

McKee Jr High School
Montgomery, AL
    Stanford Angion*

Mount Carmel Academy
New Orleans, LA
    Karla Amacker*
    Ms. Binder
    Melissa Gayé
    Mrs. Geeck
    Kristen Hode*
    Gilly Jaunet*
    Jennifer Kadden*
    Andrea Kurica
    Jennifer Smith

Poetic Achievement Honor Schools

North Iredell Middle School
Olin, NC
Sandra Ellis*

North Wilkes High School
Hays, NC
Jennifer M. Sorel*

Northgate High School
Newnan, GA
Sherry Leigh Taylor*

Opelousas Jr High School
Opelousas, LA
Kelia Singleton-Guillory*

Priceville Jr High School
Decatur, AL
Judith Winton*

Providence High School
Charlotte, NC
Ann Hopkins*

Rock Mills Jr High School
Rock Mills, AL
Brandy Pike*
Jeffery Thompson*

Sacred Heart of Jesus School
Baton Rouge, LA
Catherine Tallman*

Saint Pauls Middle School
Saint Pauls, NC
Donald Weller*

Scotts Creek Elementary School
Sylva, NC
Jill Cook
Laura H. Wallace*
Phil Woody

Smiths Station High School
Smiths Station, AL
Michelle Mullinax*

St Andrews Middle School
Charleston, SC
Mrs. Garrison
Lizabeth McGrath*

St Francis Xavier School
Birmingham, AL
Jean Lindquist*

St John Neumann Regional Catholic School
Lilburn, GA
Barbara Sneed*

St Margaret School
Lake Charles, LA
Catherine Schram*

St Mary's School
Greenville, SC
Sr. John Thomas Armour*

St Thomas More Catholic School
Baton Rouge, LA
Irene Marron*
Mrs. To*

Three Springs of Courtland School
Courtland, AL
Rhonda Newman*

Warren Early College High School
Warrenton, NC
Ryan Hurley*

Yazoo County Jr High School
Yazoo City, MS
Marilyn Reece*

Language Arts Grant Recipients 2008-2009

After receiving a "Poetic Achievement Award" schools are encouraged to apply for a Creative Communication Language Arts Grant. The following is a list of schools who received a two hundred and fifty dollar grant for the 2008-2009 school year.

Acushnet Elementary School, Acushnet, MA
Benton Central Jr/Sr High School, Oxford, IN
Bridgeway Christian Academy, Alpharetta, GA
Central Middle School, Grafton, ND
Challenger Middle School, Cape Coral, FL
City Hill Middle School, Naugatuck, CT
Clintonville High School, Clintonville, WI
Coral Springs Middle School, Coral Springs, FL
Covenant Classical School, Concord, NC
Coyote Valley Elementary School, Middletown, CA
Diamond Ranch Academy, Hurricane, UT
E O Young Jr Elementary School, Middleburg, NC
El Monte Elementary School, Concord, CA
Emmanuel-St Michael Lutheran School, Fort Wayne, IN
Ethel M Burke Elementary School, Bellmawr, NJ
Fort Recovery Middle School, Fort Recovery, OH
Gardnertown Fundamental Magnet School, Newburgh, NY
Hancock County High School, Sneedville, TN
Haubstadt Community School, Haubstadt, IN
Headwaters Academy, Bozeman, MT
Holden Elementary School, Chicago, IL
Holliday Middle School, Holliday, TX
Holy Cross High School, Delran, NJ
Homestead Elementary School, Centennial, CO
Joseph M Simas Elementary School, Hanford, CA
Labrae Middle School, Leavittsburg, OH
Lakewood High School, Lakewood, CO
Lee A Tolbert Community Academy, Kansas City, MO
Mary Lynch Elementary School, Kimball, NE
Merritt Secondary School, Merritt, BC
North Star Academy, Redwood City, CA

Language Arts Grant Winners cont.

Old Redford Academy, Detroit, MI
Prairie Lakes School, Willmar, MN
Public School 124Q, South Ozone Park, NY
Rutledge Hall Elementary School, Lincolnwood, IL
Shelley Sr High School, Shelley, ID
Sonoran Science Academy, Tucson, AZ
Spruce Ridge School, Estevan, SK
St Columbkille School, Dubuque, IA
St Francis Middle School, Saint Francis, MN
St Luke the Evangelist School, Glenside, PA
St Matthias/Transfiguration School, Chicago, IL
St Robert Bellarmine School, Chicago, IL
St Sebastian Elementary School, Pittsburgh, PA
The Hillel Academy, Milwaukee, WI
Thomas Edison Charter School - North, North Logan, UT
Trinity Christian Academy, Oxford, AL
United Hebrew Institute, Kingston, PA
Velasquez Elementary School, Richmond, TX
West Frederick Middle School, Frederick, MD

Grades 7-8-9

Note: The Top Ten poems were finalized through an online voting system. Creative Communication's judges first picked out the top poems. These poems were then posted online. The final step involved thousands of students and teachers who registered as online judges and voted for the Top Ten poems. We hope you enjoy these selections.

Top Poem Grades 7-8-9

My Imagination

Where the flowing crystal water
Meets the azure sky
Where the lone seagulls do wing
Where the moon hangs florescent
Reflecting on my dreams
Where the purple marble mountains
Meet the lonely waving sea
Where the breezy open plains
Meet solid sandy desert streams
Where the soft sun setting lights
Meet the stars once again
Where the navy black night
Knows everything
Where I fly, where I seek
Where I look, where I reap
How I live and how I breathe
Outside my life
My imagination speaks —
While I dream

TreAnna Bradley, Grade 8
Leakesville Jr High School, MS

Top Poem Grades 7-8-9

School

School is fun to an extent,
My love for school is sometimes bent,
The drama is awful, the homework too,
Teacher's words by the handful, "Oh what do I do?"

Drama says he did this, and she did that,
Teachers ask, did you get your homework?
Did you finish your math?
To all of this I just can't reply,
Too much in my head so I just sigh,

My parents want me to join extra curriculars,
But with this and that it's extra ridiculous,
Each school has its fair share of nepotism,
Every popular kid gets treated with favoritism,

Some teachers have too much power,
When they do us wrong we all turn sour,
To most of us students it just isn't fair,
So we all have to learn to just grin and bear.

Rayna Cahill, Grade 8
Priceville Jr High School, AL

Top Poem Grades 7-8-9

Music Memory

When I play my flute,
Silvery notes dance on air,
While my fingers fly.

The notes coming out,
Each shining like a bright star,
Making my heart sing.

Shimmering high notes,
Lingering upon the air,
Twist, shine, disappear.

Thick, heavy low notes
Spilling out on each other,
Oozing slowly out.

Leaving an echo;
What was once music is now
Only memory.

Katherine Lehman, Grade 7
St Anne Catholic School, SC

Top Poem Grades 7-8-9

Land of Frozen Dreams

Deep — deeper than you will ever know
They lie and freeze all eternity — they scream
One day, their colors will show
This — this is the land of frozen dreams

Those who dream but never do
Those who think but never act
All your dreams wait for you
Until you reach they stay intact

One day — when the time is right
When you see into your mind
Until you see the end of the fight
You and your dream will never bind

Your turn has come — you must remain tough
Determination is your steam
Yet it seems there is not enough
Thus is the land…of a refrozen dream

Christopher McNutt, Grade 8
Priceville Jr High School, AL

Top Poem Grades 7-8-9

Fall's First Breath

A sea of illuminating emerald upon the land
Sweet sister summer's life was drawing to an end
Audacious autumn was beginning anew
About to sing his song, so true

With a whistle of wind upon the wood, he began to sing
The majestic music first touched the tips of the tallest trees
Their leaves, now crimson and cardinal, cascaded toward the ground
Their alluring aroma spread all around

Woodland creatures delightedly dancing to the harmonious song
They have been reunited with Mother Nature's most handsome son
The whistle of the sanctifying song, wisps the birds into the sky
They too, chirp this long awaited song

The trees sway about to the tune
Their golden, glowing leaves cover the forest floor like a blanket
Scrumptious, succulent apples litter branches like Christmas ornaments
Autumn's song slows down and his jubilant journey is almost done

The luscious lullaby sang the creatures to bed
Heeding harsh brother winter's coming, close ahead
Fearing fall's final note, which was ever closer
They then dreamt of autumn's next symphony

Allison Meinert, Grade 8
St John Neumann Regional Catholic School, GA

Top Poem Grades 7-8-9

Unanswerable Questions

Laying in bed at night
My body shaking with fright
Throbbing with the question, is she all right?
The phone's ring sends chills up my spine
Please Lord, it's not her time
I hear the phone hit the floor,
Tears pouring down my face more and more
Downstairs no words are said
All the hope has left me, she can't be dead
My world is ending, should I flee?
Could this be the death of me?
Now I might sound selfish this I know,
But Lord, why did she have to go?
I know she is no longer in pain
But I wish she could still play the game
This game of life, I wish never had an end
Lord, why was it my mother, my best friend?

Stephanie Pacheco, Grade 8
North Myrtle Beach Middle School, SC

Top Poem Grades 7-8-9

And He Makes Her Sound So Perfect

He tells her she's beautiful, a gift straight from God.
He tells her she's the sweetest thing. Sweeter than sweet.
He tells her she's the reason he wakes up every day. She brightens his day.
He tells her how smart she is. She's got beauty and brains.
But she's always putting herself down. Doesn't think she is good enough.
Sad because she doesn't fit in, even though he tells her she was born to stand out.
How many times she cries herself to sleep, just to wake up the next morning to make the same mistakes.
She's always trying to hide her true potential, just because she's afraid of failing.
And she only wants a guy to show her she's special, and all he wants is for her to give him a chance.
She always falls for jerks, always getting herself hurt.
And by now, she has learned to hide her pain so well, she sometimes even fools herself.
A fake smile always on her face. But he can look through her, and see her true colors, shining
    beautifully bright.
He wishes he could take all her pain away so she would never have to cry again, he loves her smile.
But she just wants to be friends.
But maybe, just maybe, if she saw herself through his eyes,
She would know who she really is,
And then she might just love herself enough to know how much better she deserves.

Maria Tellez, Grade 7
HE McCracken Middle School, SC

Top Poem Grades 7-8-9

Tulip

Dew drops build on pink satin sheets;
they fall to the ground.
The rosy cheeks snuggle together for warmth;
the patter of raindrops makes a soft sound.

Miles of green shoot toward the sky;
for heaven they reach.
An army of ants marches up the emerald stalk;
birds fly.

A cotton-filled sky gives the gift of shade;
the sun plays hide and seek.
A kitten prances playfully;
whiskers tickle my feet.

Sheets turn to quilts;
they have entered full bloom.
Spreading far and wide,
pink fills the room.

Heather Underwood, Grade 9
Mount Carmel Academy, LA

Top Poem Grades 7-8-9

The Heart of Blue Ridge

Hills of blue and shades of green,
Drops of dew and crystalline sheens.

Mountains tickle the sky,
The heron leaps and flies.

Leaves crunch beneath the deer,
The owl sits still, his eyes near.

Trickling water flows aimlessly,
A child splashes shamelessly.

In these great hills of blue,
One can expect the heart to be true.

Love runs through the very trees,
For in this land, our home, the love is free.

Brenna Weaver, Grade 8
Fannin County Middle School, GA

Top Poem Grades 7-8-9

Luminous Leaves

I look at the ground, and what do I see?
Exquisite colors peering back at me.
Lying on the ground, too innumerable to count,
I look at them, such a vast amount.

Crimson, cardinal, scarlet all mean red.
Dwelling on the ground, becoming part of its bed.
Countlessly, conspicuously this crimson color collects.
More to come soon, I'm sure you can detect.

Emerald also gathers, fallen to the ground.
Elegantly, efficiently falling, not making a sound.
They begin to blend, as if becoming one,
But all have not fallen, still more are to come.

Gold glides glamorously down to the Earth.
Leaves fall to the ground, part of Fall's annual birth.
These leaves are beautiful, bold, and bright,
Glistening gratefully in Earth's new light.

The leaves all lay motionless on the Earth's floor.
Being part of Earth's canvas, but really, much more.
These radiant colors having now been spilt,
And what have they made, but Earth's brand new quilt.

Justin Yestrumsky, Grade 8
St John Neumann Regional Catholic School, GA

Storms
When storms come into my life
I feel gloomy.
As I watch the leaves fall
on a warm autumn day,
the warm air touches my cold face.
Diamonds sparkle in the light
I watch my friends play
in the big oak trees.
The sun brightens my dull day.
My dog, Twisty,
chases after her rubber ball!
The wind blows
a sudden whiff of cold air.
I sit and think
of my nanny all day.
I really wish she was still here
to hold me and never let go.
Jaleesa Barnaba, Grade 8
Leonville Elementary School, LA

Know the Real Me
Although I am smart
I'm a normal person at heart
I wish people would think twice
Before judging me, cause I am nice
You could be my friend
We'd be tight 'til the end
I'm actually kind of cool
And have many friends in school
Just take the time to find the real me
I think you'll like me, you will see
Myleka Jefferson, Grade 8
Alexandria Middle Magnet School, LA

The Sky
The sky is dark
It gets darker every minute
This leads to only one thing
It's going to rain
The trees and leaves are moving
I feel the drizzle
There is little wind though
The leaves are dead
No rain yet, no rain
I can hear the leaves shivering
I can feel the soft breeze of the rain
This is going to be a dark night.
Nicko Matutina, Grade 7
St Andrews Middle School, SC

Lakes
Lakes are so pretty.
The water is very dark.
People swim in them.
Tamarra Roberts, Grade 7
Opelousas Jr High School, LA

How Do You Fall Out of Love
How do you fall out of love with someone who's right there?
You sit and stare and wonder if it's over or not.
You can't stand when he calls or even when he doesn't.
You are so confused and don't know what to do.
We have a past and hopefully a future too.
But I can't predict it…so how do I fall out of love with someone who's right there?
It's easier said than done…but for now you're no longer my number one.
Kacey Rhodes, Grade 9
Goshen High School, AL

One of Them
I turn and turn looking for a way
To find those that are true
And those who never act the same day to day
You think they are somebody
Then you find that they are nobody

They try to fill you with hatred and thoughts that are just not meant to be
I have to just try to look past them and find me
Then there are those filled with kindness and love
They go all out and try to reach out above

I think I can trust you
Then I think again
Because who knows
You may just be trying
To be one of them
Brittan Coats, Grade 8
Dillard Drive Middle School, NC

Old Hannah
Nothing here is going right: There's confusion between us all.
Everyone knows that somebody better come to call.
Just then this man jumped up and shouted, "Who will take a stand?"
I threw my arm up in the air, and he shot me in the hand!

Come on down, Old Hannah, the stars are coming out tonight.
Everybody looking around to see which tide is gonna bite.

I read her letter in the parking lot; love was all she sent.
"Hey, you cannot park your car here! That time's done came and went."
"Give me one good reason why I should move ahead!"
"She ain't gonna send another letter, she's with another man instead."

Come on down, Old Hannah, the stars are coming out tonight.
Everybody looking around to see which tide is gonna bite.

Dietrich, I cannot do what you want and fulfill your cause.
My pa caught me the other day smuggling out chainsaws.
What they were for, I did not know, but I told him, "Just wait an' see."
I didn't know that you were planning a raid of the outback of Tennessee.

Come on down, Old Hannah, the stars are coming out tonight.
Everybody looking around to see which tide is gonna bite.
Asher Mitchell, Grade 8
New Hebron Attendance Center, MS

I Am Love

I am love
I wonder how people could ever hate
I hear the cries of the unloved
I see the way I change lives
I am love
I pretend that hatred doesn't exist
I feel pure happiness
I touch broken hearts and mend them
I worry for the people that have none of me to give
I cry for the people who don't have anyone to give me to them
I am love
I understand what makes people truly happy
I say I am invincible
I dream there will be no more hatred
I try to firmly plant myself in every family and home
I hope to reach every person
I am love

Danielle Gill, Grade 8
Wren Middle School, SC

The Constellations

T here are many constellations showing,
H ere on our planet, for they are always
E ver-growing, but always disappearing. Our

C onstellations can
O nly show, and
N ever
S top
T heir job. For our constellations are
E ver-showing, never off our backs. Only with a
L ovely star —
L it sky,
A nd of course our great moon too,
T he peace
I n
O ur lives can
N ever
S top showing.

Thomas Wray, Grade 7
Haynes Academy for Advanced Studies, LA

The Ghost Town

Upon the eve of September first,
All was but a ghost town in the deep south.
Generators for every driveway,
All trees were gently swaying.

Nervous vibes throughout the land,
Everyone bracing each other's hand.
Surely it couldn't be as bad as the last.
Surely this one wouldn't be so vast.
As the slight winds blew dust into mounds,
Eventually nerves slowly unwound.

Carey Camel, Grade 8
Bishop Noland Episcopal Day School, LA

Storms

Storms in my life make me feel so lost.
There's nowhere to go but home.
A place that holds all of my regrets.
Can the days let me move forward,
or will I stay in the past?
I hide behind a smile or a laugh.
No one is aware of what's behind it.
I recline in the car seat
and watch the clouds as they pass by.
Summer is a beautiful time of year.
The sun shines brightly
and the clouds are as white as snow in the sky.
I hear birds singing and dogs barking.
I feel the warmth of the sunlight on my back.
I see flowers everywhere.
At night, the sun is gone,
and the moon and stars sparkle like diamonds.
I imagine flying with the angels above me.
The fresh night breeze keeps everything cool.

Courtney Francis, Grade 7
Leonville Elementary School, LA

A Friend

I am kind.
You are meek.
I'm only weak when I'm asleep.
You get into problems waist deep.
We are different, but we are the same.
Because we all rise and fall in Jesus name.

Sonya Schmidt, Grade 9
Lawrence County High School, MS

Jingle, Jingle, Jingle

Jingle, jingle, jangle, bells tinkle on the street.
Santas are ringing, one every few feet!
Jingle, jingle, jangle, silver in the air
At the sight of the jolly men, children stop and stare!
Jingle, jingle, jangle, do you hear what I hear?
Reindeer bells magically cause people into the night to peer!
Now it's Christmas night! And it's off to bed.
Santa's coming tonight! He's flying overhead!
Jingle, jingle, jangle, there's no need to fear.
As bells ring-a-ding-a-ling Christmas is drawing near!
Jingle, jingle, jangle, snow pure and fair
Covers every limb of the tree in the square!
Jingle, jingle, jangle, Santa's round and jolly face
He rings his bell all over the place!
Now it's Christmas night! And it's off to bed.
Santa's coming tonight! He's flying overhead!
Jingle, jingle, jangle, Christmas has come again
It brings the best out of us and makes everyone a friend!
Santa's come and left Christmas has come and gone
He'll be back next year hope you like the song!
Merry Christmas everyone!

Katie Ernst, Grade 8
Haynes Academy for Advanced Studies, LA

A Season Full of Exuberance

I love how lively leaves gracefully dance in the wind
How trees are easily accentuated by their kaleidoscopic hue
When leaves can't help but appear more exquisite after a pluvial day
They never seem to cease from crisply crunching and crackling in my footsteps
Also how leaves can make a day euphoric from one glance at their scarlet, golden, and sunset shade

The weather is always impeccable
For it contains the exact minuscule amount of frigidness
Wearing a moderate jacket is just enough for the blustering wind
Rain forms a blanket of mist lightly over the browning ground
The aroma smells of the welcoming scent of yearning or this season to finally begin

Thanksgiving also occurs in this stunning season
Dinner tables are more loquacious than ever
Because relatives come from afar to have a pleasurable period of time with others
Where voracious family members turn into change gorged people after a magnanimous meal
Lastly, when everyone gets from unwearied at the beginning of the day to fatigued at the end

What is this secretive season you might ask
As if it hasn't already revealed itself
It's filled with a captivating climate
And a perfectly happy, harmonious holiday
Of course, it's fall, the most captivating season of them all

Kirsten Whitt, Grade 8
St John Neumann Regional Catholic School, GA

Where and Who I'm From

I'm from playin' Donkey Kong Island on Nintendo 64 with little brother
I'm from going to Grandma's house on Sundays
I'm from pickin' every pecan I see
I'm from playin' football with the older kids
I'm from watchin' the South Carolina Panthers play every Sunday
I'm from watchin' *Power Rangers Lightning Force*
I'm from a loving family who can be tough at times
I'm from Union, South Carolina
Now you know where I'm from; I want you to know who I'm from.
I'm from a hard workin' woman who spends all her money on her kids
Who buys us clothes when she barely has any herself
I'm from a woman who tries her best to raise two boys without a good male role model
I'm from Tammy Catrice Thompson

Stevon Johnson, Grade 8
Sims Jr High School, SC

I Thought He Was the One

Roses are red, violets are blue. I thought you was the one, kind of like a dream come true.
I can't believe I thought that, but I really did. Then you started to act like one of them childish kids.
I thought when you said you love me you meant it, but you didn't at all. You started treating me like I was a dog.
I'm going to live my life, and leave yours alone. I'm going to also delete your number out of my phone.
Live your life happily, while I continue to be sad. When I get revenge don't get mad.
I loved you very very much, and got really happy from just one touch.
Now I see you and want to die, but I promised myself that I am not going to cry.
Well there's nothing else that I can do, but live my life happily without you.
I can because I did it before you came, but I know my life will never be the same.
My words are getting short, sad to say. So I will talk to you all another day.

Damesha Haymore, Grade 8
Yazoo County Jr High School, MS

A Brickwall

The brick wall standing tall and firm,
can't be broken down,
for its build is solid,
Hard as a rock.
Its love for what's inside it
is never shown.
Built to protect.
A hard covering with an inside that is hard enough
just to keep certain emotions from swarming out.
This wall has outstretched arms
that surrounds a beautiful garden
with two small, innocent sheep.
These two sheep mean the world
to the wall, but the wall shows
compassion for only one of these sheep.
Until the wall sees
that its lack of affection towards one of the sheep
is affecting the other.
The brick wall standing tall and firm
has now become the brother
that all has wanted.

Brittany Dong, Grade 7
L E Gable Middle School, SC

Beautiful Nature

In the chair where I sit
Out the window that my eyes glimpse
Like I've never seen anything like it before.
How nature's beauty stares out galore.
All through the day I look out the window
Hoping for tomorrow to be like today.
I wait for nightfall to get in my bed.
Now in my bed where I lie
Until tomorrow morning wherever I lay
Watching nature's beautiful day.

Dylan McElhenney, Grade 8
Lake Middle School, MS

The Beach

In the morning
When I awake
Birds will fly
And the waves will quake
People will laugh
Kids will play
The sun will shine all day
When it dies
People will sigh
When they rest
Crabs will play
In their sand dunes
All through the night
The sun will rise again
In hope for a brand new day

Ross Vogel, Grade 7
Haynes Academy for Advanced Studies, LA

Crime

The law is on our side,
Crime is high almost citywide,
People take the law in their own hands,
Trying to make their laws and take a stand,
So many people are becoming a homicide,
Mothers and fathers are growing,
When they see their children take their last ride,
It is a shame the way they spread the blame,
Trying to hold up the family name,
Problems with crime cannot stay the same,
Crime will tear a family apart.
Let us make sure we stop it before it starts,
No one can make you obey the law,
But people have started to tell what they saw,
The hotline is open every day of the year,
Helping victims and families to see clear,
Crime is here, but not to stay,
People are willing to pray each and every day.

Douglas Brown, Grade 9
McKee Jr High School, AL

Our Time Together

Three years ago I watched you, my sister, from the bleachers,
With family, friends, neighbors, and teachers.

Now it's the championship of two-thousand eight,
And I watch you as my teammate.

This time next year you'll be gone,
Our uniforms together we'll no longer don.

But for now I watch you from the bench,
Wishing I had your confidence.

This time together has been the best,
I know I'll remember it above the rest.

Shelby Kendall, Grade 8
Margaret Green Jr High School, MS

Dreams

My eyes, they cry a thousand tears,
My heart it screams for years and years.
A life, a love, an eternal flame,
A dream just beyond my window pane…

Fire and ice, hot and cold,
They fill you as you're growing old…
Your hopes and dreams, a long lost love,
All youthful dreams that tend to last…

Desire burns, then disappears,
A memory from your youthful years.
Your love, you say, shall always be,
Yet when the years turn to tears, even your love disappears…

Harley Pardue, Grade 9
Challenger High School, NC

This One Time at Band Camp
It was the month of August
I was new to the school.
I didn't know much
or many people this is true.
Some were nice and some were mean.
Some were even in between.
We worked real hard all day long
to learn to march and play our songs.
We took what we learned to competition.
Where we stepped and played
with great ambition.
When it was said and done
we turned out to be number one!

Jacob Billings, Grade 9
North Wilkes High School, NC

Yoda/Darth Vader
Yoda
good, wise
trusting, respected, enlightening
Jedi, Luke, Annikan, Sith
untrusting, killing, stealing
evil, devious
Darth Vader

Danielle Horton, Grade 7
Sacred Heart of Jesus School, LA

Ode to a Flower
There I was lying in the ground,
A small embryo, scared to death,
Waiting for someone to see me sprout.
As I heard my nucleus telling me
To grow, I felt the rush of my body
Just crumble around me.

There I was a leafless stem.
I was pursuing
To become a delicate blossom.
Every day I experience the
Excitement of the world,
As I face my fears I realize I became a
Dedicated Flower.

Tashia Foster, Grade 7
L E Gable Middle School, SC

Fall Is Here
Leaves falling from trees above
On the branches a beautiful dove

In the wind leaves are blowing
And the trees are flowing

The Halloween designs are most unique
Doorbells ringing "trick-or-treat."

Ginger Elsea, Grade 7
Rock Mills Jr High School, AL

Fishing in the North Georgia Mountains
Wake up in the morning with the blinding sun in your eyes.
Man, how the time flies!
Better get up on your feet and eat a nice hot breakfast.
Grab a cane pole and some night crawlers and plop down in the cold leather seat.
Take a ride to any stream, lake, or river.
Don't forget the livers!
Once you have arrived at Cooper's Creek, look around.
Wow, what beautiful rolling mountains, their peaks rounded at the top!
Listen to the water roar over the rocks; this looks like a great place to stop!

Lindsey Ramey, Grade 8
Fannin County Middle School, GA

What Is Your Life…
What is your life?
Is you life your money?
What is your life?
Is your life the man or woman you call honey?
What is your life?
Is your life your love?
What is your life?
Do you need to think twice?
Your life is too short, don't ever waste it.
Your life is sweet, take time to taste it.
Your life is entertaining, don't be afraid to laugh.
Your life has good times, make sure they last.
Your life has bad times keep them in your past.
Your life is a chance, make sure you take it.
But always remember your life is not what I say, but what you make it.

Femaria Jackson, Grade 7
Atlanta Academy, GA

Disorienting Daylight Savings
Every year at the beginning of autumn
There is one evening where the hands of time turn back an hour.
The nights nearly seem like a never-ending nuisance
And daylight slips behind the horizon even earlier.

Daylight savings is so disorienting.
When you think it is ten o'clock because of the darkness
You look at the clock and it's really only six.
I wish someone would stop this rambunctious rollercoaster
Between night and day, day and night.

Sister Sun's time in the sky is now more curtailed
While brother Moon's time is elongated.
All the cousin stars twinkle in the sky
Like a crisp, clear, blurred illustration.
Every evening I yearn to stare at them in aghast amusement.

Yes, all the stars, the moon, and the sun
Work in harmony to give us day and night.
But still, the timing of their pattern changes
Into something that befuddles us all
With dandelion daylight and nebulous nights.

Katelyn Smith, Grade 8
St John Neumann Regional Catholic School, GA

Point of View

Instead of seeing just a bunch of words,
I see a story unfolding and flowing gently before my eyes,
Telling of villains concocting unmoral plans,
And the unexpected slipping into being
As a magical plot unfolds right under my nose.

Instead of a simple midnight sky portrayed across the horizon,
I see infinite possibilities,
Or bright gems sparkling in a patch of the softest black velvet,
Possibly even a mysterious path into the future.

Instead of a random stranger on the street,
I see a person full of brilliance and potential possibilities,
Maybe the hero or heroine of tomorrow's challenges,
But I certainly don't see,
Just another person.

Alison Anderson, Grade 8
Schley County Middle/High School, GA

Sleepless in Louisiana

Howling winds, flashing seas
This hurricane has got the best of me.

I go to sleep to rest my head,
But all the thunder shakes the bed.

Another sleepless night, I'm on a roll;
Wow! this hurricane really takes its toll.

I look outside; it's quite a fright.
To my surprise there's no one in sight.

We all look forward to the end.
I sure hope a hurricane never comes again.

Ashley Declouette, Grade 7
Bishop Noland Episcopal Day School, LA

Like a Storm

Life is like a storm —
sometimes the sun is out,
and sometimes it's rainy.
It seems like sometimes people are on your side,
but then they're like boulders in your way.
They try to destroy you like a plant in Gustav.
Often I feel like a helpless kitten
alone in the wild.
My house is like a shelter
where I feel safe.
The rain is like my tears
when I feel sad.
And the sun is my smile
that lights the room.
No matter what
I know God is watching over me!

Stephen Fuselier, Grade 7
Leonville Elementary School, LA

Georgia My Home

Born and raised in the mountains,
where I learned to live life.
Revives my soul like a spring water fountain,
fishing away my troubles and worries.
Autumn is the season,
having the trophy kill on the wall.
Wondering the right reason,
God puts such beauty here.
Play on Saturday, church on Sunday,
hometown country boy living free.
Learning like my forefathers back in the day
year after year the same old thing the old song,
it never gets old to me!
As long as I know where my feet are,
it won't be hard to see,
that Georgia is the place I want to be.

Zeke Huffman, Grade 8
Fannin County Middle School, GA

Lying in the Shadow

There he is
My ultimate fear
Just lying there in the shadow.
Waiting to strike, waiting till I fall asleep.
The guy in the hood from Hot Fuzz, the movie.
Sitting there in silence in the corner of my room,
But I'll show him I'll stay up all night if I have to
Then suddenly my eyes get heavy
I can't stay awake
I wake up brightness shining through my window
And in my corner
Nothing.

Jonathan Slimming, Grade 8
Atlanta Academy, GA

Hurricanes

When I think of hurricanes,
I think of destruction.
Imagining millions of people's homes
being destroyed by wind and rain!
Wind blows and the rain beats down steadily.
Hot humid air mixes in the gulf
to form a swirling tunnel of destruction.
A left-behind dog is barking,
begging for someone to rescue him.
No trees are left behind.
Everything is gone.
A single star is left in the black, night sky,
overlooking destroyed houses, roads, and trees.
Everything happens for a reason.
God knows what He is doing!
Morning comes — morning goes.
The sun finally goes down!

Paige Miller, Grade 8
Leonville Elementary School, LA

Then

Then, and then, and then again
Back to the fall of Elven kin.
A silent war, with no sides,
Allies shifting with the tides,
Fought with magic, wit, and lies.
Then, and then, and then again
Back to the time way back when.
Along came a girl of human blood,
Killed for the Elven Lords she loved,
As Lordlings died for she above.
Then, and then, and then again
Back to the war waged to win.
A madman's plot born of greed
With evil magic newly freed.
Thousands died for a bloody creed.
Then, and then, and then again
Back to the Houses of Blade and Twin.
A bitter rivalry put on hold,
They worked as one to form a fold.
Now, and now, and now once more
Another human opens the door.
Amber Isbell, Grade 9
Upson-Lee High School, GA

Green

Green grass is shy,
hiding near the ground.
Green trees are proud,
way up in the sky.

It doesn't matter where you look,
you see green and green sees you
even when you sprint
across the finish line.
Zachary Whitworth, Grade 7
L E Gable Middle School, SC

Horses

They run so fast, so wild and free
They run fast as the wind, so fast
They cannot even be seen
So wild that they cannot be tamed
But they can be ridden.

So many colors
They look like a rainbow
So many sizes
They look like stairs
So many breeds
They look like people.

Wild and free, or tame
They all have their own
Personalities.
Kaitlyn Hunter, Grade 8
Poland Jr High School, LA

Hurricane Gustav

Willow trees
weeping with sadness
Winds are blowing fiercely.
I hear trees cracking
Tornadoes are popping up everywhere.
Bam! The electricity is out.
Generators are running.
Shingles are flying off rooftops.
There are no birds chirping.
Moonlight glistens on the rain.
I'll never forget Hurricane Gustav
because of the damage he caused,
but I'm thankful we made it out safely.
Kristen Abshire, Grade 8
Leonville Elementary School, LA

A Hamster Named Zach

There once was a hamster named Zach
He loved to eat cake and get fat
He met a mouse
His name was Joe
And now they just go with the flow
Zachary Johnson, Grade 7
Sacred Heart of Jesus School, LA

Tell Me Why

Please tell me why
Tell me why I act the way I do,
Tell me why I love you

Tell me why I can't say no,
Tell me why I can't let go

Tell me why every time I am around you
I feel like I am floating on a cloud,
Tell me why I can't let you down

Tell me why I feel like a butterfly,
Tell me why I have to say goodbye.
Marissa Curry, Grade 8
Yazoo County Jr High School, MS

Drawing

I have many hobbies
Hunting and fishing
Like most kids do
But most of all
I like drawing things cool

Drawing helps me express my feelings
Comforts me when I'm in need
Lets me be myself
Gives me something to do
To set my mind free.
Morgan Brown, Grade 8
Hatley School, MS

Rainstorm

The rain swiftly drops to the ground,
Wet tears from the sky,
Beads of water make the only sound,
All the world seems to sigh,

Light is covered by shade,
Darkness takes over the land,
Not a beam of light is made,
Spared is not one grain of sand,

Wind blows rapidly to the east,
A damp gust is felt,
Nothing yet has started to cease,
The worst has not been dealt,

All life seems to hide,
While the storm builds up its valor,
With the wind as its guide,
The storm shows all of its power,

Then, suddenly, light shows,
The storm starts to get frail,
Everything begins to slow,
Nothing is left of the strong gale.
Catherine Kopti, Grade 8
Metrolina Christian Academy, NC

Georgia's Beauty

Georgia,
The sweet smell of fresh air,
The amazing colors of the fall leaves,
A baby cub wrestling with his brother,
Georgia,

The luscious green mountains,
Outstanding blue skies,
That you will ever see in your life,
Georgia,

Those magnificent shining rivers,
Plenty of things for me and you,
It is filled with amazing things,
Georgia.
Courtney Manning, Grade 8
Fannin County Middle School, GA

Sister/Brother

Sister
Kind, loving
Fun, fighting, sweet
Stepsister, stepbrother
Friends, relative, person
Trustworthy, dependent
Brother
Brandi Lockett, Grade 7
Sacred Heart of Jesus School, LA

Poems

Made with symbolism, made with rhyme
Being told at a legato pace
Following perfect beat and time
As if walking or running a race
Including themes and more
Rhythm, meter, alliteration
Similes and a metaphor
Poetic flow for decoration
Sonnets, limericks, acrostic too
All with their own style
About a lake or perhaps some morning dew
Some short and some can go on for a mile
Poems, with rhythm and tone
Let's go and make some of our own

Kendall Moffett, Grade 7
Boyet Jr High School, LA

Prides

Everything dark and cold is ours
and everything warm and plentiful is theirs.
We are two prides of lions,
furious and vicious.
But you can see our ribs,
while they are fit and fat, always full.
We look longingly after them.
Their lionesses are fine and the perfect predators,
ours are dirt.
We fight, and circle around and round
growls escaping through our teeth
rasping our throats.
We lunge, we don't fight fair
going for the eyes, the jaws, the legs,
breaking, tearing, killing.
They lay dead limp, unmoving, still
But they still rule.
They look down on as and we stare right back,
Not fair,
Two prides,
Two lion prides.

Zoie Reviere, Grade 7
L E Gable Middle School, SC

Harvard

Two little boys late one night
Tried to get to Harvard on the end of a kite.
The kite string broke,
And down they fell.
Instead of going to Harvard
They went to hell.
Now don't get excited
And don't get pale.
Instead of going to Harvard,
They went to Yale.

Shawn Johnson, Grade 8
St Andrews Middle School, SC

What Time Is It?

There is a time for love
There is a time for hate
There is a time to be happy
There is a time to cry
There is a time for total bliss
There is a time when nothing seems to go right
There is a time for fun
And a time for total boredom
But he can never find time for us
There is a time for work
And then there is a time for family
He denies and rejects that time for us
It is time for love but yet I hate
I hate him for leaving us
I want to cry from the pain
It is the time when nothing seems to go right
I miss those memories that we had
The memories of happiness and fun just total bliss
But in one fell swoop you took that away
And left pain and misery in my life
For that I will never forgive you

Victoria Walker, Grade 9
Greenville High School, AL

Saturday Night

Saturday was the best day ever,
We played many games, that made us sound clever.
We watched movies all night long,
And sang the words to our favorite song.
We went shopping at the mall,
And bought many clothes for spring and fall.
We stayed up all night and talked on the phone,
We never left each other alone.
We popped popcorn and made s'mores,
And when we were done we wanted more.
We did each other's hair, nails, and make-up,
And before we knew, it was time to wake up.
Saturday night was the best day ever,
And I know we will be friends forever.

Christie Saladino, Grade 9
Mount Carmel Academy, LA

Dreams

It beckons me, tells me to come,
before I know it, I am done,
I fight, I fight, hard as I can,
But the temptation is strong, I am but a man
I can resist I tell myself
But I cannot turn away from the forbidden shelf
Left alone am I again, the thing has beaten many men
I close my eyes I turn away
But from this thought, my mind won't stray
Oh! This thing leaves quite a scar
I open up the cookie jar.

Andrew Burin, Grade 7
Lusher Charter School, LA

A Life as a Dream

Life is just a dream
A beam of light that
Shines so bright
until it ends the night.

Life is just the wind
that blows when it snows.
And it knows there is a star in sight.

Life is just the moon at night
that shines so so bright.
Life is a string that extends
until it is cut.

Life is but a dream
A beam of light
that shines so so bright.
Until it ends the night!

John T. Beetles, Grade 9
Midway High School, NC

Thanksgiving

T ime to celebrate
H aving fun
A family time
N ational tradition
K ey lime pie
S tuffing
G iblet gravy
I smell Grandma's house
V elvet Chocolate Cake
I 'm full
N ext year will be even better!
G ood memories

Joseph Damron, Grade 8
Albemarle School, NC

What Is Peace

Every single person
You see them every week
Ask the same question
What exactly is peace?
I think peace is loving
Yourself and each other
Both friends and enemies
Fathers, daughters, and mothers
I think peace is not looking
At someone's race or religion
Not looking at their stuff
Or money positions
I know my definition
Is not really right
But if more people followed it
I might be able to sleep tonight

Meredith Abercrombie, Grade 7
North Iredell Middle School, NC

The Eye That Never Cries

The eye that never cries is the eye of many lies,
The eye shows no emotion or any devotion,
No one knows where the beholder goes; it depends where the wind blows,
No sympathy or sorrow to borrow, no family to love tomorrow,
The eye that never cries is the eye of many lies.

Auston Watson, Grade 9
Three Springs of Courtland School, AL

The Jaws of Life

Surrounded by slender stalks of grass,
I gaze upon a giant
with gray wrinkled skin.
Slowly trudging towards the refreshing cool watering hole.

As the elephant, tired from the journey,
wades into the rippling bathing pool,
it sprays water from its long trunk
washing itself, unaware of the danger in front of it.

Creeping slowly and quietly
with sharp teeth ready to snap
a crocodile, the elephant's predator,
floated like a log toward its prey.
The instinct to kill arose as the crocodile swam closer and closer.

Jaws wide open, the crocodile attacks,
but the sharp tusk of the elephant
pierces the predator and kills it.
The elephant relaxes in the cool refreshing water of the African jungle.

Josette Thornton, Grade 9
New Site High School, MS

Can They Hear Her Cry for Help?

As she tries to show ya'll she needs your help by destroying her body,
and all you do is stand by dumbfounded
and let her harm herself
she don't tell you she need help
but is her sulking away not enough of a sign or is it when she gone?
She needs you now don't act dumb!
In no time she might try to kill herself
she cries herself to sleep at night
and cuts herself during the day
at lunch she says she not hungry
so she can starve herself. Can you tell?
No, you're too busy to care, so when she gone blame yourself not her
she tried to get you to notice her signs of needing help.
She hurting herself 'cause she thinks you don't care and she right
you say you love her, then show it
before it'll be too late to save her
She shouldn't have to be heading down this road
act now or it'll be your fault that she's gone and not herself.
Listen to her cries, give her your hand and your love
don't ignore her cry for help!
Or soon she will be gone!

Stephanie Ingram, Grade 8
Butner-Stem Middle School, NC

Winter

Winter is my favorite season
I like it for more than just one reason
It's cold outside and sometimes snows
I have to keep warm so I wear big clothes
Houses have pretty decorations and lights
Most people try and stay out of fights
People are happy and filled with joy
Children are nice to each girl and boy
The season of winter makes me excited
I hope this poem made you delighted

Katelyn Forest, Grade 9
Mount Carmel Academy, LA

In My Heart

From our friendship has sprung my love for you.
Even though my love is strong and true,
I cannot ever admit to it. For it is wrong
to love you this way, even though it belongs
right where it is: in my loving heart.

When I see you, soft music plays light as a feather.
I see you when I close my eyes; they'll stay closed forever
so I can see your face whenever I please.
Your image makes me smile and puts me at ease
right where I need it: in my burning heart.

It is this desire for you that hurts me so;
that and the knowing that you can't know
about all of the things that I must hide.
So here they stay all broken inside
right where they lay: in my aching heart.

Justina Rieger, Grade 9
Avery County High School, NC

Inside and Out

What if you have feelings,
For someone who's attractive on the inside,
Not out?

When they walk by,
You scream and freak out on the inside,
Not out.

When he gives you a hug,
You seem to die on the inside,
Not out.

He says he doesn't have a chance,
You know he's wrong from the inside,
Not out.

But no matter what you say or do,
You know you love him on the inside,
And out.

Gabrielle Zendan, Grade 9
Providence High School, NC

Christmas

Christmas caroling around the block
Helping with all of the Christmas decorations
Rising above the anger on this very special day
Instead of receiving try giving
This is the season to be very jolly
Most of the family arrives to your house for Christmas dinner
Snow falls from the sky
Sharing with everyone on this Christmas Day!!!

Ji'Savorya Warner, Grade 7
Hubert Middle School, GA

Tired of Running

No clue where I'm going, but my feet carry me.
My soul is pierced, my mind obsolete.
I desire to be home with the ones that I love, and love me.
My temper got the best of me, and I took off, in heat.
If I did it all again, would I be here?
Would I have my siblings near?
Or my mom's tender kiss to dry each tear?
Oh, but here I am, standing in fear.
Missing my bed, that caressed my head, and sheltered my body.
The sweet buttermilk pancakes, and espresso coffee.
Why did I run away? This isn't a usual hobby.
No one even tried, no one tried to stop me.
As if they could.
If they wanted me to come home, then maybe I would.
I really do want to go now, maybe I should.
I'm tired of running. The run was good.

Ar'nekki Calender, Grade 9
The Education Center, MS

Love and Hurt

Before you hurt others,
Hurt yourself first
It will make you wise
Before you love yourself
Try to love others first,
It will make you perfect
You have the power that hurts.
He has the love that heals.
I have the light that sees.
God has the compassion that feels.
My Supreme, my Supreme, my Supreme.
How is it possible for me.
To hurt the ones
That I love deeply!
"My child, here is the proof.
That you would not actually love them."
My Supreme, my Supreme, my Supreme.
Now tell me
Do I not sincerely and deeply love you, my Supreme
Why do you hurt me so often?
If not always.

Sade Hall, Grade 9
McKee Jr High School, AL

Georgia

Rustling, colorful leaves, golden, red, burgundy, brown, a rainbow of trees, cool mornings, warm evenings, wild animals running amok, white flakes with their own design fall softly down below, to touch your cheek, head and nose, after the sun takes its wintry nap, life begins again, flowers reach up to touch the sun, birds sing their precious melodies, days get longer, children cheer for joy, traveling to beaches, the smell of sunscreen at the pool, going fishing on Blue Ridge Lake, the aroma of cookouts, watching the sun set on the mountains and the peace of a millions stars shining down upon my Georgia.

Kayla Petty, Grade 8
Fannin County Middle School, GA

All I Can See

All I can see is a ring of darkness surrounding me. All I can see is darkness. I see browning color surrounding me. All I see is black clothes on cold pale people's bodies. All I see is black vans. I see black dark hair swaying in the rain. Why won't it stop. The darkness it will not stop. All I see is the darkness outside with not a twinkle of a star. It's a cold dark lonely night. There isn't color in this world. There isn't purple, yellow, red, blue, orange, or teal. Still all I can see is a ring of darkness surrounding me. Oooops it's my eyeliner.

Sha'Myia Evans, Grade 8
Lake Middle School, MS

Jekyll

The ocean air whispering in your ears. The sand rushing toward your feet. Look, the ocean grabbing your ankles. It wants to pull you in its lair. You can hear the swish of fishing line being thrown out in the open sea. The taste of salinity in the air is overpowering. Crabs, millions of crabs, running away from the shadows of humans. Docks are full of boats resting for the night. Even though night has fallen, another day at Jekyll Island is full of wonderful excitement.

Daniel Foster, Grade 8
Fannin County Middle School, GA

My Loving Cousin

We lay you underneath the willow tree where the branches blow and the birds chirp. As we sing "Go Rest High" I feel your sweet gentle hand touch my face and I knew you were there. I still can feel you near me wherever I go night or day I can still hear that same song as I think of you. My mind wonders if I will see you again. You told me that I will see you again beyond the sky. When you crossed my mind I wept but then I remembered what you said, "Don't cry for me for I'll be with you again someday."

Jessie Ray, Grade 8
Coffeeville High School, MS

Descendent Yet an Ancestor

I am a descendent yet an ancestor
I wonder how I'll be remembered after my time is up
I hear the rolling of my ancestors in their graves at the harm I have caused
I see one day the dreary upon my descendants' faces
I want nothing else for them but for the satisfaction from which the people they came from
I am a descendent yet an ancestor

I pretend to be diligent in the hopes of satisfying the ones before me
I feel frigid stares like needles sticking in my back
I touch the earth begging for forgiveness from the ones who walked across it before me
I worry the next generation will condone the message I shall cast upon them
I cry "HELP," is it too late for me?! For I was once in darkness but I see the light
I am a descendent yet an ancestor

I understand now what you have been trying to show me
I say that I will take it all in and distribute it among others
I dream of one day everyone understanding the pain and struggle you went through
I try to reach out and pull others out of the dark hoax for which they are in
I hope one day the future can constrain themselves from such deceit
I am a descendent yet an ancestor

Cristina Paynter, Grade 9
Warren Early College High School, NC

A Loved One

I love him so much,
He was so near to my heart,
For his death, I should not fear.
At first I wanted to shed so many tears
For he was so very dear,
For you must see as I had to see,
This loved one so near and dear to my heart,
Will forever watch over me with his,
God given eternal heart.
Through all my tears and fears,
And even through all my Earthly years,
I shall remain protected through his,
God given gift,
Which I had to see,
Was give to me the day we had to part.
Thank you Papaw for guarding my heart,
For now I know we will never part.

Elizabeth Walker, Grade 9
North Wilkes High School, NC

Hurricane

A hurricane is like a beast,
Eating everything it finds essential to its needs,
Crushing every man-made object in its way,
Destroying everything you once loved and lived for
Killing the creature is only by patience, hope, and prayer.

The aftermath of a hurricane is like a deep depression,
Swallowing the hopes in the hearts of the people,
Controlling and playing with the heart like an old toy
Bruising it like a school bully
It collapses with patience and eventually goes away.

Grayson McAlpine, Grade 8
Bishop Noland Episcopal Day School, LA

Life

Every second of your life counts
Whether it's the adventures of the day
Or the sight of the moon at night
The birds that soar in the sky
The loud commanding roar of a lion
The sweet smell of fresh roses

The soothing sound of the river
As the water rocks like a baby in its bed.
Taste of a southern Georgia peach
The thought of our soldiers being killed in war
A rare disease and the doctors have no cure
A poor child being abused by their parents
A drunk driver killing your best friend
A life filled with lies and bad choices
Good times and bad
But…no matter what — your life counts.

Diamond Furman, Grade 7
Hubert Middle School, GA

The Safari Ride

Here we are in the jeep
Ready to go and hear any animals' slightest peep

I saw a funny, smelly baboon
Right before it was noon

I was fascinated by the zebras crossing the river
When a crocodile caught one, it sure gave me a shiver

I loved to look at the giraffe reach for the trees
I hope it doesn't bother a nest of killer bees

When I saw a pink flamingo
With his long legs I wonder if he can do the tango

I heard a lion's furious roar
I surely begged for more

I felt the elephant's thunderous stomp
When he headed over the swamp

Now we are going back in the jeep
And the animals are going to sleep

Brandon Markbreiter, Grade 8
Dillard Drive Middle School, NC

Love

Love has always been a battlefield.
But love is the best weapon to wield.
Love is when you give someone your heart.
Love is what keeps two people together when they're apart.

Matt Ferguson, Grade 8
Lake Middle School, MS

Saving You

To keep you safe is what I need,
And to do that I must leave,
It'll be like I was never there,
The answers you seek still in the air,
It breaks my heart to leave you alone,
But endangering your life is just so wrong,
Take care of yourself while I'm not here,
Forget the memories and have no fear,
Death seconds away and you hear a noise,
Come a little closer and hear it's my voice,
STOP!!! NOW!!! TURN AWAY!!!
To hear that voice, you decide to stay.
I've saved you before, but now I see,
It's your turn to save me.
Now *I'm* seconds away from death,
I find you in my arms and I forget.
Please forgive me for leaving you alone.
You nearly died while I was gone.
"I forgive you."

Carlos Scott, Grade 9
Greenville High School, AL

Dirt Bikes
Loud and colorful
They have different names
Fun to ride,
Until you break a bone.
Austin West, Grade 7
L E Gable Middle School, SC

Turkey
White turkey meat
tastes good like a warm, sunny day.
Turkey sounds like gobble-gobble.
Turkey smells like a fall day,
and looks like brown delicious dinner.
Turkey makes me feel warm inside.
Dustin Holm, Grade 7
L E Gable Middle School, SC

Bashful the Turtle
Bashful the turtle was
so very small,
and oh very slowly he would crawl.
He was so sick,
that he never did eat,
and after that he met his defeat.

There in his tank,
he would walk very slow.
and now in heaven, he will glow.
we always will miss him,
we loved him a lot,
and now we see him in every thought.
Kaisy Frederick, Grade 7
Henry Ford Jr High School, LA

Where Were You?
Where were you
when I was crying at night
over you and the pain
that you put me through

I told my friends that you
were the only one for me
and that you were
the best thing ever

So now I look back
and I ask myself why
and I tell myself
that I loved and got hurt

So from that sad and long day
I told myself and everyone
that my happiness comes
first in my life before anyone else
Kimmi Airey, Grade 9
Cane Bay High School, SC

New York
I love New York City just like this lady is a old bitty.
New York is where I'm from, if you don't like it go beat on a drum.
The NYC is something for you to see, but I stand tall just like the Statue of Liberty.
New York is just the place for me.
Elijah Woods, Grade 8
St Margaret School, LA

World War II
We sat in the bunker waiting for orders,
We had to defeat the Jerries using only two mortars.
I sat there cold and scared gripping my Thompson,
Lifeless, without motion there lay Private Johnson.

Swiftly I stoop, putting on my helmet,
Only to get hit by a quick German bullet.
I was moaning, kicking, and screaming bloody murder,
I was there not helping my squad, feeling like a deserter.

I could hear the Panzers coming like demons from hell,
Firing out of their cannons, shooting dozens of shells.
Like darkness and sorrow death followed me around,
As it was capturing my comrades, pulling their bodies to the ground.

All of a sudden there was a buzzing in the air,
It was our allies in Mustangs coming to make the battle fair.
They bombed the Panzers setting them ablaze,
There was a cloud of dust making a foggy haze.

We won because of our allies in the sky blue,
That was only one battle of the World War II.
Ryan Anderson, Grade 8
Mount Carmel Christian School, GA

Storms
Storms in my life make me feel so scared.
My mind just drops.
I think about the people around me
and how they are going to make it through the storm.
I wonder what to do.
Looking at people beside me,
I can see the terror and confusion in their eyes.
I imagine what they are thinking
and picturing in their minds.
Trees are swaying,
and leaves are forming tiny tornadoes on the ground outside.
Luckily, I am safe inside where nothing can happen to me.
It is very dark and hot as it grows close to night.
The wind is howling and crying.
Branches are falling with loud booms.
Stones are thrown across the highway like tiny pebbles in the wind.
Morning comes and things are ruined.
We don't know what to do.
Oak trees are down, and they have ruined almost everything
from cars and trucks to houses and buildings.
Jenna Darby, Grade 7
Leonville Elementary School, LA

A Moment

In one moment in time,
All that we thrive on can change
The question is, for the better or worse
Does a mere child have the power
To change a life in but a moment
There should be no limits to ability
No right nor wrong, just what is real
One small thought can start a wildfire
In the mind of humanity
And start of revolution of thinking
It can define a person, or even a generation
When possibility becomes reality
Even the most illogical idea
Can make or break a life
So, can one person with one thought
In one moment in time change the world?

Evan Melton, Grade 9
Ardrey Kell High School, NC

Dream Boy

There's just one type of boy that you can't seem to find
Because he only pops up once in a lifetime
But luckily one day he ran across me
And I fell into a love as deep as the sea
Little did I know his feelings were the same
And the beating of his heart he just couldn't seem to tame
And when our hands touched the magic was so real
The love that I felt was more than I ever thought I could feel
Oh those eyes were so deep and so true
Never in my life had I seen such a blue
And I lived for his smile and the way that he laughed
Though I knew in my heart it would never last

Rachel Fredricks, Grade 9
Priceville High School, AL

The Forest

Oh, how I like to walk through the forest,
There are so many sights to see,
It is like the forest is a singing chorus,
When the trees sway like a rough sea.

But then it begins to go away,
Because the trees begin to slow,
As the illusion begins to decay,
Then back into reality I must go,
To the life I remember and know.

Nathan Collier, Grade 8
Priceville Jr High School, AL

The Wave

The wave crashes down far and near
The wave crashes down like a ponderous brute
The wave does not care if it tosses you around like a ball
The wave wants to take you out to sea

Alexx Lux, Grade 7
Cathedral School, NC

The Voices of Harmony

Peace is a wish come true on a shooting star,
It smells like sweet honeysuckle;
In early spring that overturns the rage in people;
Replaced by beauty,
It tastes sugary and ripe like a fuzzy fresh plucked peach,
It feels like gentle infant skin;
With the smallest hint of warmth,
It looks like children amused with their surroundings;
Playing and laughing;
Clapping and snapping,
It sounds like a harmony of voices in a bundle of joy;
Their call carried in the wind for all to hear and crave,
The overwhelming need for happiness is not a sin;
But a feeling to be always longed for,
Gnawing, piercing, and stabbing at us;
To create it.

Chrysoula Georgiou, Grade 8
Leesville Road Middle School, NC

Hurricane in New Orleans

A hurricane is very destructive,
And all the lights go out.
It means to us more construction
With that there is no doubt.

A hurricane forms over seas;
Oh, don't come here we all plead.

As the generators start to rumble,
Sadly all the levees crumble.
Now the houses start to flood;
It's time to get ready for lots of mud.

Elizabeth Bernard, Grade 7
Bishop Noland Episcopal Day School, LA

She

The sun makes her light skin bright
With the skin so soft like a baby
Her scent smells so good that you think she's a model
The way she looks at me makes me smile
She is so beautiful
She has the most beautiful dark brown eyes
In the winter they change to hazel
When we're alone it's not the same
When we're close it makes us happy
I'm in love with her
She's in love with me
I promised her we are going to be together forever
She promised me the same thing
Tonight I'm going to call her and tell her how I feel
She doesn't know we go together
But she might like me too
I love Cari Alexis Driver

Zontavious Torbert, Grade 9
McKee Jr High School, AL

Storms
Scared — my heart is racing
and my breathing speeds up.
The cat scurries away from the rain,
and under the porch
I swing silently
as I listen to the thunder behind me.
When the lightning strikes
it brightens the sky to look like day.
I try calling my family
to see how they are doing
but the power is out.
SNAP! Lightning strikes
and breaks a tree in half.
The wind is blowing so hard
and the rain is getting to me.
I run into the house
to escape the harsh storm.
Thunder booms
and shakes the cabinets and windows.
Boy, I wish this were over!
Melanie Melancon, Grade 8
Leonville Elementary School, LA

Snow
Can it be?
In the South?
What is it I wonder?
What do I see?
It's so small,
It's so white.
I don't believe it.
It's a delight.
It's snow,
It's snow.
Oh how it glows!
It makes everything bright,
And makes everyone smile,
Oh please stay,
Stay for a little while.
Can you see?
It's so pleasing to me!!
Candace Potter, Grade 8
Armstrong Middle School, MS

Ocean
The ocean is blue.
It tastes like blueberries,
smells like fried apple pie.
The ocean looks like beautiful
mountain tops,
sounds like wind whistling
in the fall.
The ocean makes me feel
like a newborn baby.
Raven Massey, Grade 7
L E Gable Middle School, SC

A New Chapter
Childhood is something to cherish,
it goes by very fast.
There are so many memories,
and people I'll never forget.

As I have moved on to high school,
there are new halls to walk.
More paths to travel on,
and meeting new people along the way.

I must become more independent
and know my rights from my wrongs.
For there will be several speed bumps
as well as dead ends.

I'm ready to face the next chapter in life,
I'm sure I'm well prepared.
It's time to take a step forward,
but remember everything along the way.
Cecilia Vazquez, Grade 8
Mount Carmel Academy, LA

Why the Wind Blows
I wonder why the wind blows…
Does God make it whirl?
It allows the trees to wave,
The number one cause of bad hair days,
It snatches balloons from a child's hand,
Like the blustery criminal it is,
An aid for a lonely kite,
Will it ever cease?
Tesia Marie-Smith, Grade 8
North Iredell Middle School, NC

Emotions
How do I feel way up high
flying on a ride in the sky
catch me if I fall like rain
'cause if you don't I will feel pain

I want to hide in the tall corn
before I die with a heart that's torn
let me borrow a boat and sail
because I know that we will fail

I must travel through this life
with all of my strife
let us look beyond and wonder
whether we are here or yonder

I mustn't really want to cry
now I feel no pain inside
I'll take this life for what I see
and never wonder what it could be
Layla Sharp, Grade 8
Priceville Jr High School, AL

An Unknown Caller
Hello. Hello. Who's calling? Me!
Me who? I cannot tell you.
Why not? You don't believe.
Believe in what? That it's really me.
Do I know you?
Yes, you do. Do we talk often?
Yes, you call my name.
I answer you, when you call every time.
You always give a smile.
For you are my love and child.
'Cause I want peace please.
It's me Jesus, telling you my child.
Come in peace with me.
Teyairra Hendrix, Grade 8
Armstrong Middle School, MS

Fall
Looking over the hayfield
Ready for the mower
Summer's work is almost done
The days are getting slower

Trees preparing to rest
From their branches leaves are tumbling
Red, yellow, brown, and orange
Nature's beauty is humbling
Ashley Moore, Grade 7
Rock Mills Jr High School, AL

What's in My Journal?
Crushes, hatred,
Joys, troubles
If I had a journal
This is what
I would say

The bad things I think, the real me
I'm shy and quiet
But in my journal I could break free
I could say things I've done
Things I really want to do

Say who I'm hating, who I want gone
I could say what boy has caught my eye
What I really think but never say
I could slap someone
Without them knowing

I could even write a conversation
Too harsh to say
If I had a journal
These are things
That would be my Memories
Of the years I wrote and wrote…
Carisa Urrea, Grade 7
Atlanta Academy, GA

Living in Peace

Peace is laying in the sun,
Letting its warmth flow over you.
Peace is like a wave,
It starts out small then suddenly overwhelms you.
Peace is letting go of your troubles,
And letting them fly away.
Peace is heaven, peace is life.

Grayson Barker, Grade 7
North Iredell Middle School, NC

Is That Easy to You?

Is being equal hard for you?
Or being fair causing you problems?
Thinking about other people
Is that easy to you?

Is prejudging hard for you?
Being a slave of your own mind
Overlooking people by their looks
Is that easy to you?

Having a lifetime opportunity
Yet, always denying people who have talent
Just because they're disabled
Not being fair to slaves who have it

Equal, equity
Two words that are spelled alike
Two meanings completely different
What are you like?

Alexia Salazar, Grade 8
Fayette Middle School, GA

What About Now?

You see the children in Africa,
Starving and dirt poor all the time.
At one point there is nothing you can do for them,
At another, there is everything to do as help.
You must ask yourself one simple question.

You see the homeless in your town,
Cold and scavenging for food during any given moment.
Every time you walk past them it strikes you,
That you have a choice to make right now.
But will you ask yourself that one simple question?

Every day you are faced with a choice,
One that ends in giving to others to help them benefit.
Yet there is one question that stands in our way,
A question that we are often afraid to ask ourselves.
Can I wait to do this?

We have to think, what about now?

Samantha Morley, Grade 9
Haynes Academy for Advanced Studies, LA

What Music Means to Me

Strings tight under my fingertips
Sound vibrating through them to the rest of the world
Playing the music from my heart as one beat with each note
The daily show starts and my hands shake
I start and everything else fades away
Then I finish and everything explodes with sound
The curtain closes and finally I can breathe

Anthony Hulsey, Grade 9
Patriot Academy, AL

The Wonder of Nature

Here I sit brokenhearted,
A loved one and I were parted.

It is so silent,
No thoughts that are violent.

The tree limbs hugged me tight,
I see the leaves in flight.

The wonder of Nature,
The wonder of Nature.

I climbed higher in a tree,
The mysterious wind moves leaves so I can see.

The wonder of Nature,
The wonder of Nature.

I lay in a river, fish scrap me with their fins,
Everything is now washed away even sin.

Paul Fortier, Grade 7
Carolina International School, NC

Flowers

A flower is more than a speck on the ground,
It's more of a gift,
So colorful and profound.

They're Earth's little angels,
Little gifts from above.
They are usually colorful
Yet, can be as white as a dove.

As radiant as the sun,
And as calm as a gentle breeze,
They wait for their gardener to tend to their leaves.

They're as brilliant as a butterfly,
As busy as a bee,
Although their hard work is not easy to see.

They have roots that are growing way down below,
So the flowers you see can put on a beautiful show!

Sadie Martinez, Grade 7
Haynes Academy for Advanced Studies, LA

Farewell

May your troubles and worries be less
your blessing be more
and nothing but happiness comes
throughout your door.
Let the good times come
the bad times go.
The door is open,
it's time to Rest in peace
We both shall go.

Chance Wilkerson, Grade 8
Lake Middle School, MS

My Sorrow

My sorrow
Turns out that my anguish
From my environment
Comes and stays.

I always regret
What I've said
In my past life, and
My sorrow
Turns the light blue skies
Into dark gray thundering storms
My sorrow

I need help
I need someone who can
Walk through those pale skies and
Make them bright and sunny
My sorrow.

Sharice Solomon, Grade 7
Lloyd-Kennedy Charter School, SC

That I Know Is True…

Kiss me like you mean it
Kiss me like you love me…
Kiss me like you don't…
Just kiss me like the sky's falling

I'll wait for you forever
Like I know you'll wait for me.
I know that I will love you,
Way past my lifetime
And never doubt that

You can't not love the way we are…
Together we can make history…
With our love strong and true.
I love my life, almost as much…
As I love you.

I will love you until we both die…
That I know is true.

Margaret Gramke, Grade 8
Priceville Jr High School, AL

Thanksgiving

T hankful for having life and being here on earth
H aving a family that loves me and cares for me
A lways being happy for the things my family does for me
N ever being ungrateful for all the things I get
K indness to all family members and friends
S o thankful I get to see another day and another thanksgiving
G iving thanks to family and friends for all they've done for me
I 'm giving love to everyone that I talk to
V isiting family and friends that I haven't seen in a long time
I nviting people over to enjoy our thanksgiving
N utritious foods that my mom and I prepare together
G iving thanks to be able to see and eat the food on thanksgiving.

Montiah Tumbleson, Grade 7
East Millbrook Magnet Middle School, NC

My Long, Long Journey That's Only a Dream

I feel like I'm trapped, trapped in a hole.
I do believe I'm getting blisters on my soles!
Vast and alone, and yet I'm still cold.
Rain, rain go away I'm trying to make fire.
As it rises higher, something moves.
Something rustles the bushes.
It's happened this way before on the floor of the Blue Ridge mountains.
Now it's again, again!
I hear the same sound in the coastal plain.
"Hello" it calls!
It calls to me, only in a dream.
I awaken to find, I'm still confined to my bed.
I wonder back into a deep sleep.
Only to find I'm on a reef.
With a Cherokee chief.
Now I've got fire!
As I sit and wait, I see a face.
A sad face calling for my help.
I gave a yelp!
I awaken to find, I'm still confined to my bed.
It was only a dream.

Alicia Stamey, Grade 8
Fannin County Middle School, GA

Fault Boundaries

Cracks and breaks in the Earth let magma flow above ground
When the magma cools new land is found
These cracks and breaks move so very, very slow
Where two plates meet and move are called boundaries you know
Two plates that move apart have a divergent boundary
The space in between the plates becomes a rift valley
Where two plates come together the boundary is a convergent one
Which plate will sink well, density determines the outcome
Plates slide past each other in opposite directions
Here we have a boundary called transform
Crust is neither created nor destroyed by this action
Whether plates slide, converge, or diverge no matter the way
plates still move at the end of the day

Karli Walleser, Grade 8
Pineville Jr High School, LA

The Gift

Don't take for granted what you've been given

The sparkle in your eyes
or the shine in your hair
will dull if you don't take action
for the gift is yours

But you have ignored
what has been said
because you can be ignorant
with such a hard head

Your life will be wasted
with your own misery

Others are worried,
scared, and frightened
that you've taken for granted
your gift
your life

Anna Birbiglia, Grade 7
Haynes Academy for Advanced Studies, LA

Fighting the Storm

Today I feel sleepy and tingly all over.
Zap! Like a bolt of lightning,
my hands shake.
Coldness is seeping through my bones.
I'm fighting this storm inside me.
I hold onto consciousness,
hoping to resist crying.
Bizarre dreams are making my eyes flutter.
The moist scent of rain
is thick to my smell.
With wiggling toes, I fidget crazily.
Shivering in a blazing hot oven;
I have no way out.
Imagination like ocean currents;
Thrashing, pulling, and breaking their way to my mind.
Wake up, wake up, wake up!
It's only a dream.
This boulder on my back is too heavy…
Snap. I'm awake,
and I smell breakfast!

Tabby Touchet, Grade 8
Leonville Elementary School, LA

Hurricane Season

Today I feel so lazy.
When I walk outside with my cup of coffee
I see a blue sky with gray clouds.
I can tell there is a storm headed straight for us.
The sun is not so bright.
Katie walks outside
and comes to meet me.
She tells me what strange dream she had.
Mom saw a drizzle in the grass
and told us to come inside.
We go back inside the house for breakfast.
While we are walking
I feel that the wind is picking up speed.
As we walk inside dad says
that hurricane season has just begun.

Megan Stelly, Grade 7
Leonville Elementary School, LA

As If There Was Fate

flowers of the field
picked by the children
placed in a vase.
as if it was fate.
flourished and thrived
then wilted and died.
tossed away with sad heart.
the wind tears us apart.
and not looking back
we're on different tracks.
it's starting again.
from beginning to end.
in each separate place.
as if there was fate.

Jessica Wray, Grade 9
Haynes Academy for Advanced Studies, LA

Open

Open closed
Closed open
Which way does the door go?
Open closed
Closed open
Which way does life go?
Do you know why the door opens and
Closes and closes and opens?
Life opens and closes because people die
And people are born but
Do you know why the door opens and closes?

Briana Greenlief, Grade 9
Northgate High School, GA

D-day

Rocking in the unsteady boat
The soldiers waited with a lump in their throat
Bullets zipping past
A thousand soldiers running fast
Bombs dropping in every direction
Soldiers dying in every section
Getting shot down
Bodies dropping to the ground
The Earth held its breath on that fateful day
And not many can still say
What happened on D-day

Phillip Myers, Grade 7
St George Middle School, SC

Slavery

People trying to make a scheme
People trying to learn to read and write
People wanting to take an adventure
People wanting water, but can't find a river
When the moon comes out
They try to do it, but they got caught
People getting whipped almost to death
Trying for a chance at freedom
Trying to escape

Sherika Dykes, Grade 7
Hubert Middle School, GA

Track and Field

T raining to become the best
R unning to beat the clock
A ttend every meet to out do your last
C oming to every practice to help yourself
K eeping in condition to run

A lways running
N ever getting down on a bad time
D oing your best to place

F ind something to improve on
I n the heat and the cold
E veryone watching you
L oving the sport
D o your best

Bradlie Dunham, Grade 9
Warren Early College High School, NC

Rumors

Rumors are like a wave going all the way
Across an ocean
Rumors can start off as quiet as a yellow star
But soon a lot of stars appear
And rumors spread
More and more
Joking is as fun as seeing a rainbow
But that rainbow soon turns
Black
And joking turns into rumors
Rumors can turn friendships
Sideways
Upside down
Crooked
What people think about you
I hate rumors
Rumors are as horrible as a
Unicorn breaking its horn
I wish there was
No such thing
As rumors

Rachel Feldman, Grade 9
The Howard School, GA

Sitting Alone on a Park Bench Made for Two

Silent, lonely
Almost depressing
Solitude is like a silent killer
A thief in the night
Robbing you of all happiness
Like sitting alone on a park bench made for two

Most lonely people live in solitude
Never hearing another in their house
Never getting Christmas presents from anyone
Never feeling loved
Never knowing what it is like to share
Never feeling compassion
Never receiving anything out of love
Like sitting alone on a park bench made for two

Forever lonely
Never happy
Always sad
We cannot explain
Why people live in solitude
Some people never stop some do
Like sitting alone on a park bench made for two

Alayna Fikse, Grade 7
Cherokee Christian School, GA

Inevitable

We don't know what exactly will happen,
We most likely cannot change it either,
Everything that happens is inevitable.

It is beyond our control,
Beyond our imagination,
It is all for a reason.

Everything has a reason,
A reason for happening,
And that reason is because it is inevitable.

Forrest Fitch, Grade 8
Carolina International School, NC

Gustav

During Gustav I stayed with my family.
The storm had really bad rain and lightning.
It was around evening
when some trees broke and snapped.
During the eye of the storm
the frogs and birds started to come out.
Some of the rocks looked like diamonds.
One of the cars was covered in leaves.
My dream was for the storm to be over.
When the thunder roared
it felt like the Earth shook.
When the storm was over everything was ok.

Shane Latiolais, Grade 7
Leonville Elementary School, LA

Georgia

Fall is the best time of year here in Georgia.
When everything starts to change.
The air gets cooler, the wind blows harder.
The leaves crunch up and fall gently off the trees.
Everywhere you step you are stepping on leaves
As they crunch beneath your feet,
you start to smell the sweet scent of fall.

Narisa Osborn, Grade 8
Fannin County Middle School, GA

The 90's Kid

"I know you are, but what am I?"
The Magic School Bus flies right by
Plastic streamers on our bikes
Yo-yo's were things we actually liked
We ran through sprinklers in the summer
Darkness certainly was a bummer
Waldo could hide for hours and hours
We were super heroes with hidden powers
Jelly shoes, slap bracelets, Miss Mary Mack,
Playing with the teacher's Silly Tac
"In West Philadelphia, born and raised…"
By light up shoes we were amazed
Not getting your way and throwing a fit
"If you love it so much, marry it."
We didn't trip dancing to Spice Girls
'Cause our cool shoelaces had tight curls
Playing in puddles, wearing raincoats
"Talk to the hand" and writing MASH notes
Counting in Spanish, not two but "dos"
We didn't know how soon we'd say "Adios!"

Colleen Scutt, Grade 9
Fort Dorchester High School, SC

Every Day

Every day,
The sun will rise,
The rain will fall,
The waters will gush,
And every day,
We will hear the cheerful song that the birds sing,
And we will wake to smell,
The crisp smell of the world awakening,
Every day,
We will feel the warmth of the world around us,
Taste the salt blowing off the ocean,
Every day,
We will see the leaves twisting,
Twisting and twirling in the wind,
And every day,
The world will grow around us,
Every day,
And every day.

Patterson Wells, Grade 7
First Flight Middle School, NC

Fear

Fear is a silent mouse,
    Sneaking up on the unexpected
Squeaky floorboards behind you,
    Squeak, Squeak, Squeak…
You quickly turn around in an intense panic,
    What is this feeling you ask
Nothing is there but a dim candle,
    You walk farther and farther
Bang! The door shuts in a distance,
    Sprinting to investigate you see nothing
A harmless drop of sweat trickles down your face,
    Something is terribly wrong…
The candle flickers once more,
    The light disappears!
Your heart goes insane as you stand in the dark,
    You Scream
This is Fear,
    Fear,
        Fear…

Zachary King, Grade 7
Carolina International School, NC

Anger

Swelling up inside of me
like a balloon ready to burst —
anger, tension, jealousy.
Feelings that are too strong to hold in.

Red face,
hot head,
harsh words —

Silent anger —
mean glares
loose lips.

Emotions exploding all around spinning like a tornado;
hurting anyone it comes across.

Suddenly, it's gone.
You're done; content;
the winds have stopped;
heat is released.

Nikki Taylor, Grade 9
New Site High School, MS

Rich/Poor

rich
money, wealthy
buying, earning, selling
New York, California, Central America, Africa
scrounging, begging, stealing
uncomfortable, hard
poor

Ben Westra, Grade 7
Sacred Heart of Jesus School, LA

Great Day

The light burst from behind
The mist and clouds.
I know it's going to be a
Great day.
The air was warm.
It's finely time for a cool
dip in the pool.
I know it's going to be a
Great day.
Afterwards, I drink a refreshing
glass of lemonade, out on my deck.
I know it's going to be a great day.
When the sun finally sets, I say
"That was a great day."

Diedra Thacker, Grade 7
L E Gable Middle School, SC

Say Goodbye

Our love will always be strong.
Even when it's right or wrong.
I will always love you.
For you, not for your crew.
It's going to be hard to say goodbye,
When we graduate in 2009.
The New Year is near and I know
We're going to different schools.
But, I will still love you
Even if you find somebody new.
I wish we could rewind
Back in time.
Back when you were first mine.
And now, time has flown by.
Passing us saying goodbye.
Goodbye is harder than saying hi.
But now is the day to say
I love you and I realized
That it's time to say goodbye.

Haley Plato, Grade 9
McKee Jr High School, AL

My Mom

My mom is a wonderful woman,
She is always there for me.
She has taught me to live my life
To the fullest and
To be all that I can be.
I was in some beauty pageants,
My mom was there for me.
She doesn't care what she has to do,
I am always first.
My mom and I are so close,
My world revolves around her.
I couldn't do anything in life,
If my mom wasn't there with me!

Stephanie Denny, Grade 9
North Wilkes High School, NC

This World We Live In

I walk this endless land, from sea to shining sea,
The land our forefathers won so that we could be free.
Oceans span across our Earth and the skies my great outdoors.
Fish swim just outside my room, and birds fly by my windows.
I think about all of the creatures I see,
And how lucky they are to be free.
I want to soar among the clouds, and swim beneath the reef.
I exist for this world we live in, and this world exists with us.
We live inside this world of ours, but also with its wondrous lands.
Boundaries are the ties that bind, the walls that close us in.
When we escape this state of mind, this box that keeps us blocked.
I will move worlds and keep going forward; no more will I be human.
I will be with the animals, in this crazy world we live in.

Evan Bridges, Grade 8
Armstrong Middle School, MS

The Sky

The sky is a mystery that can never be solved
The sky is an endless wonderland
There are big puffs of white candy floating around
The background is blue like the reflection of the ocean blue
There is a yellow ball of heat that will punish you if you stare at it
All the stuff in the sky is wonderful…But…
What were those white crystals falling from the sky
I do not know much of the sky but I would say…
The sky was crying crystals

Jacob Tanas, Grade 7
Cathedral School, NC

A Song of Greatness

When I hear the old men, telling of great deeds, of ancient days,
when I hear that telling, then I think within me, I am one of these.

When I hear the people, praising great ones, then I know what I, too,
shall be esteemed, I, too, when my times comes, shall do mighty things.

Kenya Ingram, Grade 7
Laurin Welborn Middle School, NC

What Is a Best Friend?

What is a best friend?
Someone who's there no matter what,
someone that calms that bad feeling in your gut.

What is a best friend?
Someone who's there when you get in a fight,
someone who is always wrong so that you're right.

What is a best friend?
Someone who's there when your hamster dies,
pulls you into a big hug and tells you that it's ok to cry.

What is a best friend?
Someone who's there when that jerk breaks up with you,
looks him in the eyes and tells him you're a jerk through and through.

Kasey Edwards, Grade 8
Yazoo County Jr High School, MS

Extended Metaphors

I am a turtle

Moving slowly on through life.
Greeting new people as I go.
One day I will stop and live on peacefully.

I am a tree

Never moving from my place.
Always watching everyone play.
Getting older as the day goes by.
Never getting younger.

I am an airplane

Always traveling the many miles.
Going to places I never knew.
Needs to be refueled with gas to travel.

Christopher Yang, Grade 7
L E Gable Middle School, SC

Black

Black is the night when stars are hidden
It walks alone, careless and untame
Black engulfs the world where light cannot go

Black is my mother's hair
silky and smooth
It stands out telling everyone to back off
Black has a mind of its own

Kaylee Hilton, Grade 7
L E Gable Middle School, SC

I'm Ticklish

I am ticklish!
Yes, it's true.
There are some things I might do.
Bump into stuff.
Hit something made out of fluff.

Run around.
Fall on the ground.
Yell, stop!
I hope I won't pop!

Jordi Wright, Grade 7
East Millbrook Magnet Middle School, NC

Motion of the Ocean

I see birds hunting for fish amongst wave breaks
I hear the over turn of the oceanic waves
I feel sand amidst my soggy toes and fingers
I taste moist, salty pretzels
I smell the humid, briny air
I know I'm having a superior time on the coast

Hannah Davis, Grade 7
East Millbrook Magnet Middle School, NC

Come Back to Me

I wish you were with me.
I miss the things we used to do.
I miss the time we played our games.
I missed when the phone rang and I knew it was you.
Do you wish I were with you?
I hope you are doing well.
I also hope you're happy with the person you're with
I also miss our song and the things we did together.
I dreamed that you would come back to me.
But dreams are dreams they don't come true.
And wishes are wishes.

Brittney Wilkerson, Grade 8
Lake Middle School, MS

About Frogs

A frog,
   green and smooth,
croaks and moans,
   loudly.
Amphibian.

A tadpole,
   tiny and wet,
twists and squirms,
   bonelessly.
Baby.

The lily pad,
   still and motionless,
floated and stayed,
   quietly.
Plant.

D.J. Bordelon, Grade 7
Haynes Academy for Advanced Studies, LA

A New Purse

When I was a child
Being a girl meant having purses,
Purses, and more purses.
A blue polka-dotted purse
A pink striped purse
A red purse with swirls
A purse with key chains
I wanted all of them
Anywhere I went I saw purses
Sitting in the store window
All alone
With nothing in them
And then, as I was staring in the store window,
I realized
I don't need a billion purses,
I need a
Fur coat!

Lindsay Merritt, Grade 7
Atlanta Academy, GA

My Friends, My Family

My friends, my family are the world to me
A world where even the blind can see
A place where everyone wants to be
It's a place known to many
But still unknown to some
For I know it all too well
It is where I live
It is where I roam

Some people say their life is a living hell
Well mine isn't the best either
But there are two things
That could make it better
You should already know
What those two things are
They're my friends, my family
My world forever more

Kayla Ledbetter, Grade 8
Eclectic Middle School, AL

Music

Music speaks for the words that cannot be spoken,
And expresses the emotions that cannot be expressed.
Music intrigues the mind and soothes the soul.
Music tells stories with song.
Music hypnotizes the mind with its beautiful melodies,
Sometimes soft, gentle, hard, or irate.
Music is in and around us.
Music is life!

Amelia-Kate Johnson, Grade 8
St Joseph Catholic School, LA

I Am the Future and Change

I am the future and the change
I wonder what the future holds
I hear the clock ticking as time goes by
I see people waste away the days disagreeing
I want people to stop being segregated
I am the future and the change

I pretend I don't see the wrong
I feel the hate
I touch the hearts of people
I worry that people will never walk hand in hand
I cry when I see abuse
I am the future and the change

I understand we are not perfect
I say it will stop
I dream people will walk hand in hand
I try to prevent segregation
I hope to change the views of people
I am the future and the change

Jessica Maynard, Grade 9
Warren Early College High School, NC

Football

Football is intense every Sunday
Fans gear up and come to scream
I hope you've rested because here it goes
Everyone screaming go team go!
Half-time the score is tied
Now things begin to intensify.
Fourth quarter ten seconds left the score is tied.
Out comes the kicker for the other team
Oh no, he's the best in the league.
He's going for the win
With a fifty-nine yard field goal.
Wow, it's in!
You lose your first game.
Better luck next time don't feel lame.
Fans are sad but next week flies
Back to practice, coach is mad
You run, toss and tackle
Until your muscles hurt bad.
After practice you know you'll play your best
To win next Sunday's game.
Will you pass the test?

Matthew Alikhani, Grade 7
Haynes Academy for Advanced Studies, LA

Races?

Why so racist?
Everyone's colored.
We are,
Pink when we're embarrassed,
Red when we're burning up,
Orange when we're fake tanned,
Yellow when we're infected,
Green when we're bruised,
Blue when we're freezing,
Purple when we're punched,
Brown when we're out at the beach too long,
Black when we're dirty,
White when we're sick,
And most of all,
We're gold in our hearts.
Why so racist?

Rosa Park, Grade 8
Jay M Robinson Middle School, NC

Blindness

Everyone in the world is blind,
But not in the way you would think.
There is the blindness of heart and the blindness of sight.
Those who can see the light of day
Judge people by the way they look,
So they are blind of the heart.
But those who are truly blind and can only see the night
Can look deeper into the hearts of others
And find the light within.

Katie Bougére, Grade 7
St Joseph Catholic School, LA

Dark Rains

Rain falling.
    Darkness covering us like a blanket,
Suffocating our happiness and joy.
    But soon the darkness slowly uncovers,
Leaving us an unforgettable mess.
    But also teaching us that even in darkness,
There is always a bright side of life.

Jason Reed, Grade 7
Margaret Green Jr High School, MS

The Day I Started Dance Class

Here I am getting dressed for dance
Waiting for my mom to call me down the steps
I'm hoping dance will be easy, and fun
Hoping that she won't make us run!

Walking in the door in front of everyone,
Also being the shortest one,
Doesn't seem really nice
It feels like the lowest number on a dice!

We start stretching to music,
Which really hurts,
Don't confuse it,
It's a lot of hard work.

We start working on our routine,
Even though I feel as if I just ran a mile,
The pain is easing off,
And it's getting really fun!

Now it's time to go,
She gives us candy on the down low,
I'll be coming back soon,
Tuesday afternoon!

Makia Davis, Grade 8
Dillard Drive Middle School, NC

Horrifying Weather

Storms make me feel scared
Winds are very strong,
and clouds cover the sun.
Green grass flows with the wind
Frogs have nowhere to hide
Many memories go through my head.
I think God is here somewhere.
It feels like the earth is moving
a thousand times faster.
I am inside watching through my window.
The storm calms down a little bit,
Finally the storm is over
and we go outside
and look around
to see the damage.

Amanda Tujague, Grade 7
Leonville Elementary School, LA

Love

What really is love?
What does it actually mean?
When will you find it?
When will you feel it?
When will you see it?
Have you ever found love?
When did you find it?
How does it feel?
What did you see?
Love is unexpected,
Love is trouble,
Love is happiness,
Love is true,
Love is forever,
Love is everything you feel!

Megan Robles, Grade 7
Haynes Academy for Advanced Studies, LA

Looking Back Through Heaven's Eyes

Life I had to live
Paths I had to choose from
Friends I had to betray
Times I looked away
Good deeds went downstream
Greatest broken dreams
Reasons why it happened
Lives my choices impacted
Signs the good Lord showed me
Ways my heart's been broken
Regrets I need to say
Minutes 'till I pass away
People I ask forgiveness
Hugs I gave today
No doubts run through my mind as I see my Jesus

Lauren Leistman, Grade 8
Alexandria Middle Magnet School, LA

A Nobleman's Daughter

I am the daughter of a wealthy man;
I do not worry over food or clothes.
It's sad that I must wed a man I loathe.
Before too late I must devise a plan
To get away from that old grouchy man.
My precious world will end when I betroth.
To hurt my father by my choice I'm loath.
His health is poor. I please him all I can.

Though I should not, I love the miller's son.
To wed him now would be my greatest wish.
Into his waiting arms fain would I run.
Our lives are new and fresh. They've just begun.
My future now can only bring anguish.
Our custom triumphed over love and won.

Aynsley Pruitt, Grade 7
Tishomingo Middle School, MS

Losing Me for Me

There is this friend of mine whose love is always kind and when something good happens they're always on my mind,
I can't show you for tomorrow what there is to come; but I know I don't have to worry because I know where I come from.
I know I might seem tough and sharp around the edges, but you've only seen one part of me and that part is not enough,
I cannot tell you everything that crosses on my mind, it's all because I'm a person who is just too hard to find.

I can't show you who I am, I wear a sad clown face and, if I were to take it off I fear that you would race,
I know I might sound fake but this is how I'm real, 'cause I have a broken line that shows you what I feel.
I feel as though I'm a geisha, painting my face to hide all the huge emotions that are building up inside,
But when I'm with my friend all of that fear goes from me 'cause they're the one person that just always sees.

My paint I wash away, the brush I give to them, the powder blowing in the wind, the lipstick is worn thin.
My smile is quite bright, my eyes can finally breathe, everything is ok, until they have to leave.
You see they know the routine, the process we go through, it is well done now because, they are my friend so true.
They give me back my paint brush and tell me to stay true to who I am inside even when I'm blue.

The love we share today will be greater and more tomorrow, because we both can understand that there is no more sorrow.
For I will lose my paint, I will stick it in a jar and put it high, in a cupboard, and leave it there to dry.
I will show my real skin off, leave it bare for the world to see and I will have no fear, no more! Because I will be me!

Imani Mobley, Grade 9
Holly Springs High School, NC

Secretly How I Love You

Secretly I've been watching you and admiring your beauty. How beautiful you are that you look like an angel. When you smile your white teeth glisten and your cheeks get rosy red. When you talk you look straight into a person's eyes and your blue eyes sparkle. When you eat anything the crumbs get on your face. When you speak you sound a little manly and there is a sweetness to your face. When you walk you seem to glide. When you get all excited your ivory face turns red. When you dance you look like a graceful goddess. When you drink tea you sip very slowly so that your tongue doesn't get burned by the hotness. When you play sports or skateboard you have a demeanor which is so appealing. When you read manga it seems like you just read a page in one second. When you brush your long, straight, brownish-black hair you act like a child. When you see someone in trouble you help them out. When you get angry you become violent. When you get sad you start crying and write depressing poetry. When I see you, I just blush because I am in love with you and your nature. I love you, yet you will never love me back. For you are the girl of my dreams, and I am your worst nightmare.

Pranati Puri, Grade 9
Brandon High School, MS

Freedom and Love

How delicious is the winning of a kiss at love's beginning,
When two mutual hearts are sighing for the knot there's no untying!
Yet remember, midst you wooing love has bliss, but Love has ruing
Other smiles make make you fickle tears for other charms may trickle
Love he comes and love he tarries just as fate or fancy carries,
Longest stays, when sorest chidden laughs and flies, when pressed and bidden
Blind the sea to slumber stilly bind its odor to the lily
Bind the aspen ne'er to quiver then bind love to last forever
Love's a fire that needs renewal of fresh beauty for its fuel
Love's wing mouth when caged and captured only free, he soars enraptured
Can you keep the bees from ranging? No nor better love from dying in the knot there's no tying.

Jessica White, Grade 9
Marion High School, AL

The Wind

The wind smells like fresh air, the leaves looking like wild men fighting to the death.
The noise is music to my ears. It tastes like honey as the honeysuckles get blown away in the air.
The wind feels nice and I feel better.

Caleb Knieper, Grade 7
First Flight Middle School, NC

Hurricanes

The hurricane is coming
as the sun sets down.
Many trees are blown down
as the wind picks up its speed.
The streets of New Orleans, Louisiana are empty.
The levees break
as water rushes over them.
A ton of water from the Gulf
takes over the whole upper 9th ward.
Many cars are damaged
and homes are lost.
So many people and pets are dead,
but just as the days go by,
the hurricane disappears out the sky.
Then when I think back of this disaster
I remember that it's only
Mother Nature is our master.

Zakayle' Bellard, Grade 8
Leonville Elementary School, LA

Nature

Grass is green,
The sky is bright,
Wind is blowing,
Water splashing onto the rocks,
Everything is nice and calm,
Like nothing could go wrong,

Leaves falling from the sky,
Everything falling,
But you still feel like nothing is wrong,
All is normal.

You can't change nature,
If you could it wouldn't really be nature,
It happens naturally,
Changing it would not make it nature.

Maria Piacun, Grade 7
Haynes Academy for Advanced Studies, LA

Georgia

Georgia, what a wonderful place!
Come here and spend many days.
Bring your family and friends.
Oh! How the fun never ends!
You can come and camp on the lake,
There are many souvenirs that you can take!
There are many activities you can do,
from hunting, fishing, and camping, too.
Join the fun and delight,
and watch the stars shine so bright.
We ride four wheelers, and pack in the fun
and ride all day until the day is done.

Lindsy Walker, Grade 8
Fannin County Middle School, GA

Heroes

Heroes can be anywhere in the world
They may be young they may be old.
It doesn't matter whether they're short or tall,
All that matters is they are there when you fall.
They can be your friends or family,
Or you don't even have to know who they are.
All my friends and family are my heroes,
They know when to help and know when to go.
Sometimes teachers are even my heroes,
They might get on your nerves
But all they are doing is helping you.
They have a lot of wisdom and so do parents,
Even though they make us mad you should listen.

Samantha Harrell, Grade 7
Albemarle School, NC

Friends

Friends aren't easy
They start off rough
And end up sad
Friendship is all about
Loving and caring for one another
Being there with them, and at their pace
Looking out for one another
And just having fun
They're the ones you can trust
The ones you can love
The ones you can count on
Every day you go through with them
They're the ones who try to keep a smile always on your face
I can't really explain what a friend really means
But a friend is what we all share
I thank you now for being there every step of the way

Khadiga Konsouh, Grade 8
Carolina International School, NC

Like No Other

Someone important to me is my mother,
She is mine and like no other.

She has taught me all I know,
Such a good job doing so.

She gives me advice
So helpful and nice.

She tells me what to do
When I am feeling so blue.

She watches over me
Making sure I am the best I can be.

What would I do without my mother?
Let me tell you, I wouldn't want any other.

Sarah Bourgeois, Grade 9
Mount Carmel Academy, LA

A Silent World

Only if the world were silent
It would speak peace.
It would express the word calamity.
If there were a silent world.

The world could be a mocking bird
Without it's beak.
It seems so easy but could this be?
If there were a silent world.

A billion words people speak
The tracks of records played a week.
If there were a silent world
It would finally contribute
To the true meaning of harmony.

Janay Taylor, Grade 9
Leesville Road High School, NC

Wow Christmas

Peace, joy, hope
WOW Christmas is almost here
We hang our stockings, row by row
Playing in winter snow
On Christmas Day
We hope for toys
We've been
Good girls and boys

But we must never forget
On Christmas Day
To thank the Lord when we pray

Ashley-Olivia Kennedy, Grade 8
St Peter Claver School, LA

Brown

My hair is so soft, so long, so nice
It has all the colors of spice
A little black and brown
With even sides all around
Now my hair is twisted into little spikes
It looks just like my cousin Mike's

Jarvaris Fuller, Grade 7
L E Gable Middle School, SC

Mom

Mom is such a little word
And yet it holds inside
A wish for happiness
Always and forever

It holds a world of gratitude
For all you say and do
It holds a wish for happiness
Always and forever

Corey Boothe, Grade 8
Three Springs of Courtland School, AL

Our Lady

A new place a new world just waiting to unfold.
I have become estranged to my native land, forgotten the smell of its civil sand.
I miss the sound of the Liberty Bell, and the long story it has to tell.

Laura Herring, Grade 7
Home School, SC

Tick Tock — Tick Tock (The Killer)

Time; it's a precious thing
in a blink of an eye you have plenty of it
…I wouldn't blink again if I were you
because next time, your time might disappear
Tick tock tick tock goes the clock
It sits on the wall, mocking, laughing, all towards me.
You were a young soul even if your skin was old
but there was so much, so much life inside your body
…but then I blinked
Now it's different, you're an empty shell of the person I once knew
Your blank stare and your empty mind; they don't suit you
I'm still blinking, but nothing's changing
Tick tock tick tock goes the clock
…more time slipping away more time with you gone
Your shell, it sits there trying to put words together
I'm sick of this but time's not changing
Tormenting, playing with my mind…stupid time
Time was on my side, but then it turned
Now, time is a cold-blooded single-minded killer
Tick tock tick tock goes the clock
…I wish that clock would just stop…

Kayla Alexander, Grade 9
Haynes Academy for Advanced Studies, LA

My Love

My love is the sun that lights our way,
with brilliant rays that light your darkest days.

My love is the moon in the still of the night,
while the stars are shiny, so beautiful and bright.

As they flash and shimmer with the twinkle in your eye,
When the daylight comes, my love is your bluest sky.

My love is the raindrops pouring down through the mist,
It's wonderful bliss.

When we're together…

You are my knight in shining armor and your love is your sword,
You stand and protect me from evil horde.

My love is the leaves that blow in the wind,
As I tell you I love you time and time again.

A wife, a mother, a lover and a best friend am I, and I promise you,
My love is yours…yours, until the day that I die and forever more.

JeBresha Jackson, Grade 9
McKee Jr High School, AL

High Merit Poems – Grades 7, 8 and 9

World

The world,
    Monumental yet benign,
Revolves and spins
    Perpetually.
Earth.

The Earth,
    Living yet dead,
Explodes and tremors
    Unrelentingly.
Disaster.

A disaster,
    Natural yet overwhelming,
Quakes and storms
    Ceaselessly.
Nature.

Matthew Guo, Grade 7
Haynes Academy for Advanced Studies, LA

A Flickering Light

Alone in the hallway stands a dimmed light,
Flickering ever so bright.

I crept down the stairs to see what it was; a flickering light,
The light reminded me of myself, standing alone in the world.

I stood there silently and alone without another to help shine,
The light was me, shining independent and free!

Maribeth Morgan, Grade 8
Margaret Green Jr High School, MS

Steady

As the world turns,
and out there impossibilities
are becoming realities.
Women of all races,
making their dreams come true.
But here am I, sitting and watching her,
day after day after day, throwing her life away.
Watching her world turn outside
these four walls through two glass shields.
I watch her stay scared and alone,
not knowing the current of a mother.
Desperate for change but not action.
And just sitting.
As if her world depended on it.
Staring and thinking.
Thinking of a world with no danger at all.
Imagining us as total aliens.
As if I, I were a stranger.
And slowly, and slowly pushing me away.
She's what I watch
Day after day after day.

Joy Bailey, Grade 8
Bell Street Middle School, SC

The Small Comforts of Life

The dew on the grass in the morning light,
The quiet chirp of crickets at night,
The fresh scent of crisp and cool air,
The gentle breeze that blows through my hair,
The soft pitter-patter of a persistent rain,
The silent echo of a far off train,
The rumble of the car when Dad gets home,
The meowing of the stray cat as he roams,
The gentle waters lapping up from the lake,
The tantalizing smells while my mom bakes,
The innocent bark of a neighbor's dog,
The goodbye from my sister before her jog,
All of these little things make me happy.
They complete my days with peace and comfort.

Gabrielle Roe, Grade 9
Mount Carmel Academy, LA

Memories:

Memories are things you can never see.
You can remember memories if you think of something sweet.

You can search for years but never find a single memory.
However, you wonder and wonder you are losing the sight.

You are crying and crying you want to flee
But you can never see the last memory.

Then you think, can you ever see
The precious memory that lies beneath?

Soon you lay dawn the memory comes back to you
Can it be? It is true
You can see the memory that has come back to you.

This is the journey of a single memory that has lost its path
Then it began a new journey that just begun.

Niccolo Roditti, Grade 7
Carolina International School, NC

The Worst Storm

During Hurricane Gustav,
I felt like I just wanted to let the hurricane take me.
There were thousands of trees
    knocked down by the storm.
My dog had to come into the house for the storm.
School time is longer now because of the storm.
No electricity for several days
    made me feel uncomfortable.
Could not see the grass because it was flooded.
All of the trees were knocked down.
The sun did not shine as bright.
Many of my dreams were pretty scary
    until the sun came out again!

Blaine Davis, Grade 7
Leonville Elementary School, LA

Basketball

The basketball
Quickly
Soaring
   Through the air
   To the goal
   Through the hoop
Who made the shot?

Terrance Fryson, Grade 7
Sacred Heart of Jesus School, LA

The Great Blue Ridge Lake

If you ever have a heartache,
Do you know where to take it?
I hope the answer is,
"Of course, the great Blue Ridge Lake!"

With its trickling streams,
The laughter of people,
And the birds chirping
This place is very relaxing.

It's not just relaxing,
It is fun!
When I'm tubing,
I feel as if I'm floating on air.

As this lake has advantages,
It also has disadvantages.
Sometimes a dead fish washes up
AND IT STINKS!

Whenever you have a problem
You know where to take it.
Just take it on a great vacation,
To the great Blue Ridge Lake!

Anna Birchmore, Grade 8
Fannin County Middle School, GA

Music

The beat of a drum,
The strum of a guitar,
All flow together to form
Music.

The tune of a saxophone,
The whistle of a flute,
All flow together to form
Music.

Young and old,
Small and tall,
All come together,
To make
Music.

Christopher Spedale, Grade 7
St Thomas More Catholic School, LA

Drawing

Images flashing through my mind
Which one should I choose?
Then I finally pick

Touch the paper
And gray lines appear
They start to take shape
And form a picture

Now's the time for color
Now I make it shine
The picture is now complete
When I see
The image that was in my mind

McKayla Brown, Grade 8
Hatley School, MS

My Sanctuary

My house
My place
My prison
My peace

Relaxing
Stressing
Clumsy
Clean

The trees
The grass
The balcony
The wind

My special place
My getaway
My house
My prison
My peace
No one knows where it is
But me

Cristina Guerra, Grade 8
Atlanta Academy, GA

Place for Me

Georgia, Georgia, oh so free
Such lovely weather, the fresh outdoors
Our backyards as wild as can be
Birds chirping, rivers flowing
Sounds like Georgia is the place for me
Georgia, Georgia, oh so free
Going camping, visiting lakes,
Even going to the sea
Family get-togethers and festivities
Georgia is the place for me.

Kaitlynn Baugh, Grade 8
Fannin County Middle School, GA

Rain Dance

Tapping on windows
Our cold roofs are their dance floors
Thumping and beating

Meghan Pavelka, Grade 7
Martin Middle School, NC

Storms

When storms come I feel sad.
I am thinking of swimming.
I am feeling tired.
Winter is my favorite season.
A frog jumped on a lily pad
Sunrise looks like gold
when the storm is over.
The sun from the sunrise
also looks like fire.
I can hear the dog
barking in the distance.
Dark clouds soon go away,
as the angels come.

Seth Mistrot, Grade 8
Leonville Elementary School, LA

peace

what is peace?
it is a world without fighting
no enemies pain or hunger
no suffering or killing
peace comes with laughter
and with happiness
peace feels like a beautiful morning
right when you wake up
it saves peoples lives
because they're not at war
it repels all grief
from a world at peace
to me peace is like
being under a shady tree
eating a fresh baked apple pie

Caleb Gilleo, Grade 7
North Iredell Middle School, NC

My Love Song

Love is a spring-green song
It blossoms with vividness
It is fresh
A new occurrence
It sings in my heart
And joy claims me
The music floats on the air
And I float with it
I am calm
I am happy
Because love is a spring-green song

Kathleen Wilson, Grade 9
Mount Carmel Academy, LA

Attitudes of Life

Make choices that are right for you
In the end you will benefit and others will too

Treat others the way you want to be treated
If you don't you will be defeated

Never think you are superior to others
Or else you will suffer with your lovers

Believing in yourself is a must
You will then live a life of just

Overcome your fears by keeping your lights on
And all your dismay will vanish and be gone

Life will throw many riddles at you
And you will have to figure out how to overcome those too!

Important life principles are listed in this poem
Just always remember to never forget 'em!

Zeshan Velani, Grade 8
Fayette Middle School, GA

My Hurricane

Hurricanes can destroy everything in your life.
All the animals can feel it coming beneath their feet.
Hot strong winds start to pick up speed.
There is not a cloud in the blue sky.
Everyone is waiting to find out
whether to leave or not.
It is evening and everything starts to calm down.
The big storm is on its way.
All we can do is pray to God everyone is safe.
It is here!

Taylor Dalfrey, Grade 8
Leonville Elementary School, LA

Thinking

Sitting at the window
Staring outside
Wondering why.
Sitting outside
On sun-warmed grass
The scent of flowers
And the warm summer air.
Sitting outside
Wanting to know why.
What has the world come to?
Fights, wars, hunger, and cold.
Homeless people wandering the streets.
Who did what?
Why did they do it?
Why? Why? Why?

Malerie Eiserloh, Grade 8
Haynes Academy for Advanced Studies, LA

The Season of Summer

Summer is my favorite time of year
It's a time of fun and a time of cheer
Ice cream, popsicles, and snowballs too
All you wear is tank top shirts and flip flop shoes
None of the teachers have to teach
Instead all the teachers can go to the beach
Summer camp is also fun
We do crafts and eat hot dogs on buns
We sit by the pool in our lounge chairs
It is as if we have no cares
My favorite thing is our annual cruise
My family and I have fun and snooze
Right before dark we watch the sunset
Summer is a time I will never forget

Caitlyn Betbeze, Grade 8
Mount Carmel Academy, LA

I Am One

There I lay hopelessly on the street
The dirty, muddy, lonely street
I watch the joyful people going along with their everyday lives
Not even glancing in my direction
I am alone, and one
I have no partner
No mom, dad or even a sister to argue with
I am one
Dinner…that's gourmet
I dig through the garbage every night
Only to find empty boxes of delicious foods
When the fall of night arrives
I snuggle up into a flat screen TV box
Or in the tube slide at the local park
I wonder what my life could have been
A doctor, a lawyer
Or anybody with a life
I continue my lonely life as one
No partner
Just one
I am one

Deema Al-Ghandour, Grade 8
Dillard Drive Middle School, NC

When You Left

It was a morning so dark and dreary
My heart was broken, sad and weary

You'd left this world and me behind
Your heavenly home you surely did find

Without you here life is not the same
I dream of you often and breathe your sweet name

And yet I know this isn't the end
The day will come when we will meet again

Deven Alexander, Grade 8
Lake Middle School, MS

Friendship

Abby is my best friend
She will be there 'til the end
She will always be there for me
As far as I can see
We will be friends forever
As long as we stay together
Friendship is a great thing
That makes me want to sing

Kori Lackey, Grade 7
Lake Castle Private School, LA

Music and Storms

Lungs breathing, heart beating.
Veins pulsing,
eyes blinking.
Music makes me feel alive.
Babies being born,
loved ones dying.
Happiness and sorrow,
smiles and tears.
It helps me escape all of this.
All of these storms
happening around me.
I need a place
that calms these storms.
Where it feels like I'm floating
on the clouds.
Where it feels like I'm soaring
through the stars.
And I've found it
in all these little beats and rhythms.

Sawyer McMicken, Grade 8
Leonville Elementary School, LA

Papa's Healing

We got the bad news today
We got the bad news this morning
Papa has cancer it made him cry
We got the bad news this morning
Papa has cancer he cried
We go to the doctor today
We got the bad news this morning
Papa has cancer it made him cry
The bad news came this morning
The doctor said he wouldn't live
Papa has cancer he cried
We go to the doctor today
They said he wouldn't live long
The Lord took Papa today
We got the Good news today
He's not in pain
Papa is in a better place today
He has no more pain in his body
Papa is HOME!

Caitlin Rogers, Grade 7
L E Gable Middle School, SC

Dark to Light

As a dark and rainy day comes over us here,
I sit in the classroom and think.
But why?
The picture's already very clear.
The rain beating hard on the Earth,
Making puddles as big as my fist.
Lightning striking more than once.
The thunder very tense,
Like a child kicking and screaming or a dusty rug getting a beating.

Then out of nowhere it stops;
Dark clouds disappear
The sun comes out showing what mighty things it can do.

Birds sing;
Clouds so white linger;
A blue sky clings to our eyes.
Birds flying left and right out of surprise,
Flying high and flying low.

I sit in the classroom and think.
Then give the sun a little wink.

McKinnon Skeen, Grade 7
Margaret Green Jr High School, MS

Broken Window, Shattered Dreams

I look out the window to witness that beautiful place.
To see your loving eyes, the sunshine bounce off your perfect face.
An image of great beauty, of many great things.
An image of a wonderful life, of us dancing together, eternally.
I begin to reach for you, as you reach for me.
The window shatters, I realize, it was all a dream.
A dream of our past. I'll stare out that window forever,
wishing the next time our hands meet,
the glass won't shatter, so I can be free.

Kristi Dorsey, Grade 8
Lumberton Jr High School, NC

I Miss You

Do you know how much I miss you?
Do you know how much I care?
Do you know how much I wish you were standing right there?
Do you know how much I love you and wish that I could hear your voice?
But I know how to deal with it when I'm missing you.
By looking at a picture or writing a song or poem.
It's been some time I know but still I miss you.
I miss the sound of your voice.
I miss the look of your eyes.
I miss how you and I used to play a lot of games.
I just miss you in all.
But somehow I just can't cry.
I really really miss you and I wish I could see your face one last time.
A picture is not enough to remember you.
I wish that I could see you, hear you, and spend a little bit more time with you.

Carole Stout, Grade 7
Meridianville Middle School, AL

High Merit Poems – Grades 7, 8 and 9

Why Do We Have Thunderstorms
Rain falls down on the window
Rain falls down on the ground
Rain falls down on the dock
Rain falls down on the sound.

The heavens cry for the young and the old.
The heavens cry for the healthy and weak
The heavens cry for the rich and the poor
The heavens cry for you and me.

The clouds crash angrily because of poverty
The clouds crash angrily because of illness
The clouds crash angrily because of war
The clouds crash angrily because of the people it misses

The sky flashes for hope
The sky flashes for love
The sky flashes for joy
The sky flashes from up above.

Ana de Pedro, Grade 8
First Flight Middle School, NC

Try Not to Miss Me
Try not to miss me, my love, my sweet,
Know it is you for whom I weep,
Leave me alone, but not for long,
Wake me, with a kiss, from my somber song,
Love me tender and hold me near,
Know that, in my heart, you'll always be near.

Hailey Holmes, Grade 8
St Scholastica Academy, LA

Become
Feel the sky,
The trees,
The air,
And all living things.
Feel life itself…
Let nature guide you
Calm you, absorb you,
Engulfing you in a world of all living things
Where the pressure of life alone
Falls away
Dissipates.
Leave our world,
Material world.
Let nature itself guide you,
To support, comfort,
Relaxation.
Become…
One,
Everything around you,
That is you,
Feel, become all.

Maddie Laethem, Grade 8
Woods Charter School, NC

Friends
Laughter, the same in every language.
Every culture, every life.
Forgiveness happens a lot.
Be thankful, forget about.
Awkward moments are all the same.
Embarrassed, very outspoken.
Sarcasm is often used.
Very rude, always playful.
Encouragement is to stick up for.
Very clever, being bold.
Understanding is for the better.
Listen to, connect with.
Friends, they seem to know:
How to forgive, how to forget,
How to be outspoken, how to embarrass you,
How to be rude, how to be playful,
How to be clever, how to be bold,
How to listen, and how to connect with.
Just to have one good friend, is a handful.

Abigayle Lista, Grade 7
Haynes Academy for Advanced Studies, LA

Love
Love is a waterfall cascading down,
into a relaxing and smooth river;
It smells like sweet Thanksgiving day,
the most wonderful scents fill the air,
It tastes like warm mouthwatering chocolate cake,
that engulfs people with happiness,
It feels like a roaring fire place on a freezing night,
heating your soul,
It looks like the sunset raising over the ocean,
breathtaking and overwhelming,
It sounds like humming birds,
singing all kinds of love sick tunes,
The calm peaceful atmosphere brightens life

Alexis Ford, Grade 8
Leesville Road Middle School, NC

Where I'm From
I'm from Power Rangers and Ninjas,
Hamburgers and milkshakes,

I'm from video games and the computer,
I'm from, "Turn off that TV" and "Get off that computer"

I'm from Will Smith
And Coldplay,

But most importantly,
I'm from my family.

Doug Clarida, Grade 7
Atlanta Academy, GA

Love

Love is a powerful thing,
it can bring you closer or tear you apart.

Love is so powerful,
that it consists of two important factors.

Trust and Honesty!

If you don't have these,
your love isn't powerful.
So

How powerful is your love?
Azia Hill, Grade 8
Yazoo County Jr High School, MS

Just a Girl

I am just a girl
A girl in love
With a guy
Who does not see
How I stare
The way I think of him
How I dream of him
The way I am nervous around him
My friends notice
But he does not
I don't know what to do
I am just a girl
Kristen Mauldin, Grade 7
Carolina International School, NC

Plane Flight

Up Up
Higher and higher
Through the clouds
Fluffy white
Bright light
Ears — popping
Soaring high like a bird
In the sky
Looping through the air
Fearing rain
Praying for sun
Soon we will be there and done
Excitement
Getting closer to the ground
Slowly
Slowly
Going
Down
Lower
Lower
We touch the ground
Ashley LaFrance, Grade 7
St Mary's School, SC

Night Shift

The night cold
The wind brisk
And the moon high;

The raven crows
And the hour begins
The midnight hour that is

As the leaves sway
And the old cemetery gates
Creak when they swing

With the wind
To help visit the cold ones
Who have recently passed;

In the night
In the brisk
Under the moon

On the other side.
Tyler Johnson, Grade 9
North Forsyth High School, GA

Ode to a Desk

A desk sat sadly.
Wondering why people
mistreated it
like they do.
It thought what would it be like
to stomp all over
a human!
Put its legs all over them.
See how they like it.
I bet they
wouldn't.
A bell rang and many kids
piled into the classroom,
sitting where they please.
But no one came
to sit in the desk.
Why had no one
out of the million people
in the room
sat in him.
The desk sat rejected and sad.
Gabriel Ballou, Grade 7
L E Gable Middle School, SC

Halloween

On a crowded street
Beneath the harvest moon
Through the dark night
Scary children are running
Dylan Thompson, Grade 7
Rock Mills Jr High School, AL

Fall

The cool crisp air
Red and yellow leaves
Grab a jacket to wear
Or you'll freeze

Crunching and crackling
Underneath my feet
School bells ringing
Sounds like music to me!

The days become shorter
Football season is here
Halloween is around the corner
Trick-or-Treater's will soon appear!

Hay rides are a treat
Carving pumpkins are too
Grab some chili to eat
Hope the ghosts don't scare you!

It is time for the earth to rest
This is why
Fall is the best!
Rebecca Dugger, Grade 8
Priceville Jr High School, AL

A Deer That Is Near

Climbing quietly in a tree,
Sitting calmly to see,
If a deer is near,
That has no fear,
Rising out of my seat,
It's gone in a heartbeat.
Ashley King, Grade 7
Rock Mills Jr High School, AL

Gustav

I see people
walking in water.
People come back
to find they have no homes.
People crying
and even dying.
Trees are falling
and crushing homes.
Dogs are left behind.
Water washes away homes.
The sky is gray and fierce.
It hurts me to see
all this going on
but when the storm is over
all we can do is live on.
God is with us
through it all.
John Coleman, Grade 8
Leonville Elementary School, LA

Glue

Stuck on me,
Stuck on you,
This white stuff won't undo.

Thick or thin,
As pasty goo,
This white stuff won't undo.

Spread it heavy,
Spread it few,
This white stuff won't undo.

Stuck on me,
Stuck on you,
This white stuff must be glue.

Taylor Waguespack, Grade 7
Haynes Academy for Advanced Studies, LA

His Last Day

Just like yesterday, the memory still there.
Mom arrives at school and the news was out.
That word…I thought I would never hear…CANCER.
Walking in the house seeing him in his hospital bed.
The nurse was there
he could not talk, but he could hear us.
I reminded him of our trip to Ohio
knowing he knew it was me.
I love you so much and I miss cooking with you.
Talking, tears gently glided down my cheek.
Through the night all was quiet in the house.
By eleven o'clock family began to gather as
he was slowly fading away.
Crying about his passing started.
Waking at dawn to the sound of weeping, knowing he had left.
His skin pale and cold, as if he fell asleep in the snow.
The doctor's words confirmed my fear…
HE WAS GONE.
Knowing for him no more pain, but tears for me.

Brittany Dempsey, Grade 7
L E Gable Middle School, SC

Hurricane Fear

The hurricane is coming,
The people are running,
Wind is blowing and throwing,
Water is growing and flowing,
The hurricane is here.

The hurricane is here,
People are in fear,
Buildings are boarded,
Cars are loaded,
The end is near.

Shaheryar Khan, Grade 7
Bishop Noland Episcopal Day School, LA

Christmas Eve

Trees, lights, presents, Santa Claus, cookies…
These words seem to smile at me
The smells, sights, sounds, soft singing
It is simply heaven to me

Tiny hands going across the wrapping paper like race cars
Santa bringing presents, reindeer heels clicking…
It is simply heaven to me

Being with the one you love
Caroling, baking cookies, seeing people happy…
It is simply heaven to me

Do you know what time it is?
It's Christmas Eve…

Emily Courtney, Grade 9
Springfield High School, LA

New Orleans

New Orleans, my home, my heart, my everything.
The birthplace of Jazz and many other things.
The smell of crawfish filling the air.
The cool, but humid breeze whipping through your hair.
The streets filled with tourists admiring our wonderful city.
People laughing and chatting in restaurants.
Savoring every bite of our delicious Cajun food.
The hot sun beating down on your face.
Your feet keeping a steady pace.
Mardi Gras floats parading down the streets.
Kids screaming for beads and many other treats.
The blistering heat in the summer time.
And the icy cold in the wintertime.
The musical and joyful mornings.
And the cool, peaceful nights.
The sounds of children playing in the parks.
People walking dogs and hearing their steady barks.
The sight of people dancing and having a ball.
Families and friends invading the malls.
Living in this city has filled me with glee,
Because it is home to you and me.

Morgan Petersen, Grade 8
Mount Carmel Academy, LA

The Destruction of Hurricane Gustav

During Hurricane Gustav
Saw trees waving at me
As the animals ran wind blew
Through midday of destruction
The houses drew through the day
as if grass came upon the sky.
From the light of the day
was like coal from the shadow
When I glazed through the sky.
My thoughts would still follow the hurricane.

Darius Narcisse, Grade 7
Leonville Elementary School, LA

People

People come in many different shapes and sizes
They all have different attitudes when a new situation arises
Emotions of all kinds
Happy, sad, angry, or frustration goes through their minds
People can be tall, fat, short, or thin
All sorts of figures, I don't know where to begin
But the best ones, no matter how small
Are the ones that are there when you call

Betsy Primes, Grade 8
Mount Carmel Academy, LA

Fear

Thrumming in my eardrums
Screeching in my chest
Fear has gripped me
With its icy metallic claws
Thrashing and screaming inside me
Pleading to be let out
And yet having total control
I search in desperation
For some way out of
Fear's tangled fingers
They're woven together
Escape is impossible
There is no way out

I sit in silence
My heart beating rapidly
My breathing even more
Little crystals of terror slide down my face
I cannot flee fear's tangled fortress
I am being consumed by
Fear

Abby Benjamin, Grade 7
Carolina International School, NC

Charlene

Legend has it one night of Halloween
A girl died, her name was Charlene

People say every Halloween in the fall
She can be seen in her house haunting the hall

One day a boy whose name was Paul
Was joyfully playing with his new football

A pass through her window fell in her hall
When he went in to get it, he heard her call

He ran home in fear
And there shed a tear

The saddest thing of all
Was he lost his football

Cody Towler, Grade 7
Rock Mills Jr High School, AL

Shy

What is shy?
Afraid to look someone in the eye.
Too scared to talk to a girl or a guy.
Walking down the street, always being passed by.
You are so sad, you want to cry.
So you look up at the sky,
and wonder why,
this had to happen in junior high.
Maybe you should just start new.
'Cause then you wouldn't always be blue.
It really is time that you break through,
the walls you put up around you.
I'm sure your friends will help you through.
Some may even come to your rescue.
By the time you are finished, you will be renewed.
And you will see life through a new view.

Jade Franke, Grade 8
Haynes Academy for Advanced Studies, LA

Running

The thrill of running
the pride of winning
was in the hearts and minds
of the great racers that day
Across great mountains
and down rugged roads
runs the greatest racer
named Jack "The Pacer"
The time is running out
just one hour left
yet Jack keeps on running
his heart is drumming
but he won't stop running
Across the finish line
he's just in time
to claim his great trophy
all others left behind
As he starts to walk
he doesn't talk
because if he boast
he won't be admired by most

Marc Kober, Grade 7
Cathedral School, NC

Hurricane Gustav

During Hurricane Gustav I felt scared.
My heart full of pain
thinking of all the families left without homes.
Watching people's belongings fly through the streets.
Listening to the wind at night.
Inside our houses all was still
but outside everything was treacherous.
I felt as if the world was coming to an end.
Angels surrounded me through this crucial moment

Shelbie Guidroz, Grade 7
Leonville Elementary School, LA

Panic for Nothing
Looks like a hurricane is barreling through;
It is well over a category three too.

Gaining speed faster and faster,
Gustav looks to be a disaster.

Should we go, or should we stay?
We must not procrastinate to the last day.

Seven hours in a car sounds no fun;
We will stay; we will not run.

The day is here without rain in sight,
And, wait, there is still light.

The gorilla-like hurricane is finally here;
Our city is calm for there is nothing to fear.
Quinn Walker, Grade 7
Bishop Noland Episcopal Day School, LA

Fall
My favorite time of the year is fall,
it's when the trees raise tall
and drop their leaves,
so they won't freeze

I love the feel of the crisp cool air,
and all the rides at the county fair
the sounds of nature hush my ears,
and makes me want it to last for years

The smell of my grandma's pumpkin pies,
as the days go quickly by
and before I know it,
fall vanishes in the blink of an eye.
Lauren Speegle, Grade 8
Priceville Jr High School, AL

Penguins
See how they swim,
See how they slide.
Watch them run up,
They jump, and they dive.

Gliding through water,
Looking around.
Up for some air,
Before they run out.

Fish all around them,
Squirming about.
The penguin gets ready.
Whoosh! Food in its mouth.
Sorena Dadgar, Grade 7
East Millbrook Magnet Middle School, NC

Waiting for a Roller-Coaster Ride
While standing in a line
Waiting for the time
To be mine.
Little kids begin to cry.
Although their parents tell them it's fine,
They still act as if they are going to die.
Screaming and yelling I hear
As the ride goes round and round.
Now everyone begins to fear.
In the line I still stand
Constantly chewing my nails
Hoping the ride before me would never end.
As it's time for me to step on board
The guy at the gate lets me go.
I get on the ride and then we soar.
Up a hill and around a curve
We go faster and faster
Then I feel the ride destroy my nerves.
Slowing down to stop ahead
The ride is now over
And no one is dead!
Evan White, Grade 9
Sylvania School, AL

Storms
During Hurricane Gustav
I was going crazy.
All the trees were moving side to side.
Finally the sun went down.
Insects were everywhere.
My house was not hurt in the least bit.
The air was dry and the ground was wet.
It seemed like God was by my side
every step of the way.
Bright and big the sun was finally up.
When we went home the weather was great.
During the storm it seemed the world was still
but it was not.
Christian Bourgeois, Grade 7
Leonville Elementary School, LA

This Is Peace
What is peace?
Is it when the wars are over,
But one country still has hate for another?
How about when people keep mean thoughts to themselves?
Will victims be ready to come out of their shells?
What is peace?

Peace is when we finally love each other,
Because no one is better than another.
If the world would just open its eyes,
Maybe it would realize,
This is peace.
Evie Brooks, Grade 7
North Iredell Middle School, NC

The Essence of Nature

From the spherical planets
To the spacious Earth
The Essence of Nature
Shines for all its worth
First is the sky
A sapphire blue
Then the plush feathery clouds
An ivory hue
Then the glowing sun
Warmth and light so grand
And the silver moon
Which shines on the land
After that comes the trees
So great and tall.
Then the peaceful saplings
So delicate and small.
Then the gorgeous flowers
So sweet and fine.
The Essence of Nature
Is tremendously divine.

Sharlaina Harris, Grade 7
Red River Jr High School, LA

My Life

Where do I see my life going?
Well, I hope to grow up in one place,
get a good job, marry a good girl,
have two kids, and one dog —
When I'm too old to work,
I want to travel the world —
And all of the United States
The thing is —
You never know
What is in store for your life.
Even the best planning in the world
can't predict your life.

Chance Fuller, Grade 7
St Andrews Middle School, SC

Storms

Storms make me feel…
scared and fearful.
The trees sway back and forth
Animals are scared and crying
I know I am safe inside.
I feel the earth shaking.
I know angels are watching.
The sky is dark, and the fence rocks.
A stone hit me on the side of my leg.
This time of season scares me;
nights were very scary,
and morning were dark.
I wished it was all a dream
but it was not.

Natalie Marks, Grade 7
Leonville Elementary School, LA

Sadness

Sadness is a lonely puppy dog that has no home and no where to go.
It smells like spoiled milk that sits until it turns into cottage cheese.
It taste like a salty soup that no one wants to eat.
It feels like you're drowning under a pool full of tears that you can't escape.
It looks like a homeless man on the street begging for money.
It sounds like babies crying everywhere.
To me sadness is something that happens to anyone in their life.
It causes depression and that's a emotion no one likes.

Dalvin Johnson, Grade 8
Leesville Road Middle School, NC

Love

Love is a battlefield
It has its ups and down
The ups are the best part
That is except when you get your heart broken
Then it hurts

What do you do when you get your heart broken?
I sit and cry.
Or sometimes I call my friends too and they come over
It's not good to watch soap operas and each chocolate ice cream

The first time I was in love it drove me insane
We would stay up all night texting back and forth
Also, we both would get excited when we would see each other

My heart would jump and beat every time he said "hi"
I know it sounds cheesy but…
That is what true love is

Shelby Katz, Grade 7
Haynes Academy for Advanced Studies, LA

Don't Give in, Keep Your Head Up!

No matter how life goes, just remember you have values,
Set your goals high and never let go.
You may have obstacles, deeper than the sea.
Been around the block and back, you may think you know the way.
Well march with me, my brother and sister.
Living life now are the old times of the future.
Shall you give up? I don't think so.
Tied down like slaves, now we're stronger than ever.
People back then almost lost their pride,
But that doesn't mean you should push yours aside.

Speaking of the past reminds us about the life we are living now.
I'm still young, but I haven't been through it all.
If all of us go down, then together we fall.
Giving up is like a tumbling brick wall.
You may think that you are weak, but your strength walks with you.
Becoming stronger is a process we all need.
Are you a sky scraper, always wanting your elevator to go to the top?
No matter what gets in your way you should never let up.
Don't give in; just keep your head up!

Y'Nicha Davis, Grade 9
Warren Early College High School, NC

High Merit Poems – Grades 7, 8 and 9

Lincoln Memorial

The Lincoln Memorial,
hard and smooth,
sits and amazes
serenely.
Reminder.

The tourist,
excited and thrilled,
wiggle and chuckle
energetically.
People.

The officers,
tired and watchful,
stand and watch
protectingly.
Guard.

Braden Billot, Grade 7
Haynes Academy for Advanced Studies, LA

Mountains

Mountains are big like a giant but small like a mouse
Mountains are tough like a rock but soft like a pillow
Mountain tops are cold like a freezer but hot like pepper
Mountains are strong like an elephant
But delicate like a newborn baby
Mountains are tall like a giraffe
But short like a two year old child
Mountains could be big or small
Short or tall

Maisha Delph, Grade 7
Hubert Middle School, GA

The Fisherman

The fisherman is fishing
hoping to catch a big one.
He feels a tug on his rod
and gets excited.

The rod doesn't feel heavy
and he still pulls it in.
The fish comes out of the water
and the fisherman is sad.

The fish is too puny.
He gets an idea
to use the puny fish as bait
to lure the immense one.

He sets it and something pulls on it.
He is excited once again
It comes out and he catches the immense one
and goes home happy.

Diego Castillo, Grade 9
Leesville Road High School, NC

Friends

Friends are something to cherish.
Friends are vital to happiness.
Friends comfort you in hard times.
And friends listen to all your gripes.
Friends will treat you with respect.
And friends are like your brothers or sisters.
Friends stick together through thick and thin.
I know I have a friendship that will never end.

MK Burgess, Grade 8
Wren Middle School, SC

After All

Nobody knows I'm here
as I walk outside to sit
under the old oak tree.
It is midsummer,
and it is very hot outside.
I want it to rain,
or a good breeze would be very nice.
I see a rabbit scurrying
across the yard in a hurry.
The sun shines like gold in the morning sky.
The old oak tree stands tall
and proud in the yard.
I look up and I imagine
I see two angels looking
down on me from the heavens above.
I guess somebody knows
I'm here after all…

Brandon Hollier, Grade 7
Leonville Elementary School, LA

Just Listen

There are so many things
I want to say to you.
I can never tell whether you are listening to me…
Or hearing me
There is a difference, you know.
Listening is when you make an effort just to hear something.
Hearing is when you pay attention to what someone is saying.
With you, I can never tell.
On days when you are in a good mood,
You actually respond.
On days when you are having a bad day,
You look off into space or say "oh" or "huh."
I feel like
You don't care sometimes.
You say you love listening to me.
But, as you have heard,
Listening and hearing are
Two separate things.
There is just one question I have for you:
Are you actually hearing me…
Or are you just listening?

Renata Roussell, Grade 8
Haynes Academy for Advanced Studies, LA

Sad Willow Tree

A hot summer night,
Sitting under a willow tree.
Listening to the leaves blow,
Waiting for a change.

The beautiful, sad tree,
Sitting here alone.
Waiting for a friend,
Here I come,
Sad willow tree.

Looking at the sad tree,
The smell of fresh cut grass.
The willow tree waits,
The poor willow tree,
All alone in the world.

Here I come,
To sit under the willow tree.
Kaitlyn Dickens, Grade 7
First Flight Middle School, NC

Snow

Dark November skies
Snow falls toward the green grass
And gone in a blink
Stephanie Gilbertson, Grade 8
First Flight Middle School, NC

John

Me and John
Sister and brother
Going through thick and thin
Always sticking together

Thinking of memories
And places we've been
Fighting and loving
Smiling and crying

The beach, the sun
The snow, the cold
Walking on hot sand
Throwing snowballs
Wrestling on the trampoline
And fighting over the computer

Turning 16
The days of fright
When he drives away without me
It seems, there is nothing I can do
Wanting to cry when I see he is gone
But knowing he is happy
Is what I've wanted all along
Laurin Hunnicutt, Grade 7
Westchester Country Day School, NC

Georgia's Coastal Region

The beach is a wonderful place to be!
The waves,
The way they crash upon the shore sometimes,
Hiding seashells in their bubbling and foaming water.
A seagull flies by floating like a feather into the ocean
with a splash to catch a meal.
Dolphins jumping out of the water are so gorgeous and graceful!
You might think that their fins look like shark fins,
but dolphins won't hurt you.
Miranda Bennie, Grade 8
Fannin County Middle School, GA

Halloween's Hold

On Halloween, when shining sun takes its rest
Darkness spreads its sleek cape over the night
Hideous and haunting, glowing in the dark, auburn jack o' lanterns
Light landscape loaded with incognito youth clamoring for candy
Spooky sights supply sensational scares

Home to home hoarding hundreds of sugary sweets
Delirious devils and animated animals scuttle through the streets
Blissfully badgered by scary skeletons they cling to their care givers
Rabidly racing, they eagerly eat their tasty treats
Delectable delights deliver divine dedication

After all this, youth yearn for a break
Many merrily munch on the treats that keep them awake
Shiftlessly sitting they intensely eye
The creative costumes that pass them by
Finally finished friends frolic freely

They get up wanting to finish the spree
When the youth look around what do they see
All the lights in the street have already dimmed
It is finally time for them to go in
Hundreds holler haunting Halloween's hold
Anthony Moraes, Grade 8
St John Neumann Regional Catholic School, GA

The Volcano

I feel so helpless now. My house is underground,
'Cause the volcano just exploded and the lava's pouring out
And I'm remembering all the facts, that I learned in science class,
And the lava's coming fast, and it's burning all my grass.
I remember when you were magma, and you were still in Earth's middle.
Now you have exploded, and I'm in such a pickle
Stop laughing at my words you've got me in distress.
You're lava's going everywhere.
You think that you're so tough,
That you're a ring of fire,
But you are no kin, or queen or sire,
But I've gotta give you props, 'cause you're a real "trier."
You said you wouldn't hurt me, you big fat liar.
And it's making such a mess.

Kasey Morgan, Grade 8
Pineville Jr High School, LA

Reality

Global warming is a reality
It's happening, like it or not, and we need to accept it
Everyone needs to help, or there'll be much mortality
Do what you can, use the knowledge you've got
Help us all, do what's wise and do your part
Let's join together and show we've fought
To keep our planet a work of art

Sarah Farrar, Grade 8
Dillard Drive Middle School, NC

Wonderful Day

Winter is a jolly time
   filled with holiday cheer.
This bustling season has a story
   that everyone must hear.
This wonderful story is of Christmas;
   it's the day our Savior was born.
And on this wonderful day
   the angels sounded their horns.
All of the wisemen and shepherds
   had heard about it that day.
They followed the star to Bethlehem
   to the manger where Jesus lay.
They gave Him the finest of presents
   gold, incense, and myrrh.
They filled the entire stable
   where Mary had just given birth.
Over two thousand years ago this happened;
   in a town called Bethlehem.
Our Son of God, Jesus was born,
   and He is going to return again!

Bobbie Jo Smith, Grade 8
Priceville Jr High School, AL

The Loss of a Loved One

What do they see when they look at me?
A beautiful, strong, female is she!
She walks with her chest stuck out and her head high.
She walks into school with such great pride.

Nothing brings her down today.
A frown may appear but then it fades.
She's overcame such a devastating stage in life.
Her heavy load is now much more light.

She's now leaving the pain behind.
No more starving and no more crying.
She still has memories of such a great friend,
And every time she thinks of her she grins.

She swore to never cry again,
Unless it's more devastating than losing a friend.
So since then, I'm smiling from now on,
Because I know she's looking down on me from up above.

Shakia Carter, Grade 9
Warren Early College High School, NC

Nature

Nature is awesome,
it is beautiful in the night.
You can't see in the night,
but I like to listen to the air.
We play games by jumping in the leaves.
We drink hot coffee in the fall.
If it is cold enough we make hot chocolate in a cup
that is very, very, very hot.

Alex Satterfield, Grade 7
L E Gable Middle School, SC

A Thousand Tears

The many young men who go off to war,
Come back with family who adore.
But for those at the end, who stand by a grave,
Wish to see their loved one is what they crave.
We lay in our beds and when we pray,
We pray for war to go away someday.
For every day there's a thousand tears,
This war we are fighting has been going on for years.
Every day lives are lost.
But why must the lives be the cost?
Mothers look at the graves of their sons,
This was all done by men and guns.
So before you go to bed say a prayer,
Because there are families in deep despair.
For everyday there's a thousand tears.
This war we are fighting has been going on for years.

Samantha Bissell, Grade 7
Lake Castle Private School, LA

Ghost

Gliding floating
On a bed of the past
Done deeds hang heavy on your shoulders
Wandering through the hallways
At the midnight hour
Your footsteps echo through the darkness
Breathing slowly
With a whisper soft as silk
Locked in eternal grief
Just as you are frozen in time
Did you lose your love?
Did you kill a child?
Are you feuding with your family
Angry and wild?
Or perhaps you were murdered
In your bed
People see you with a feeling of dread
Gliding floating
On a bed of the past
Done deeds hang heavy
On your shoulders

Jennifer Beadle, Grade 7
Boyet Jr High School, LA

Grandfather

You are young and wild. Flying across fields,
Your feet pounding the earth, feeling freedom swell under your rib cage.
Throwing caution as far away as possible. Flinging it to the mercy of the trees.
Shrill, childish laughter fills your lungs and consumes your mind, making you giddy.
You live for the moment. For the sweet breeze that tousles your curls. For the breathing dirt beneath your feet.

You are middle aged and strong. Taking risky business opportunities, and calibrating your finances.
Under a layer of thick confidence, an awareness, alert and wary. After a long day at work you are weary and sore.
You come home to a beautiful wife, and two adorable children.
You prop your feet up in your favorite chair, and soak in the evening.
You open a glass bottle of Coca-Cola and allow the carbonation to tingle in your nose.
Satisfaction becomes a small candle, warming the underside of your belly. Peace settles in the marrow of your bones.

You are worn and wise. Your skin has long since been tanned.
Your arms, open and strong, ready to welcome a stray grandchild.
Pulling them into your embrace. A comforting smile, a rich laugh.
Your knowing eyes observe everything. From the yellow butterfly, struggling in the wind.
To the hummingbird, silently hovering near the feeder. A new house indicates a new start.
Out by the lake, you are wrapped in a blanket of tranquility and safety.
Every sunset becomes a new adventure. Your favorite movie, replays in your backyard.
You watch the blazing sun conquered by the horizon. Thin fingers of red, orange, and pink stretch out.
Trying to find some kind of anchorage. They scramble to stay in view.
The sun's declaration. Telling you that it will be back again tomorrow.

Bailey King, Grade 9
Lexington High School, SC

From Spring to Summer

In spring the leaves are back on trees
blowing in the gentle breeze.
Spring is one of my favorite seasons because flowers show their faces.
The flowers look and smell so wonderful.
I could just sit and relax or make a bed in them.

After spring has come and gone, summer has finally knocked down the door with heat that cannot keep flowers beautiful.
However, summer is a good time to dip in the pool, but missing the flowers is hard leaving me to desire to plant more.

Rachel Upton, Grade 7
L E Gable Middle School, SC

Where I'm From

I am from 120 acres of rolling hills and terraces; from Diet Pepsi and saltines with Peter Pan.
I am from a home in Bonham where my great grandfather was the "Night Mayor."
I am from azalea bushes and dogwood trees that are so beautiful in the spring.
I am from planting on Good Friday; corn, green beans, okra and tomatoes.
I am from farmers and hard-working textile workers; cash only — credit wouldn't do.
I am from England, Scotland, and the Cherokee Nation.
I am from banana pudding with Nilla wafers and hand rolled chicken and dumplings.
I am from God, my creator, and His son, Jesus, my Savior.
I am from Brown's Creek where my Maw-ma and Paw-pa helped restore the church that I attend today.
From the time Maw-ma was 15 and Paw-pa was 13
She asked his daddy if she could have him and he said, "Yes, when he is 18;" and she did.
I am from memories of summer vacation; the reading of the Christmas story on Christmas Eve;
And humble sunrise services on Easter.
I am from photos in Mama's bottom dresser drawer, along with baby teeth and a birth bracelet.
Special things that remind her of the baby I once was.

Conley Trammell, Grade 8
Sims Jr High School, SC

Here Comes the Rain

Here comes the rain.
Pitter-patter like little feet
Slowly growing louder
Now like glass shattering
Swirls of wind dancing
Like ballerinas with razor blades
Waiting to destroy
Any and all things in their path
Crackling limbs swaying
Branches flying about
Only to slowly fade away
Leaving a trail of shattered debris
And broken dreams.

Ian Gibson, Grade 8
Bishop Noland Episcopal Day School, LA

Family on the Field

A pure game of determination,
The game I love.
I would play all day if I were allowed.
The adrenaline rushing through you like a flooded river.
Every step you take, every shot you make,
You feel so alive.
Nothing in the world matters to you once you step on the field.
The only thing in your mind,
Is what will I or they do next?
Could we win, could we possible lose could we come back?
Your team,
Like family on the playing field.
We all work as one, together we are unbeatable.
The fans cheering you on.
Giving you support, always at your side
Even when you mess up
Your team and fans are there to support you.
But when you score or make a good cross,
You feel like a new man,
Loved by everyone.
Soccer is my passion, the game I love.

Austin Jobe, Grade 8
Atlanta Academy, GA

Leaves

Falling to the ground
Without making a sound

Yellow leaves covered with dew
Not so fresh and not so new

Orange pumpkins glow so bright
Listening for things that go bump in the night

Children prance around piles of leaves
All of them at ease

Prestin Winkles, Grade 7
Rock Mills Jr High School, AL

Guys

Guys are so obnoxious.
Guys what do they think they are.
Guys want to be everything.
Guys think they know everything.

Guys are always wanting attention.
Guys who do they think we are.
Guys what do they want from us.
Guys only want to think of themselves.

Guys are always worrying about their clothes.
Guys are always wanting us to see them.
Guys think they are everything.
Guys, Guys need to get over themselves.

Amber Marcangeli, Grade 8
Lake Middle School, MS

One Step Ahead

Power, place, and passion and symbols of the heart.

The peace is good for the mind.
Don't let your faith fall behind.

Hurt and sorrow is what you feel.
Just let the "Good Man above be your shield"

The emotion that you feel is at a steady pace.

The importance of power is your breaking point.
I promise He has love, peace, and passion to anoint.

Your soul is cold and unpleasant as if you were dead.
You're dead in body form but not your spirit.
Use your will you're almost there
You're only "one step ahead."

Kierra Stewart, Grade 8
Lake Middle School, MS

A No Good Guy!

Low down no good jerk.
He thinks he is the best at mostly everything.
He plays basketball, football, and baseball
He is very good at it.
Well he is pretty average with blue eyes,
Beautiful shaggy looking blonde hair.
When he looks at me I melt.
I know if I could be with him nobody else matters.
All he does and wants is something.
I can't give.
He could have been the best down to earth guy.
But he doesn't have the brains to keep one
When he has to dress up for a sport.
He is the most gorgeous thing
That walked the planet!

Faye L. Royal, Grade 9
North Wilkes High School, NC

Swing and a Miss

I focus on the pitch,
It's like a riddle,
A fastball down the middle.
Swing and a miss,
Strike one!

I wait for the pitch,
A curveball to the inside,
That was quite a ride,
Swing and a miss,
Strike two!

I wait for another pitch,
Another fastball up high,
So I let my bat fly,
Swing and a miss,
Strike three!

I walk back to the dugout,
My head is down,
"Boo, you suck!" the fans shout.
Sure, my team won!
But that does not help the fact,
The fact that I did not have much fun.

Jeremy Ritter, Grade 9
Leesville Road High School, NC

Trees

I am a tree
I am big and strong
I am afraid of nothing
But the sound of an axe
Chop, chop, chop
Sends shivers down my bark
There are many types of trees
I am the giant sequoia tree
My friends are
Oak, cedar, redwood
Willow, pine, maple
But birch can be a real…jerk
Also, animals love me
Because I give them a home
I am a tree

Paul Giraldo, Grade 8
Carolina International School, NC

Oranges

Oranges are oranges,
But this one's different,
There's a seed and a heart,
Both determined and efficient,
But what pleases me,
Is near the heart is me!
And boy, is it sweet!

Tristan Leger, Grade 8
St Andrews Middle School, SC

Why Like, Why Love, Why Care About

Why like, why love, why care about?
Just so they can take your heart and rip it out.
So for the rest of your life you can do nothing but pout,
Because deep in your heart you know you've chosen the wrong route.

Why like, why love, why care about?
Because it takes all of the hurt and pain and anger out.
You're so happy it's impossible to pout.
Inside your heart you know that your life is on the right route.

Why like, why love, why care about?
You're too afraid you'll be left alone, forgotten, and thrown out.
You're so bitter and hurt that your face is a permanent pout.
You've been deserted on every single route.

Why like, why love, why care about?
To have someone to stick with you in and out.
Who will try to fix all your problems when he sees you pout.
Someone who will stay with you on every route.

Why like, why love, why care about?

Heather V. Campbell, Grade 9
Prattville Christian Academy, AL

Football

Football is my favorite sport and running is my favorite thing.
When I'm running down the field I hear the fans chanting and screaming.
I like to play I like to run
You should not fight you should just run.

Hykeen Horne, Grade 8
Laurin Welborn Middle School, NC

Memories

I lay here awake, memories of you dancing in my mind.
The pain of knowing you were once mine, clouds my soul.
It makes me envious seeing you with someone else.
I stare off into space,
Seeing your face kills me on the inside.
Though, I cannot let my feelings for you show,
I doodle your name all in the margins of my notebook.
People ask me why I am obsessed with you;
And I simply tell them,
He was my one and only love.
I write about you in my diary every day.
Yet, to you I am invisible.
I love the way you walk and the way
Your hair just slightly curls in the front.
I pay close attention to every detail of your wonderful body,
Like the way you wear your collared shirts with two buttons open,
And the way your clothes match your skin tone.
The memories of us riding in cars,
And singing our favorite songs.
I miss those memories
And wish I had them back!

Heather Mitchell, Grade 7
Weir Elementary/High School, MS

Kaeley

Kaeley has light brown hair
Big blue eyes
Lips that bud off like rose petals falling from the sky
With a small puggy nose and pointed ears
She has small hands with rounded fingers
She wrinkles from head to toe
Kaeley also has long skinny feet no longer than my thumb
These are the things that make her who she is

Jessica Wagoner, Grade 9
North Wilkes High School, NC

I Do

Saying I do
Is more than saying I love you
It goes beyond describing how my love is true
Because words are not enough to express my love for you.

Saying I do
Is like saying I'm here for you
That I am ready to see what the future may bring
Because we are together in everything.

Saying I do
Is saying I am now complete because of you
That the pieces of the puzzle called my life
Becomes a beautiful picture called our love.

Now I am saying I do
As I walk down the aisle with you
This is a lifetime promise that I will hold
A promise I make until we grow old.

Osmar Celaya, Grade 9
Leesville Road High School, NC

The Choice

Every day there is a sea
Of familiar faces around me.
At every corner I meet an ocean
Of mouths moving in endless commotion

I am in a group, and I have a chair
Each day waiting for me there
Among the people I call friends
But I fear this vision is close to an end.

The sight is happy but very unclear
Since no one can see or even hear
What goes on in my head while I am about
These people who laugh, talk, and shout.

Each time I am with them,
I feel that I am
At a crossroads of destiny
With options for me.

Ali Perez, Grade 7
Haynes Academy for Advanced Studies, LA

Librarians' Jokes*

Librarians always seem so serious,
They're always acting so mysterious.
People think they're answer ladies,
But I'm starting to think they may be crazy!

'Cause the library ladies are in the back —
(I hope they don't have a heart attack!)
They are laughing so hard back there —
(Did one just fall off her chair?)

They are having so much fun:
Are they laughing at someone?
Or is it at a private joke?
(Oh no, I think she's about to choke!)

I wish I could really show
Or even let some people know,
That librarians aren't all mean,
And they are much more than they seem.

But — if they want their reputation clean
And have us all still think they're mean.
They need a room that is sound proof
So we can't hear them raise the roof!

Somer Rowe, Grade 9
Lamar County Comprehensive High School, GA
*Dedicated to the Barnesville Librarians

The Apple That Led the Journey of Fright

My uncle was mowing behind the shed with glee,
I asked him why and he said to me, The grass is way too tall.
He made a mistake by surprising the nest.
I stayed inside for a fifth of an hour,
When I came back out I was greeted with power.
I grabbed an apple and subconsciously sent it flying.
It hit my target, the nest of the yellow jackets.

It didn't cost me a dime.
But I was impaled five times.
I ran to my neighbor's and on my way,
I stumbled onto a dilapidated bridge.
I rang the doorbell and she answered my request,
When she saw me her face turned its whitest.
I went back outside and ran to my house.
Then opened the door and Granny looked at me.

"What happened" is what she asked me.
I said I was attacked by a powerful army.
She looked at me like I was crazy.
So I clarified, the Army of Yellow Jackets.

The Apple that led the Journey of Fright
Was a Journey of utmost terror and delight.

Mikie Finley, Grade 9
North Wilkes High School, NC

Headstrong

Yes, I'm different
Not like anyone
I use it to my advantage
I never feel the need to run

Try as you may
To make me break
But I'm headstrong
I know I'm not fake

No label can describe me
Because I'm headstrong
Put me under a stereotype
And you'll still be wrong

Ask me to describe myself
In just one word
I'll tell you it's not possible
My voice will be heard

So listen up
Hear what I'm all about
I am headstrong
If I have to, I will scream and shout
Doha Hindi, Grade 8
Dillard Drive Middle School, NC

Heavy Storms

Storms make me feel excited
The wind howls as it blows.
Home protect those who live there.
The seasons change very fast
Nighttime is when it is calm.
Animals find shelter from the rain.
Plants are crushed as the rain falls.
Moonlight tries to break free.
My dreams feel warm and bright.
The rain sounds like angels crying.
Mallory Wyble, Grade 7
Leonville Elementary School, LA

Lollipops

Lollipops lollipops all types
of lollipops some lollipops
are filled with centered tasty
treats, such as… "Tootsie Pops,
Blow Pops, Gum filled Pops."
Classic Hubba Bubba lollipops.
Lollipops so sweet and
Delicious scrumptious lickorous.
The mouth watering treat that
You lick till it's gone!
So many scrumptious colorful flavors
It's very hard to pick.
Cody Ian Estrada, Grade 7
St Andrews Middle School, SC

Stormy Weather

When storms come into my life
I feel so lonely.
Strong winds are blowing.
Heavy rains are coming down.
Animals are looking
for a dry place to stay.
I see roofs fly off the houses.
Electricity is out
and people are hot.
There are trees down on the roads.
The weather is cool.
I see people outside raking leaves
and picking up branches.
Now the roads are clear
and I can return home.
Jordan LeBlanc, Grade 8
Leonville Elementary School, LA

Summer

Summer Summer
Beautiful Summer
The sweet smell of flowers at every turn
The crisp breeze blowing at your face
The sun gazing down at me
The flowers smiling at me
The aroma of them tickling at my nose
It is a beautiful summer day
A beautiful summer day
Summer Summer
Rachel Womack, Grade 8
Sylvania School, AL

A Letter to Grandpa

My name is Monica, I am 12 years old
I am your daughter, Molly's, daughter
Therefore I am your granddaughter
You died before mom and dad even met
I wish I could have met you
I heard that you were funny
I would have laughed at all of your jokes
Even if they weren't funny
Even though we have not met
I miss you so so much
Monica Hotard, Grade 7
Lake Castle Private School, LA

the hurricane

strong force winds howl at our windows
us trying to keep our hats on,
trees frassling in the howling wind,
thunder crashing, rain, pounding,
and wind blowing at our house…
after the storm trees are down,
trash everywhere…but we are still there.
Blakeney Armstrong, Grade 7
The Education Center, MS

Bubble Gum

I'm walking to the candy store
With one thing on my mind…
Bubble gum
The only thing I can't wait to find

With its different colors and flavors
And its unique shapes and sizes
These tasty treats
Can be explosive surprises

When you plop one in your mouth
You are tempted to blow a bubble
But make sure you're not in school
Because you may get in trouble

Delectable treats like these
Can be found almost anywhere
Whether under your shoe
Or even in your hair

Bubble gum's awesome features
Clearly beats the rest
No other candy compares
Bubble gum is simply the best
Daniel Freund, Grade 8
Dillard Drive Middle School, NC

Stormy Weather

When storms come into my life
I feel so self-broken.
The storms make the rain
pour like springtime.
Fire explains it
in great detail.
Diamonds show life
like a sparkling way.
Friends do not know
how bad it hurts.
Sunrise helps me get over it.
All animals make noises
in sign of help.
The sun sheds tears.
Dreams make my day a blur.
Bridges collapse and hearts break,
but we can never forget a day like this.
Brooke Artigue, Grade 8
Leonville Elementary School, LA

Bad Day

Today was a bad day.
The teacher said "no play!"
Even though I wanted to play,
I stayed in my seat the whole day.
Does this remind you of your bad day?
Dejan Bligen, Grade 7
St Andrews Middle School, SC

Yard Work

As we work willfully in the yard
Leaves keep falling at a never-ending pace
The rakes make a scraping sound
As they gather up the bothersome burden
Yard work is extremely excruciating enchantingly boring

We have the leaves separated into piles of ten
We go in and come out again
The yard is recovered in the tree's scarlet clothing
We must rake it again
Yard work is simply time consuming

The leaves, a vibrant bright crimson
Anyone would love to have these colors in their rooms at night
They make a dazing delightful array of colors
We all hope they land in one of the piles of ten
Then we won't have to pick them up again

When we are done we decide to disperse for a break
Our dog runs rapidly out to the labor's lumps of leaves
She jumps into one and comes out the other end
And then she goes back again
Now all leaves are apart again
And we must rapidly pick them up again because the sun
fell back an hour and the days end early.

Michael Reddaway, Grade 8
St John Neumann Regional Catholic School, GA

Playing at the Pumpkin Patch

A giddy young girl and her boldly brave brother
Imagined a pumpkin patch like no other.
They found it while climbing up the orange tree.
The young girl said, "You mustn't tell mother, you see."

They remained in their pumpkin patch all the long day.
The pumpkins were always there ready to play.
The precariously perched pumpkins speckled their patch.
Each one was unique; no two were a match.

In their pretend pumpkin patch, butterflies were bats.
Ghosts shone through the leaves as they watched for black cats.
Black birds became witches as they jetted through the sky.
They thought they saw goblins as the evening drew nigh.

The full moon was discernible as their mom called them in.
Girl looked at her brother and said, "Let's do that again."
As luminescent light shone bright with all its might
They both went inside and soon said goodnight.

Then the next morning their mom had something to say:
"We're going to the pumpkin patch today."
The young boy was bewildered as his mom sat.
"But Mama," he said, "we already did that!"

Maria Olwine, Grade 8
St John Neumann Regional Catholic School, GA

Soccer

I play soccer with my gang.
My feet are like two switchblades.
They will cut you if you get in the way.
The soccer ball is what we are fighting over.
We have to cross over the other side
in order to win more territory.
I play with all of my heart and soul —
my victory is your defeat.

Walter Cervantes, Grade 9
North Wilkes High School, NC

My Grandfather

This is a poem to my grandfather
I have taken the time we had for granted
All those mornings you spend exercising
All those times you fell asleep while the TV was still on
When you would snore
Waking up everyone but yourself
You told me stories
About the animals you had
About the old military life
About your years in doctor's college
When you were talking about the research that you did
I thought you were crazy!
When you talked about the surgeries you performed
I thought you were a hero
You seemed to know absolutely everything
But now I know,
You can't know everything
But you can be proud of what you do know
This is a poem to by grandfather
Who's watching right now from above

Joyce Li, Grade 9
Ardrey Kell High School, NC

Rags to Riches

Trying to go from rag to riches
Living my life with all these wishes
Going from bad
To stay in class
Everybody wish they would have passed
Tired of being on the bottom
Trying to make it while it's autumn
So I can get off the bottom
The time of the year when I ball
The time of the year when leaves fall
Also when God made trees stand tall
When the leaves are bouncing off the wall
She always told me there is a time to stand tall
Now that it is cold
I will always stay on my toes
Staying away from all the bad roads
That's a life
We all intend to fight

JaJuan Lee, Grade 9
McKee Jr High School, AL

Spring

Springs is a season
It's when flowers start blooming
The weather feels right

Tunhi Duong, Grade 7
Opelousas Jr High School, LA

Boxer Dog

B est friend
O ur family dog
X -mas dog
E xtraordinary
R eady to play

D igging in the dirt
O ur favorite pet
G ood guard dog

Carson Spivey, Grade 7
Albemarle School, NC

Words Hurt

Maybe it's because
We having nothing better to do
We just run our mouths
Without thinking it through

We find the first person who is different
And we find fault in him
Maybe we'll apologize later
But the chances are really slim

Maybe it's the way you talk
Or even the style you lack
Could you really call us your friends
Or will we stab you in the back?

We'll always criticize you
Like being stomped in the dirt
No matter what they say
Words really do hurt

Brittney Taylor, Grade 8
Lake Middle School, MS

Mystery

A wesome and unique
M ember of the Christmas committee
B ringing joy to
E veryone that I love and care for
R ealist person in the world

S he comes with elegance from
M other Earth, she's never
I nterrupting anybody, anyone can
T rust and believe in her
H onesty

Amber Smith, Grade 7
Lloyd-Kennedy Charter School, SC

Mother Nature's Magnificent Mosaic

Autumn is a kaleidoscopic pallet of paint.
As her brush sweeps up and down,
Tenderly painting everything around.
Diligently and gently her brush glides,
Leaving the whole world with a majestic surprise.

Tickling the leaves, she lets out a minuscule breeze.
The leaves elegantly flutter around,
Until she places them gently on the ground.
Quietly, quietly, they will stay,
Awaiting the release of the mellow wind that sweeps them away.

As these magical colors glide through the air,
The sky is brimming and nothing lay bare.
She emits a deep breath and they swirl everywhere.
Satisfied, she watches them with infinite care.
Dancing, dancing all around, there is nothing melancholic to be found.

Majestic colors begin to fade away, and the pallet becomes darker day after day.
Exultant children dream of what next autumn will bring,
And imagine the hues of the season with glee.
Will stunning shades of orange, gold, brown, and red be found?
I pray she ensures such multiplicity of color will always abound!

Megan Bazzell, Grade 8
St John Neumann Regional Catholic School, GA

Gustav

First you hear worried voices,
Saying Gustav is out at sea.
You turn on the weather;
There it sits spinning and twirling.
Not a second one you think;
Then the man on the screen starts talking.
He says it's headed right at you;
Just two days away, you wonder what to do.
After deciding to stay, you wonder how to prepare.
You get a generator, water, and canned food.
As you hunker down, you hear it has turned towards New Orleans.
With great joy you hear it's not coming towards you.

Robert Knox, Grade 8
Bishop Noland Episcopal Day School, LA

Where I'm From

I'm from dancing with Papa; standing on his feet
I'm from dolphins; dancing in the sea
I'm from Amazing Grace; Making people glad to hear
I'm from proud parents; cheering and clapping in the background
I'm from Thanksgiving; making families come together
I'm from bowling; abolishing all the pins
I'm from the rainbow; giving you all the colors of my mood
I'm from God; sending peace down to Earth
I'm from Mother Nature; giving everything everlasting life
I'm from my trumpet; playing peaceful music
I'm from the Goins family

Brandi Goins, Grade 8
Sims Jr High School, SC

Just Because I Am Black

Just because I am black
It doesn't mean I like to be judged by my skin color
It doesn't mean I am illiterate
It doesn't mean I don't know how to be respectful.
Just because I am black,
I can speak my mind and use BIG words while doing so!
I can go to college and become successful.
I can make a difference!
Just because I am black,
I do listen to what you have to say
And give you good advice that doesn't have to deal with violence
I care, I love, I am like everyone else and it is,
Just because I am black!

Cheyenne Reed, Grade 9
Warren Early College High School, NC

Love

Whoever said it was a good feeling
Must have never really felt it
'Cause what most feel is pain and heartache
You'd think they'd be too young
To feel this kind of pain
But I guess they're never too young for anything
They'll try so many times to express their feelings
But would open their mouth and silence would escape
They could pour their heart out on paper
But never in speech where it really counts
The hurt the pain
The restless games
Goes out in different serving amounts
Love
Whoever said it was a good feeling
MUST have never really felt it
'Cause what most feel is pain and heartache
You'd think they'd be too young
To feel this kind of pain
But I guess they're never too young for anything

Carol Matsey, Grade 9
McKee Jr High School, AL

Technology

All of this is to entertain the human mind,
Old or new,
It keeps the world wondering what we will be next.

Electricity runs it all,
Computers to lap tops,
Keyboards to touch screens,
There will always be something new to ease our daily lives.

TV rots our brains,
Internet provides us with knowledge,
Video games save us from school,
What will technology do for you!

Cameron Moore, Grade 7
Carolina International School, NC

Siblings

Siblings
The annoying gibberish in the background,
The person singing a jingle out of season,
The one tapping your shoulder while you're working,
The people fighting over whose turn it is,
The one rolling the die to a board game,
The person who asks for help in math,
The one who helps you master a video game,
The person who will always stand by your side,
A future organ donor,
The one who passes the ball in the backyard with you,
The people who look up to you,
The people you look up to,
The ones who are always looking out for you,
Siblings

Matthew Nelson, Grade 8
Dillard Drive Middle School, NC

Week of the Hurricane

During the storm
I felt good and confident.
The thing that scared me the most
would be that the tree we live under
would fall on my house.
We left my house to go meet a friend
in a brick home where it was safer.
Most of the day we stayed outside,
and with the wind blowing
it felt good.
The backyard was flooding,
water was at least a foot and a half deep.
My dog played in the water for a little while.
We went back to the house
when the storm was over.
There was no damage done
nothing had a dent or anything!

Derek Leger, Grade 8
Leonville Elementary School, LA

Wonderful Times

Thanksgiving is a wonderful time,
With family, friends, and foods of all kinds.

Thanksgiving is a peaceful time.
All the people are so happy.
It's just a nice state of mind.

Thanksgiving is a fun time,
With games, people, and all the good food.

Thanksgiving is a thankful time.
I am glad that God made us
So we can enjoy so many good things.

Kyle Taylor, Grade 7
Magnolia Springs Baptist Academy, AL

Live Your Life

Live, laugh, love strong words sent from above
Keep your head high and live with no regrets life is too short to always be upset
Love your enemies and all foes for you might need them one day, who knows
Laugh while you can and be merry be who you are and love fairly
People will always come and go the reasons why can be hard to know
Instill in your heart a place to forgive and be happy with the merry life you live
Associate with others and keep a best friend who will always be there with a hand to lend
Look towards your future and hope for the best know that you're strong enough to withstand any test
However, still cherish your past and remember what you've been through you can sometimes learn various things you never knew
Your dreams are your own and can be fulfilled only if you know, only if you will
Realize your faults and learn from your mistakes therefore knowing the same bad decisions aren't to make
You're your own person and no one can tell you it's not true you can be whatever you want and succeed in everything you do

Chassidy Cherie Whittaker, Grade 9
McKee Jr High School, AL

Finding Myself

I'm figuring myself out.
I can feel the sunlight pouring out of my mouth as I tell people honesty
I wish to fly to a place that I can dream forever; dream of happiness.
But happiness only exists in fairy tales.
Today I am flying, tomorrow I am trying to dig myself out of this hole my emotions have buried me in.
I try holding in my feelings to not show weakness, but every day my struggles get worse.
I held a butterfly and watched its glowing wings become one of me.
Each day I am preparing myself for a new hope.
I have learned to fight off these serpents who wish to control me, with a sword full of peace.
I am determined to make hate a useless term and love fill the air.

Tiffany Lester, Grade 8
West Craven Middle School, NC

Face of Fall

Alluring amber acorns fall from broken branches,
Stunning skies of silver allow no more for summer's dances.
Lovely leaves lie lazily upon the luscious loam,
Fallen frenziedly from their fathers as they hastily left home.

The wind glides through caressing branches as it sings its happy song,
While trees are painted golden all season long.
Tangible tears fall from overcast clouds above,
As they see scarlet taking from them the gorgeous green they love.

Rambunctious rabbits rapidly run round,
While squirrels scramble from sycamore to sweet gum without a sound.
Deer dance among the daisies dazing into the dawn,
As they wonder where brother fall will take them and where sister summer has gone

Although fall's face has immaculate beauty, it's the inner qualities that really shine,
The righteous redwood, the just jackrabbit, and the virtuous vine.
Fall is fair as it relinquishes the rations of sister summer's troubles,
Scant supplies for the sluggish but for the diligent double.

The face of fall appears to be faultless but it too has flaws,
With its brisk breezes that billow by, badgering without a cause.
Fall is free, a season of dance, to run and do as you please,
When brother winter comes round to cover the ground we sorrowfully miss fall's face in the trees.

Barbara Anne Kozee, Grade 8
St John Neumann Regional Catholic School, GA

An Apple

At first sight, without
knowing her, she is an apple blossom.
But this is without details,
if you saw who she hangs out with
you would surely change your mind.
She hangs out with the caviar of society.
Her friends are the most beautiful
apple blossoms, in their mind.
They are rather full of themselves,
which insinuates that she is one of those
repulsive apples you eat before they are ripe.
You would think she could care less about you.
You'd think all she ever thinks of is herself,
how rich her pigment is,
how beautiful her shape is and so on.
But she is not the repulsive apple,
she is the grade-A, harvest time apple.
If you see what's on the inside you'll
see how down to earth she really is.
She isn't the stuck-up bragging apple, as all her friends.
She's just that kind of crisp apple, that does not boast.

Stewart Schrieffer, Grade 7
L E Gable Middle School, SC

The Magic Box

The magic box is very small
The magic box has four walls
It may not be heavy
It may not be light
But what's inside it
Is a great delight

On the box are tiny figurines
That unlock the doors to my dreams
Different dreams are all alike
They pop up in my head day and night

This box has always been special it seems
Without it I would never have dreams

Jennifer Kennedy, Grade 8
Mount Carmel Academy, LA

Georgia on My Mind!

Georgia, this is my place.
With the Blue Ridge Mountains you must embrace.
The mountains all in line,
The majestic view will blow your mind.
It's about nature and life.
The way the moon fills the sky at night.
It's like being mesmerized, being ravished by beauty.
The mountains take your breath away.
Georgia, a place of silence and sweet peace.
A perfect place to stay!

McKayla Barriault, Grade 8
Fannin County Middle School, GA

Fall in Georgia

Fall is the best time
of the year in Georgia.
You can see all the different
colors of leaves swiftly
floating through the air,
just to slightly lie on the ground.
By the end of fall,
there are no leaves on the trees,
and you can see the whole state of Georgia
through the tall bare trees.

Sierra Brown, Grade 8
Fannin County Middle School, GA

Unforgettable Storms

When storms come into my life,
I feel so scared and worried.
I hear the crickets and frogs communicating
during the tragic days in my life.
The summer is the worst time
for storms and deaths.
I see his diamond blue eyes
sparkling in the night sky.
I can feel the wind on my face
when it is all over.
I will never forget the day
when the storm hit and took him away.
When I am outside
staring at the sun going down,
I wonder if he is with me
holding on tight and never letting go.
I hope all the angels above
are as loving as he is or will be.
During winter I want to be with him
always and forever.

Brittany Benoit, Grade 8
Leonville Elementary School, LA

Outspoken

What is being outspoken?
Being loud and making noise.
No, outspoken is more.
Being able to be seen but hear 1000 words.
Having poise and intelligence.
Pay attention and looking good.
Having confidence and talent.
Walking with your head held high fearing no one.
I am outspoken can't you see.
I am proud to be me and I am seen.
Heard but only in a good way.
I am funny, smart, kind, beautiful, peaceful,
confident, generous, loving, gorgeous,
graceful, and much more.
And you can see that better than you can hear that.
I am outspoken don't you see.

Jhone Egerton, Grade 7
Weldon Middle School, NC

My Best Friend

You're wacky and you're weird.
You act a little strange
But even though you act this way,
I don't want you to change.

You're zany and you're zoopy
You always make me smile.
Your loud long laugh
Can be heard from as far as a mile.

Although you're a little different,
Your love will never end
And I am so so happy
That you're my best friend.

Amelia Williamson, Grade 7
Fayette Middle School, GA

Student

Being a student isn't fun
without someone
guiding you the right way

A student couldn't learn
if the teacher
didn't learn with them

A student would never listen
if the subject
was never interesting

A student is not
a pleasant thing to be until
you earn your teacher's respect

Chelsea Babb, Grade 7
L E Gable Middle School, SC

Blind Date

Watching, just watching
Hoping and wondering what it might be.
Secretly waiting patiently.
Hiding, scarcely behind the door.
Waiting excited, I can wait no more.

Nervousness, happiness,
What might it be? Or Who?
What if he's hot?
What if he's not?
Who could it be or what might it seem?
Patient, excited, filled with glee,
For the thing I'm not knowing.

I'm cringing and hiding,
From what I might be finding
Ring, ring, it's the doorbell.

Christine Bowen, Grade 8
Dillard Drive Middle School, NC

There Comes a Time

there comes a time when children have to spread their wings and fly
there comes a time when moms and dads have to say good-bye
there comes a time when birth is the beginning and death is the end
there comes a time when an angel, God can send
there comes a time when people lose everything they ever loved
there comes a time when God sends down His love
there comes a time when you gain friends and lose them
there comes a time when God makes up for ten
there comes a time when you can cry and forget
there comes a time when you can smile and forgive
there comes a time for laughing and smiling
there comes a time for skies and sunshine
there comes a time when heaven is sent
there comes a time when your path is bent
there comes a time for helping and mending
there comes a time for troubles and blocks
there comes a time when God is your soldier
there comes a time when the world is weighing down your shoulders
there comes a time for everyone and when to be
there comes a time and now the time is for me

Kaitlyn Stone, Grade 9
Cape Fear Christian Academy, NC

An Old Dirt Road

An old dirt road lay amongst a yellow wood
and I was fortunate that I could travel it.
Being a lone traveler I thought for a while, I was actually gung ho,
acting like a child, noticing this was opportunistic.

As I began my commute, with much gusto,
I realized my path has began to change,
for I was distracted by the wonders around me
that I have noticed my course was not the same.

It was quite an adventure, just like a dream,
filled with excitement and joys and wonderful things,
but now it's over, my journey has ceased,
and all of my energy has been released.

Jay Sanford, Grade 8
Schley County Middle/High School, GA

Thoughts

So what if I'm not as you expected! I'm different, I'm not like you.
Is this a reason for me to be neglected? I do my own thing; to me this world is new.
My thoughts and opinions are not to your liking, but I love how I am.
I know you find my personality shocking, but I'm only human.
I don't want to conform; I like to stand out
On this I stand stern, to be an individual! I shout.
But you try to tie me down, clip my wings so I cannot fly.
If I conform, all you'll see is my frown. I feel smothered like I will die.
So what if I'm different! Love me for who I am!
You do know that I'm God sent; but I feel as though my life is a sham.
I'm not going to change to please you! You say I rebel
But is this really true? Sometimes my life feels like a living hell!

Joseph King, Grade 9
McKee Jr High School, AL

Gustav

When Gustav was seen in the gulf
I felt nervous.
No one had accurate answers
as to which direction it was heading.
The storm was in the gulf
picking up speed and gaining power.
Once it hits land
it slows down
It just hit my territory.
Looking out the window,
all I see is strong winds and rain.
Tornadoes will be twirling everywhere soon.
As I continue to stare out of the window
it gets very calm.
Heavy rain drops hit my roof.
I hear a loud noise "boom;"
a tree has just come out of the ground.
Now I am shocked with a blank feeling.
Now what happens.?

Tattianna Yarde, Grade 8
Leonville Elementary School, LA

Death by Love

So now you know my feelings I have shown
yet you don't seem to show, your face doesn't glow

I thought I was clear can you not hear?
I just poured out my heart yet you don't even start
you don't run away but do you still want to stay?

If you don't talk soon I may run away
I gave up too much to just sit here and wait

Answer me now please don't frown
my head is spinning around as I fall to the ground
I see out of the corner of my eye you walk away and sigh

Now I understand

As my world goes black
I can see clearly
I was your tool
You used me every day as I slip away
A tear falls and fades

Samantha Quiel, Grade 9
West Johnston High School, NC

Love

Love is strong love is true
Love is what I'm thinking about when I see you
When you love someone you don't give up
You keep on fighting, making yourself tough.
Love is forgetting, and it is rough.
Time is passing, I just can't get enough.

Breyia Compton, Grade 7
Poland Jr High School, LA

This Place I Call Home

When I step out of the door in the morn,
I just can't help but to feel reborn.
With the deer prancing around in the yard,
the clouds up above are looking a little charred.
The dew on the grass gleaming in the sun,
makes me want to dance around and have fun.
I look around and smell the sweet scent of honey,
I couldn't sell this place for any value of money.

Emily Green, Grade 8
Fannin County Middle School, GA

What Happened?

Going forward,
Feeling that lurch in my stomach,
Hearing the mourning everywhere.
Seeing her.
But in so many ways,
It wasn't her.
I couldn't see her natural beauty,
And happiness in her face.
There was no life in her.
Just her.
All I saw was her skin so pale and fake,
Like porcelain
And hard as a rock.
Not believing it was real.
Thinking at any minute,
She'll wake up from a deep sleep,
But didn't.
That's when it hit me.
You will always lose someone you love.
And it will always happen.
It did happen.

Susan Favrot, Grade 7
Haynes Academy for Advanced Studies, LA

Peace and Hatred

Peace represents blue
Hatred represents red.

Green represents the border
That separates blue and red from each other.

When there is peace, hatred cries out
When there is hatred, peace cries out.

Why is this?

Peace doesn't like hatred
Hatred doesn't like peace.

They are just two things that don't go together
They are like fire and ice.

Marquis Miller, Grade 8
Palmetto Middle School, SC

My World
Chocolate chips and marshmallows
Sweet aroma of cookies
Crunching crumbs beneath my feet
Softness of those marshmallows
Cookies so sweet you would not believe
I could eat my world in a day
Ashley Carter, Grade 8
Alexandria Middle Magnet School, LA

Volleyball
The volleyball
quickly
flew
through the air
on the ground
in the stands
Will it go over the net?
Hannah Hotard, Grade 7
Sacred Heart of Jesus School, LA

Smile!
A smile is the sun
It makes the bees hum
Seeing one each and every day
It makes you turn gay
In the depth of darkness
It helps you find your happiness
It covers up your anger
And lets you see others clearly
Each smile opens up a new world
It tells you who you really are
A smile is the life of light
Barbara Thao, Grade 9
Challenger High School, NC

Zack Clark's Place in Poetry
Infinite, dexterous, extravagant smooth
the mist of Poseidon himself
over the edges of reality
new way of life
defying gravity
a red dawn
Mississippi
Zack Clark, Grade 8
Fayette Middle School, GA

Winter
Winter
Cold, frost
Freezing, shivering, sledding
Snowman, wind, pool, ocean
Swimming, hiking, surfing
Hot, dry
Summer
Jade Jefferson, Grade 8
St Peter Claver School, LA

Do You Feel Lonely?
Do you feel lonely parrot,
in a cage of parakeets?
Do you feel lonely turtle,
in a pond of trout?
How about you, smallest of the big,
or you, biggest of the small?

Do you feel unique?
Parrot?
Turtle?
The smallest?
The biggest?
Do you?
Or do you feel lonely?
Cassidy Ray, Grade 9
Smiths Station High School, AL

China Doll
There she sits,
Lightly, delicately,
Semblance of a china doll:
Glassy marble eyes,
Stony white skin.
Graceful, beautiful,
Her ruffled emerald dress
Folding neatly beneath her.
Fragile, breakable:
Skin like paper,
Bones like glass.
Make sure you let her down easy.
Leah Marie Fox, Grade 9
Indian Springs School, AL

I Am a Young Teen
I am a young teen
I wonder where I'm going
I hear nothing
I see nothing
I want everything
I am a young teen

I pretend to be on top
I feel under the bottom
I touch my character
I worry about my inside
I cry tears of fire
I am a young teen

I understand why I have friends
I say everyone has a purpose
I dream happiness
I try to work hard
I hope success in the future
I am a young teen
Kenneth Kearney, Grade 9
Warren Early College High School, NC

Love
Love is kind
Love is the best
Love is beautiful
it is judgeless.
Love is like a love bug
together your whole life
when you're apart
feels like being stabbed
with a knife.
Love is someone always having
your back.
They never back down
or crack.
They say the family that
prays together stays together
Isn't that love.
If that isn't love
it is none of the above.
Kardarius McClendon, Grade 8
Lake Middle School, MS

Clouds
The clouds come
when rain forms.
They form together
when bad weather comes.
The color of the clouds
makes you want to fly.
Annchester Williams, Grade 7
L E Gable Middle School, SC

Baltimore
Baltimore, the place where the
Championship is held

I'm ready, at least I think so
We play in 30 minutes

I have 30 minutes to dream
Libby Kesler, Grade 7
L E Gable Middle School, SC

How and Why?
How had the world come to be
How could it have come to me

Even though we cannot change
It makes us look from a different range

Why do we deserve to live
If we do not care to give

The footsteps of my Father have shown
To light the way of the unknown
Lindsey Schexnayder, Grade 7
Sacred Heart of Jesus School, LA

Working Together to Achieve a Dream

Hold your head up, be brave,
Harm will not come,
This world can be saved,
There is so much to overcome.

You and I can help,
We can all do our part,
So we feel like Michael Phelps,
A champion at heart.

How do you do this, you ask?
It's easy as 1, 2, 3
If we all do a task
It starts with you and me.

Emily Williams, Grade 8
Priceville Jr High School, AL

Pancakes

Pancakes, pancakes, tasty and sweet,
The more you smell the more you'll eat.
Round and fluffy, they sure are delicious.
Can't wait to eat them, I'm very ambitious.
There are many flavors, as you can see,
Like chocolate, cinnamon, and strawberry.
Syrup on a pancake is necessary too,
just like pancakes are necessary for you.
Warm, fluffy, a scrumptious treat
When I am hungry this is what I eat.
On Sunday mornings when Mom gets out the batter,
I'm the first one to get you on my platter.
I could eat you for breakfast, dinner, or lunch
Straight into the fluffiness I love to munch.
Pancakes, pancakes, tasty and sweet,
You're the one I love to eat!

Ashleigh O'Donnell, Grade 8
Haynes Academy for Advanced Studies, LA

Here I Am…

Here I am having a bad day
Here I am fussing everybody out
Here I am keeping all the anger in me

Here I am having a bad day
Here I am not doing my work because of frustration
Here I am getting annoyed

I feel this way because I don't feel good
I feel like throwing up
I feel like going to sleep

Here I am trying to take the pain away
Here I am trying to make the best of it
Here I am wondering when is it going to leave me alone

Susie Binganisi, Grade 7
East Millbrook Magnet Middle School, NC

The Wicked Witch in the Woods

Standing alone under the dark, lonely night
The stars illuminated under the lowly twilight
Enigmatic and mysterious happenings arose all around
There was evil around me that could not be found

Upon the woods lay an ambiguous witch
Hidden in daylight through the nocturnal switch
Masked behind the tormenting trees
She lay manipulating the revolting leaves

The wicked witch from the Western way
Who was never approached during night nor day
Had a controlling force that could not be seen
For she haunted the town on Halloween

Watching the world through the spooky sky
Nobody knew if she was dead or alive
She hid in the woods alone and waited
If her legend was true, it was always debated

For this was Halloween and fear was arising
The woods were forbidden and the whole world was hiding
But come November first, she was labeled a myth
And the fear of the witch drifted away in the mist

Daniel Tanghal, Grade 8
St John Neumann Regional Catholic School, GA

Feelings and Storms

Storms make me feel nervous.
There are birds stuck in a tree.
My dog is ill and hurt.
Many storms are arriving at other locations.
The sky is like Mother Nature.
My house is like a big mess,
full of trash from the storm.
I look out the window every day.
So many cats and dogs are hurt badly.
My mom and dad are hiding in their room.
The storms are getting close,
and closer to my house.

Tevin Thibodeaux, Grade 7
Leonville Elementary School, LA

Stand by You

I will stand by you through thick and thin.
When you get in your dreary moments I will be there for you.
When you feel that there's no one you can express to,
I will stand by you whenever you need me to.

Some more shall I say…
I will stand by you like a true best friend would,
Like no other would.
This is me telling you that I will
"Stand by you!"

M'Kenya Gray, Grade 8
Lake Middle School, MS

Sun vs Moon

Sun
Smoldering, sweltering
Blistering, gleaming, blazing
Temperature, fever, inferno, fire
Reassuring, soothing, glowing
Pallid, glaring, chilled
Moon

Alex Giddens, Grade 9
Northgate High School, GA

Land/Water

Land
grass, dirt
shrinking, shifting, producing
solid, unbreakable, drenching, moving
growing, splashing, covering
cold, warm
Water

Leslie Landry, Grade 7
Sacred Heart of Jesus School, LA

Winter Wonderland

Winter makes you feel cool
bring out the wool sweaters.
We never regret the white blanket
over our yard.
You get the wonderful winter cards.
Sad emotions
now snow melting away.
The children's faces now turn to dark.
Walk outside and you're standing
in slush.
It's melting away very slowly.
Have a tear.
No time to play.
Next hear chimes of spring all day.

Lauren James, Grade 7
Cathedral School, NC

Hurricanes

When I think of storms,
they make me want to cry.
My family and I are inside my house
and all the animals go into hiding.
At twilight, I go outside
and see the moon
shining down on the flooded grass.
The rain makes the grass grow
My momma dreams of her mom.
As the night goes by,
I dream of wonderful things.
I wake up
and see the sun.
It's another day!

Drissa Maiga, Grade 8
Leonville Elementary School, LA

Florida

My place of them all is Florida.
I have lived in Florida all my life and I respect my city.
I have been everywhere in Florida and traveled by car and it was a long ways.
I love the beautiful ocean and beaches they have
And there are amazing places I still want to see.
My city is Gainesville, FL.
We have a big city and we keep it clean
There are only Gator fans in Florida.
There are only four major cities in Florida.
I am a witness to that, and we are the very best.

Chuck Hooks, Grade 9
Three Springs of Courtland School, AL

Love

Love is a passion
Time for family and friends
To get together and
Love each other
And pick up some red roses
To the person that you love
You could give it to your mother or father
All of your family members need to love each other
You don't have to hate each other just love each other
The ones that are in the army you should still love them no matter what
You should always love the people in the army because they are
Fighting for our freedom
Love is something you give away
We should never hate each other
That's what love is all about — loving each other!

Sherrece Howard, Grade 7
Hubert Middle School, GA

Away Away, I Run

With this heart that pounds like thunder, from your might I may wander.
Far away I hope to stay.
Away away, I run.
These wounds that burn like fire, cinders never to retire.
In the flame I remain, but maybe soon I will reign.
Until that day comes,
away away, I run.
For so long you've been my captor, forcing things upon me.
Your brutal words fly like dragons, storming down my fortress.
But here my castle still stands, in front of you I am.
I am not afraid of you, only what you have put me through.
Soon my agony won't hold me down,
away away, I run.
I see the weakness in your face, regret in the actions taken place.
Knowing places the blame into you. Soon you let go, not to pursue.
Away away, I run.
Now you are weak and I am gone. Feel the tormenting pain you once thrust upon,
this soul that is no more yours to control.
I have gained the strength to remain. No longer the same is the pain,
I gave it back to you. Never to come back to you, while you can no longer pursue.
Away away, I run.

Courtney Morgan, Grade 9
New Site High School, MS

Dreams

I peacefully lay my head down
My eyes begin to close
I have many things on my mind
Some good, some bad

My dreams can be imaginary
Like raining cats and dogs
Dreams can be like funerals
Very sad moments up in the air

Take me away
To a secret place
No one can follow me
You can't see me, but I can see you

My dreams can sweep me off my feet
Take me away to a winter wonderland
Or around the world
Then take me back to my pillow as I wake up.

Carly Dolniak, Grade 8
Carolina International School, NC

John Deere Tractor

A tractor
Once used for plowing fields.
Once used for stringin' barb wire.
Missin' those times o' hard work and fun.
Once used to pull a hay baler.
Wonderin' where his driver is.
Hopin' and prayin' he won't be sent to a scrap heap.
Rememberin' his glory days.
Wantin' to know if he'll ever see the light o' day,
Or be shut up in the barn.
Wonderin' if he'll get sold.
A lonely tractor broken down.
Once used for his driver to yield.
A tractor
Large faded John Deere green with yellow numbers
Just an ordinary ole John Deere tractor.

Michael Beckwith, Grade 8
Lake Middle School, MS

Cops

A cop is
like a savior,
he helps you do good things
and not bad things.
He helps you feel safe in
your community or town.
A cop is always there for you.
A cop discourages you from using drugs
by talking to you or taking you to jail.
Cops are not always the bad guys because
they can be the good guys, too.

Zamion Pearson, Grade 7
L E Gable Middle School, SC

Sparring

We stand and we wait,
we stare each other down.
Bow,
yell,
hear that special word — begin.
Kick,
punch, punch,
kick.
Spar with all my heart
like never before.
Using everything I have —
jump,
scream.
Point.
Block, block,
counter.
Stay in the moment,
lunge.
The time is now —
spin, hit
win.

Emily Dokken, Grade 7
Cherokee Christian School, GA

A Diabetic Is Not a Pleasant Thing to Be

A diabetic is not a pleasant thing to be.
Without having to endure some pain.
The pain of a needle sticking you in the skin.

A day without it
Would not involve
The endless blood
That is taken from me.

There would be no pain.
No needles
No blood
And the end of scarred skin.

Paul McGaha, Grade 7
L E Gable Middle School, SC

Krupa Dabhi

Krupa
Sensitive, funny, active, thin
Daughter of a strong father, and loving mother
Lover of volleyball, family, and friends
Who feels happiness, love, and joy
Who fears nightmares, guns, and dying.
Who needs support, energy, success
Who would like to see the Great Wall of China,
the Statue of Liberty,
and Hawaii.
Dabhi

Krupa Dabhi, Grade 8
Statesville Middle School, NC

Thanksgiving

A time for bonding, a time for sharing,
Eating tablefuls so tall.
Parents talking, kids chatting,
Laughing through the wall.

Chowing down on turkey, plates filled,
Thinking more the merrier.
Appreciating what time we all have together.

Food being devoured, bite by bite.
Spoons and forks are all out of sight.
Parades and football games are all on TV
While Mom has already set up
The annual Christmas tree.

So while we bond and share
And eat tablefuls so tall,
Let us all be still,
Thanking God for all.

Jalil Moore, Grade 8
Magnolia Springs Baptist Academy, AL

My Free Sprit

The rose is like a gentle kiss
Thoughtful, for a specific person
The sunflower is like a new adventure
Bright with endless opportunities

The rose's dance is like a ballet position
Tight and motionless
The sunflower's rhythm is like a jazz routine
Swaying and intertwining with each other

The rose is as precious as a first impression;
It's something that lasts forever
Although it eventually dies
It's a memory that is endless

The sunflower is as optimistic as a ray of sunlight;
Forever lasting, shining upon faces
Growing tall and strong
Nurtured as a young child

I will forever adore the rose
But I am as free as a sunflower

Madison Ott, Grade 9
Ardrey Kell High School, NC

Stars

Depression, anger, pain
These are the feelings that darken the day
But when it gets dark enough
Look up and you can see the stars

Jonathan Schmitz, Grade 9
Sanderson High School, NC

My Perfect Date

My first date with my boyfriend Kris
We sat on the beach and he gave me a kiss
We had sat there all night long
He made me laugh to his funny song

We had ice cream from the BP gas station
Kris had chocolate as did I
We sat on the beach to watch the sunset
The ice cream melted because we had barely touched it yet

As the ice cream dripped down our hands
Little brown blotches plopped on the sand
They started to look like a little pile of dirt
I laughed when Kris dropped some ice cream on his shirt

As we left we laughed as we ate
I knew right away it was the perfect date
When push came to shove we said our goodbyes
As we did we laughed so hard we started to cry

Stacy Troutman, Grade 9
North Wilkes High School, NC

Turic

You are the best
You beat the rest
Can't believe you're mine
If I could I would give you control of time
So we could lay together forever
Never knowing what will happen tomorrow
Not feeling the sorrows
Just the happiness and warmth
Of being in each others arms
Through the thick and thin
Being together to the end
Wishing you could be here
Holding you so dear
I love you so much
No need for a hunch
For you are the tune to my lyrics
My dear Turic.

Kathleen Crocker, Grade 9
Lumpkin County High School, GA

Love

Love is sweet,
Sweet like candy!
We need love,
And I need love!
So just love one another
and just be you,
Because Love don't come by itself
You have to earn and show a little love TOO!
Love is sweet, sweet like,
Honey!

Tichina Broden, Grade 7
Saint James High School, LA

Things I Like

I like…
The loud lime green on bedroom walls,
A busy winter day in a nice warm mall,
The smell of cinnamon on a crisp winter day,
The feeling on my hands when I play with clay,
The smell of a fireplace, a-crackling and a-blazing,
Cheetah and leopard prints are amazing,
When the smell of strawberries fill the air,
When my mom frosts a cake with gentle care,
Writing on a dry erase board, all nice and neat,
The taste of yummy candy, wonderful and sweet
Roses, daisies, tulips and sunflowers too,
Flowers of all colors like purple, red, and blue,
British accents, sharp and crisp,
On a boiling, hot day, running through mist
Cold caramel frappuccinos from Starbucks Coffee,
Little, tiny babies laughing in glee.
Of these things that I like the best,
I could not tell you which rose above the rest!

Katelyn Aquilo, Grade 9
Mount Carmel Academy, LA

Christmastime

Tree
Many lights twinkle bright
Hung all around this Christmas sight
Presents wrapped in Christmas bows
Everyone hopes that it snows
I love this special time of year
Everyone is full of Christmas cheer
Reindeer and Santa always come to mind
But Jesus is the most important person of this time
Christmas morning is the best!
Waking up to the Christmas smell
Everyone knows is so swell
Friends and family gather around
All soon for a Happy New Year
In
3
2
1

Hanna Dugas, Grade 7
St Mary's School, SC

The Ocean

Watch the marvelous foaming waves crash on the beach.
As you walk across the steaming hot sands,
you begin to feel blisters form on your feet.
When you finally splash into the ice cold water, you feel relaxed.
You can smell and taste the salty air.
Then your feet start to tingle.
The mist is hitting you in the face
making little water droplets fall from your hair.

Morgan Chastain, Grade 8
Fannin County Middle School, GA

Goodbye

You would think goodbyes would never come
But they're finally here at last

What once was our bright future
And is now our dim-lit past

The pathways we have traveled down
And the corners we have turned

But we hold onto the memories
The lessons that we learned

So make your goodbyes ones to remember
Those are the ones that will be treasured

All the sad sorrow feelings change
They become new beginnings

So all your unknown feelings
Become into new Hellos.

Ander Gilreath, Grade 9
North Wilkes High School, NC

The Elements

The wind
   peaceful and relaxing
Flowing and moving
   gracefully
Breeze

A fire
   strong and powerful
Destroys and burns
   unfriendly
Blaze

The water
   graceful but quick-tempered
Moves and flows
   peacefully
Rain

Nick deVeer, Grade 7
Haynes Academy for Advanced Studies, LA

Get Active

Getting active
You should always get active and get off your butt,
You can be the quarterback and yell "hutt hutt."
You can be the starting point guard,
And strike down the court really hard.
You can play baseball and hit a home run,
But after that you won't be done.
Whatever you do get active and play,
Keep on doing it day after day.

Arman Smith, Grade 8
Fayette Middle School, GA

Oceans

Oceans
Mysterious, beautiful
Full of life
All different kinds everywhere
Waters

Scott Maloney, Grade 7
Sacred Heart of Jesus School, LA

Planet Earth

Down on the river shore is sand,
Slipping through foot and hand.
Rivers once mighty, now tamed by man,
Flow in brooks and streams.
Forests rise, then fall, then come again,
Green kingdoms of past live, again.
Creatures of all, past, present, future
This is planet Earth.

Deserts wide, sandy, hot like ovens,
Ice caps cold as freezers,
Icicles hang like daggers,
Lakes of midnight dew,
This is planet Earth.

High in the sky birds fly,
Deep in the ocean fish swim,
On the ground animals roam,
Everywhere humans go,
This is planet Earth.

Sameer Chawla, Grade 7
Margaret Green Jr High School, MS

In My Thoughts

Storms in my life make me feel so sad
because they remind me of people
in my family who have died.
I always keep my grandma,
Mama G., in my thoughts.
God took her into his home.
Now she is with the angels
above watching over me.
The place I think of her
the most is outdoors.
I watch as the leaves fall
and change to orange and brown.
I walk outside and feel the cool
breeze as it caresses my skin.
It is close to twilight.
I'm in my bedroom, now.
I am all alone and now one is
around to hear me cry.
I sit on my bed and watch as the
gray clouds cover the moon
with a blanket of sadness.

Meleigha Lazare, Grade 7
Leonville Elementary School, LA

Red

Red is a color I have always remembered, all the way back when I was three.
A cheerleading suit, of wolfpack red, I remember it to be.
From that time on, I have loved red, every shade there can be.
Crossfire, flowerpot, candy corn, this color stays with me.
Fire engine, scarlet, and maroon.
I hope to see red soon.
For red is my favorite color,
no color could be better for me.

Go Pack!!

Mary Parker, Grade 8
Dillard Drive Middle School, NC

Nature

Nature beautifies the universe
With its magnificent plants and trees.
However, they are more important than you think;
They help everybody to live.
From seeds to plants (or otherwise)
They grow slowly
Without dying abruptly.

Again I say, nature grows.
The plants begin small,
But their larger size will make history.
Their larger sizes will appreciate us;
Their helpfulness (and usefulness)
Make us assume that they are so crucial to us.
In fact, they are always helpful, big or small.

Nature spreads around the world,
Making it a fantastic reason to live.
Without plants, it is impossible.
Grass, shrubs, trees, and other plants
Should be proud of their growth.
They are surrounded by their loyal friends,
Building the environment, and thanking God for their long existence.

Kamau A. Grant, Grade 7
Carolina International School, NC

Georgia's Wonders

Georgia, Georgia
Your wonders never cease to amaze me.
All those sparkling lakes glistening in the sunshine,
Colossal horses carved into stone,
Amicalola Falls pounding like the roar of a lion,
Radium Springs blue as a gem,
Bottomless Providence Canyon echoing in the breeze,
Tallulah Gorge with its jagged cliffs,
Warm Spring's volcanic relaxing water,
The crisp aroma of leaves in the Blue Ridge Mountains during autumn season,
And the spongy bog of the mysterious Okefenokee Swamp.
It's no surprise that everybody enjoys coming here.
Georgia, Georgia, a wondrous place.

Sean Callihan, Grade 8
Fannin County Middle School, GA

First Love

Looking up, anxious to see
Those baby blue eyes looking back at me
Lost in the sea of blue
I struggled to catch my breath

Heart thumping the first time
Our hands touched,
Sending an arc of electricity between us —
Long talks, first date, fireworks bursting
Getting to know the other's heart

Love slowly blooming
Like a rosebud slowly opens
Revealing the beauty that's held within
My first love.

Marta Pedroza, Grade 9
North Wilkes High School, NC

My Little Sister

I've dreamed to teach you right from wrong.
You keep your head up firm and strong.
You will be with me day and night.
For a minute you'll never be out of my sight.

You are so beautiful with you bright brown eyes.
My little sister will light up our big, dark skies.
My little angel I'll always treasure.
To take care of you will be my pleasure.

Every night you appear in my dream.
Along with the tears which form a stream.
I cherish you with all my heart.
To this day I wish we weren't torn apart.
When I wake up I wish I were there.
I know soon that you'll be near.

You gave me the courage to do real good.
Just like you told me I always should.
I want to tell you that I love and miss you.
And someday I'll be there
to bug and play with you.

Destin Casey, Grade 9
Three Springs of Courtland School, AL

Down by Two

There is a minute, twenty seconds left on the scoreboard.
If he doesn't call me in I'm going to be floored.
Finally I hear my name.
I get the ball and think what a shame.
We are down by two and it's my turn to kick.
I think to myself I'm going to be sick.
I kick the ball hard and hear the crowd roar my name.
The ball clears the field goal.
I tied the game.

Stacy Fortenberry, Grade 8
Lake Middle School, MS

Hurricane of the Past

See the winds and rains fly by.
See the patch of sun in the eye.

Flying trees and crashing waves,
Only God's mercy is what saves.

New Orleans, a bowl that filled.
So sad the number it killed.

See how strong its winds blow.
See Lake Pontchatrain overflow.

Houses upside down and inside out,
That ended the summer's drought.

How much teamwork it takes to fix
A demolished home from giant sticks.

It made sea cover land,
But we held on hand in hand.

Now our times are around the bend,
Mandatory to say, "The End."

Alejandro Uribe, Grade 7
Bishop Noland Episcopal Day School, LA

Light

A light is happiness
A light is joy
A light is the uniqueness that shines inside of you
Let that light shine
Show everyone who you are
Be a role model
Shine bright in a room full of darkness
Light up the dark and don't let it take over
A light is a shining star that leads others
Be like a light, and become a star
Be a leader wherever you are

Aba Hutchison, Grade 7
Carolina International School, NC

Remember

Remember the pain.
Remember the games.
That he played with my heart
Remember the days of my life and
The days that I lost.

I lost the one who I loved.
I wish that I could have him back.
He broke my heart like a broken plant.
He made me smile when I was down, man!
I wish I could hear his sound just one more time!

Chasity Jacobs, Grade 7
Laurin Welborn Middle School, NC

When Storms Come into My Life
When storms come into my life,
I feel so sad.
I feel the need to be outside in the rain.
My brother bothers me
because he is bored.
I notice that I can't even see
the beautiful moon at night.
Floods wash away items
we once cared for.
It is hurricane season
and this is its mighty power.
Our grass has died
from drowning in the rain.
Lightning strikes a tree
causing it to fall.
Rocks fly everywhere in the wind.
When storms come into my life
I feel so sad!
Lane Thomassee, Grade 8
Leonville Elementary School, LA

You Said
You said you loved me
you said you cared,
but yet you were never there
you said you needed me,
that you wouldn't survive without me,
but yet you left me broken hearted
you said you would be truthful
and that you would never hurt me,
but truly that was a lie for
you tore my heart in half
you truly hurt me
you truly broke me,
but yet I'm still alive.
Christina Mathews, Grade 8
Priceville Jr High School, AL

If I Could Fly
So glad as a bird,
I sing and chirp in good mood…
If I just had wings.
Jamaal Dance, Grade 9
H L Trigg Community School, NC

October
O outside
C alling all of my friends
T o come over
O ff we go
B est of friends
E veryone is scared
R oaming through the woods
Brailey Hall, Grade 7
Rock Mills Jr High School, AL

Night
The sun slowly fades away
As the night comes to view
Not a place or time to play
Plus other things come too

As the night comes to view
Nothing should or shall be seen
Plus other things come too
Giving the moon its cue

Nothing should or shall be seen
Darkness covers every inch of land
Giving the moon its cue
Almost trying to show that you can

Darkness covers every inch of the land
Not a place or time to play
Almost trying to show that you can
The sun slowly fades away
Rachel Blomquist, Grade 8
Alexandria Middle Magnet School, LA

Friendship
Friendship is love,
Without friendship love means nothing!
Without friendship love is empty,
Without friendship love is boring…

Friendship means sharing,
People learn to share from friendship,
Share everything they have in life,

Friendship is like stars,
Even though we always see them together
Always mean to each other,
But,
Sometimes they argue!

Friendship is like flower,
Soft but strong!
Friendship is like sun,
Bright and beautiful!

Friendship is everything in life.
Akasia Costley, Grade 7
Saint James High School, LA

Music
Music
Peaceful, melodious
Moving, relaxing, encouraging
The rhythms move me
Songs
Maribeth Burton, Grade 8
Dalton Middle School, GA

Short and Tall
Some people are short,
and some are tall.
They are different in many ways,
but we need perspectives from all.
In the end, short is short,
and tall is tall
Even though these heights work together,
no one size fits all!
Anna Stuteville, Grade 7
Lake Castle Private School, LA

Working Boy
Farm
Exciting, hard
Self-building, working, struggling
Cows, tractors, student, son
Encouraging, trying, loving
Tough, honest
Adam
Adam Smith, Grade 8
Appling County Middle School, GA

The Hippo
In the dark of the night,
Within the light of the moon,
By the mysterious lake,
Near the deserted lagoon,

Spookily,
Slowly,
Secretly,
And full of suspense,

Rested a

Salad-eating,
Fierce-appearing,
Purple-colored,
Soundly-sleeping
HIPPO
Carol Lewis, Grade 7
St Mary's School, SC

Sleeping in the Beauty of Georgia!
The silence crept in,
Like a cat in the night.
The moon went down,
Like a man in the world
The Georgia state shines,
Like a star in the sky
As I sleep soundly,
In a wonderful place,
On Fannin County soil.
Collin Owen, Grade 8
Fannin County Middle School, GA

Pup Dog

They romp, they play, they rip, they tear
Though they can be rough, I still show my care
When they're puppies they're cute and innocent
Seeming like angels heaven sent
Soon they've grown to a rebelling age
Having to be kept in the forbidden cage
Pretty soon they're faithful friends
Always there to fend
Then they're old, humble, and meek
All too soon, getting weak
Remembering their days of puppy youth
Then all too soon they know the truth
Show your love and care most there
They've lived a wonderful life

Laarni Lapat, Grade 7
Bertie Middle School, NC

Summer

As the days pass
I watch the time go by
I wait for school to come again
Friendships I made
Ones I lost
Places I've gone
Everything lost
Everything gained
Summers to come
I will never forget
The ones I lost
The minutes I spend
The places I've been
I will never know
What the meaning of summer is
But I know this summer is a summer to keep

Anna Klingenberg, Grade 9
Ben Franklin Academy, GA

Dear Someone or Something

Dear Someone or Something
The trees' windblown branches creak and sing
A haunting melody, their branches follow
And lure the animals from many a hollow
The chatter of squirrels and the chirp of birds
And the grazing of deer in their groups and herds
They wander the land not knowing what to do
Except look at the sky, a curious land of blue
They live in meadows with sunbathed flowers
And wait away the long summer hours
Until the sky darkens and the sun goes down
Each star shines like a gem upon a king's crown
And the animals go back to their hollows and herds
And wake the next day with nary a word
And that is nature

Heather Wells, Grade 7
First Flight Middle School, NC

Children

C hildren are the most loving people to
H ave around. They enjoy playing
I n parks. Their
L aughter brings joy to people who are depressed.
D ontè is my name and going to school is my game.
R especting others is what I was taught to do.
E njoying teaching my brother is something I like to do.
N othing can ever change that special bond.

Dontè Whichard, Grade 8
St Andrews Middle School, SC

All Kinds of Colors

The rain is here
Then it goes away
It brings out the rainbow
All bright in the sky
Red, Orange, Yellow, Green, Blue, Indigo, Violet
Are all the colors of the rainbow

Monique Brooks, Grade 7
L E Gable Middle School, SC

Best Friend

You are there when I need a hug,
You are there when I need to talk
You are there when I have problems
You are there when I have no one there
You are there when I feel lonely
You are there when I have boyfriend problems
That is why I have best friends!

Haven Gibson, Grade 7
Laurin Welborn Middle School, NC

Global Warming

Global Warming: friend or foe,
which one is it, I think I know.
The temperature's rising, bit by bit,
penguins at the North Pole are having a fit.
Sea level's rising as we speak,
soon we can only see Mt. Everest's peak.
Hurricanes are becoming faster and stronger,
tornado season's getting longer.
Extreme flooding is devastating people's lives,
frequent wildfire is spreading like hives.
But what is causing all this chaos?
It happens when human and nature crisscross.
WE are polluting our lovely Earth,
even as we sit upon our smoky hearth.
Too much Carbon Dioxide in the air,
come on, to the Earth this is not fair.
Turn off the lights when not in use,
forgetting to is not an excuse.
Renewable energy is the key;
to protect the people, animals, and plants you see.
Global warming is a foe: don't let it trick you.

Molly Koochekpour, Grade 9
Haynes Academy for Advanced Studies, LA

Bad Storms

When storms come into my life
I feel afraid
Cold winds blow hard
Feels like the Earth is upside down
Boulders surround my mind
People surround me to see if I am okay
Crickets play sad music
Stars remind me of him
Red roses are blooming over a new life
I make a wish in a tall wishing well
As the beautiful sun sets,
I cry knowing that he is gone forever.

Kelly Disotell, Grade 8
Leonville Elementary School, LA

First Trail Ride

My first trail ride on a Polaris 90
It was on a spring day in my dad's trail
A shiny day in July
Riding with my brother Luke

Going up the steep, rough hills
It felt good that I did it
Then my brother flipped on a hill
It was bad and I was worried

My uncle hurried down fast
The quad was on top of him for a while
I had to get it off of him
It turned out he was all right after all

He was just cut and bruised
Everyone was scared he was hurt
But he just shook it off
He is riding good from now on

Heath Bryant, Grade 9
North Wilkes High School, NC

Storms

Storms make me feel nervous.
My body feels motionless
as I wait for the storm.
The weather is cloudy and gloomy.
Frogs are croaking
and crickets are hopping.
The trees are swaying back and forth.
It just became evening time.
The earth feels like it's breaking apart.
The air is peaceful and calm.
It's almost the end of summer
There are so many emotions
running through my body.
Dreams are flowing in my head
as I woke up to another day.

Christopher Hutchinson, Grade 7
Leonville Elementary School, LA

Do You Remember?

Do you remember when we first met
Back then all we thought about was being good friends

Now as I look at my best friend in the eyes while I put on my gown
I go back to us sitting on the playground

Going on throughout high school we all kept in touch
Now it's time to see old faces as well as new ones

The music begins as I walk down the aisle
I see my friend who went off on a softball scholarship
And the one who plays in the NFL

But when I stop I see the one that I have been waiting on
From our first hello to our last goodbye

I had the love of my life
And nothing or anything could ever change it.

Brittany Cobb, Grade 9
White Plains High School, AL

Life Literature

Lions roar, eagles soar,
old men will be wise forever more.
Pigeons fly, and cars drive,
when I visit my family it brings a tear to their eyes.
Sun is to morning as moon is to night,
some wake up in the middle of the night in fright.
Schemers scheme,
while children live their live smooth then go to sleep and dream.

D'shon Early, Grade 7
Hubert Middle School, GA

A Good Dream

A good dream
is like flying through the air
A good dream
is like being in your own world
A good dream
is like having a friend and knowing they will always be there for you
A good dream
is like going on an amazing and unforgettable trip
A good dream
is like doing something bad and knowing there's no consequences
A good dream
is like spending money for no reason
A good dream
is like sleeping with not worrying to wake up
A good dream
is like watching a sunset or being in the ocean alone
A good dream
is like knowing if you love someone
A good dream
is like going to heaven.

Bianca Borough, Grade 8
Atlanta Academy, GA

What I Do in a Game

The color green and white
always in my heart.
When I put the shirt and shorts on
how proud it makes me feel.
When I walk on that field
I begin to get butterflies all in my stomach
and then when I grip the bat
my hands start to sweat.
When I go to the plate
my heart thumps faster and faster.
Then I grip the bat and watch for the ball
Oh no! Here it comes! Here it comes!
I got to hit!
And it must go far, far, far away.
Oh I pray I pray it goes far
then I must run fast as I can
to get to the base, and when I do
I breathe a sigh of relief,
I pray I will get to the home plate
What a joy it will be to
add a point for my team.

LeAnn Boyles, Grade 8
Lake Middle School, MS

Friendship

Friends are the ones,
Who know when you're down,
Or can see when you're hiding your frown,
They are always there for you,
In times of gray and times of blue,
They are there to lend a helping hand,
And can withstand,
Everything ya'll go through.

Phoebe Castro, Grade 7
Lake Castle Private School, LA

A Terrible Hurricane

During Hurricane Gustav
I watched several trees fall.
Trees that were very big and pretty.
I love the time of day
when the sun goes down.
My dogs were barking loudly outside…
Shingles flew off the roof.
The water in front of my house
was full of branches.
We watched the fire as we burned the branches,
and listened to music.
Indoors, we watched movies
because of the generator.
Helicopters were flying often
in the skies after the storm.
Our prayers were answered
when the electricity came back on…

Chase Grimmett, Grade 7
Leonville Elementary School, LA

The Storm

Nobody knows I'm here.
I feel invisible.
No one hears me.
No one sees me.
But, I'm here.
Everyone must be blind.
Storms in my life make me feel so paralyzed.
I feel scared, sad, and worried.
My imagination controls me.
I can see lightning bolts striking.
Forceful winds are slamming into the glass windows.
I hear the rain and the pain of those that sit by me.
It rains. It pours.
My niece is in my thoughts and in my mind.
When she hurts, I hurt.
My grandma is in my thoughts, too.
I always know she's here with me.
I look outside my window, and now all I see is fog.
I wipe my window.
Do you know what I see? Me.
But, nobody knows I'm here.

Lyman Jackson, Grade 7
Leonville Elementary School, LA

A Day in the Life of a Flower

Swish, Swoosh, Swish
The wind is blowing my leaves.
One spring morning, I will awake
with my big friend the sun.

In the winter, I die but
my son or daughter will come out
and be a great supermarket to all their friends.

Swish, Swoosh, Swish, Swoosh
My seeds are falling and I am dying.
I'm cold and in pain and my leaves have fallen.
I feel like I'm going to break in half.

Swish, Swoosh, Swish, Swoosh, Swish
I wish I could be a human who sees the sun every day.

Swish, Swoosh

Rafael Garcia, Grade 7
Carolina International School, NC

A Day Outdoors

A day outdoors is always fun.
To be outside in the sun.
To be outside with friends and play.
Oh how I wish I could stay outside all day.
And when the sun goes down and the day ends.
I can't wait for the next one to begin.

Madison Dillard, Grade 7
St Thomas More Catholic School, LA

Where I'm From

I am from a fresh new pair of Nikes and chugging a glass of Dr. Pepper before having a burping contest.
I am from a nice country-style brick house in a small neighborhood surrounded by family.
I am from the towering trees that surround my home, the bushes I hide behind while playing paintball.
From the muddy field I play football in.
I am from arguments on every subject and laughter after each one.
From being who I want to be and not paying attention to those who try to put me down.
I'm from Union County where we love mashed potatoes and fried chicken.
From the stories of my papa's time in Vietnam, the haunted house we'd lived in when we were younger,
And the tornado my dad saw.
I am from all the pictures hung in my grandma's living room of my family from now back to the Stone Age.

CJ Gardin, Grade 8
Sims Jr High School, SC

The Valley of Joy

Leaves rustle; mud bubbles pop, the wind races and the very animals holler and shout in joy!
The father sun has risen to welcome all its children, of all the valleys and rolling hills, the Valley of Joy rejoices above all.
The leaves each fall one by one and dance in the whirring wind.
The mud bubbles pop in a musical sensation which the leaves spin and whirl to the mud's rhythmic song.
The animals of the forest reveal themselves from the shadows and rejoice as they celebrate the rising of their father.
Midday returns, everything slows, all creatures tire.
As the sun sets, its blazing rays wave goodbye and then the sky turns dark.
Leaves return back to their bare trees, the mud dries and slumbers
And the animals slowly returning to their homes, awaiting the morning, when their father rises again.

Gavin Jeganathan, Grade 7
Carolina International School, NC

I Am From

I am from cornbread and pinto beans.
I am from my grandma's banana pudding, collard greens, and Sweet Baby Ray's pork chops.
I am from smoked chicken and riding four-wheelers.
I am from my grandpa's juicy delicious, delicious steaks.
I am from getting whoopings and talking too much.
I am from fishing and lying on riverbanks early in the morning.
I am from backward things said and done.
I am from old Tennessee and back yard hunting.

Brandon Shetley, Grade 8
Sims Jr High School, SC

Aubrey

Little sister, you drive me crazy. You drive me crazy when you break things that belong to me. You drive me crazy when you kick and bite me. You drive me crazy when you draw all over my homework.

Little sister, you make me aggravated. You make me aggravated when you will not let me come into my own house. You make me aggravated when you put stickers all over my wall. You make me aggravated when you tell on me.

Little sister, you give me a headache. You give me a headache when you scream in my face. You give me a headache when you hit me in the head with your toys. You give me a headache when you don't stop talking.

Little sister, despite all that, you make me laugh. You make me laugh when you make funny faces. You make me laugh when you run around the house. You make me laugh every day.

McKenna Tucker, Grade 8
Mount Carmel Academy, LA

Drugs

As my head spins like chromed out rims my friends influence me that all I need to succeed is to take a puff of this weed but I know better I have dreams of becoming a actress a novelist you may laugh and my dreams are ballistic but I refuse I refuse to be another school statistic.

Chailin Joseph, Grade 7
Saint James High School, LA

The Outfit
Then
The color was blue.
The jeans were blue.
The socks were blue.
The shirt was blue.
Now
The jeans have holes.
The socks are old.
The shirt has holes.
The girl is blue.

Courtney Spann, Grade 7
L E Gable Middle School, SC

Music
Country, rap, hip-hop, rock and roll,
heavy metal, blues, opera and soul.
All describe a wonderful thing called music.
There is at least one type of music for everyone.
Songs are relaxing, songs are inspirational,
songs are soothing, and some songs are just pure fun!
Download it to an iPod, burn it to a CD,
turn on the radio and happy you will be.
Music is uplifting, it creates a good mood
turn on the radio and pick a good tune.
Music is played at almost any function you will go to.
It is played at the highest volume that speakers go up to.
Music has been around for a very long time.
The tunes are ongoing,
adding different styles all the time.

Abbey Peterson, Grade 9
Mount Carmel Academy, LA

Following My Dreams
I'm going out to college
to achieve my goals.
I'll only stop to make a change,
I make my choices and follow my dreams,
So life goes as it seems.
I will stand and be me,
So I can be who I want to be.

Kaylan Tankersley, Grade 7
L E Gable Middle School, SC

The Window to Heaven
He used to hold me in his arms.
We used to lay there and count the stars.
He taught me how to ride a bike.
He used to tuck me in at night.
Now God holds him in His arms.
My daddy's now in heaven helping hang the stars.
The Moon is his window, and my shining light
And I know he watches over me from it
Each and every night.

Destiny Tune, Grade 8
Lake Middle School, MS

Evacuating Gustav
Vroom, vroom the plane engines went
Heading down to Mexico from Gustav.
Bang, bang the guns went
As the doves fell to the ground.
Vroom, vroom the van went
Coming to pick up to report to camp.
Talk, talk the TV went
Talking about Hurricane Gustav.
Vroom, vroom went the engines
Heading back to the target of Gustav
Sigh, sigh went the people;
It was no more than a rainstorm.

Jack Boyer, Grade 7
Bishop Noland Episcopal Day School, LA

Everything Will Be Fine
I looked into the mirror, what do I see?
Pale brown eyes looking back at me.
I asked myself "How are you today?"
And came tears all down my way.

What? What is it dear, is something wrong?
And all this came out, just like a song.
"Everything here troubles my heart,
No one to talk to, no one to look up at."

"I am just so lonely only one friend I had,
Now she's gone and everything's so sad.
She was the only one with who I was at ease,
Suddenly, everything's over just like a breeze."

Here I am writing thoughts of my past,
And all I got to say is that I shall not be aghast
No matter how bad it's been,
Everything will be fine while this remains but a bad dream.

Akanksha Sinha, Grade 9
Leesville Road High School, NC

My Coming Death
Slowly, though, I do not recall
My existence here is becoming raw
My body is numb from head to toe
My fingers are gnarled and my feet are curled
Even while I deteriorate
I still know what made my life great
I felt feelings
Such as true love and great happiness
As my life ends, my heartbeat just drops
Everyone will weep,
And then they will stop
My body will be buried,
My spirit will fly,
As I watch over my family
Until I meet them at the end of time.

Anthony Nguyen, Grade 8
Haynes Academy for Advanced Studies, LA

Father, Son, and Georgia

The little boy looked
Eyes filled with wonder
At the big green hills
That roll like thunder.
He stopped to blink
Then turned to the lake.
Of Georgia's deep beauty
He was about to partake.
His father smiled down,
"Come along son!
The fish won't bite,
If you don't come on!"
The little boy smiled
And got in the boat.
These memories with Dad
He's never demote.
Mikayla Dittman, Grade 8
Fannin County Middle School, GA

Sweet Weeds

Flowers
Colorful, sweet
Blooming, swaying, growing
Have a sweet aroma
Plant
Brooke Walker, Grade 8
St Margaret School, LA

Ice Cream

Creamy, sugar sweet
Melts, excites, makes smiles appear
But yet they disappear when it's gone
Ice Cream
Erin Gurney, Grade 7
Cathedral School, NC

What Does Springtime Bring?

Sitting sideways staring
Whoosh! A cool breeze blows by
Just like on a windy day.
A butterfly flutters past and
Someone goes after it while it is
Zooming all around.
There are little cheetahs,
Down the hill they go,
Trying to catch the butterfly.
The butterfly stops and
Holds its wings out to me
As it is landing on a beautiful flower.
Someone tries to catch it and
It zooms off again.
It settles on a pink flower,
Folds its little wings,
And that is what springtime brings!
Heather Dodson, Grade 7
Broadview Middle School, NC

Storms in My Life

Storms in my life make me feel so blue, it's true.
One storm I had to overcome is when my Mama died.
I was only 9 months old,
and it was on Christmas Day.
I look at the people outside on the playground.
They all look happy and are having fun
while I am still here alone in my bedroom.
The season is winter.
It is still my favorite season,
even though that is the time that I lost my mom.
It is cool outside and I can hear leaves
as the wind rustles through them.
Then, it starts to rain,
and I start to feel the pain in my heart from losing my mother.
I hear an owl hooting in the night as a black cat runs past my window.
Even diamonds and pearls cannot take the sadness away.
Sydnei Hall, Grade 7
Leonville Elementary School, LA

Unwanted Visitor

As the darkness slowly creeps in,
You realize it's time.
The trees start to moan;
The windows start to shudder.
The lights start to flicker;
You gather the blankets,
The candles, and the flashlights.
You turn off all the lights and electricity.
You huddle up together to await the storm's destruction.
You rejoice when it's all over and restore the cheerful mood,
But you will always remember the feeling of being scared and alone.
You will carry on with your wonderful life until it comes again.
Yassara Shaikh, Grade 8
Bishop Noland Episcopal Day School, LA

Where I'm From

The projects, the hood,
Whatever you call it, I live there.

They ask how do I live,
When negativity is everywhere?
This is actually where we choose our path, our way
Mostly the fast life because your momma got bills to pay.

It's a shame because our talent is wasted,
"They ain't nothing; we better than them," is what they are all saying.

Slanging and jacking is the way we are told to get it;
We come from negative ways of living.
Running from police sirens, ducking and hiding,
We ain't scared when the guns get to firing.

But me, I got a plan,
Get out and get it like a real man.

Jovon Denzel Thompson, Grade 9
Donaldsonville High School, LA

Believe

You think you can't
Your palms are sweaty,
Your voice is shaking,
You've forgotten everything

You don't trust yourself,
Your confidence is gone,
You've lost your strength,
No reassuring can help

Then you remember…remember
The thought is coming to you
Like an ant trying to squeeze
Its way into a crack

How could you have forgotten?
It's something your mom had always told you

If you think you can
You will achieve
All you have to do is
Believe.

Mikayla Raleigh, Grade 8
Dillard Drive Middle School, NC

My Glory

The feeling you get from an accomplishment,
when there's no reward not a dollar nor cent.
That is glory.
The pride you feel from a job well done,
or on the field when the game is won.
That is glory.
Doing what's right when nobody's there,
like never cheating and playing fair.
That is glory.
My glory is my purpose.
My glory is my soul.
Temptation which brings my downfall.
I must resist.
This is how I protect my glory.

Justin McNair, Grade 8
Fayette Middle School, GA

Careful What You Wish For

"I'm evacuating!" said the boy.
Whisper where you're gonna go.
"I don't know."
The whirly wind glided over rooftops,
But barely damaged the wing of a crow.
He wished for bad weather, but he meant snow.
"I don't care 'bout no rain."
But sadly his fear came in to place.
Yes, the little boy had an all-time low.
He wished for bad weather, but he meant snow.

Erika Evans, Grade 7
Bishop Noland Episcopal Day School, LA

Storms

When storms come in my life
It's very odd
and good things happen to a great many.
People dancing around merrily
so happy, yet some sad,
praying for happiness to come from the angels above.
The crickets chirping
and frogs croaking all with great joy.
Winter, savory cold and fun
The snow as clear as a crystal.
The sparkle of rain drops
reminds me of diamonds
as also of silver jewelry.
The smell of many foods
made from the people so carefree
and some are yet even a mystery.
All at an evening of twilight so
peaceful and beautiful.

Robert Austin Tankersley, Grade 8
Leonville Elementary School, LA

That Love Thing

You say you love me
But you don't show
You say you care
But when it's something
Important to me you're never there
When I say I'm home alone
It's like you jump through the phone
But when I tell you I'm home sick
The excuses come quick
When you talked to me it made me melt
Tell me is that how you felt
When I pour my heart out to you
You get all quiet like you're confused
You say that's because you gotta think
Think of what you should know in a wink
You say a lot of things
That I don't think you mean
So is this that love thing
Or just another fling

Doriann Broaden, Grade 9
McKee Jr High School, AL

Friendship

Friendship is a bright yellow pillow,
Cushioning you as you fall.
It gives you a place of rest
And a soft spot to cry on.
It cheers up your day
And lets you release your frustrations, all.
Friendship is a bright yellow pillow
Giving you courage to go on.

Emily Koehler, Grade 9
Mount Carmel Academy, LA

Hailstorm Calls Tornado
The cold wind freezes the cloud water
It falls to the earth
The wind repeatedly
Lifts Mother Hail
Back up to the sky
The wind gets stronger
Bubbles form in the sky
Completing the weather ritual
The wind speeds up
And swirls in giant circles
A funnel appears
Summoning Father Tornado
DeQuadrick Jefferson, Grade 8
Alexandria Middle Magnet School, LA

Defeat
Deep in a hospital
She runs to stay alive
You hear complete silence
A bang and a crash erupt

She runs to stay alive
It starts again
A bang and a crash erupt
You hear footsteps

It starts again
But now she's dead
You hear footsteps
A door slams

But now she's dead
You hear complete silence
A door slams
Deep in a hospital
Nick Bailey, Grade 8
Alexandria Middle Magnet School, LA

Fire
Fire is thirst and lust
Overcoming your conscience and trust
Fire is passion and scorn
Fire is from which all emotion is born
Fire is man
Benjamin Archer, Grade 9
Chapel Hill High School, NC

The Cycle of Life
Life is like a circle
There is no way out
Wherever you go
You will always land
In the same place.
Manar Joudeh, Grade 8
Dillard Drive Middle School, NC

Love
Love, love is a roller coaster
Sweet-smelling roses and chocolate
Until…
Chaos, disagreement
Destruction of your soul
Hurt, anger, surrounding you
Bad luck stalking you, waiting for attack
Depression, crying
But for now…
Peace, happiness
Basking in a sea of hope
Thinking about the future
Dreams coming true
Love, love is a roller coaster
Nirvana Madho, Grade 7
Carolina International School, NC

Trick-or-Treat
On a chilly night
Full of scary sights
Up and down the streets
We "trick-or-treat"
Brittany Arrington, Grade 7
Rock Mills Jr High School, AL

Baseball in My Life
Standing on the mound
Looking at the ground
I sweat my heart out in the baggy jersey
Realizing that I have to hurry
The next pitch I have to throw
The next batter I can't let go
He must go out
Or we will all scream and shout
They'll jeer and sneer
But it's just the start of my career
The batter swung late
Because I threw too fast
And even though we won
Our team still came in last
BOO HOO!!!
Charly Van Norden, Grade 8
St Mary's School, SC

Basketball
I am good
that I will put you on the wood.
If you play me it will be a sud.
You probably will not be glad
I put you on the court.
You don't have a chance on me.
If you bring the ball by me
I will zoom right past you.
Erling Chanson, Grade 7
St Andrews Middle School, SC

Storms
When a storm comes into my life
I feel like I am waiting with false hope.
It's autumn right now
and the weather is changing.
The air is getting colder as I walk.
I stop and sit on a boulder.
It's getting darker as I sit and wait.
I hear a familiar voice in the distance.
As the wind blows stronger
his voice gets louder.
The voice is behind me,
but I don't look back.
As I know it's just another storm
coming into my life.
Ricky Arnaud, Grade 8
Leonville Elementary School, LA

I Pace Myself
I pace myself through every lap
my energy reserve on tap
I pace myself both to and fro
endless laps I have to go

endurance builds with every turn
store of calories I've yet to burn
"Step up" is heard and I climb aloft
the buzzer sounds and then I'm off

my heart it races strong and true
I blister forth into the box of blue
my legs they tighten, my arms a rage
a blitz of energy like notes across a page

my lungs they burn from lack of air
my pride, my courage will get me there
seconds pass like time standing still
I see my goal, I muster my will

victory greets my journey's end
this is my sport…
I LOVE TO SWIM!
Julianne Cooper, Grade 7
L E Gable Middle School, SC

Race Day
Once, at Dorman Freshman Campus
I ran through
sloppy, wet puddles,
while wind hit me in the face,
I think of nothing —
Thump, thump,
Thump, thump
except for WINNING!
Madyson Coggins, Grade 7
L E Gable Middle School, SC

Detained

Oh my, oh dear I'm terrified
Locked up in room G-9
What a horrible place called ISS
From which, I wish I could hide

The fan and intercom are all that's audible
The sounds that confirm I'm alive
My companion and I are frightened
Inside the trailer called G-9

Maybe I should bolt, I wonder
I'm contemplating my escape
There's no place for me to run
So I guess I'll just sit here and wait

Oh my, oh dear I'm terrified
Locked up in room G-9
This place is called ISS
From which, I wish I could hide

Save me!

Ashleigh Mitchell, Grade 8
Alexandria Middle Magnet School, LA

Snowflakes

Dancing among the skies above,
they flutter with the grace of a dove.
Fairies falling,
the fire calling,
nothing could go astray.
One, two, three, four, fall on your tongue,
as soon as they drop, you feel young,
that one little flake has a presence of its own,
the cold quick feeling makes itself known.
As soon as it comes, even sooner it goes.
Was it there? No one but you will ever know.

Keith Coffman, Grade 7
St Mary's School, SC

Blister Blue

I met a gypsy in a shoe, her name is Blister Blue.
She's very pretty and unique, she even has her own boutique.

Meagan Melancon, Grade 7
Sacred Heart of Jesus School, LA

Skip School for Hunting

Have you ever skipped school for a shot at a monster buck?
Well I have so many times and so many days.
Sit for an hour and not see a thing out of the corner of my eye.
I see horns.
I count 1, 2, 3, 4, 5, possibly 10 or more.
I see a shoulder and I shoot.
It was a good day.

Allen Brown, Grade 9
North Wilkes High School, NC

Why?

We all know the Nazi Hitler,
He was villainous and bitter,
This led him to become a killer,
He filled many with horror,
And to the innocent he would torture,
Why would he cause so much pain?
Maybe he did it for the fame,
What he did is such a shame,
For over a million deaths he's to blame,
When I think about the innocent people I begin to fear
So I end this poem with a tear.

Cullin Goodly, Grade 8
St Margaret School, LA

My Heart

My heart is so lonely that I don't even feel alive
I wonder if anyone can see the pain in my eyes
My heart is very torn and also very sad
I often try to find the love that I had
Although, it's waste of time
Because when I look it's not love that I find
It's pain, sorry, fear, and doubt
My mind is telling me to take another route
I'm afraid to go another way
What if it turns out to be the same thing I go through every day
My friend says it's not my fault
It's the person who took me out
Out of his life to be with someone else
To care and feel the pain they felt

Sekiyah Jones, Grade 8
Seminole County Middle/High School, GA

To Whom It May Concern

To whom it may concern,
I've something to say
Even if you don't feel the same way
To whom it may concern,
Ever since that first night,
Everything has been different
Each day after has been clear
To whom it may concern,
You make my days brighter and happier
Give everything a completely new meaning
To whom it may concern,
You've given me a gift no one else has
You've taught me things that nobody else could
To whom it may concern,
You mean more to me than you're aware
Our friendship is my most prized possession
Our love most precious
To whom it may concern,
No. To whom it does concern,
I love you
With all my heart and soul and being. And more.

Aimee Bourdier, Grade 9
Ellender Memorial High School, LA

Two Days Past

Two days past fifteen
Moving down the county seat
Wasn't a good beginning
Because you tried your best
Not to fight
You tried your best
To do it all by yourself
In the end
You did your best
Two days past fifteen
Moving down the county seat
Wasn't a good beginning
For starting all over
It was hard
In the end
It was worth it all.

Brandi Renee Griffin, Grade 9
North Wilkes High School, NC

Georgia

Georgia, Georgia,
You're always on my mind!

To hear the waves
Crash onto the shore,

To see the beautiful nature
In this resourceful state,

To smell the beautiful wildflowers,
To feel the wind rush by you,

You wonder how
You could ever leave.

Georgia, Georgia,
You will always stand out in my mind!

Kelly Ross, Grade 8
Fannin County Middle School, GA

Emptiness of Storms

Storms make me feel empty
as if my family had disappeared.
If I didn't have a heart,
I didn't have a home to go to.
The world didn't have a center
dreams that never came true
animals who were left alone
as if the sun didn't shine.
When sunrise came,
the birds didn't chirp
and flowers never bloomed.
Overall, I know
God is watching me!

Brianna Barron, Grade 7
Leonville Elementary School, LA

Happy Pills

My Adderall is a red capsule.
My Seroquel is a round pill — white.
One is to help my concentration,
The other is to help me fall asleep at night.
Because of my diagnosis, I take these pills,
With these real special medications my concentration heals.
These outlandish medications have gotten my brain so addicted,
Without these medications my brain is real afflicted.
These medications help me make it through each and every day,
Without these medications it feels there is not time to play.
Using these medications makes my body feel fine,
When taking these medications my body will shine!
I take these medications because they make it easier to think,
I take these medications because of the recommendation from my Shrink.

Eric Luttrell, Grade 9
Three Springs of Courtland School, AL

The Facility That Changed My Life

They treat us like slaves you can call us a blacksmith
But they don't know they're pushing me closer to that cliff
My days don't get better by the second they get better by the shift.
In poetry I am legend you can call me Will Smith.
They always say the sky is the limit but what if the limit is the sky.
So we can fly high in the sky with fire burning inside like a phoenix.
But no one cared about me but Mr. Motes and Miss Lenox
Some say I'm a man I don't cry but they really need a Kleenex
My life is passing by so fast like NASCAR.
They tell me don't give up because you came too far.
OK Mrs. Dunlap is way too smart to be a science teacher.
And Mrs. Faye is the cleaner.
Mr. Motes is the preacher.
And Mrs. Russell is the leader.
And Mrs. Newman is the teacher who wants to drive a beamer.
Or maybe a Lincoln navigator.
Some people call us the Navihators
Ok Austin is the country type he says tatters
And Charles doesn't care about nothing but them Gators.
But we just want to be loved not called traitors.

Martwan Evans, Grade 9
Three Springs of Courtland School, AL

What Is a Dream?

What is a dream.
Can you hold it in your hand?
Or is it a treasure you find in the sand.
Is it like music; soft and sweet?
Or is it loud like a toddler's feet.
Does it move as fast as a plane?
Does it drop like rain on the window pane?
Does it move swiftly across my mind?
Or will it creep slowly across my floor,
Escape out my door, and fly into the night.
Laying in my bed one night, I wonder this; my eyes shut tight.
Now I know! Now I know. Dreams are happy pictures in your mind.

April Crumpler, Grade 8
Carolina International School, NC

Good-bye

Saying good-bye to a school I know very well.
Every day I come here has been so swell.
I will never forget the walls of blue.
And having to wear certain shoes.
All of the teachers are so great.
I don't think that there is one I hate.

Although these 10 years have gone so fast,
I can always think of memories from the past.
I have come to know and love all of these people.
I will always remember them even when I grow old and feeble.

I don't want to leave Lake Castle and go to high school.
I have heard the teachers there are very cruel.
My fondest memories are created here.
When I think back, I start to shed a tear.
I'm sure in 10 years we will all be doing fine,
I will love you forever Class of 2009!!!

Conner Luscy, Grade 8
Lake Castle Private School, LA

Question and Answers

I don't like to read instead I ask questions
Sometimes I don't even get answers
And everybody always says ask questions
But sometimes there are no answers to my questions

Answers don't always have questions
There are answers to questions that haven't even been asked
That is there are questions and answers
Where nobody knows where they come from

PiaMonae Titus, Grade 8
Laurin Welborn Middle School, NC

Free

As I look out this window made of glass
I think of my kids sitting in class
Thinking about how pain is so immense
I also look at that old barbed wire and chain linked fence
I just want to be free
As I write her she writes me
I went up for bail
I should have known it would fail
All I could do was cry
Remembering how my kids were so shy
It is also sunny
I could be making money
I am now out from behind bars
And now I see so many cars
I can't rob another store
Or I will be locked up once more
I just want to be me
So I can be
Free

Matthew Brown, Grade 9
Three Springs of Courtland School, AL

Great Things of Georgia

The beautiful smell of Georgia roams the air.
The sound of rain hitting the ground, then making puddles.
Smelling the flowers as you walk by.
Birds singing along in a great sounding tone.
Kids playing in the school yard.
The great smell of hot-dogs and nachos in the air
As it gets darker, you walk.
Slow and steady the wind blows.
Slowly moving your hair backwards
With a good sight of the mountains, as you sit down
It gets quieter as the night goes along
Suddenly it is complete silence, not even the wind blows
Then you feel a few drops hit your arm.
Then another, and another
You decide to call it a night and walk home
That is what is great about the state of Georgia.

Austin Pittman, Grade 8
Fannin County Middle School, GA

My Violin

Playing the violin is my favorite thing to do.
The strings play a solid tune.
It soothes the body to play.
Legato is smooth.
It is peaceful.
The notes float in the air.
Orchestra songs are played like a bird chirps.
Passion speaks in the music.
Playing the violin is my favorite thing to do.

Anna Boyd, Grade 8
Hatley School, MS

It Was a Dark and Stormy Night

I want to tell you something, so please just take a seat.
A hurricane is coming, and we might wind up dead meat.
Evacuate to a safer place so that you may survive.
The rest of us will stay at home and try to stay alive.
The wind is whistling outside as the rain rips up the roof.
It hits so hard; it sounds like a giant horse's hoof.
It's pitch black in the kitchen; you can't see anything.
The rain has quieted down a bit; it sounds like just a ping.

It's strangely quiet outside; we've finally reached the eye.
I'm so scared; I feel like I'm going to start to cry.
The winds begin to pick up; the clouds begin to stir.
This one's a big one; I think we all confer.
The wind is whistling outside as the rain rips up the roof.
It hits so hard; it sounds like a giant horse's hoof.
It's pitch black in the kitchen; you can't see anything.
The rain has quieted down a bit; it sounds like just a ping.

The hurricane has finally passed,
And everyone shouts, "Hurray! At last!"

Mary Fentiman, Grade 7
Bishop Noland Episcopal Day School, LA

Hunting

Twigs snap.
I look around, and I see movement far ahead in a bush, it's shaking.
Soon the adrenaline takes over and click goes the safety.
I search for the beast through the scope, looking for brown fur and antlers, but I don't see anything.
Snap! Another twig behind me, I look around the woods behind me, but I see nothing.
I hear the rustling of leaves far to my left, still nothing!
The hairs on the back of my neck stand up and the fear and dread run through me, what is it?
Is it a bear, a wild hog, who knows?
Then a twig snaps to my right and I jump out of my socks blazing away with my semi-auto .243 at a...squirrel.

Joshua Lasley, Grade 8
Fannin County Middle School, GA

Love

One of the most complicated things to figure out in life, scientists can't even understand,
How could one four-lettered word be so complicated and hard to comprehend?

The world love is what I'm speaking of so simple and easy to say.
Yet how could such a simple word make you feel so hypnotized day by day

Is this word a feeling, a stage, or just a simple emotion?
Again, how could something that seems so tender and solemn toss you like an ocean?

Some say love is like a roller coaster, when you start it looks good like everything is going up
But once you've seen what you've gotten yourself into, going up, down, and all around
you really wish you never would've

My question is what is love? Is it good, or bad, happy or sad,
Can it make you smile or cry, could it make you even want to die?

How could one word be so powerful? I'll tell you why,
Sometimes emotions can overtake us, and you could become a new person inside.

One of these emotions happens to be one of most powerful above,
The four lettered word that I'm talking about's name is love.

Nia Anthony, Grade 8
Wren Middle School, SC

Look at What We Have Done

What are we doing? Do any of us even care about what's going on? I guess we have given up hope for the human race, life, and the world itself. War is ripping the world apart and it seems like we don't even care. We go around with our fancy cellphones, nice cars and big houses for what? To feel like we're important when someone walks by. Do we even understand what is happening today? Kids a lot younger, a lot older, and some even the same age, are starving and most people couldn't give a care in the world. Most people probably wouldn't care as long as it didn't involve them but, it does. Every time you go out and don't do something to help someone else, you're doing something. When you go out and laugh and mock other people for not wearing or dressing like you want them to, then you're doing something. Every action that you do while you are living and breathing affects every other person on this planet.
So step back and look at what WE have done.

Katelyn Mayberry, Grade 8
North Iredell Middle School, NC

Missing You

You have been gone for a while, almost a year, but I never stop thinking. You and I were so close, it's making me cry. All the time I wonder why you had to leave. I miss you so much that I wish I could be with you. I remember all the times we shared you finally left me. I cry and wonder why and cry. Missing you.

Donyelle Butler, Grade 7
Saint James High School, LA

Abandonment

When you left, I didn't know why.
I was too young to understand.
When I realized you weren't coming back
it made me feel worthless.

Did you think I didn't need my mother's help?
Or that you didn't have to be there
when I scraped my knee
or was scared?

Because of you leaving,
I had to put up with a new mother
and a brother who I hated.
I had to put up with unfair favoritism
from my "mother" towards my step-brother.

Sometimes I lie awake at night
wondering what life would be like if you were still here.
But most times I just lie awake
and hate this living Hell you put me through.

Alex Ward, Grade 9
New Site High School, MS

Fire

Fire is like a burning pain clawing at my conscience;
It is like dark abysmal pain that eats at my soul.
Fire is like lake of sadness that swallows us all;
It is like a reflexive demon that tears me apart.
 It smells like the ashes of a stale ashtray;
It is like a steel band tightened around my chest.
It sounds like drums pounding in my head,
It tastes bitter like dry herbs;
It looks like the steely stare of a surgeon.

Travis Holt, Grade 9
Northgate High School, GA

A Place to Be

Georgia is a place to be!
The mountains whisper, as a cool breeze blows
through the waters.
The depth of the lake holds secrets, still yet to
reveal in Blue Ridge.
It tells a story one has never heard.
It's history is remarkable to say the least!
It's not what's said or what's done.
It's nature and it has begun!
With the grass, the clouds a ray of blue.
I know, do you?
Up in the mountains a mist may rise,
and hide the starry skies.
It's still there, but where, in love, in death, where?
You tell me, up on the peak, see!
Where? There, I fell in love here!

Amber Gilliland, Grade 8
Fannin County Middle School, GA

Tears

Tears are strange I know,
When you cry they start to flow,
I wish they would go away,
But with me they're here to stay,
They are there when you are sad,
Sometimes they come when you are glad,
But tears of joy I do not shed,
My body is here, but my spirit is dead,
I should go, I'm getting sad,
This paper makes me mad,
Why I'm crying I do not know,
Goodbye, I think I'll go.

Crimson Coleman, Grade 8
McKenzie Elementary & High School, AL

The Forest's Sounds

A morning walk
To relieve the mind
And empty my thoughts
Among the trees
And in my peace
The wind starts to blow
And the leaves dance
A whistling sound
Sweeps through the trees
The bushes and brush that scatter the ground
They walk and waltz to the wondrous sounds
I run around to see it all
To see the birds flutter
And chirp a tune
And watch how the bubbling stream flows
And listen to the wondrous sound
But my walk has ended
And I must go
To wait for tomorrow
To hear the forest's sound

Taylor Cameron, Grade 8
Alexandria Middle Magnet School, LA

The Hurricane

When we were getting ready for the hurricane,
It nearly drove my mom insane.
It was all very hard work;
My brother turned into a real jerk,
But I knew all would be okay
So I went outside to play.

When it was all over,
I went to Chase's to sleep over.
All was well in our little town;
Barely any trees had even fallen down.
A few days later I went back to school.
When I got home, I wanted to ride my bike;
Then Mom told me about Hurricane Ike.

Jonathan Allen, Grade 7
Bishop Noland Episcopal Day School, LA

Summer Days
Lying in the grass
looking at the sky,
Oh what a surprise
a bird flies by.

Running around the yard
are the kids next door.
While mom's in the house
sweeping all the floors.

Sonny's in the back
barking up a storm.
While Joshua's off at college
sleeping in a dorm.

Summer days go so fast,
you never know what has past.
Don't look back now,
let's get ready to go to town.
Jessica Henderson, Grade 9
Smiths Station High School, AL

Night
Night is a shadow all around you
It watches every step and move you take
It stalks and scares you
During the day, night hides from the sun
Night makes fun of little children
You try to avoid it but it doesn't go away
You can't escape it
When you are no longer scared of it
It is nothing but a little darkness
After that it goes away
It tries to find another child to scare
Eddie Bacharach, Grade 7
Carolina International School, NC

Pain of Life
Life has an end
life has a beginning
running a race
while I'm just sprinting
I am just beginning
I don't want to finish
do this race, I don't want to
see the ending
I stop...
I replenish
thinking of my ending
only sprint 13 meters
But I'm in it
to win it
and I'm gonna make it to the finish
Zachary DeShawn Jennings, Grade 8
Lake Middle School, MS

The Wonder of Nature
Nature is a wonderful thing.
Peace and happiness is what it brings
I love to go and play outside
It even provides a place to hide
For many creatures small or big
And you can grow things like figs.
No matter what species, human or pig
Nature, Nature it's a wonder for all.
Even when you think it's bad
Nature is the thing that holds us together.
Trevor Sheehy, Grade 7
Carolina International School, NC

Homer Hero
I love this brainless character
Whom I've watched throughout the years
He may not be the brightest
But he always brings on tears
I'll probably never follow
His steps for I recall
Every show where these footprints
Have led straight into walls
I call this toon my hero
For he helps me understand
That there's no mind more simple
Than inside the heads of man.
Rachael Howard, Grade 9
Northgate High School, GA

My First Turkey
I shot my first turkey
first day I had been.
I shot my first turkey
when I was ten.
Last day of the season
is when I killed him.
I shot my first turkey
in a clearing I saw him.

He popped his head up
Then I called for him.
He was walking forward
when something scared him.
He stopped and looked
I called again, he raised his head.
I fired at him.

He dropped to the ground
with a big puff of smoke.
I killed my first turkey
First day I had been.
I killed my first turkey
When I was ten.
Michael McLean, Grade 9
North Wilkes High School, NC

A Mouse
A mouse, with his fragile body
Intently listens to the dark.
Scared of what may come.
His past — haunting him daily,
Makes him anxious and worried.
He must stay in his group,
To be protected by the others.
Especially one important guy.
This guy loves him,
In fact he is the only one,
The only one he loves.
The mouse is tense,
All of his inhibitions show
Through his soft fur.
He won't — can't let go.
His small eyes show fear,
Like danger is in the air.
The mouse is protected —
Far from any harm.
But he still has no intentions
Of letting go of his fears.
Ansli Stanford, Grade 7
L E Gable Middle School, SC

Dear Someone
Dear Someone,
Well whoever cares,
Sometimes I want to die,
Sometimes I love everything,
Sometimes I just cry.
I don't like a lot of people,
People don't like me either,
I always get made fun of,
But I don't care, anymore,
I have gotten used to them,
But I'm trying to love more,
And hate less,
I don't think it is working out so well,
But I'm trying my hardest,
Well my life sucks, a lot of times,
But I'm trying to get over it,
So I think I'm doing good.
Sincerely,
Alexis
Alexis Ashton, Grade 7
First Flight Middle School, NC

Friends
Friends
Loyal, loving
Helping, talking, playing
Friends are always there.
100%
Akeena Edwards, Grade 8
Armstrong Middle School, MS

Riding Down a Hill
Riding down a hill
on my skateboard
the wind in my face
while poppin' ollies
and dodging rocks on
the ground hoping that
one won't get stuck under
the deck and end my
much enjoyed ride.
Speeding 'round corners
is fun but I'm staying
on the sidewalk today
riding over each crack
carefully if I'm lucky
my wheels won't get
caught and send me flying.
But just as soon as I
start it is over skurd!!!
I power slide to the bottom.
Nebraska Wiggins, Grade 7
East Millbrook Magnet Middle School, NC

Death
When someone dies, someone cries.
Every night we say a prayer
"Dear God, please let them be all right,
please don't take them away from me!"
but in the end they never come back home.
We wished on that star and we prayed real hard
but God said no, it's time for them to come home.

When someone dies, someone cries.
We're all grown up and we've learned to understand
but we're mad at the world
and we blame the Lord Almighty for our problems.
"Leave me alone and go away!"
We lash out, pushing away the ones close to us
but when we go home and sob in our pillow,
we imagine our loved one there
comforting us and saying it's okay.
Shernell Harrison, Grade 7
Broadview Middle School, NC

I Am a Leaf
I am a leaf.
I sway in the wind like clothes hanging out to dry.
In autumn, I fall from the limbs like snowflakes from the sky.
My colors are like a box of crayons.
During the winter I crumble up like sheets of paper.
My body comes in all shapes and sizes like a jigsaw puzzle.
My stems are pointed like sewing needles.
During thunderstorms, rain beads up like sweat on athletes.
I fly through the sky like birds traveling south.
Bugs nibble on me like a mouse nibbling on cheese.
Terrence James, Grade 9
Georgia Washington Jr High School, AL

The Game of Baseball
People say baseball is America's pastime,
Created over a hundred years ago.
But still it never has left our hearts,
In fact, some of us have it stuck in our minds.

There's not much you have to do,
To play this fantastic game.
Just swing a stick of wood,
And hit a tiny, spherical ball.

Now once you hit the ball,
Don't think about what to do next.
Just run with all your might,
To the first square lying on the ground.

After rounding the first square,
Head for the second one that catches your eye.
After you reach that base,
Head for the final square.

But you can't stop now,
Not after all your hard work.
Head for home plate,
And be the hero of the team.
Daniel Knepper, Grade 9
Leesville Road High School, NC

I Hate Hurricanes
Hurricanes can hit like a freight train.
Its acid rain can cause real pain,
And you'll run like a Great Dane.
It is hard for me to explain
How a hurricane conducts its inhumane campaign.
The shake of the window pane almost made me go insane.
Once the rain started to restrain,
Then I started to complain
That I hate hurricanes.
Devin Denison Wicke, Grade 7
Bishop Noland Episcopal Day School, LA

Storms in My Life
When storms come into my life
I feel so apart.
Rain floods into our house.
Trees fall down from powerful winds.
Schools get ruined.
Plants get washed away.
Canals and bayous get polluted.
The skies are gray with no sunshine.
I get sleepy from being stuck in the house.
My dog stayed by the door in fear.
I worry about others being safe.
But luckily we are all safe.
Antonio Maddie, Grade 8
Leonville Elementary School, LA

Never

Never let go if you still want to try
Never wipe your eyes if they still want to cry
Never settle for any answer if you really want to know
Never say you're over him if you can't let him go.
Never show your hurt, your pain, or your fear
Never let go if you still want him near
Never fall in love again if you know he's heaven sent
Never let go when he's the one meant.
Never seem to be down, heart broken, or through with it all
Never hit the floor and not recover from your fall
Never give up on life if he was the world to you
And never lie to your heart when you don't know what to do,
Now when your life gets hard — you just gotta stay strong
Hold your head high, pray, and then move on

Jacquaniese Washington, Grade 8
William J Christian School, AL

New Beginning

Fall is a new beginning
When special friendships are made
When leaves change all their colors
And when there is plenty of shade

Fall is starting school
When locker combinations are changed
When friends finally get to reunite
And when crushes' numbers are exchanged

Fall is new events and activities
Such as sports, dance, and cheer
When fathers and sons make a special bond
From boating, fishing, and hunting deer

Fall may be just a season to you
And it might not mean a thing
But to me it is much more
Fall is a new beginning

Karlie Rowley, Grade 8
Caddo Middle Magnet School, LA

Just Because…

Just because I'm short
Don't mean I can't play sports
Don't mean I'm a bad friend
Don't mean I like to get picked on by my height.
Just because I'm short
Don't mean I'm scared
Don't mean I'm smart
Don't mean I'm perfect.
Just because I'm short
Don't mean I can go small places.
I can't wait til I get taller,
Just because I'm short — please leave me alone.

Keon Harris, Grade 9
Warren Early College High School, NC

African Life

Living freely on African plains,
hunting for food,
and drinking dirty water.
Women cooking and cleaning,
while the men work.
Dancing and singing at ceremonies.
Decorating and painting faces.
Children running around
outside their huts.
Boys becoming men,
girls taking on their mother's job.
Elderly telling old folk tales,
while the children crowd around to listen.
They don't have everything we have,
but they love their humble life.

Kaila Holloway, Grade 7
Haynes Academy for Advanced Studies, LA

Hurricanes

Every year hurricanes come
to take away the things we love.
They lurk outside our homes
as we sit, scared, wondering if we'll be its next victim.
Fall and summer are the times we love,
but also worry about.
Animals run in fear
while some animals can't hide and are taken with it.
I worry that our home or even my family
might not be there much longer.
When all is over and nightfall comes
everyone is glad to be able to see
the diamond-like stars again.
People pray and hope God will protect them,
but He can't protect everyone.
Trees are even tossed around and picked up by the roots
when these storms come.
In the morning the sun feels
like a bright warm fire burning behind the clouds.
Once it's over everyone can finally go outside and play
without worrying about the hurricane.

Megan Bordelon, Grade 8
Leonville Elementary School, LA

Shining Secret

It rises in the morning
sets at night
warms me up when I'm cold
makes me happy when I'm sad
It brightens up my world
shines through the trees
sometimes so bright I have to wear special glasses
makes me want to go swimming
It would be nice if I could stare at it without hurting my eyes
guess what I'm talking about?

Ashley Endress, Grade 8
Sylvania School, AL

A Silvery Scene of Superb Sights

Wrapped in crystalline streams of endless sequined holly,
In company of silver bells twinkling with jolly,
Comes an outpouring of sweet evergreen scent,
Piercing the soft icy sky like a towering tent.

Crystal beads on pine branches of deep forest green,
Sparkling poinsettias placed in such a divine scene,
Glorious angels locked in a poise of praise,
Never to lose their comforting glow in all their days,
Bringing joy to weary souls in a variety of ways.

All dangling on spiraling strands of silver,
Ornaments of doves begin to trill and quiver,
Silent ballerinas slowly spin and sway,
All perched on branches pointing every which way.
Boxes of different sizes enveloped in royal paper,
Beneath red velvet bows professionally cut and tapered,
Resting inside is a childlike toy
That will soon bring the owner a wave of everlasting joy.

This fascinating feat catches a variety of eyes,
Keeping the holiday cheer and spirit well alive,
The most breathtaking top is seen from afar,
Eternally shining rests the stunning star.

Ellen Willis, Grade 8
St Mary's School, SC

My Father the Soldier

I asked my mommy if it was true
If men really fight for the red white and blue
She sat me down and told a story
My dad who fought his name is Cory
She held my hand and started to cry
And told me why my daddy had to die
With the simple words that meant so much
She had said with one simple touch
Your daddy died but is still here
So don't you worry don't you fear
He fought for me and for you
He fought for life of the red white and blue

Fame Galloway, Grade 9
Spalding High School, GA

Ice Cream

Oh, my! I dropped my ice cream.
That really makes me want to scream.
Don't laugh, it's not funny.
That ice cream was Blue Bunny.

Can I borrow a dollar to buy another?
Or do I have to get money from my mother?
I think I'll have a strawberry swirl.
That's the best flavor in the world!

Kirra Smith, Grade 8
Appling County Middle School, GA

Scared

Storms make me feel scared.
The grass sways
like waves in the ocean.
I'm wishing the trees
won't fall on my house.
Telling God to watch me.
Hoping and praying
that all of my family stays safe.
Watching my dog
as he looks back at me.
The rocks in the driveway
fly everywhere.
I am so scared
that one will break a window.
It is so scary!
The wind blew so hard
it broke my aunt's window.
I had a bad dream that my house got crushed
by a tree and my family died.
Help me
I am so scared!

Addison Ortego, Grade 7
Leonville Elementary School, LA

The King of the Jungle

The king of the jungle.
Who is it.
What is it.
No other than the mighty lion.
With mighty jaws,
Killer instinct,
A grand hunter,
A force to be reckoned with.
Not just a mighty hunter,
A loving father;
Teaching the necessary skills
To young cubs.
Never disgraced,
Dishonored:
Always traveling in prides.
Soon young cubs become new members of the pride
Following in the footsteps of the elders
The king of the jungle.

Peter Belleau, Grade 7
Haynes Academy for Advanced Studies, LA

Gone

There he is tiny and quiet
Laying on my mother's bed
Time goes by and we're here again
But this time for something bad
Family looking down in fear
They've all at least dropped a hundred tears
Now he's gone

Austin Williams, Grade 7
Carolina International School, NC

Blue Ridge the Beautiful

Smells of honey,
Sounds of the birds.
The beautiful tall mountains,
The cool breeze against your face.
Hiking the tall mountains,
Swimming in the ponds.
Catching foot long trout,
And hunting in the trees.
Throwing a football,
Eating in the park.
Camping under the stars,
And laying in the long grass.
Leaves falling to the ground,
Trees as tall as your house.
The Beauty of Blue Ridge!

Kristina Chastain, Grade 8
Fannin County Middle School, GA

Piano

Smooth ivory keys.
Melody and harmony
Playing in unison.

Fingers playing smoothly,
Legato, freely.
Now they play short,
Staccato, crisply.

Fingers dance. They fly.
Rhythm and soul,
Are second nature.

Notes getting louder —
Steady, steady crescendo.
And, climax!

Now softer —
Steady, steady,
Decrescendo.
End.

Sarah Milowic, Grade 8
Cathedral School, NC

Life

Life.
Life's sometimes fun.
Life is sometimes boring.
Life is a pain in the neck.
Life is a strain as an architect.
Life can bring you down.
Life can bring you up.
Life is the world around.
Life is what you've found.
Life.

Matt Blackmon, Grade 9
Leesville Road High School, NC

Family

F amily helps through your toughest time.
A lways loving no matter what happens.
M om for always loving and caring by always pushing me to do better.
I can never stop being apart of this family.
L oving sister for discipline of telling me when you think I've done wrong.
Y ou are my family and I will always love you.

Aquira Cook, Grade 7
East Millbrook Magnet Middle School, NC

Checking the Chickens

My dad and I walk outside in the moonlight.
We are doing the last chore of the night on the farm
We are going to check the chickens after a long day of work.
So many different sounds surround us as we walk down the path.
The owl shouts like an Indian's war whoop
The frogs sing in a throaty chorus
An opossum rustles through the leaves
We look behind us and see glowing eyes
They get closer and we can hear growling
We are beginning to get alarmed
Now we can see it is only my two cats checking on us.
The katydids are as melodious as an orchestra
The moon is a pearl in the sky
The stars are glowing beacons of hope,
There is a wish on each one.
I have no reason to fear the night
The darkness is like a blanket,
Warmer and softer than my patchwork quilt
It envelops me, a comforting cloak,
I am alert but at home in the darkness,
Checking the chickens with my daddy.

Gretchen Lund, Grade 7
St Francis Xavier School, AL

A Masterpiece

I paint with my feet, draw with my hands,
And I sketch with my eyes.
When I am on stage,
I know I am home.
Nothing else matters when I am up there.
It is just me and my tools.
My life is full of tap shoes and stockings,
Bobby pins and leotards.
After I am finished with my performance and hear that crowd roar,
I know that I have done my duty.
All the sweat and tears I have shed to get here,
I know it is worth it.
This is my life,
I will gladly give up a weekend for it.
The dance is no longer just a thing you do,
It is an example of fine art, a masterpiece.
I am proud to say that I am a dancer,
And as my duty of a dancer…
I entertain!

Faith Allen, Grade 8
St Joseph Catholic School, LA

Mission Accomplished
Clock ticks faster and faster
Exhausted teammates race down the court
The ball pounds the court
Sounding like an earthquake with every dribble
Fans sitting still
Anxious for the ball to be shot
Mid-court line
Defenders race up to block your every move
Piece of cake!
The ball reached the paint
The shot goes up
World comes to a sudden halt
The ball comes down in slow motion
Players are frozen with fear
The ball reaches the rim.
It spins and spins
Swirling down to the net
Score!
Players and fans jump with joy
The mission was accomplished!
Mackenzie Cozart, Grade 7
Cherokee Christian School, GA

Waiting
Sitting on the floor
Waiting for the storm to come
Wondering what
Will happen to
My beloved home.

Strong winds, heavy rains
What havoc will be done?
Scared stiff
What if
We never see the sun?
Jacqueline Landry, Grade 8
Bishop Noland Episcopal Day School, LA

Why!!!
Why do people have to get hurt?
Why do people have to be crazy?
Why do people have to steal?

Why do people have to lie?
Why do people have to be sad?
Why do people have to be mean?
Why do people have to cry?

Why do people die?
Why do people have to do bad things to other people?
Why do people have to do bad things to everyone?

Why do people have to blame me for the things they have done?
Just ask yourself why.
Blake LeMaster, Grade 7
L E Gable Middle School, SC

Stormy Days
Storms make me so angry inside
I watch out my bedroom window
As the water feels upon my face
When morning comes, my mom wakes me
to go pick up sticks and stones.
Some storms leave things everywhere.
When night falls, I think of sad thoughts.
Diamonds and tears appear in my eyes.
Besides God and angels are watching over me.
It feels like storms are a part of me.
Armanni Bennett, Grade 7
Leonville Elementary School, LA

Friends
Friends are people you can trust,
When you need them they are always there,
In your memory they will never rust,
And to forget them is very rare.

It's great to have friends,
And if you find the chance to have more,
Take them by the tens,
And you'll have a crowd by your door.
Akshay Gopal, Grade 7
Lake Castle Private School, LA

Bleeding Out Loud
Through all the abuse, the hatred, the sickness, and lying
I'm sitting through it all just thinking and dying
I'm crying on the inside it's all bleeding out
Lord please heal the pain that I'm praying about
Remember you told me it'll be all right
You told me to get out of the dark and follow the light
I didn't know any better I was stupid and foolish
But I knew in the long run you would help me get through this
Is this some kinda act, some play, some silly little dream
Or am I just overwhelmed with what life seems
Raven Nycole McZeal, Grade 8
St Margaret School, LA

Sometimes I Wonder
Sometimes I wonder if living on the Gulf Coast is fun.
Sometimes I wonder if Lake Charles is fun.
Sometimes I wonder if Hurricanes Rita, Katrina, and Gustav
Meant to hit us and why.
Sometimes I wonder what happens to the shores.
Sometimes I wonder what happens to all the people
That live on the shores.
Sometimes I wonder what happens to the houses.
Sometimes I wonder,
And then I know.
Sometimes living on the Gulf Coast is fun.
Sometimes living in Lake Charles is fun.
Lebrue Stevens IV, Grade 7
Bishop Noland Episcopal Day School, LA

Our Day

Day
Bright, blue
Easy to see
Time to be awake
Light

Noon
Hot, sunny
Time for lunch
Too hot to play
Halfway

Night
Dark, black
Seeing is hard
A time to sleep
Peaceful

Daniel Jacob, Grade 7
LA

Homework

Homework
It's not fun
Suppose to be helpful
If not done you're in trouble
Not even the teachers like it
Why do we have it
Know one really knows
Teacher's excuse, practice
Homework
The most boring thing on Earth!

Cameron Milks, Grade 8
Dillard Drive Middle School, NC

The Veterans

I will never forget
The people who gave
Up their lives
To protect you and me.
They were courageous
Soldiers to fight
For what was right.

I will never forget
The freedom they gave us,
To have fun every day
To see the next day.

Bobby Phetsynorraj, Grade 8
Magnolia Springs Baptist Academy, AL

Thanksgiving

As I watch nature
I think about God in Heaven
And thank Him for me.

Phillip LeMaire, Grade 8
St Margaret School, LA

Goodnight Daddy*

Daddy you and I were together once,
And now you and I are separated.
You're in a deep sleep and you will suffer no longer.
You and I had a close relationship and you will always be in my heart.
I love you deeply because you always, treated me like I were your own.
You are my loving father and now I'm heartbroken because you are gone.
All I wanted for you is to be happy but, without all the pain.
I love you so much and I just wanted to say,
"Goodnight Daddy I'll see you again someday."

Emily Bellamy, Grade 9
Loris High School, SC
*Dedicated to Anthony Gerald Richardson (Tim) my loving daddy

Envy

Envy sits alone,
her jet black hair spirals to the ground,
crashing at her feet.
Her long arms wrap around her bare knees.
It is here, in this empty room, that she watches.
Her friends — Happiness, Love, and Excitement — are outside.
"I don't need them," she cries to herself.
"I don't need anyone."
Envy won't admit it to herself, but she hates her friends.
She hates them for being everything she isn't.
She hates them for being better than her.
But through this struggle, Envy has made new friends.
Jealousy, Hatred, and Pain take the place of the others.
Yet still she sits, watching them,
Envying them.

Taylor Maxson, Grade 9
Middle Creek High School, NC

Remember

Remember that girl?
The one who could make you smile but couldn't make herself smile.
Remember that girl?
The one who could brighten anyone's day,
Even though she couldn't brighten up her own.
Do you remember her? I do.
She tried, and tried to smile.
She seemed so strong.
Who would have known she'd fall?
I couldn't see she was broken inside, could you?
Do you remember her?
She used to be your best friend, your lover, your life.
Remember you used to love her?
You would have done anything for her, what happened?
You broke her into pieces when you left.
She needed you,
But you couldn't be there for her even if you wanted to.
Do you remember her? I do.
Never thought someone could fall so much for a person.
But she did and you couldn't see that.
Now do you remember her? I still do.

Hannah Moncrief, Grade 9
Prattville Christian Academy, AL

The Wonders of Food

Yum, mmm, tastes so good,
That's just the power of food,
Oh, all the wonderful tastes,
Whether it's a cookie or a turkey that bastes,

There's sour, salty, bitter, and sweet,
Tastes like steak just can't be beat,
The chicken I love is almost my favorite,
But the quesadillas I make, you can't compare it,

Here comes the appetizer, entrée, dessert and with it they bring,
Mmmmm, an appetizer of barbecue hot wings,
Entrée is pizza, an explosion of sauce and cheese!
My taste buds welcome it, love it with ease,

Finally, to go out with a bang,
When I took a bite my taste buds sang,
The dessert was cake, chocolate to be exact,
Anyone can love it, that is a fact,

Yum, mmm, tastes so good,
That's just the power of food,
Oh, all the wonderful tastes!
Whether it's a cookie or a turkey that bastes.

Abigail Collins, Grade 7
East Millbrook Magnet Middle School, NC

The Beauty of the Sea

The sea is a beautiful thing,
Seagulls flying and trying to sing.
You can hear dolphins laugh as they play
Flipping in the air all day.
Snow white foam spraying in the salty air,
Any worries, you just won't care.
The sound of waves crashing on the sandy shore
That we hear while we wonder what hides on the ocean floor.
And when the sun shines on the blanket of mass
It twinkles like a sea of glass.
No matter if it is day or night,
The sea is a beautiful sight.

Mallory K. Gill, Grade 7
St Thomas More Catholic School, LA

Cherokee Indians

We threw them out like they were nothing,
they died because we wanted their land.
They had a good life,
then we came in and destroyed it.
What kind of people are we?
The land was beautiful, now it's ugly!
We ruined the Cherokee Indians!
They are no longer here.

Brittany Hill, Grade 8
Fannin County Middle School, GA

Friends

A friend is someone you can trust;
They are a definite must.
They won't judge you on what you wear;
They keep your biggest secrets close.
When your sick, they'll make you toast.
They won't talk about you behind your back;
If you get out of line, they'll give you a smack!
Friends are the best.
Hold them close;
They're the ones that matter most.

Gabby Gibbons, Grade 8
Priceville Jr High School, AL

The Prairie Is My Garden

The prairie is my garden.
By snow the lupines have been marred, in
Time the scars will heal while the pollen romances
The bee as spring soon swells over Kansas.

The prairie is my ballroom.
Waltzing wildflowers wave and bloom.
I feel the music as a daisy dances,
While a pile of plucked petals prances.

The prairie is my seed that's been sown,
A place to land always my own.
Though people come, the bright future advances,
It will still be mine, so I'll take my chances.

Though people come, the bright future advances,
I'm as a bee when spring swells over Kansas.

Elysia Moon, Grade 8
Covenant Christian School, GA

Fire! Fire!

Boom! I ran to the glass door,
Sounds like a noise from a movie of gore,
When I looked outside to see,
I said to myself "Oh gee!"

I saw fire in the woods,
I gasped and I then knew that it was not good,
I said to cut the game off,
We ran out and started to cough.

We tried to put the flames out,
However my grandma had plentiful doubts.
The whole woods were set in flames,
My brother was playing games!

Let's never do this again,
How I felt about this I could not explain.
Took a long time to put out,
But my grandma did not shout.

Jordan Dezern, Grade 9
North Wilkes High School, NC

That Friend

I like to sit at home sometimes
And think about my past,
Of memories and days gone by
I'd wished would always last.
I wonder what the future holds
Without the warmth of friendships old
Life is different, always changing —
Turning around and rearranging.
Everything I thought I knew,
Won't always stay the same, it's true
Although that's good in many ways
New things will happen day by day.
Everything old becomes new again
But I hope I keep that cherished friend.
Summer Walls, Grade 8
Priceville Jr High School, AL

Cats

Look around and see the cats —
Because of them there are no rats.
Black, white, red and gray —
All they do is sleep all day.
They prowl the streets on dark nights
And sometimes get into big cat fights.
They love it when you scratch their back,
But touch their belly and they will attack.
From great heights they can dive
Without losing one of their nine lives.
Cecelia Morise, Grade 8
Mount Carmel Academy, LA

Storms

Storms make me feel so sad
They make me think about my aunt
As I look out of my window
such a gloomy day
I sit and listen to the loud thunder.
This afternoon has been very boring
When I hear bullfrogs croaking
The trees sway back and forth
My house is quiet and boring
Clouds are hiding the sun
People say this means
that God is crying
Today the air is filled
with awkward sounds.
Morgan Gauthier, Grade 7
Leonville Elementary School, LA

Frogs

Frogs are all colors
They eat all kinds of insects
Some are big and small
Brittany Andrus, Grade 7
Opelousas Jr High School, LA

Do People Like Shiki

Do people like shiki
I guess they do
The restaurant is always packed
Teriyaki and hibachi
Makes my mouth water
American food is so great
When it is cooked by foreign people
Jesse Walker, Grade 8
North Iredell Middle School, NC

Why I Didn't Do My Homework

Well, I didn't do my homework,
 'Cause nature called me to play.
The squirrels told me to come running,
 And the birds did quite the same.
My cat meowed a song for me,
 A dog did a little dance.
Some clouds begged me to stay outside,
 And I simply could not say no.
Nature has a wonderful call,
 That nobody should deny.
Now you know why my page is blank;
 I just could not stay inside.
Emily Bowers, Grade 7
St Thomas More Catholic School, LA

One Day

One day I stepped inside a place
That was like no other
It was only I
Not my brother nor my mother
I went in alone
But was not scared or afraid
For I have been there once or twice
On a cool and calm day
I have met some great people there
That are now so close to me
I care so much for them
And I hope they care for me
Because one day
I won't go in that place
Ever again.
Ashley Bran, Grade 7
Henry Ford Jr High School, LA

Freedom

I want to be free
to look here and there,
to see new things
to see new faces,
I don't want to be alone forever
I need someone to hold me,
I wish I had freedom.
Taylor Ferguson, Grade 7
L E Gable Middle School, SC

Tybee Island

The water shines like the sun.
As dolphins play, the
Gulls dive snatching diamond fish.
Shells litter the shore
Broken and wasted they lay
Waves crash like cymbals
The sea oats wave in the breeze
Soft, sandy island.
Jimmy Dyer, Grade 8
Trickum Middle School, GA

A Day at the Ocean

I taste salt in the water
I hear the waves hitting the rocks
I smell the salt in the air
I see the waves coming in
I feel cold water
The ocean makes me calm
Dallas McKinney, Grade 7
L E Gable Middle School, SC

Fall

F amily together
A mazing time of the year
L eaves falling everywhere
L asting a few weeks and then it's gone
Dillon Sumrall, Grade 7
Rock Mills Jr High School, AL

Fun Times

Staying up the night before
Anticipating the trip ahead.
The forever long flight
'Til we finally arrive.
Waiting in line to board the ship,
So happy and excited.
We just can't wait.

Seeing all my family,
For the first time in months.
Happy to be all together,
And eager to begin our vacation.
Departing from the dock,
And feeling sick at first.
Getting used to it, after all.

Waking up early in the morning,
Can't wait to begin our first day.
Putting on bathing suits and sunscreen,
Ready to visit the islands.
Taking lots of pictures,
And planning what we're going to do.
It's finally here!
Savannah Wellington, Grade 8
Westchester Country Day School, NC

Slow and Painful

It all happened so slowly
All the aches and pains
I don't remember much
There was a train and everything slowly faded away.
Now I'm here in this darkness
I can hear voices speaking of my condition
I'm not going to make it!
I have lain here for days silently fighting
Then the voices begin to slowly fade
I see a light that is oh so very bright
Then I am so abruptly awaken
I see streets of gold and pearly gates.
I hear a strong voice calling my name
This can't be possible!
Am I really here?
I can remember it all
Waking up on the tracks, the train, and the hospital
I look around
This can't be right
But I'm really here
I'm Dead!

Whitney Garrett, Grade 8
Lake Middle School, MS

Alex

I have a best friend whose name is Alex
We always have fun
We always go crazy
She is like a sister to me
She is the greatest friend anyone could have
Even though she died last month
She is still my best friend

Katie Billeaudeaux, Grade 8
St Margaret School, LA

School, School

I woke up this morning and said "yes!"
I ran to the closet to find my best.
I looked up and down the racks and what did I see
A white shirt and blue jeans for me
I went to the bathroom to wash my face
And under my breath I said I'm out of this place
I then remembered last year, as I walked to the bus stop
No more DVD player to forward, rewind, pause, or stop.
Then I heard a roar come over the hill
And immediately I felt a chill
I was so happy to see this bus
If it was crowded, I would not have even fussed.
What I'd hope for since last year
Was about to happen and I had no fear
I was going to have me some friends
That I couldn't wait till the school began.
Finally class has started and I have a smile
I'm no longer homeschooled, feeling like the only child!!!

Shekinah Bass, Grade 8
Dillard Drive Middle School, NC

All Alone

Nobody knows I'm here. I'm all alone.
I feel like there is no one else in the world but me.
My mind goes blank.
I don't know where I'm at.
There is no one else here.
Only the forest creatures are in sight.
As I walk by, they all go away.
This place is so dull.
There are millions of trees all around me.
I want to get away from here.
The trees are changing colors.
I can barely see the path
with all the leaves covering the ground.
The clouds get darker and darker.
Cool bursts of wind come from out of nowhere.
I start feeling drops of water.
I just want to go home.
I pray to God that I'll be all right.
The night begins to come.
The sky is getting even darker.
I hope I can find my way back to where I belong.

April Stelly, Grade 7
Leonville Elementary School, LA

Hurricanes

When I think of hurricanes, I feel sad.
Children unaware of what is going on
Wind bangs hard and knocks over buildings
A dog in its dog house scared.
The sun trying to shine
but clouds get in the way.
Boulders flying in the air
like little feathers,
bridges being destroyed.
I am indoors and it is horrible.
Angels protecting us all the way.
It has only just begun!

Emily Bergeron, Grade 8
Leonville Elementary School, LA

Blue

Blue is the color of the sky
It is so beautiful, it almost makes you cry

I see white clouds up above
And then there goes a beautiful, white dove

As blue cars pass my face
It looks like they are in a race

Bright, blue sky up above
It makes you fall in love

JJ Green, Grade 7
L E Gable Middle School, SC

I Am From

I am from family and friends,
All year long.
I am from Christmas in Charlotte,
And summers at the beach.

I am from dance,
Two nights a week,
And church every Wednesday night.
I am from shopping all day,
And watching movies at night.

I am from playing in the snow with my dad,
Then going inside for a cup of hot chocolate with my mom.
I am from church on Sunday morning with my mom,
Then a crazy lunch afterwards with my aunt and uncle.

I am from kisses from my dog,
And taking him out.
I am from giving him tummy rubs,
And cuddling on the couch.
I am from family tradition,
With loving and laughing.
I am from High Point, North Carolina.
The place I love the most.

Megan Caffey, Grade 8
Westchester Country Day School, NC

Winter, Summer, Spring, and Fall

Snow is covering everything,
All around jingle bells ring,
This is the merriest time of year,
The winter season is here!

This is a time of no school,
Kids will be laughing at the pool,
In the sky's a bright yellow sun,
Summer's the time to have fun!

Rain and showers,
Sprinkle down on blooming flowers,
Animals wake from a long winter's sleep,
Spring's when we hear the bird's little peep!

Jumping into a leaf pile,
Makes all little children smile,
Right now Thanksgiving and Halloween,
Are the holidays that are seen,
Celebrated by one and all,
It's the season of fall!

Winter, summer, spring, and fall,
What's the best season of all?

Nicole Hlebak, Grade 7
St Mark Catholic School, NC

9-11*

9-11 is our biggest fear
That's the day that is already here

It comes to show that the men were brave
They gave their life for us and now lay safe in a grave

We love them so dearly it hurts to show
That the tears that had fallen in a river they'll flow

The men that have fallen have fought with all their might
We'll see them in heaven with a flag in sight

So take this time to remember them again
And just remember that it's not the end

So many people have lost their lives
Some lost their husband some children and wives

They took over the plane oh its a shame
They took their shot and hit their aim

People who lost someone may never know
Why their loved ones had to go

Christopher Doddridge, Grade 8
Rock Mills Jr High School, AL
*Dedicated to all those who helped that day.

Snow

It is the snow, that covers all tragedy,
that can stop all problems,
and that can freeze the land into a place of universal joy.

It is the snow, that summons memories of childhood,
evoking the sights and sounds of our youth,
where all was new, exciting and exhilarating,

It is the snow, that covers the world in a soundless blanket,
muting everything, stopping everything,
and gives us a chance to step back, and look forward

It is the snow, that cleanses the land,
that washes away all traces of life in the melt,
that is nature's force of rest and renewal

It is the snow, that can be as gentle as a flurry,
as steady and intense as a blizzard,
or even as fiercely lethal as an avalanche.

It is the snow, that is forever changing,
that is never the same and always something new in life,
and nothing is the same,
as Snow.

Thomas Wright, Grade 8
Dillard Drive Middle School, NC

High Merit Poems – Grades 7, 8 and 9

Happy Days

I can't breathe, my nose is stuffed up
I can't see, my eyes are filled with tears
I can't remember the good things my dad said we did
I can remember the stories my dad has told me

You my mom, who cared so much about me
You my mom, who did anything for me
You my mom, who had O.C.D.
You my mom, who had 3 children, plus me

Your beautiful pictures smiles at me every day
Pictures cannot possibly show how beautiful you really were

You had love in your eyes
You had hope in your soul
You had happiness written on your face
You had kindness in your heart
The heart that will never beat again

So as I walk to your grave on this beautiful Mother's Day
I can't see, I can't breathe
But I can now remember
The stories
Of those Happy Days

Madison McKinney, Grade 7
Atlanta Academy, GA

Winner

And the winner is…me
I'm the winner of me
Who else could it be?
I'm the winner of courage and perseverance
And much confidence
I'm the winner of great peers
Filled with no fears
I'm the winner of me
Who else could I be?

Falisha Pierre-Louis, Grade 8
Dillard Drive Middle School, NC

Hurricane Havoc

It was a late day; I was playing with my brother
Out in the bay, when I heard a call from my mother.
My brother was scared; he was frightened so.
It was a hurricane like the one that had happened so long ago.
The trees were swaying and we were praying.
Sticks fly and winds rush,
But then there was a hush.
All was quiet; all was well,
But then we heard a sound quite like a bell.
It started again, but ended in minutes.
We had nothing left but cuts in our tendons.

Hunter Rogers, Grade 7
Bishop Noland Episcopal Day School, LA

Rescued

Baby don't you hold back,
Trust me you have nothing to lose.
You're lost like everybody else.
I don't know you,
However, I know pain. (Pain runs deep)
You're scared of being judged,
What about the fear of making it 'til tomorrow?
I know lost, abuse, and hurt.
You listen here, speak what you want.
You're drowning in self-pity.
Nobody cares anymore.
Passion is flowing.
Let it all go.
You stop, the world keeps on spinning.
You're lost, way lost,
In this world of nothing.
All you want,
All you need,
Is to be
RESCUED.

Nicole Niedrich, Grade 9
Leesville Road High School, NC

Men of War

A swordsman,
  powerful and persistent,
slashes and smashes,
  slowly.
Warrior.

An archer
  keen and swift,
aims and shoots,
  precisely.
Bowman.

The commander,
  strong and wise,
orders and fights,
  passionately.
Leader.

Brennen Acosta, Grade 7
Haynes Academy for Advanced Studies, LA

Hurricane Gustav

The heavy winds blew
As the water level grew.
Was I dreaming, or was it all true?
The night sky was black and blue.
We had a big, huge barbecue.
We all hoped our houses would pull through.
I'm sure glad we didn't have a curfew.
When it was all through,
We all said, "Thank you."

Garrett Harless, Grade 8
Bishop Noland Episcopal Day School, LA

Little Girls

Since we were little girls,
We watched with a stare.
Since we were little girls,
We wanted to be out there.
Since we were little girls,
We wanted to do the same.
Since we were little girls,
We dreamed of cheering at the game.
Since we were little girls,
We cheered in the stands.
Since we were little girls,
We longed to do "one mans."
Since we were little girls,
We waved our pom-poms high.
Since we were little girls,
We looked at them with glowing eyes.
Now that day is here,
As we still stare in awe.
And when they leave we'll shed a tear,
But remember they taught us all
Since we were little girls.

Kaitlyn Gladwell, Grade 8
Priceville Jr High School, AL

Day and Night

Day is a time of play and fun
A time of happiness and cheer
It is a time of shining light
That is until it becomes night

Night is a time for sleep
It is a time for rest
All through the dark and the fright
Until day comes back with its light

Joseph Schenck, Grade 7
Lake Castle Private School, LA

Breaking Peace

Hidden in a circle of trees,
Nestled in between two,
Mountain peaks.

So calm,
So serene.

Then splash!
The silence breaks.
Ripples fan out in every direction.

Dark as night it is,
Cool as a glass of water.

It's now calm,
Back to peace.

Zach Smith, Grade 7
First Flight Middle School, NC

One of a Kind State

Georgia is a one of a kind state.
The Blue Ridge region is the most marvelous region.
There are so many things to do in the Blue Ridge region.
You can hike the mountainous land to see spectacular views.
I love to fish on the gleaming stream.
Hunting is fun too; you get to hunt all kinds of things.
Shopping is fun to you, visit all of the antique shops.
The weather is beautiful in the winter and the summer.
There is rarely any bad weather so usually always beautiful.
The fall season is when leaves change; is the most beautiful season.
Fall is also football season.
Rafting on the lake is very awesome.
The Blue Ridge lake is very beautiful!
Swimming is an awesome feeling with the cool water.
Running through the mountains is like a movie with all the pretty scenes.

Justin Young, Grade 8
Fannin County Middle School, GA

You

As I rest my head upon your shoulder I listen to your rhythmic heart pound
Being with you makes my feet lift off the ground
Knowing that I have you makes me able to do anything,
I can climb the highest mountain and swim to the deepest trenches of the ocean.

You love me unconditionally
Despite all my flaws
I know you have fought long and hard to win my heart
While I just tore it apart…

Now I'm beginning to feel the same love that you feel for me
Secret words and unspoken things
You never have lied to me or actually hurt me
Your honesty about your past has made me love you even more

Other people may say things about you and ask why I chose you
I say because it's my choice and they don't understand what you do
I never thought when I first met you that we'd be where we are today
I didn't even think I'd go out with you…

I'm glad I did
Because now I am able to say I love you with my whole hart not just half…
I love you!

Shanquea Jamison, Grade 9
McKee Jr High School, AL

Anthony Paul*

The way you looked at me with those big brown eyes,
The way you could smile and light up the sky,
The way you left this world in calm and peace,
The silent kiss I put on your cheek,
The way my legs started to shake,
The more I wish it could've been fake,
It's now been two years since you've been gone and I am still all alone.

Cheyenne Cromer, Grade 8
Schley County Middle/High School, GA
**In loving memory of Anthony Paul Wodzinski.*

Mother Nature's Majestic Mural
Mother Nature is an artist
There are many breathtaking things she creates.
She puts so much time and thought in it,
It is something that you can relate.

One of her beautiful paintings,
Its amazing name is fall.
It shows how mesmerizing and calm autumn can be,
And how all the bad things stall.

She adds scarlet and honey hazel
To the leaves in the wind that are frazzling.
Also puts in brown-green grass.
Oh the beauty is just so dazzling.

Then she paints children,
Outside and having so much fun.
And puts in lovely mothers cooking ham,
Turkey, and deliciously, sweet honey bun.

Finally she puts in a touch of pink skies
And a glowing sunset that is fainting.
This is how fall should be
In Mother Nature's painting.
Natalie DeJesus, Grade 8
St John Neumann Regional Catholic School, GA

The Best Things About Georgia…
The best things about Georgia is the scenery.
Do you know what that means?
The rivers flowing, the wind blowing.
Fish flopping, deer hopping.
The bushes rustling, the children hustling.
The food here is great!
What's really good is the steak.
You have baked beans and corn bread.
Don't let it all get to your head!
See, I know what it means.
The question is, "Do you?"
Morgan Ross, Grade 8
Fannin County Middle School, GA

Life on the Gulf Coast
Living on the Gulf Coast
We often have rain,
All kinds of weather,
Sometimes hurricanes.

Katrina, Rita, Gustav,
And now possibly Ike.
High winds and rain all,
But no two are alike.
Hurricanes here and there,
People scattering everywhere.
Walter Klumpp, Grade 7
Bishop Noland Episcopal Day School, LA

It Will Be All Right
Soar on wings and be free
That's all I've wanted you to be
Go explore don't be shy
I'll be right here by your side
It will be fine give it a try
You might like it in the end
Go say hi, never say goodbye

You can go wherever, it will be all right
To be free you have to reach for the sky
It may seem a little scary on the very first try
But you will have to trust me, it will be all right
Jordan Widas, Grade 8
Dillard Drive Middle School, NC

Gettysburg
A visit to the battlefields on an autumn day;
The monuments stand in white and gray.

Cannons along the battery wall;
I cannot believe I saw them all.

Our uniforms now stand up in gray;
The soldiers fought all through the day.

The third day brought death and sorrow;
It seemed as though there was no tomorrow.

Finally the battle was done;
The sadness was with everyone.

Gettysburg helped solve many a mystery;
And I have now seen my family's history.
Thomas Hart, Grade 7
St Anne Catholic School, SC

Ignored
If I have to smile one more time
While looking at you stare her way
I think I'll break down
And never look up
I think I'll break down and just give up

In my mind we were made for each other
But I guess to you you're just like a brother
She walks your way and you just ignore me
But you look my way and I can hardly breathe

I want you happy I really do
But you with her that I don't want to be true
If it's just you and me I see the world
But with her around I'm just another girl
Joyce Bryer, Grade 8
Carolina International School, NC

Fairy Tales

Sometimes we wish our lives were like fairy tales
Where good never fails
With the never ending laughter
And the beautiful princess marries the handsome prince and they live happily ever after

But our lives aren't like that here
Evil can seem to overcome and laughter isn't always near
And some of us don't find the one to complete our heart
Then when we do, sometimes it falls apart

You see our world isn't a perfect place
And not everyone has a smile on their face
Our world is full of hurting, longing, and sorrow
Some people believe that there is no hope for tomorrow

We need to come together and take someone's hand
So we can make this world a little more grand

Sarah Wootten, Grade 9
Sylvania School, AL

Sorrow

The tension in your face muscles burn.
Your lips curve slightly downward.
Your nose beings to tingle, and your eyes form a glassy shield.
The shield breaks loose, and a clear crystal tear runs down your smooth pale cheek.
Your hand starts to tremble and your fingers as if they were strumming strings on a guitar.
The tears come faster and double in size.
Nobody can help or make this pain go away… the death of the cell phone!

Emilie Schneider, Grade 8
Mount Carmel Academy, LA

Cheerleading

Cheerleading is a sport in which you use your mind and you use strength.
You use your mind when you think about what you are supposed to be doing.
Strength comes in when you are holding someone up in the air.
This is a sport of endurance.
It is not just about the uniforms, make-up, and looking cute.
Cheerleading is about working hard at something that you love doing.
Sure the routines are intense and hard and the practices are long and tiring.
When hitting that competition floor everything that you worked on counts at that moment.
It is then you realize that making every little thing right in the routine pays off in the end.
So if you think cheerleading is just about yelling cheers that rhyme, there is more to know.

Ashley Hotfelter, Grade 8
Mount Carmel Academy, LA

The Lonely Volleyball

I am peeling and I am flat
Every day I wait patiently for someone to take me out of the basket and toss me around a bit.
But every day I am left. No one likes me. I am all alone.
I am not new I am not clean.
But if you give me some air I can give you what you need.
I can help you get that serve over the net or pass to the setter.
We could be a team. We could work together.
But until now I am the lonely volleyball dirty and out of air.

Gabby Davis, Grade 7
Westchester Country Day School, NC

Night and Day

Waking up in the day
To the chirping blue jays
Stretching and yawning to the morning's bright sun
Waiting for today's fun

Night is approaching
And it's time to get some rest
I don't know what I'll do tomorrow
But I hope for the best.

Sophia Tran, Grade 7
Lake Castle Private School, LA

9/11

Planes went Insane
Crashing and flashing
All that was left was
Tears along with fears

At every house at every home
Many felt alone
Loved ones and friends dead and gone
Families trying to hold up their heads
Not knowing what else to dread

At ever nose there held a tissue
Holding a picture of a loved one saying I love you

Wives hurting with humble cries
Husband's hearts cut with knives
Girls without mom's, boys without dads
All was left alone and sad

America will never be the same
America asked; who's to blame
Together we stand; united we fall
We join together both big and small

Arronice Jones, Grade 8
Crisp County Middle School, GA

Once I Lived a Life in Sin

Once I lived a life in sin,
I had no joy or peace within,
I did not know where to go or what to do,
Then I met a man one day,
Who gave me joy and peace this day,
And now I'm saved within the Cross of Calvary.

He'll give you joy, peace, and love,
If you'll only come to Him
He only cares where you're going not where you've been.
So let His blood cover you and His son be a guide to you,
Then you'll be saved within the Cross of Calvary.

Justin Scott Duncan, Grade 9
Three Springs of Courtland School, AL

Fear No More

All at once
A man's freedom can be taken away
By people out there who do not mean well.
But the will of a man
And his faith in God
Can be the best defense.

With this thought
We can go into the world.
We can no longer fear
The evil set upon us.
And even if something evil does happen,
God is there, to protect us and guide us.

Patrick Seelinger, Grade 8
Cathedral School, NC

Storms

Storms make me feel hollow
like the tree in my backyard
so empty and dark
cold and lifeless.
Today I feel so calm
like the ocean on a cold winter night.
The cool breeze brought chills down my spine.
Not even one boat in sight
nor even a swimmer.
The sand is cold,
and so is the water
I even thought I saw dolphins
jumping for only a moment.

Kristy Fontenot, Grade 7
Leonville Elementary School, LA

Darkness

Deep in the darkness is where my heart lays.
At the bottom of a pit were it slowly dies.
The lies it is filled with,
The hurt inside.
Inside my heart is were sadness hides.
The loneliness stings with pain.
As outside the sky is my emotion,
Filled with rain
I can't escape the silence.
The violence inside my heart is powerful.
Memories linger with strong grievance.
The looks, the stares, and the ugly glares.
Only makes me feel worse.
As my heart grows hoarse.
With only a shimmer of light.
Slowly fading, slowly disintegrating
My heart is blank, in the silence
Without feeling, but with much love
But do you know what?
This process is only the beginning!

Jazzmyne Johnson, Grade 8
Reid Ross Classical School, NC

Courage

There you go again
walking by
I know I'll never have the courage
to say anything to you
thinking of all my chances
though I can say it in my mind
I'll never say it in words

Not sure if you know it
though I try to show it
trying to think of words to say
scrambled in my mind
but there's no way
maybe I'll just try some other day

Chris Aiello, Grade 7
Cathedral School, NC

A Loving Friendship

You say I'm really annoying,
And sure, I may laugh,
But at night when I think about it,
I always feel a draft.

You hate it when I follow you,
But love it when I'm there,
You're living your life alone,
And you don't really care.

I have funny feelings,
When I'm close to you,
But when you walk away,
I get the downright blues.

So listen to me now,
Or you'll forget me forever,
I'll love you always and always,
Whether it be now or never…

Kacy Campbell, Grade 8
Eclectic Middle School, AL

Storms

When storms come into my life,
they bring depression.
Mosquitoes fill the humid air around me.
Birds are no longer cheerfully chirping.
Many people have evacuated.
The streets are deserted.
Only clouds drift in the sky above me.
Debris fills everyone's yard.
Trees have collapsed everywhere.
People's homes are now destroyed.
Smiles are very limited.
Hopefully God is watching over us.
He'll help us get through this.

Emily Robin, Grade 8
Leonville Elementary School, LA

Reasons

The reason we should not be together is simply because,
We like each others company but we are not truly in love.
We smile in public,
As if nothing is wrong,
But behind the scenes you will find a very different sad song.
To many observers around,
Our relationship seems perfect.
But when I'm sad at home,
Feeling depressed and alone,
I ask myself: is all of this pain and heartache REALLY worth it?
We both care for each other deeply and feel strongly for each other,
But half the time I feel like it's not a feeling of true passion,
But the kind of care that I would feel for a brother!
We argue, we fight, we scream, we shout.
And it's stupid because the next day neither of us remembers what it was even about.
In our relationship others always seem to interfere,
And this is the reason we have been breaking up and getting back together for a year.
I think that we both know this and it's very plain to see,
That we are not meant for each other and we simply cannot be.

Jailyn Montgomery, Grade 8
Armstrong Middle School, MS

The Wonder of Nature

Nature is such a wonderful thing to see.
The best time to see the wonder of nature is in the fall.
Fall is when most of the trees' leaves change color and fall off.
Other wonders of nature can be tornados, and nature itself can be wonderful.
Nature can also be a wonder of nature in the spring when most plant life and
animal life comes back out from being in hiding from the cold winter.

Alex Hedrick, Grade 7
Carolina International School, NC

Change for the Better and Worst

My nail polish is black instead of pink
I'm letting my guard down and feeling more confident
But other than me something is changing
Twenty percent precipitation means it's raining
Global Warming means Global Warning
Get out New Orleans
I'm not running it ain't gon' be hurting me
Flooding with toxic crocodile streams
Change for the better
Change for the worst
The country is voting for what I call the obvious
The same policies so you can complain or a better hope for your children
We are sinking in an oil puddle and it's too sticky to get out of
The viscosity doesn't run off
Another typhoon here we go
They said gas is going to be five dollars a gallon
Change for the better
Change for the worst
That's what happened this weekend
But can you guess which one it is my birthday it's three months from now
I hope I can get a fourteenth candle

JeVonda Wright, Grade 8
Avondale Middle School, GA

Rain, Wind, and Water

So many fallen trees
So many memories
Blue roofs everywhere you go
You'll keep the memories
Even the ones you wish not to know.

The rain that flew
The wind that blew
The dark, black sky
The water, oh so high
The hurricane of '08.

Nicole Ferriss, Grade 7
Bishop Noland Episcopal Day School, LA

The Holidays Are Coming

Thanksgiving is finally here
We have been waiting for this all year
We know we will eat too much we fear
As the leaves begin to fall
We start to have a ball
We get ready for the big meal
and dread the full way we will feel
Next, Christmas comes
We get to sit on Santa's lap
then after that we can take a nap
On Christmas, we decorate, we gather, we eat
Bring on the stuffing, bring on the meat!
After we set up the tree
We sing, we dance, and of course we eat!
Early to bed, early to rise
Don't you love a good surprise!
We are so thankful for all we have
and remember all those who have not
Christmas is a holy time
Jesus is the reason
Happy Holidays everyone!

Hannah Lund, Grade 9
Mount Carmel Academy, LA

My Glory

As I run down the sidelines with the ball in my hands;
Scoring the winning touchdown, everybody cheers in the stands.
I prove myself to everyone watching the game,
I earn my glory and also my real name.

Finishing my routine, I stick my dismount.
I look at the scoreboard, as it reads 10.0 with no doubt.
I earn my glory once again,
This time with a gold medal hanging from my neck.

With one second left, I shoot the basketball and make my wish.
The crowd goes silent and then we all here a "swish!"
With loads of happiness, we all rejoice.
And I know inside that my glory is my true voice.

Danish Dhanani, Grade 8
Fayette Middle School, GA

Memory

I close my eyes late at night
expecting to see a sudden fright
I see myself and another child,
the resemblance is only mild.
The children run, and sing, and dance.
They laugh, and play, and prance.
They ask if I want to join,
They ask me if I want to join.
I say I can't I have to go,
for this day it will surely snow.
They beg, and plead, and ask some more,
and for some reason I feel torn.
Seeing my face and another,
then I see my precious mother.
She sits on a bench with a bag in hand,
the children yelling as they ran.
Then I remembered a long lost thing,
the memory of a long lost dream,
the joy and wonder that comes when I sing.
But all I feel when I wake
is the feeling of my heart about to break.

Salathiel Jones, Grade 8
East Central Middle School, MS

Love Causes Pain

Love causes pain
Wherever you go.
You can try to hide it,
But it'll always show.
You might not know it,
But it's there.
My heart's full of pain,
While you're oh so near,
For the love I have for you,
It's oh so hard to bear.
I watch in so much despair.

Angela Cherry, Grade 8
Seminole County Middle/High School, GA

Last Time I Saw You...

Seems like we have known each other forever
But we don't know a thing
Seems like we were closer than ever
But that all changed
I saw you standing there
With your wife and kid
I didn't know what to say
But I guess I never did
I only remember the stories
Of how alike we were
But looking at you now
Everything's a blur

Bailey Williams, Grade 9
Northgate High School, GA

A Letter to Grandma

I know you're up there
So proud and free
When you were here
You were in misery
I hated to see you go
But when I think about it
I know your watching over me
I feel safe
As if nothing can happen
But if anything does
I know one thing
I'll be with you
So I can't possibly fret
Because when my time here is done
I'll be with you once again
Madison Fontenot, Grade 7
Lake Castle Private School, LA

Colorful Monsters

I cried my eyes out,
Monsters covered
In yellow white and red.
Then I shout, one of them was Fred.

He comes towards me juggling balls,
I stand and hit he falls.
I run quickly scared and in fear,
I stop to hear.

He's laughing,
I finally look at him.
I stopped shedding tears I wake up,
I take a glare and nothing was there.
It was just a dream.
Benjamin Williams, Grade 7
First Flight Middle School, NC

The Killing of Kindness

As leaves decay
my heart goes to clay.
Knowing winter is near
how it make me fear.
That I will not make it
nor have the fight.
To see the light once more
just as before.
The sickness
fell upon my kindness.
And without
kindness throughout.
It made a monster
The disaster.
I am today.
Anyssa Maltba, Grade 9
Avery County High School, NC

Pain

Pain
Rain
Tears fall
Your heart tugs
Water streaming
Soul screaming
Longing for someone to hold you close
You cry out
And the sky answers

Pain
Rain
Looking up
Hands clutching
Thunder calling
Spirit falling
You collapse to your knees
Chills shake you
All alone, in
Pain
Crying in the
Rain
Whitley Grindle, Grade 9
Lumpkin County High School, GA

Motorcross

Racing my orange 200 xr dirtbike
Last lap went wild
Gear showing red as racers spread
Chomped on the gas
So fast
Split ruts and hit the jumps
Messing up on the jump was some junk
I went to first with a burst
Last jump
When I jumped
I soared past victory
This made me jump
You should have seen the golden cup
Dalton Anderson, Grade 9
North Wilkes High School, NC

Winter

Snow is falling on the ground,
Signs of winter are all around.
Teary eyes and runny noses,
Wintertime is slowly approaching.
Wind in the air, blowing your hair,
Signs of winter are everywhere.
Drinking hot chocolate to warm you up,
Sipping it from your favorite cup.
Snow is falling on the ground,
Signs of winter all around.
LeAnté Craft, Grade 8
St Peter Claver School, LA

Thanks

I give thanks for my family,
They're always around for me.

I give thanks for my freedom,
It lets me worship wherever I want.

I give thanks for my friends,
They are always there for me.

I give thanks for my sisters,
They keep me on the right track.

I give thanks for food,
It keeps me alive.

I give thanks for church,
It teaches me right from wrong.

I give thanks for my parents,
They take good care of me

And when I need something
They get it for me.
Amber McCormick, Grade 7
L E Gable Middle School, SC

My Special Friend

You make me laugh,
When I want to cry.
You're honest with me,
You'd never lie.

You make my fears disappear,
You make my problems seem so clear.
If he breaks my heart or hurts me so,
You're there for me, I always know.

I hope our friendship will never end.
You'll always be my special friend.
Bethany Gingerich, Grade 8
Priceville Jr High School, AL

Sunrise

It's bright and glowing
It's a sign of a new morning
It has a light,
That is sheer perfection
It could be like a heart,
Shining with love and affection
As you wake in the morning,
You see it rest in the sky
Then you know,
You are taking in the beauty of sunrise.
Jenna Deer, Grade 7
Boyet Jr High School, LA

Frolicsome Fall

Colorful, captivating, leaves crunching beneath my clogs
Swirling, twirling, whirling past me like small children
Pleasing pigments plummeting towards the earth
A crisp feeling in the air, invigorating with every breath

A pumpkin patch abundant with plump pumpkins
Tickled tots trying to take the biggest one
Several are scant, some are stout
Many wander about the pumpkin patch

Camouflaged children cackling in their costumes
The succulent smell of sweets in the air
Terrifying tall tales being told
Halloween is here, yes, hair-raising Halloween is here

Scrumptious, savory scents spilling from the kitchen
Families have fixed looks on the football game
At last, the thickset turkey emerges from the oven
Everyone giddily gathers at the table to enjoy the feast

Frolicsome fall has at last arrived
Families gather to eat and enjoy each other's company
The temperature finally dropping, drawing everyone to the fire
Frolicsome fall has arrived at last

Suzanne Brady, Grade 8
St John Neumann Regional Catholic School, GA

Teenagers

Teenagers get put into difficult situations
And have to make many hard decisions
We are not perfect and never will be
But we try out best for all to see

Peer pressure is something we all experience
But all we have to do is listen to our conscience
We might make the wrong choice along the way
But to get back on track we just have to pray

We like to have fun at parties
But often mix up our priorities
Education should always be number one
But we are still kids who just want to have fun

We get distracted easily
By not listening to God completely
We should not listen to the drama going around
Because most of it is not profound

Being a teenager is easier said than done
We always have to please everyone
Our parents give us rules to follow
Sometimes they are hard to swallow

Kelly Quern, Grade 9
Mount Carmel Academy, LA

Life

Life is like a road,
you start off on a fresh slate,
then as you grow up,
the road starts to get bumpy
and changes happen along the way.

School gets hard and life gets tougher,
but then you meet the perfect one
and stay together forever.
Along the way you have to deal
with things you don't feel like messing with.

In the end, the road might have been rough
but you just have to stick with it
until you get old.
Then after death,
you begin a whole new slate.

Carlie Cox, Grade 8
Poland Jr High School, LA

The Veteran

The veteran is the man we honor
He fights for our rights
He dies for his beliefs
A true hero by any standard

The veteran is the woman we remember
Her home a foxhole in the field
Her fuel the desire to fight
Her will composed of iron

The veteran is the young man dead in the plains
A victim of unnecessary bloodshed
An innocent dead by the hands of a savage
Worthy of our sorrow

The veteran is the factory worker
His occupation the nation's lifeline
His product the arsenal of democracy
The unsung hero

Richard Spohn, Grade 8
Carolina International School, NC

Winter's Delight

I feel the air turn crisp as I begin to shiver
My hands search for my pockets as my lips quiver
My toes are surrounded by warmth in my cozy boots
I look around as the wind seems to hoot
Suddenly I feel the moisture on my tongue
The snow has begun
I no longer feel the cold as I dance around the streets
Ready for anything I may meet on this winter night
At times like this all feels right
Because this is winter's delight

Jacquelyn Saunee, Grade 9
Mount Carmel Academy, LA

Family

Some have a lot,
Others not enough.
But when you need them most,
They will always be there.

Yes you fight and disagree,
Sometimes become mean and greedy.
But when you fall,
They will pick you up.

They're your family,
Your closest friends,
The one's that make you, you,
So be thankful for your family,
Because they will get you through.

Hunter Rick, Grade 8
Wren Middle School, SC

My Backyard

Storms make me feel
as though I am alone.
My mind goes blank;
no one is happy.
All you can ask is,
"When will it be over?"
Sky is gray and dark,
not blue and bright
Sounds of the wind
whipping houses.
Watching as shingles
fly across my flooding backyard.
The best thing to do is pray,
There is no moon,
there is no sun
there is only darkness.

Kayra Paul, Grade 7
Leonville Elementary School, LA

Snowfall

Show falling on the window sill
Frosty panes

Fire crackles behind my back
Shadows dance on the wall

Warm socks wrapping
Keeping toes toasty

Baking cookies fill the air
Lights twinkle in the distance

Holiday cheer close at hand
Christmas is coming
The falling snow whispers.

Conner Gallagher, Grade 8
St Andrews Middle School, SC

Gymnastics Competitions

Winning at a gymnastics meet gives me such a tickled feeling,
I'm ready to let out all the excitement which I have been sealing.

The many medals around my neck of silver and gold,
There's a shiver through my body and I'm not even cold.

This shiver is good because this doesn't seem real,
Then I realize I did great and how accomplished I feel.

Taking pictures with my teammates and all of my new medals,
Everybody is so happy as the excitement starts to settle.

After all the fun is over, reality checks in,
Tomorrow it is back, to another hard, workout at the gym!

Miranda Ross, Grade 7
Boyet Jr High School, LA

The Creek

A creek runs by my house.
The rushing waves sound like the church's chimes.
The water is always cool even in the hot, arid, sunny days.
Little fish, plants, and frogs lived in my creek once.
Vacationers came around for the summers and found my creek.
They threw garbage in it and destroyed my animal friend's home.
Now the creek isn't clean or clear, in fact it has no life at all.
Its waters are stilled and the wave's chimes are not hear anymore.
All the nature was taken away from my family and me.
The clean, pure air we once had is no longer clean, but polluted.
I don't live by the creek anymore, but I visit from time to time.
I sit on the big rock and look at it remembering my past.
Thinking of the time I would jump in the water on the tire swing.
I think of feeding my friends, the fish, turtles, and frogs.
One of my biggest treasures got taken away from me forever.
However, my memories of the creek will last a lifetime.

Natalia Gonzalez, Grade 7
Haynes Academy for Advanced Studies, LA

Not Ready to Let Go*

I was left alone, but I can't be alone, yet,
Hard to conceive that she is gone, I couldn't believe,
Lucky thirteen is when she left me, still, I am strong and solemn,
A ghastly sight to see a leaving is what I saw,
It hit me, will she ever come back? I think not,
It made me forlorn to this day, knowing she is safe,
She made me a stronger person, knowing I can handle the pain,
The pain is reducing since the leaving.
The heart, the soul, the mind, all gone,
I need, to set her free, but still, I can't.
The pain is not evanescent to me,
Now, during the serene moment,
I can make her happy,
this is my eulogy to her, and only to her
Still, I am not ready to let go.

Thomas Schmitt, Grade 7
Haynes Academy for Advanced Studies, LA
*Dedicated to my Aunt 02-13-07

This Heart

This heart that was once full of love,
Is now full of hate

Because you took it,
And broke it into pieces

Now it's colder than an iceberg,
And hard as a rock

It's empty like a barrel,
With no feelings what so ever

No matter how hard I try,
I can't find those pieces

Every time I look in the mirror
It's not me anymore;
It's the person you have created.

This heart doesn't want anymore darkness,
This heart just wants to rest in peace.

Yazmin Obregon, Grade 9
Warren Early College High School, NC

Winter

Winter time has surely come
The cold weather makes my hands numb

A white blanket covers the ground
Children play in the wonderful sound

Hunters find it's a good time to go
Their enthusiasm surely shows

The days are short and the nights are long
The air is filled with holiday songs

Christmas is the time of the year
Everyone is nice and sincere

This is my favorite season
And those are all my wonderful reasons

Devin Trulin, Grade 8
Albemarle School, NC

Drama

Being a teen isn't easy.
Sometimes it can make you a little sneezy.
It might make you cry
You might want to curl up and die.
Drama is a part of life.
I suggest you let your drama pass you by.
Shake it off, ball it up and throw it away.
Do as I say and your drama will be gone that day!

Jessica Harris, Grade 8
Carolina International School, NC

Imperfect Girl

I look up in the mirror to notice this girl,
a life of mistakes in a big crazy world
I've hurt the ones who cared most
to get others to care.
Followed tracks to the wrong road,
but turned back into nowhere.
I can only ask for forgiveness and
dig my way as I go,
out into a better path from
inside this tiny hole.
The more I try to make it better
the worse things begin to seem.
My intentions become nightmares
from what started as a dream.
I've figured it all out
I'm an imperfect girl,
but I have to learn nobody's perfect
in an imperfect world.

Briana Searcy, Grade 9
Lamar County Comprehensive High School, GA

Music

Music is something important to me,
I think about songs all the time in my head.
Sometimes when I'm in my bed.
It always makes me happy.
Whether I'm listening to classic rock or heavy metal.
I love listening to Led Zeppelin
Once you hear Robert Plant's voice you know it's them,
It's cool listening to Nirvana
Hearing Kurt Kobain's hard gristled voice.
It's a shame he committed suicide.
I don't know what I would do without music.

Tony Salas, Grade 8
Cathedral School, NC

My Dad

Anthony
Dad of my sister and I.
Brown hair and green eyes.
He loves my mom, my sister, and I.
I love to do things with him,
and he loves to do things with me.
He has a big heart and is open to care.
He is my one and only dad,
and he is also my hero.
He is always there for me,
and I am always there for him.
He is my favorite.
He is my dad.
And I love him.
That's my dad!

Ethan Elliott, Grade 7
Haynes Academy for Advanced Studies, LA

Life

Why can life be so hard
But it can rule
Life is a big test
You meet people you don't like

You meet people who get on your nerve
They lie on
They don't care how you feel
They just want to make your life horrible

You meet people who start things with you
They hurt you
They pick at you
They just dislike you

You meet people that are ugly to you
They are disrespectful to you
They just want you to hurt
They want you to cry the rest of your life

Life is not easy nor hard
Don't let others bring you down
Don't let life scare you
Just live your life

Aliayah Daney, Grade 8
Manning Jr High School, SC

My First Deer Hunt

Deer hunting is an exhilarating antic
Sitting in the frigid cold hiding
Waiting for those colossal animals to run
As I watch the ravishing sunrise, over the hills.

The cool breeze flying through my hair
Sitting in tranquility in a tree or on the ground
Patiently waiting for a cornucopia of deer
Suddenly I hear a thunderous BOOM.

I grab my gun and lay low
By now the sky is a kaleidoscope of hues
A prize winning buck is in sight
I take a deep breath and aim.

My hawk-eye never ceases to fail me
My heart is racing faster than ever
The enormous buck senses my presence
Slowly he moves abroad with the herd nearby.

Chances must be taken in order to not miss opportunities
My grand chance is gone
My auburn heart sank as my opportunity left me
Maybe there will be a next time.

Victoria Forrister, Grade 8
St John Neumann Regional Catholic School, GA

Sandbox

One day a girl was playing in the sand
And there came her sister with a childish demand
She said move aside and let me play
But the girl said you can play another day

Sarah Booth, Grade 8
St Margaret School, LA

Where I'm From

I'm from fish fry's and cookouts
I'm from high top tennis shoes and overalls.
I'm from mud pies and dirty hands and feet
(Which tasted like an off brand cookie).
I'm from the country where the tide gets high,
And the swamps leave a smell that could make you die.
I'm from church on Sundays to serve for the Father above.
I'm from Papa J.D. whom I truly love.
I'm from feeling my mom's soft and tender touch
During a thunderstorm.
She surely did make me feel warm.
I'm from Apple Bottom jeans and boots with the fur
I see everybody looking for sure.
I'm from getting the kids pack at the movies
And enjoying my Fun-Dip which I can't deny.
I'm from being the only child with my mom I love.
Picking flowers that smelled like cleaned dishes.
I'm from myself that has many dreams and makes many wishes.

Mikayla Prioleau, Grade 7
Chapin Middle School, SC

The Power of Reading

Books are a passageway
to get away all day
nothing can stop me
if I want to read not play

A movie I see inside my head
when I stay up reading all night in bed
wrapped in my blanket tightly
in my nice and cozy big shed

In the morning I awake to my dismay
it had snowed all night and day
while kids run out and play in the snow
I jump and say "I can read some more. Hooray!"

I make some hot chocolate
and feed my dog Hobbit
I eat my breakfast quickly
so I can get back to my book *The Closet*

The more you read
it can take you anywhere you want to be
books can really be addicting
so read, read, read and you will feel free

Natalie Villacis, Grade 7
East Millbrook Magnet Middle School, NC

Heaven

What is life?
Is it an imaginative trick our minds play on us?
Is it real?
Is it a cruel fantasy we can't escape from?
Or is it far away in a distant land
that is so complex our minds can't even comprehend it?
It is all of these things and none of these things.
Life is an intricate web we all weave.
It is a story with no end.
It is a broken record that keeps repeating,
Or it might be all in our dreams.
In a world where there is no darkness,
A world where you can be anyone and do anything,
The sky is the limit,
And when our souls are released,
We go to a place where the blind can see,
And the deaf can hear;
We go to a place called Heaven.

Jordan Lunstead, Grade 9
Northgate High School, GA

Being in Love

Being in love is very sincere.
Whether it's with yourself or someone that's not here.
When you are in love you can't fight that feeling.
Your true feelings desire whatever you want are willing.
You are so special like a dream come true.
Every single day I think of you.
You are the one that stole my heart.
I'm hoping that we will never fall apart.
I'm so glad that you are in my life.
Whether it's just a friend or as a wife.
My love for you is like a rose.
One that never dies or has to regrow.
Loving you will always have a place in my heart.
So from the first moment I saw you.
I knew you would be the one for me.
When you looked into my eyes you see love.
I felt my heart melt and I knew at that time I must be in love.
Being in love is the feeling of joy.

DeAnte Lawrence, Grade 9
McKee Jr High School, AL

Blue

Blue is the pretty sky
For the beautiful birds to soar and fly.
Blue is the water that helps the plants grow
Blue is the string that I use to sew.
Blue is the colored pencil that I use in school
Blue is how we feel when we break a school rule.

BLUE is everywhere you go.

Raina Brenen, Grade 7
L E Gable Middle School, SC

Imagine

Imagine what it would be like
If everyone went away,
There would be no sound, no joy in the world,
Only you, what would you say?

What is there to do,
Because there's only the world and you,
Do you cry, or do you run,
But where do you run, who do you run to?

Do you run to the sun if it is light,
Or the moon, if it is night,
But if you cry, there's no one to cry to,
No matter how hard you try.

The people are gone, the liveliness is gone,
You loved the people who went away
And you wish they would come back,
But this time, to stay.

Emily Gurtner, Grade 8
Mount Carmel Academy, LA

Heavenly Tears

Two young people so deeply in love,
a gift that is given from the angels above.

Enclosed in his pocket was a wedding band,
for he was on his way to ask for her hand.

This tragedy occurred all so fast.
The headlights blinded him, the two cars crashed.

Having lived a life of innocence, this was not his fate.
But when they reached the hospital it was already too late.

The proceeding day the drunk driver was put in jail,
and she soon afterward received the ring in the mail.

With nothing left, in sorrow she died,
while above the world, the angels cried.

Amberlyne Gilley, Grade 9
Challenger High School, NC

Live Your Life

Live your life to the highest extent every day,
because you don't know when it will be taken away.
Make people laugh, make people smile,
make it last for awhile.
Jump for joy, breathe fresh air,
live without the slightest care.
Enjoy the now, don't move too fast,
remember you learn from the past.
Take life day by day and God will show you the way,
and when all else fails — pray, pray, pray!

Michaela Snavely, Grade 9
Cape Fear Christian Academy, NC

The Rhythm of the Storm
I feel a sense of urgency
any time of day.
I'm mixing rhymes in my head.
It burns
like a fire in my soul.
My rhymes are valuable to me —
like diamonds.
I can freestyle
any time or place.
It is like God put the words
in my head and
I just make them rhyme.
Be aggressive
like a wild wolf.
Rhymes shoot through my head
like comets.
Storms are a great inspiration to me
because they show you have to be fierce
and make yourself known.
Jaymarlon Stevens, Grade 8
Leonville Elementary School, LA

Fall
Leaves paint the ground,
when fall comes around.
We rake the fallen leaves,
and jump in, no telling when,
then when we're all done,
we start all over again!
Bridgette Hamack, Grade 8
Fannin County Middle School, GA

Mysteries
I peer out over a cavern
Where I look, things live
These things are not to be seen
Not to be seen by humans
Humans who abuse the world
This world that holds more mysteries
Mysteries that outnumber us all
'Us,' people
Evil, self-absorbed people
Only I can see them
'Them,' mysteries
If I had more power
The power to let all
'All,' the world see what I can
The mysteries want to be seen
Want to be heard want to be believed in
You can see them too
Look hard enough and they
'They,' my mysteries
Can be seen and heard by you too
Believe, and one sees
Kristen Bryant, Grade 8
Alexandria Middle Magnet School, LA

A New World
I am a little bird in an egg,
I am warm and safe, but when it hatches I am the exact opposite,
I have a new world as far as the eye can see, I am free,
Gone with the wind! Except in this world I am new,
I am a beginner so things might not go as planned,
But as soon as I learn everything I need to know I will not be a little bird, I will be a
big, beautiful, vibrant bird. And I will spread my wings and fly!
So high in the sky.
Zion Buxton, Grade 7
Hubert Middle School, GA

Dawn of Time
Through the dark shines a light.
It warms the world.
Like sun shining through the night.
This being in the Light was neither boy nor girl.

This being stretches its enlightened finger through the cold and the dark.
Like a piece of paper it separates.
It was a being spreading happiness like the sun at the park.
There came creatures, buildings, streets, and states.

Wind blew and time started.
People stood and played.
Animals spread and parted.
Forever the Light lived and never decayed.

It is true what the Light did.
No matter what they called the Light.
It is what it is.
It is all that shines hope in your darkest of night.
Thomas Bui, Grade 9
McKinley Sr High School, LA

Hilton Head
"Ring Ring"
School's over
We jump and shout
In excitement
It's summer
We pack our bags
We're "hitting the road to Hilton Head"
"Are we there yet?"
The whole ride there
I was imagining
"Sticking my toes into the sandy beach"
Splashing in the cold salty water
Racing to see who could find the coolest shell
The laughter we have when we're burying each other in the sand
The joy of creating a sand castle with my mom
At last
We were there
— Hilton Head
Kendall Morrison, Grade 7
Atlanta Academy, GA

Spectacle

Spectacles are depended things.
The clearest ways to see, it brings.
You could see afar,
possibly even look upon a star.

But is it good,
the capability to see things as they are and should?
Is it better,
to see the stretched out road further?

To me, I say
that it's best either way
Such things in the world
shouldn't be spoiled

But to get to where you want to be,
put on those spectacles to see clearly
Off you go with your head held high;
greet those on your path with a hi!

But have your spectacle case ready
to wear your spectacles quickly,
or to store it the time when you don't want to see
as you descend down the destined road.

Ellen Vang, Grade 9
Challenger High School, NC

Sense the Changes

Listen to the breeze
As it passes right through you
You don't want it to seize
Making you feel lighthearted instead of down in the blue

Watch the blazing sun
For it just might make you grin
Enjoy it before the day is done
So you just might win

Smell the air as the weather changes
No one may know
Until the rain or maybe snow just wages
The weather continues like so

Something is always noticed
Even when you are not focused

Adora Anadi, Grade 7
Boyet Jr High School, LA

Life

It's here,
Then it's gone
Life is what you make it
You only have one chance
So live it right

Shianne Wadsworth, Grade 7
East Millbrook Magnet Middle School, NC

Mixed Emotions...

Why is all this happening to me?
I did nothing to deserve this hatred.
All the lies make me want to scream.
Rip my heart out and scream!
Then I start to laugh.
No way of knowing why.
Just knowing that something can make me feel this way.
But then you think
After all this, I feel all lonely!
How can just this one boy make me feel this way?
I don't care what everyone else thinks!
He is wonderful, sweet, and different.
People say you shouldn't be different.
But, why be the same
When everyone hates you as you are.
Being the same won't make you loved.
I just want to be loved!

Lori Hollingsworth, Grade 8
Lake Middle School, MS

Music

My guitar
Black and wing shaped
Strumming and picking
Purely
Sound

Amplifiers
Small and big
Electronifies and distorts
Loudly
Noisy

Music
Aggressive and soft
Pleases and relaxes
Differently
Instruments

Gage Haas, Grade 7
Haynes Academy for Advanced Studies, LA

The Final Game

It was the last game of the season,
both teams had to win for a reason.
It was the championship game,
and both teams' records were the same.
The score was close all game long,
and the crowd cheered a winning song.
When the game was won,
and the season was done.
Both teams felt like winners,
and they went home and ate pizza dinners.

Zachary Watts, Grade 7
St Thomas More Catholic School, LA

Childhood Tree
It glimmers in the dark
With colors so bright.
It's full of honorable memories
Waiting to be shared
Only one time a year.
The time is near,
So close your eyes
And hear the rustle
Of pine needles blowing
As it rises to its stature.
All the ornaments and ribbons and bows
Coming together on one huge plant
To make my Christmas
Cheerful and bright.
Standing in front of me
With power and might
Is an adorned Christmas tree.
Emily Gomes, Grade 7
Fayette Middle School, GA

The Shell
Gritty sand between your toes,
a crashing thunderous roar,
water playing,
trickling at your feet,
loud merrymaking nearby,
magnificent applause.
As this is all around you,
with every step you take,
you see something,
so neat, so sweet,
it could not be fake.
Like a little bell it rings,
in a quit whisper…
oh how sweet it sings,
a crash and a roar,
echoing around your ear,
as glorious applause.
Caleb Lloyd, Grade 7
Cherokee Christian School, GA

The Things I Love About Winter
The things I love about winter
   Lots of snow,
           Hot cocoa,
  Skates and skis
             Fluffy trees,
Silly hats
             Thermostats
Snowball fights
          Fire lit nights
Out of school
           That's so cool!
Tyrielle Ward, Grade 8
St Peter Claver School, LA

Dancer
A dancer
Leaped
Gracefully
   Across the stage
   Around the audience
   Over her partner
What will she do next?
Anna Katherine Dazzio, Grade 7
Sacred Heart of Jesus School, LA

A Daughter Is Not So Great
A daughter is not
a great thing in hard times
lots of pain and sorrow

Losing family
ones you love
strive to go on
it's hard sometimes

Other times easier
although we miss those we have lost
trying to move on
still trying; strive

A daughter is not
a great thing to be only
but maybe someday it will be
Bre Spry, Grade 7
L E Gable Middle School, SC

Hail to Hail
Hail to hail,
Those jumpy pieces of ice
Bouncing off the windshield
Like a cat, pouncing its prey.
Look up in the sky,
It smacks you in the eye.
Doesn't mean any harm,
It's not their fault.
So close to snow,
But not close enough.
It'll do.
It'll do.
Hail to hail,
Hard chunks of ice,
Pelting against me:
Melting as it splashes on the sidewalk.
Then, its three minutes
of fame are over.
   Gone.
    Done.
     Hail to hail.
Virginia Lambert, Grade 7
Fayette Middle School, GA

Hurricanes
For Hurricane Gustav
I was both scared and amazed.
During the storm
the wind was horrible,
trees got blown down.
Luckily, no one was hurt!
Water covered everything;
I wonder how the others felt.
I could see the fear
in their eyes.
In their voices,
I could hear the worry.
Nights after the storm
were dark and depressing.
God helped us that day.
Kolin Robert, Grade 8
Leonville Elementary School, LA

Volleyball
Volleyball
Jump, hit
Bump, set, spike
A fun sport to play
Volleyball
Gabrielle Landry, Grade 7
Sacred Heart of Jesus School, LA

My BFF
I have a best friend
She got my back no matter what
We go to the same school
Her birthday is Nov. 21
She makes me laugh
When I'm down she makes me smile
We are going to be friends to the end
September Ferrell, Grade 7
Laurin Welborn Middle School, NC

Flying
Once in my room,
I flipped open
my worn music,
played a C on the piano
and I
let the
notes fly out
of my mouth.
It was like
I was swimming
down a river,
with no bumps.
When it was over,
I smiled.
Melissa Pehling, Grade 7
L E Gable Middle School, SC

Black Rose

You're all alone in the dark
Nothing to hear but the beating of your heart
Then one, no two knocks a pound your door
Then all you can hear is your heart beating once more
Your door flies right open to see who has upset you
Then not one but two
Two ghostly figures of a boy and a girl
And it's like the everything even the world…STOPPED
You grab for something to throw at them
Then they disappear in thin air
Nothing behind but a Black Rose.

Brieun Fagan, Grade 8
Brown Middle School, GA

The Nature of Life

This is the rose.
This is the rose my dad wore
The night he went to get married
This is the rose
The night he went to get married, and the bell rang,
This is the rose my dad wore
The night he went to get married, the bell rang,
And he was so happy his rose fell off.
This is the rose my dad wore
The night he went to get married, the bell rang,
He was so happy his rose fell off,
And he grabbed the rose and said, "I will."
This is the rose my dad wore
The day he went to get married,
The bell rang he was so happy his rose fell off,
He grabbed the rose and said, "I will"
And slipped the ring on my mom's finger.
This is the rose that started the big love
And I am happy as much as my dad,
Happy as a laughing clown in a
Purple small car.

Xayasith Xaikhamharn, Grade 7
L E Gable Middle School, SC

Cookie

My dear cookie, oh how you were so good.
I'm happy to say that you tasted how you should.
I remember momma bringing them out,
so I let out that big shout.
I walked slowly around,
trying not to make a sound.
While Momma turned her head,
my face turned red.
I opened my mouth,
and sorry to say…you went south.
Again my dear cookie I didn't mean to,
I do regret eating you.

Brittanie Covington, Grade 8
St Andrews Middle School, SC

Do Drums Like Getting Hit?

Do drums like getting hit?
I guess they don't mind.
They just sit there taking hit after hit.
Sometimes they even break, but still take the hits.
They always produce sound after each hit.
Drums are not a selfish piece of art.

Jared Mitchell, Grade 8
North Iredell Middle School, NC

Georgia Mountains

The stunning mountains stand above,
you only wish that you were a dove.
The sky so blue, the sun so bright,
And then it goes from day to night.
The stars beautify the dark sky,
a light breeze hits your face.
It's that time of year — fall breaks,
the leaves fall lightly from trees.
Yellow, red, green, brown,
beautiful colors hit the ground.
You step outside, the trees provide shade,
flowers dance around each and every day.
The morning starts dark and clear,
the fog lifts, it looks like smoke is near.
Closer and closer soon it's here,
every day goes by so fast.
You only wish it could last,
Georgia mountains are the place.
If you ever just want to see clouds race,
a wonderful day starts here in Georgia.

Ashley Neal, Grade 8
Fannin County Middle School, GA

Our World

The world is a magnificent place;
It rotates at its own pace.

The grass is so green, the sky so blue;
But this is only noticed by few.

The lakes are so clear;
But the pollution I fear.

The air is so fine;
I want it to be mine.

The beauty I love;
Like that of a dove.

Even through the changes of weather;
We all work together.

We're small from outer space;
But Earth is a terrific place.

Daniel Monazah, Grade 7
East Millbrook Magnet Middle School, NC

War and Peace

War is a part of life
It's the nightmares that come every day
It's the pain we have to hear
It's the torture we have to see

Many hate this
Others enjoy hearing this
More people oppose but refuse to speak
They refuse to share

The good will prosper
The world will have peace someday
Wars will be banned
The people of the world will speak up

Peace can come upon us
Peace will come upon us
The world has more good than bad
As one we can and will win

Kayla Castello, Grade 8
Carolina International School, NC

The Lake

Swimming when the
water feels good,

Picking blackberries and
walking in a wood,

Soaring on the tube
and catching air,

Watching the sunset
in a fiery flare.

Eric Monk, Grade 8
Priceville Jr High School, AL

When Gustav Came to Town

During Gustav,
I thought it might flood.
Wind was blowing heavy
while it was passing.
Branches of trees
were falling on people's homes.
No electricity, no water
Raining off and on for days.
The town felt like it was dead
for a couple of days.
But today I feel so lucky.
I hear God calling my name.
The sun is starting to set,
and frogs are jumping on the lily pads.
The weather is changing to winter.
I see angels in my mind.

Taylor McCoy, Grade 7
Leonville Elementary School, LA

The Passing Seasons

Pitter patter, drip drop rain is falling with no signs of stop
Splashing on the flowers' heads sprouting up from their flower beds
What could this mean? What could it bring?
Time for beautiful, beautiful spring

The sun is warm across my skin we'll swim so much we could grow fins
You'll need sun screen, ice cream, and a pool if you want to stay cool
This is a season that couldn't get funner look out world!
It's time for summer!

Leaves dropping here and there floating through the crisp air
The smell of a fireplace starts to linger a cozy glove on each little finger
It's my favorite season of them all.
None other than colorful fall

It starts to turn dark and cold snow is in the forecast told
Jack Frost is doing his job but Christmas is near so no need to sob
This icy time gets your attention centered
Bundle up, it's a long winter

These are the seasons of the year appreciate them while they're here
Each one passes before you know it
We love them all and it's time to show it!

Tori Lambert, Grade 7
Haynes Academy for Advanced Studies, LA

The Midnight Sky

Every night at twelve o'clock midnight I would go outside on the balcony and look at the dark blue sky. I love to go out on the balcony and feel the breeze on my skin and through my hair and pajamas. I make a wish every night I go outside and pretend that I am soaring through the night sky. I imagine that I can fly so high that I can touch the moon and stars. One day I really hope that I can fly and go so high that I can touch the stars and the moon, but as I think about it, what if the stars wish that they can come down here on our surface. As I am starting to feel sleepy, I make one more wish. I wished that the stars could come down on land and maybe we can light up the Earth surface. I put on my star pajamas and I go back into my room and get under the covers and dream about the night sky and the stars.

Danesha Crawford, Grade 7
Hubert Middle School, GA

Rage

I am fire.
I am as unjust as the wrongful imprisonment of an innocent child.
I am what drives vengeance.
I am danger in its worst form.
When I take control I will never let go.
I am the torture of one's inner being.
I am highly explosive and can kill anyone who lights my fuse.
I even thought I can be as powerful as an untamed beast.
I can be control by the self-will, wisdom
and having the right key to unlock the shackles of rage.

Marcus Davis, Grade 9
Georgia Washington Jr High School, AL

Majestic Colors

It happens every year
People don't seem to notice
But when the wind gives a cold chill
The land becomes covered in beautiful colors
Red, gold, brown, and orange
It is truly fascinating
But it lasts only a short time
The wind blows harder
And the climate freezes
All these wonderful colors that floated in the air
Vanish and drop to the ground
Yet we can still admire these amazing colors
Not from the air, but the ground
This is fall

George Robert Mohr, Grade 8
Carolina International School, NC

Song of Myself

Wind sings sweetly, song of myself
Whispers about my full lips
And warbles my lion's mane
Swirls past my dark eyes

Wind sings truly, song of myself
That I am a fierce and proud lion
Murmurs that I sometimes act like the queen of the jungle
Drifts away to harmonize another life

Megan Boyanton, Grade 8
Lake Castle Private School, LA

Answering the Call

God is calling. Can you hear?
He says, "Do not be afraid, for I am near."

Will you listen or choose to ignore?

"Face your fears," he says, "all things
are made possible through me."

Will you listen or choose to ignore?

"But wait," you call,
"what if I stand up only to fall?"
"Then I will lift you up."
"But what about the darkness?
It frightens me."
"I am the eternal light."
"What about the —"
"I am the Almighty Creator and my
plan is to work through you.
I change the world, one person at a time.
And now it's finally your turn."

Will you listen or choose to ignore?

Rebecca Otwell, Grade 8
Fayette Middle School, GA

Remember

Many people lost their lives that day
Not knowing their fate
Many jumped and many fell
Like rain on a cloudy day
Smoke rose to the air while fire burst inside
Some died inside the tower
And some died from the fire
Families lost their loved ones
And many lost friends
Many people survived
Many did not
Some were found
Some were not
The tragic day has brought us all together
That day has started a war
And the war is still raging
Just because of hatred on that day

Khilar Jackson, Grade 7
Hubert Middle School, GA

That Terrible Day

The lives lost
The families' grief
The 3,000 lives,
That couldn't be saved
Flight 93,
Though destination never reached,
Killed one twenty five,
Innocent lives
The day the world came together,
To mourn the loss of human life
The shock and amazement,
That America could be breached
Those who didn't understand what a terrible thing,
Had truly happened on that terrible day

Emily Froelich, Grade 8
Leesville Road Middle School, NC

Love, What Is It?

Love, what is it?
What am I supposed to do?
When it just comes out of the blue?
What is the price I'm supposed to pay?
When, suddenly I ran out of words to say.
Love.
Can it be real?
Can it be true?
But you just act like a fool.
At the end of the day
I'm still stuck on what to say.
But, really?
What is love anyway?

Lariel Simon, Grade 7
Saint James High School, LA

My Dog Mikko

I have a pug and his name is Mikko, and boy is he one neato. He knows lots of tricks like shaking hands, sitting, and staying, but his favorite things to do are just watching TV and laying. His nickname is smushi, because his face is pushed in. He is a nice dog and doesn't bite, so your in good paws when your in his sight.

Jeremy Lester, Grade 8
St Margaret School, LA

Confusion

Confusion is losing your compass on a hike through the woods,
It has the scent of sour milk in a vacant fridge, in a vacant house,
It tastes like eggs right out of the frying pan, scorching your throat, not knowing why you don't slow down,
It feels like watching a fire burning away your favorite childhood home with all of your memories inside,
Your hearing is impaired from the wind howling in your ears,
Not being able to hear your best friend talking to you, right next to you,
Confusion is rain on a sunny day keeping me inside — in the dark.

Kailei Trippi, Grade 8
Leesville Road Middle School, NC

Love Is

Love is
Like the stars at night
The sky is dark
But the stars are bright
Love is
Something you dream of at night
When you dream of love
You see light
When you're with the one you love
Everything feels so right
Love is
The feeling you get when you're with the one who's right for you
Love is
The feeling you get when you're with the one who's true to you
Love is
The feeling you get when you're with the one who tells you that they love you
When you're with the one you love it feels like you want tot fly
When you're with the one you love you want to be with that person whether you live or die

DeLashay Sanner, Grade 9
McKee Jr High School, AL

She Did

As he held her arm off the edge
of the boat he calmed her.
He made her realize she didn't have
to do it.
She said, "I'll never let go."
But when she was pulled
over the railing, she did.
As her fiance became jealous of the arm that was holding her tight, she said, "I'll never let go."
But when she was pulled over the railing, she did.
Now her fiance was gone, and she could focus on her saviour for that one night.
They courted and spent lovely days and evenings together.
Their world began all too soon to sink.
She said, "I'll never let go."
But when she was pulled over the railing, she did.

Destinie Duckworth, Grade 9
New Site High School, MS

Spring

Early on one sunny morn,
There I sat till dawn.
I watched the sun shine bright as gold,
And was staying till day was gone.

The air smelled as fresh rain,
While daisies stretched from the ground.
And then I knew, by the glistening dew,
That spring was truly bound.

For it was on that cool, crisp morn,
My mind soon had a thought.
And I then began to praise the Lord, saying,
"What a glorious day You've brought!"

Isabella Bolter, Grade 7
Proverbs 1:7 Christian Academy, SC

Happiness

Happiness is sitting outside in a meadow
On a breezy autumn day
It smells like the soft scent of grass
While it is carried through the air by the breeze
It tastes like a homemade glass of lemonade
That is freshly squeezed and made to perfection
It feels like diving into a refreshingly icy pool
After being outside on a hot summer's day
It looks like the sun setting in the far off distance
It sounds like a newborn baby laughing
The diversities and cultures of the world are the joy in my life

Brian Campoli, Grade 8
Leesville Road Middle School, NC

Ponder

I grew up with it, but it's not
Wrong or rejectable for that.
Whoever had the shirt saying how little I hold
Cannot make me over into what I already am,
Still cannot set me against it.
They and I may stand forever
Regardless of how much I inch toward them,
Without a thought for the answers I always find,
The bridges I know I need to build.
I remember the way the words felt when I first
Gathered the courage to recite them,
The way my heart felt when I knew what they meant.
I tremble now too, with their weight.
And I tremble again as the music
Dangles my faith over a fire and a flood,
It is not a thing you can ignore.
With racing pulse I try the words on my lips,
The melody in my throat.
It feels good. It feels right.

Dakota Brady, Grade 8
Parkton Elementary School, NC

Snowflakes

Floating in the winter air
The snowflakes fall gently as I stare
They become a white cover for the yellow grass
I wish this moment would never pass
They glide
They float
They fall
They land
They seem to call me to stand
Outside in the cold in the snow
I lose all other thoughts
I was thinking about before
The snowflakes falling
Are mesmerizing
Are gently landing
Could make me fall asleep
As they creep
Into my thoughts
As they fall and land
As they cover the yellow grass
I wish this moment would never pass

Elisabeth Noblet, Grade 7
St Mary's School, SC

Pink

The color of beauty and design.
Pink, the color that is painted in my mind.

I see pink flowers in the Spring
That makes me want to sing.

Pink the color in the morning, in the sky.
It is so beautiful, I cannot lie.

Asia Suber, Grade 7
L E Gable Middle School, SC

Weather

A tornado
Furious and dangerous
Gasping and swirling
Swiftly
Cyclone

The wind
Cold and elusive
Rushing and gliding
Alone
Torrents

The cloud
Billowy and mellow
Floats and hides
Away
Mist

Jeb Kirn, Grade 7
Haynes Academy for Advanced Studies, LA

Love?
LOVE?
What is it?
An emotion
A feeling
Or just an expression

LOVE?
Makes you believe
It makes you wonder
Who is?
My love

LOVE?
Is one of the best things in the world
And one of the worst
Don't let it spoil your life
Nathaniel Tilque, Grade 7
Carolina International School, NC

Hurricanes
When the water hit it was devastating.
The wind hit you like a sheet of ice.
There wasn't a cloud in the sky.
All animals fled for safety.
Trees swaying from side to side.
Bridges and houses are destroyed.
All I thought about is why?
Water is everywhere
People picking up branches and debris
All we could do is pray to God
Hoping it will be okay.
Megan Lanclos, Grade 8
Leonville Elementary School, LA

Politics
It's all the same.
No one's to blame.
The issues don't matter to some.
It's all about the fame.
Mason Veillon, Grade 8
St Margaret School, LA

Shattered Glass
The shard in my side tears me apart.
Wearing me down,
Feeling the numbness in my hands,
Seeing the pieces on the floor,
Seeing the emptiness up in the sky.
What used to be there was an object,
What lies beyond is up to you.
Sharp sparkling points all staring at you,
Showing you what used to be,
The understanding,
And the spirit within me.
Michelle Rucker, Grade 8
Valley Point Middle School, GA

The Sweetest Girl
What is the sweetest girl to me?
She isn't eye candy for the world to see.
She wouldn't break your heart if she had the key.
Her love for you is like a tree.
It grows and grows never reaching a peak.
She is the only one you think about before you lay down to sleep.
The image of her face in your heart you keep.
When you see her she makes your knees grow weak.
She is very independent she can stand on her own two feet.
She is a girl that would make you forget all others.
She is a girl that would be your mother.
She is a girl that would never lie to you.
And if something's wrong she would come and cry to you.
This girl can't be found in an hour.
She is as strong as a lion,
But is as delicate as a flower.
She is your universe.
She is your world.
Now that is my idea of the sweetest girl!
Brendon Brown, Grade 9
McKee Jr High School, AL

Cancer (My Life)*
When I woke to a cry of "no."
So little so frail. I didn't know till I got there.
They drew blood and did tests. They wouldn't let me rest.
I cried, I screamed, I bit. They knew me as the one who throws the fits.
They gave me a drug called chemo. That they said would cure the AML.
They said it was rare I didn't think anyone cared. I started to lose all my hair.
Strangers would stare. I made friends that were at the hospital too.
My friend Tory died Jamie, Candas, and Katie did too.
The tender age of 5 I had radiation and a bone marrow transplant.
I couldn't go outside. I asked the doc.
I thought what a bummer after a transplant.
I guess I should thank God for letting me live.
Giving me good health, and just enough wealth.
It may sound rough, but you have to be tough. It made me special.
I still wish I had not been told, "It's CANCER," but then I wouldn't be ME!
Nichole Mathus, Grade 7
St George Middle School, SC
**Based on my real-life experience.*

You Are Awesome
It amazes me how Your power works in my life every day.
Your inspiring love grows on me every time I pray.
In Your abiding love, You show me all new things,
With all my faith in You, I am prepared for whatever life brings.
I close my eyes, wake the next morning, and know that You are blessing me again.
You know me well and always have a ear to lend.
With my back turned on You, somehow You still bless me.
I begin taking the wrong path when You created a light for me to see.
You never stopped loving me and I know You never will.
The least I can do is live for You because You've already paid the bill.
Chalice Pack, Grade 9
Southside Christian Schools, SC

Skating

A skateboard
    addicting and fun
olling and flipping
    dangerously
Wood

A ramp
    sloping and curving
stalling and airing
    bravely
Concrete

A rail
    speed and balance
sliding and grinding
    haphazardly
Metal

Zachary Israel, Grade 7
Haynes Academy for Advanced Studies, LA

Sculptor

You brighten my dull, colorless life with shades of yellow.
When you smile, your face lights up like golden sunshine.
The way your nose wrinkles and your eyes sparkle
Fill me with deep, orangey-yellow warmth like glowing coals.
Your contagious laughter glitters
Like twenty-four carat gold flakes floating in water.
No matter how bad I feel, even when I am as numb as a stone,
I watch you laughing, and it builds inside of me until I smile,
And then laughter erupts from deep inside of me
Like bright yellow sparks from a sculptor's chisel.

John Marshall Diffey, Grade 8
Margaret Green Jr High School, MS

My Boo

His brown eyes brighten my day
He helps me through my bad ways
His shaggy hair glowing in the sun
He makes my day loads of fun

He touches my heart
He's just too smart
The cutest smile I've ever seen
I know he would never be mean

As the day ends, we set apart
I feel the beating in my heart
The sweet scent of his breath
Now we both got to jet

He brushes his cheek against mine
It makes me feel just fine
Our love is unbreakable
We are always lovable

Alisha Chowdhury, Grade 7
Haynes Academy for Advanced Studies, LA

Fall

Celebrate because fall is here!
There're many great things to do in fall
It is the greatest season after all
Goodbye swimsuit, hello sweater
Fall is near and it can't get any better
Nothing is better than the changing of leaves
Fall is awesome, that's what I believe
Not as cold as winter, not as hot as summer
When fall is gone, it would be a bummer
The only thing I don't like about fall
It feels like the shortest season of all.

Dustin Guillory, Grade 8
St Margaret School, LA

Lovely Christmas

We're going to have a lovely Christmas
Oh what fun it'll be
With toys and gifts and Christmas lists
It seems so sweet to me

We're going to have a lovely Christmas
Just see for yourself
With cakes and hams and Christmas jams
You wouldn't want to be someplace else

We're going to have a lovely Christmas
Come and join along
With family and friends and video cams
And Christmas sing-along-songs

We're going to have a lovely Christmas
Have some pleasure with me
With laughs and jokes and a lot of folks
It's going to be a treat

We're going to have a lovely Christmas
I don't want it to end
With presents in sight and Christmas delight
I want all joy to begin

Ashantia Pittman, Grade 9
McKee Jr High School, AL

The World on Our Shoulders

The world is on our shoulders
We need to take charge of it
We have all the water we will ever have
One atmosphere is all we got
Whatever you do makes a difference
Whatever you say changes everything
Now's the time to act, waiting won't help
Have faith, and hope and
Remember, the world is on our shoulders

Bailey Eichman, Grade 7
Carolina International School, NC

Night and Day
The day is a time to play.
The children are all laughing.
The birds and the bees are all buzzing.
What a beautiful day.

The night is a time to rest.
The children are all sleeping.
The grasshoppers are humming.
It's time to get some rest.
Ashley Ramirez, Grade 7
Lake Castle Private School, LA

Party
We are out of time!
I heard the chime!

He will be here soon!
The man on the moon!

Soon we will celebrate!
There is no time to decorate!

Forget the party!
He might be tardy!

Please don't hurry!
It makes me worry!

All this rhyme!
We really have run out of time!
Kathryn Meyers, Grade 7
Sacred Heart of Jesus School, LA

Hurricanes
I hate hurricanes
They are very destructive
They show no mercy
Raven Handy, Grade 7
Opelousas Jr High School, LA

Ode to Mom
Mom, the person
that helped me to my feet.
The person who
catches me when I fall.
The one who
held my hand for a while
and my heart forever.
The one who
stands by me through the
bad and the good.
The only one
who told me I could.
Elisabeth Pagan, Grade 7
Fayette Middle School, GA

Georgia
The simple elegance of a single tree,
the beaming sun,
the glowing leaves,
and to hear their rattling song.
The beauty caresses my star struck eye
as I grasp the beaming sun,
the wayward air,
the entrancing smell of pine.
A mountain arise in my gleaming eye,
as I behold a majesty of God,
the swiftest stream seldom gleam…
As it sings a beautiful song.
Nick Riley, Grade 8
Fannin County Middle School, GA

Pain Is and Shows Love
Pain is like love
you always get hurt,
Pain is like fear,
leaving the body,
Pain feels wondrous
at times, but then
Pain feels like torment,
Pain creates distress,
it reveals love,
Pain gives agony,
Pain leaves a wound,
then when the day ends
there is grief for
the affection
you once showed to
the one you ignored.
Dustin Royal, Grade 9
North Wilkes High School, NC

All to Myself
Yes, I say as Sean leaves
The house all to myself
As I run inside
Jumping and screaming
I thought to myself
That this is what life really feels like
I stop
I listen
I wonder
I'm bored
I realize that I miss him
And it is not the same without him
I stop
I listen
I wonder
What do I do
Without Sean?
Ian Moran, Grade 7
Atlanta Academy, GA

Waves
Huge ferocious beauty,
Yet in their beauty lies a rage,
We'll tell all you and me,
Of how the sea got so angry.
Not at you nor at me,
But at all humanity.
We've polluted hurt and killed,
In that poor poor innocent sea,
All that pollution and animal murder,
I don't wish to see.
Many don't want to believe,
Including me,
That it's we,
Killing the sea,
But we must face facts,
And it's true,
So let's stop poaching and pollution,
Me and you.
Meghan Blanton, Grade 7
Hornbeck School, LA

I Am Yours
My God I will praise Thee.
I will tell the devil to flee.
I will not take Thy name in vain.
I will keep myself sane.
I'll live my life for You.
Just tell me what to do.
Tell me when, I'll start now.
Just tell me how.
I'll go anywhere, here, there.
Just tell me where.
God I am Yours,
Use me for Your will and Your glory.
Emilee Piersanti, Grade 8
Sandhills Middle School, SC

A Colt
The colt stands in the field,
Small and lanky.
Its youth showing,
Proudly handsome.
Its timid yet still proud stance.
The colt runs in the wind
Wild and free spirited.
He has no boundaries,
No cares, no worries,
And much to learn
From the older distinguished stallions.
The colt trots, runs, and shakes his head
In hopes of standing out in the crowd.
He jumps over the fence
To find himself in a world of unknown.
Kylie Easterlin, Grade 7
L E Gable Middle School, SC

High Merit Poems – Grades 7, 8 and 9

Riding Four Wheelers
Riding four wheelers is one of the best things ever,
with the wind blowing in your face.
It makes you feel as free as a bird,
when you're in the open space.

Going through the woods is so much fun,
you can hear the leaves going crunch crunch crunch
under your wheels.
Then you realize you need to go,
remember you can come back another day though.

Dannica Holloway, Grade 8
Fannin County Middle School, GA

What Lies Within
The walls of My Book
Keep things back
Like a cage keeps a raging lion back
Many stories good and bad
Anger brewing like a wild fire
Calmness and understanding
Like a cool wind just rolling on into eternity

Feelings no one has ever felt, But me
Jokes that give you cramps from laughing so hard
Thing I have kept folded into the veins of my heart
Honesty like no other
Experiences
That takes you to the depths of my heart
Secrets
Woven into the string of my life

As daring as jumping off Mt. Everest
And strong enough to survive the fall
Beyond the walls of My Book
Untold secrets and journeys just waiting…
To spill out like water from an overflown lake
The Key to the gates of My Life…that only I have seen

Kara Matassino, Grade 8
Atlanta Academy, GA

Storms
Storms make me feel upset.
Bolts of lightning strike my house.
It's very dark outside.
The clouds are gray and dark.
Wind blows the flowers outside by my house.
There is no sun outside.
Everyone says it is 3:00 in the morning.
I'm in my house looking outside the window.
In the air birds are flying around.
My house is fine
and there is no damage done to it.

Taylor Nezat, Grade 7
Leonville Elementary School, LA

The Little Flower
Where were you when I was lost and lonely?
Where were you when I was fading away so slowly?

I was cold and sad, and nobody knew.
Until I looked around one day and found a little
flower that grew.

I thought of all the good things in life.
And I did not think of all the things that I despise.

I thought of my friends and family.
I turned my day around all by myself.

But where were you?
Not with me!

Jordan Skinner, Grade 7
Cathedral School, NC

A Thankful Time of Year
Thanksgiving is the time of year
That all worries fade away.
Families meet for a meal of plenty.
Hugs and kisses are seen everywhere,
Being given by both young and old.
People pray for all their blessings
Just before they eat.
So as you look at orange, red, yellow leaves,
Be thankful for all you have,
And let God know how thankful you are.

Lauren Dillard, Grade 8
Magnolia Springs Baptist Academy, AL

Perfect World
Our natural world is beautiful
With all we ever need to live
And thrive
But with that, we take advantage
We abuse and profane its generous reserves
We defile the air, water, earth
And do little to give back to it
To give thanks for our survival
And yet, Earth remains indulgent
Allowing us to continue
Our selfish misuse of our only home
But at the same time
We have a world where mankind is virtuous
Living with integrity and honesty
Existing for others as much as themselves
So no matter how much
We want to change the world for the better
We can't
So we accept it
Our already…
Perfect world

Sophie Nguyen, Grade 9
Ardrey Kell High School, NC

Spring
Spring comes once a year
It is very colorful
Springs makes me happy
DaKayla Washington, Grade 7
Opelousas Jr High School, LA

Cats/Dogs
Cats
Soft, tiny
Cuddling, licking, chasing
Mice, string, bones, tricks
Playing, fetching, barking
Friendly, loyal
Dogs
Laycee Mercer, Grade 8
Appling County Middle School, GA

Butterflies
Butterflies
Pretty, colorful
Flying, catching, watching
Pretty as a picture
Life
Sydney Cook, Grade 7
L E Gable Middle School, SC

No More Deaths…Please
Why is there death in the world
can't we all stay here together forever
I want no more death…please

Two grandparents gone never will I see
one great-grandparent I never saw
an aunt that I want to know more about
I just want no more death…please

A sister that has passed away,
but will I die to see her?
I want to stay with my family
I want no more death…Oh! Lord please!
Deja Haywood, Grade 7
L E Gable Middle School, SC

Rubber Bands
How do rubber bands
Help to get your teeth straight?
I guess they pull them together
Like bungee chords on a trailer
Keeping them snug and perfect
Eliminating gaps and overlaps
Each little band, an angel from a bag
To help you have
The straightest, most beautiful teeth
So you can show that smile!!
Emily Jones, Grade 8
North Iredell Middle School, NC

Lemonade and Sunshine
God is my lemonade and sunshine,
Knowing I have had someone to love me before I knew myself
And family is going to love me no matter what
is the best feeling in the world.
My little sister is my lemonade and sunshine,
just to play with her hear her laugh and see her smile makes my day.
My mom and dad is my lemonade and sunshine,
Knowing I am loved by them is the warmest feeling in the world.
My grandma is my lemonade and sunshine,
She is there when I need anything and her food is the best in the world.
My best friend is my lemonade and sunshine,
She is there to talk to every time I have a problem
And she never tells me to do anything wrong.
My family is my lemonade and sunshine,
Knowing a group of people love me no matter what relaxes my worries.
Erika Harris, Grade 9
Georgia Washington Jr High School, AL

Autumn
Autumn wind blows throughout the air,
Bringing bright smiles to everyone.
It is time to put up all of your summer clothes,
Because autumn brings a shiver to your body,
So add warm pants and jackets to your fall wardrobe,
Children play in the bright colored leaves
As their family takes many pictures of them.
Round orange pumpkins are being picked at the pumpkin patch,
By many eager families to carve their pumpkin,
Thanksgiving meals are being prepared
The smell of pumpkin pie fills the kitchen air
Families are all gathered at the kitchen table,
Saying their prayers,
Thanking God for all of their wonderful food.
Firewood is being placed in the fireplace,
And hot smoke begins to fill the cold air.
Autumn is a time of joy,
And is always a remembered season, but the season does not last forever,
So when all of the bright, multicolored leaves turn to gray,
The wonderful season of winter is soon on its way.
Olivia Rodriguez, Grade 8
Mount Carmel Academy, LA

Seasons
Seasons come and seasons go
beginning with a winter snow.
Furry animals sleeping in their den
waiting for winter's end.
Water falling that's just springs shower soon to follow fields of flowers.
The air is hotter and the grass is green summer is the newest scene.
Children going back to school
weather getting really cool.
Leaves are changing orange, brown, and red. Making up the forests bed.
Seasons come and seasons go.
Joey Turberville, Grade 8
Priceville Jr High School, AL

A Season of Wonder

Scarlet, amber, bright yellow, brilliant orange,
The hues of autumn foliage,
Clinging to the tree ever tightly.
But as the wind blows,
They fall kaleidoscopically to the ground.

The wind moves effervescently.
It rollicks through the trees.
Howling, it brings the cold.
Pausing briefly, the breeze dies down.
Letting the sun shine warmly on the earth.

Turning pluvial, the days get darker.
Bringing rain, the clouds close in.
For days, it feels like the water will never stop pouring,
Until one day there is nothing but dew.
With this, the world turns cooler, welcoming winter.

The season of change, the season of color,
Leaves turning to breathtaking shades,
Rain coming and going throughout this time of year,
Blustering wind never seeming to cease blowing.
We are caught up in a season of wonder.

Jennifer Ashenfelter, Grade 8
St John Neumann Regional Catholic School, GA

First Time Hunting

First time hunting was a blast,
Didn't know a thing.
I was only eight years old,
Was hunting with a twenty-two caliber rifle.
Was with my dad.
Went to Uncle Ray's to hunt.
Got told big deer roamed there.
It was so peaceful in the woods,
Birds were singing.
Even though seen no deer, I loved hunting.
From eight to now,
I hunt every year.
Haven't killed a deer, yet!

Colby Whitley, Grade 9
North Wilkes High School, NC

A Snowy Day

Falling from the heavens like white pixie dust,
Snow is a weather in which playing is a must.
Though, long it doesn't last,
In it I'll have a blast.
Even if it's cold and wet,
It's a day I'll never forget.
Snow makes me feel extremely silly,
Especially when I'm cold and chilly.
Snow, oh cheerful snow,
Please don't ever go.

Alix Griffin, Grade 7
St Mary's School, SC

Eyelids Block the Dark

The warmth of a perfect sun
Carefully positioned so I'm surrounded
Trapped in my lovely bubble
But my setting will leave some dumbfounded

This summer scene
And bright noon sky
Is truly in a room at night
Warm and cozy in the bed where I lie

Extra blankets kick out the cold
Eyelids block the dark
Music outshines every competing sound
Maybe sung by a nearby lark

Every muscle relaxed
Amazingly content
To live in my midnight noon
My reality happily bent

I fall asleep gently
A smile plays at the edge of my lips
Where will I fly next,
On my wintry summer trips?

Katie Myers, Grade 8
Westchester Country Day School, NC

Last Kids in New York

I walked down the snow covered streets
Like heaven on Earth
My black hair flowing through the wind
Snowflakes getting caught in it

Tyson walks besides me
Blue eyes like the sky
Skin pale like snow
His hair black, flowing back

We walked through the streets of New York
No one here in our minds
Just us,
Alone

I closed my eyes
Dreamed of the stars in the sky
I lift my head
And a snowflake kissed my brow
He kissed my brow

Even with people all around us
We felt like
The only kids in New York

Tatiana Brown, Grade 7
East Millbrook Magnet Middle School, NC

Creature

Once upon a time my dear child,
There was a creature, nameless to all,
And never once felt any emotion,
He never seemed to care, not one little bit.

Hush now child, the story is not over.
He had no family, only dolls,
He capered with them night and day,
They were dolls of everyone in the city,
Almost like voodoo dolls, except one,
Who he couldn't take control of.

Sit still dear, you will want to hear the rest.
He kept one doll close to him, he called the doll Sally,
No one knew why he kept this doll, hidden from plain sight,
But some say it was the doll, of the woman he loved dearly,
But she was murdered, he was heartbroken.

Be quiet, the end is near.
He still lives alone, and many say you can still hear his moans of sadness,
And he only comes down on Halloween, and I must say he isn't a creature at all,
But a man, a very handsome man, who steals the hearts of many, but only one was lucky.
Ah, I can still remember his voice, but it was for the best…

Dana Varden, Grade 8
Eclectic Middle School, AL

A Day in the Woods

There I was, sitting in my deer stand. I could feel the cold wind blowing in my face, I looked down to check my gun, but my glove slipped out if my hands. I didn't notice in the distance that there was a buck, a 6 pointer, just standing there, while I got my gun up to get ready to shoot. But as I was trying to get my gun up, the big buck noticed me in his point of view. I saw him look up and I tried standing still as could be. As he looked back down, I did a big phew and could see my cold breath coming out. The wind blew my breath back at my face. As I tried once more to get my gun ready, I heard a gun shot about two miles away. I looked up at the buck but he had already left my food plot. I called my dad on the radio, and told him the whole story. He said he was coming to get me. I got my things together, and as he pulled up, I climbed down the deer stand, and got into the truck.

Carolina Berryhill, Grade 8
Armstrong Middle School, MS

The Words I Learned from My Mother

I've known her for so long, she's always a part of me. She reminds me of a song, sang in harmony.
Her beat is constant, like a heart that pumps so strong. The tune is sometimes sweet and exciting like a gong…
She helps me in my struggles, but like a steady song…she never fails to find the rhythm, even in things I've done wrong.
She listened very carefully…to the words I failed to say…unknowingly to me, she would help me find my way.
I've asked myself this question many times, what is love?
My mother stated; it's in a song that said, "It fits like a hand in a glove…"
So I asked her, what is love? I want to understand…and she said to me quietly, as she took my hand…
She said, LOVE is like a quiet storm, rolling across the sea. It hits the shores raging…it can bend the strongest tree.
Love helps but never hurts; it can heal the deepest wounds. It flows like silk, and it's soft as a sweet tune.
It never fails to be there, and you will surely find…it's the first thing you might run to, and the last thing you leave behind.
Love is the foundation that holds you up, and also has your back.
It keeps you strong, keeps you focused and always catches your slack…
Love is deep, warm and not of madness…it is a happy feeling; that sometimes produces sadness.
These words I live by and take forward in life as no other. I will be blessed one day, to have love in my life…
Just like I learned from my mother.

Cody Chalk, Grade 9
McKee Jr High School, AL

Leaves of the Trees

I wonder if they like being leaves?
The sound of the crisp crunches as we walk across them
Drifts of cold wind catch them and make them fly
There they go across the fall sky
Wondering where they will land
Will it be on a rock
Or on the nice soft grass?
Can't wait to see them again next year.

Daniel Smith, Grade 8
North Iredell Middle School, NC

Ode to the Road

In everyone's life there is a road
A road with twists and turns.
A road that has divides
and chances for us to learn.
The road we take is not always marked
and the paths not always clear.
What is certain about our road
is it divides between chance and fear.
If we take the road of chance,
we may try and fail
but if we take the road of fear
there is no chance to prevail.
Chances are scary and may cost us much
but if we fear to try
we may never succeed in life
And in failure doomed to die.

Jared Frye, Grade 9
Avery County High School, NC

To Matt

Like a dream have gone
the last seven months.
Memories in photo books,
winking glances and loving looks.
Kisses so light and hugs so strong,
have we really been in love that long?
You tell me that I'm your girl
the love of your life, your whole world.
Watching movies, singin' along,
to a classic love story song.
Talkin' on the phone way too late,
laughin' about our first date.

I told my daddy when I was young,
I'd marry a cowboy when I was grown.
Not quite eighteen, but I'm real sure.
You ride, you shoot, you wear muddy boots
you hold onto your pride and roots.
Things are exactly as they seem —
Matt, you're the cowboy of my childhood dreams.

Darian Dantzler, Grade 9
Clarendon Hall School, SC

Hurricanes

Hurricanes large and small
causing trouble as the trees fall.
Shelters filled with homeless and worried people.
People so worried they're up with the sun
and still awake as it rises again.
Homes are shaking as bodies are aching.
No air nor lights
it feels like going back in time.
In stores fighting
over macaroni and baloney
Homes flooded and
bodies floating ashore
Earth looking as if it's at the end of its course
When this journey ends,
people come back to their home
and notice everything's gone.
Tears running down their cheeks
as they pray for help from up above.
Towns empty and off the map,
but still they thank God for keeping us safe.

Dalaina Johnson, Grade 8
Leonville Elementary School, LA

Hurricane

Waves of destruction crashing 'round.
Pieces of our lives littering the ground.
Tears of the people mixing with the river.
The wind blows and the trees shiver.
Loved ones lost; hearts are broken.
People gather; no words can be spoken.
Pets left out in the cold.
Cars float down the road.
Water rushing overhead.
Once again our town is dead.

Katy Credeur, Grade 8
Bishop Noland Episcopal Day School, LA

Take Me to Your Dreams

Hold me in your arms
Take me away in your dreams
Where I can spread my wings
Where my heart won't be ripped at the seams
Take me to a place where a broken heart can mend
Where my faith won't bend
I want to dream
With just you and me
Can you show me a place?
Where reality is gone
Where time is at a slow pace
This is where all my feelings are real
Can you promise to love?
That's the deal
Please don't rip my heart at the seams
Just take me to your dreams

Mabel Soe, Grade 8
First Flight Middle School, NC

Time

Oh no I'm late!
Oh no. Don't even start.
What is time to you any ways?
A boundary between certain seconds?

No.
Time is nothing to me.
So what is it to you?
Is it a clock?
Is it a watch?
Is it important?

No?
Then stop complaining.
Relax a little.
Stop being so bunched up
In a certain schedule.
Come on, live a life.
Without boundaries.
Have fun.
And relax.

Moriah Rae Goodman, Grade 8
Carolina International School, NC

Latina

Many people think family means
having the same blood,
or they are the ones that adopted you.

For us, Hispanics, family means
everyone who we care about.
Sure, we can be a little bad,
but still, we have big hearts!

I am a Latina,
and I care for many people —
because they are part of my family!

Kenia L. Cruz, Grade 9
Leesville Road High School, NC

Young Love

Being in love feels so right,
I just want to be held tight,
Love makes me do crazy things,
It makes me feel like I have wings,
I stay up on the phone so late,
Talking with my soul mate,
I get feelings deep inside,
Some so strong, that I can't hide,
I laugh and smile all day long,
It feels like there is nothing wrong,
I've changed the way I am and act,
I'm in love and that's a fact!

Hialeah Navarro, Grade 8
Dillard Drive Middle School, NC

Roller Coaster

When you drop
You hear a pop
As people scream
You see a beam
A flash of white light
Is the people's last sight
As they go through a tunnel
That looks like a funnel
Now we have to take a flight
With the kids a-fright

Logan Hearn, Grade 7
St Mary's School, SC

Thanksgiving

Thanksgiving
It's that time of year
Where you hear
The children's laughter
And smell the
Homemade pumpkin pie
My grandma's pie
Tastes like silk
On your tongue
It's the time of year
Where everyone's joyful
And the turkey
Looks so perfect
That it's almost like it's not real
And you just want to
Gobble down the mashed potatoes
They feel fluffy and warm
In your mouth
It's my favorite time of year
Because everybody's
Peaceful and thankful.

Megan Munson, Grade 7
First Flight Middle School, NC

A Friend

A friend is like a flower
All different and unique
They come in many sizes
Tall, short, large, and petite.

A friend is like a tree
Standing tall and strong
They shelter and protect you
And keep you from harm.

A friend is like the wind
They come and they go
But you know in your heart
They will never cease to show.

Lauren Fogarty, Grade 8
Mount Carmel Academy, LA

The Beat of Nature

The sway of trees gets me going
The droplets of water give me a beat
As the autumn leaves start to fall
They crunch beneath my feet

The clouds come together
Old man winter comes to town
He lays down a giant white blanket
There is not a single frown

The sun wakes back up again
Shining his warming rays
Flowers start to sprout
With the sound of blue jays

The sky's on fire
There is no shade at all
You thirst for some water
As you rest against a wall

Seasons go around in loops
Like repeated notes in a measure
But we just go with the flow
Taking in all the pleasure

Taylor Hill, Grade 8
Dillard Drive Middle School, NC

The Stranger at the Beach

I throw a frisbee at the beach,
Over my head and out of reach,
Then lands far away.
A stranger stands in my way

The stranger happens to be cute.
Now, suddenly, I am struck mute.
So there I stand
All tongue tied
Nothing to say.
Now she is walking away.
Ok bye

Hayden Prentice, Grade 8
Priceville Jr High School, AL

Just Being Me

I can't help myself
I just love being me
Yes, I'm messy and loud
And a bit annoying,
But I can't help it.
I'm just being me.
C'mon,
You know you love me
Just the way I am.

Patrick Hampton, Grade 7
L E Gable Middle School, SC

Saturday Night in Baton Rouge

Saturday night in Baton Rouge,
A day when football reigns,
The day is full of grilling and fun,
But at night the stadium fills,
And the crowd is ready to watch LSU win,
They cheer and chant their team to victory,
Because it's what they love,
That's what a Saturday night is like,
In Baton Rouge.

L. Brennan Messina, Grade 7
St Thomas More Catholic School, LA

The City

Tall buildings standing high
Look like they could reach the night sky

Bright lights are a Milky Way
So many shades of black and gray

Many people are walking in the street
All I can see is their fast feet

Loud honking horns from taxi cabs
And people on their cell phones going blab, blab, blab

Flashing police cars rushing by
They look like comets in the night sky

The city is a very busy place
It can be hard to keep up with the pace

Gabriela Christian, Grade 7
St Francis Xavier School, AL

9-11

We will never forget the day we were struck.
Some learned of the news by the sound of a fire truck.

Suddenly two planes in a building had crashed.
People were running in a hurry and mad dash.

The buildings began to fall and tumble.
The noise was so loud, just a huge rumble.

The impact was heard from miles away.
While the ashes burned throughout the day.

The search for people lasted hours and hours.
Scattering through the streets and broken towers.

People boarded the planes jeopardizing their life.
Although they did not know they would have died by night.

No one will ever forget that sad day.
Still on September 11th, America still prays.

Taylor Eanes, Grade 7
Carolina International School, NC

Love Words

The words you say every day
The words that take my breath away
The words that I just can't stand
The words that give me a chance

"I love you" that's what you seem to say
"I love you" you say every day
"I love you" it just won't stop
"I love you" keeps ringing in my head on and on.

Kimberly Ponce, Grade 7
Stokes Elementary School, NC

I Am Me She Is She

I am me she is she.
Everyone says they see her in me.
She is Kim.
I am Bobbie Jean.

I am me she is she.
She is twenty-two.
I am fifteen.
See different ages.

I am me she is she.
They see her face in mine.
They see her actions in me.
They say I'll be her when I grow up.

I am me she is she.
They call me by her name.
They mix me up with her.
I hear hey Kim or what's up Kim

I am me she is she.
I hate being mixed up with her.
She is her own person and so am I.
But hey for the last time I am me and she is she.

Bobbie Jean Gavigan, Grade 9
Warren Early College High School, NC

Bad Weather

Storms make me feel alone.
Rain crashes against my window.
Trees crash and fall to the ground.
Houses topple over.
The outside looks like the end of the world.
Sunlight is nowhere to be found.
God watches over me.
Animals cannot escape the strong winds.
Water floods in as the door to the house opens.
Gravel from the sidewalk has been shot in the air.
It looks like daytime turns into night.

Tyler Hammond, Grade 7
Leonville Elementary School, LA

My Hero
Christy
Mother of two boys and one girl
Wife of Jerry Porrovecchio
Hazel eyes and brown hair
Loves to shop
And share
She always has a heart
Open to care
But beware
If she gives you the stare
Mom is rare
Like my grandpa with hair
She's my one and only
Top priority
My mom, friend, and hero.

Alexis Rizzo, Grade 7
Haynes Academy for Advanced Studies, LA

The Beach
The smell of the salty sea
The gently rolling waves
Falling on the soft sand
The sun, shining down

The laughter of children playing in the sand
The sound of a bouncing volleyball
The delicious smell of a cookout
The sun, shining down

The sight of surfers, body boarders, and skimmers
As far as the eye can see
People swimming, floating, playing
In the endless deep blue sea

The sun is slowly setting,
The night about to begin
Casting shadows on
The darkening beach

Adam Russotto, Grade 7
First Flight Middle School, NC

Live Life
You live your life every day
So live it at the fullest
'Cause you'll never get a day back
So live your life the best you can
What you did is already done
You can't go back and change it
So forget it, and just stay in the present
Cause the future hasn't come so just relax a little
Live in the moment, and enjoy it
Cause that's what you'll look back on and remember

Daisy Gutierrez, Grade 8
Piney Grove Middle School, GA

Christmas
Watching the snow
Fall down on the ground,
Looking at the star
On top of the tree.
Giving out presents for us
To share and decorating the
Christmas tree we set up
To show we care.
Outside the snow falls down.
Kids run and jump
For happiness as they make
Snow angels on the ground.
We sit by the warm fire
And drink hot chocolate,
As we sit together
To enjoy each other forever.
Christmas is the time
For love and laughter
And celebrate the day
Christ was born and
Each other.

Mariel Valino, Grade 7
East Millbrook Magnet Middle School, NC

Hurricane Terror
Rain falling from the skies up above
Clouds a darkish gray
Wind blowing miles and miles per hour
Dehydration from the endless temperature of heat
Nervously relieved when finished
Feelings of breath
being taken away.
Heart beats skip
Animals continually roam
the wet streets.
Leaves slowly
drift from trees.
Families losing loved ones.
Houses destroyed
Windows broken
Shattered glass throughout
Lights out…it's over!

Coriana Hayes, Grade 8
Leonville Elementary School, LA

Love Forevermore
We miss them now more than ever
We wish we would have changed our ways when we were little
To show them more love
Even though they knew we loved them ever more
They passed away a short time ago
Leaving only memories we know
There is no need to grieve anymore
They're in heaven forevermore

Regan Bennett, Grade 8
Lake Middle School, MS

Thinking

As I sit here thinking,
Of what life must be like,
Outside these four walls
People must be playing,
Laughing, singing, dancing.
While I sit here thinking
Quietly thinking.

I lookout the window,
And see the sun and clouds
They are free, not stuck inside this room.
But being here, surrounded by these walls,
Is not as bad as one might think.
It's peaceful here, and I have time to think.
Gently think.

As I sit here thinking,
The bell sounds, it is time for me to go.
But the day is not over yet,
I still have many more rooms to visit
But I don't really mind,
For I know I'll be there thinking.
Simply thinking.

Cody Ward, Grade 9
Smiths Station High School, AL

We're Only Friends

She gets upset quite a bit,
Almost every other day.
He'll ask her what's wrong, she'll say "not a thing,"
The same response; same words, same way.

She could never admit it since she was gutless to say,
"I love you and you'll never love me back."
He walks down the halls with a beautiful girl,
He's the one worst person to lack.

They always have been the most closest of friends,
From years and years ago.
He'd never think of her in a romantic way,
Even now, when she loved him so.

She was wishing for him with all her might,
To noticed when he tried to impose.
He told her he loved her, that he'd be hers for life,
And handed her a single rose.

Years have passed, she loved him more than ever,
And knew that their love was true.
As she looked deeply into his beautiful eyes,
She smiled and exclaimed "I Do!"

Sydney Travers, Grade 8
Fayette Middle School, GA

Mamma Rose

Now that you're gone
I will never smile again.
Now that you're in heaven,
I may never laugh again.

You were my light
And my role model.
I wanted to grow old
And be just like you.

But you're gone now.
I still hear your voice
The last words you said to me.
When the wind blows, I hear
Your voice cheering me on.

Even though you moved on
And are in a better place
We will never forget you
Mamma Rose

Kymie Byrd, Grade 7
Haynes Academy for Advanced Studies, LA

Love

What is love, a word we take for granted,
A word that is commonly misused,
A feeling that can take over your common emotions,
Until they become emotions that we abuse.
How many times have you said "I love you,"
But never knew what it meant?
Have you ever stopped to think,
About the message that you have sent?
What is love,
Something we feel for that someone we care about?
It's a feeling you cannot always explain and should never doubt.
When "I love you" is said those words have a meaning,
That should stay in your head.
Love is not just a word but a feeling,
That will never die 'till the end.

Alyssa Scurria, Grade 8
Mount Carmel Academy, LA

Inspiration

I magine a world without hope;
N ote the small things in life;
S ave anyone that needs salvation;
P lace everything where it works best;
I nspire anyone who needs encouragement;
R etrospect if you can benefit from doing so;
A ppreciate people for who they are;
T ake what's given;
I nsist on the best;
O pen your mind to new ideas;
N ever make the same mistakes.

Hiba Tahir, Grade 7
Margaret Green Jr High School, MS

Peace?

I wonder what the fingers are thinking
When they flash the
PEACE sign.
I wonder what the lips are feeling
When they yell to a friend
PEACE.
I wonder how the pencil feels
When it is used to doodle
PEACE signs.
I wonder what the trigger is feeling
When it is pulled to kill for
PEACE.
I wonder what the soldier feels
As he's dying for
PEACE?

Ashley Hanna, Grade 7
North Iredell Middle School, NC

Stormy Weather

Today is very sad
Watching the water rise
Staying inside the house
Hoping no more trees fall down
Lots of debris
flying in the air
animals hiding
behind boulders
angels are watching over us
The eye is here
Everything is still
People outside,
looking around
It starts again
Is everyone okay?

Laura Stelly, Grade 8
Leonville Elementary School, LA

There's No Going Back

There's no going back
when you say something horrible.
There's no going back
when a friend moves away.
There's no going back
when you lie and feel miserable.
There's no going back
to the start of the day.
There's no going back
when you do something dreadful.
There's no going back
when you say that you hate.
There's no going back
when you lose your temper.
There's no going back
to fix those mistakes.

Lydia Chappel, Grade 7
Discovery Middle School, AL

The March of the Mouse

The mouse marched soberly through the barren meadow,
Thinking about the unlawful loss of his battle.
He had just gone looking for a nibble of cheese
When a pair of golden, glowing topazes stared back at him.
Then through the dried grasses the great cat appeared,
Its glossy groomed coat shining in the boiling hot sunshine.
The giant beast stalked around him,
Smiling and showing his knifelike teeth.
The great animal pounced on the timid creature.
The mouse was smuggled but not for long,
He scurried beneath the cat, limping with effort
Until he made it to the almost dried-up spring,
And from there, he marched soberly through the barren meadow.

Emily Merrin Leamy, Grade 7
L E Gable Middle School, SC

He's Gone

I loved him…but he's gone…
Like a leaf in the wind;
I'm not sure if I can live now…
The past year of my life has been spent with him…

I wish he could come back…
To kiss me one more time…
But to feel his gentle arms hold me tight is something of my dreams…

There is one other, but no, I can't!
It would be so wrong;
He was his best friend! I'm lost…

I'm lost in confused emotions.
— He's gone…that's it…I can't do anything about it;
I can't take the drunken state of mind
Out of the man that killed my love…
I couldn't take him out of the burning car;
As he sat there pinned to the dashboard, dying…

I can't move on because of the simple reason that — He's gone…

AnnaMae Barber, Grade 9
New Site High School, MS

Who

Who was born on December 25th, who was born in a manger,
Whose mother's name was Mary, and was called a perfect stranger,
Whose father's name was Joseph, and they had no room for him in the Inn,
Whose blood was shed for you and me, and covered all our sins,
Who walked across the water, and calmed the raging sea,
Who laid His life on the line, and died for you and me?
The answer to all these questions is JESUS, the one who paved our way,
Right now I just want to tell Him I'm glad He was born on this day.

Happy Birthday,
JESUS

Devin Mitchell, Grade 8
Armstrong Middle School, MS

Terror

We've all been through this once before,
Here it comes, pounding at our doors,
The heartbreaking, house-shaking storm,
The beating of hearts, waiting to get back to the norm,
The terrifying vacancy in all of the streets,
The rattling of the ground, shaking at our feet,
The subtle cries of families' fear,
The flashes of lightning, coming so near,
Hopefully soon, it will all be through,
Pray for clear skies to come out of the blue.

Sarah King, Grade 8
Bishop Noland Episcopal Day School, LA

Storms

Storms in my life make me feel so sad.
As I sit in my room
and look out my window at the terrible winds and rain,
I start to get scared.
I pray it all stops and goes away.
I am sad when I hear about all the people's houses
that got messed up in the hurricane.
When I think about what happened to all of the beautiful trees
that fell down in the bad weather and killed or hurt people,
I feel so bad.
As I sit next to the big stone in my back yard,
I look around and thank the good Lord
for not letting it be *us* that got hurt in the storm.
When I wake up in the morning,
I always go to see my animals first.
I make sure they are all okay.
Then, I thank God for answering my prayers
and letting my animals be safe.

April Darby, Grade 7
Leonville Elementary School, LA

I Am

I am a strong, black woman
I wonder why God keeps me here
I hear the voice of God talking to me
I want to be used by God
I am a strong, black woman.
I pretend to like all people, when I don't
I feel like giving up
I touch the stars, while climbing and striving to be better
I worry about people who don't care about themselves
I cry when close people die
I am a strong, black woman.
I understand that most teenagers are stressed
I say people can be whatever they want to be
I dream that when my day comes,
I will be worthy in Jesus' eyes, and he will say
"you have done well my faithful servant"
I hope I finally get myself together,
I am a strong, black woman

Alexis Williams, Grade 9
Warren Early College High School, NC

Broken

A heart is with love,
They could have holes,
Or they could be sealed,
You could be heart broken,
By a special someone,
You have to trust that person you know,
Only if they love you back,
Send them cards, flowers, and chocolates,
If you really love them,
Tell them you do,
Before your heart gets broken.

Carley Leach, Grade 8
St Margaret School, LA

jesus, our savior

jesus is life
jesus is the way
he died on the cross
he rose on the third day
we are the knife
he is the handle that holds us up
he is the house the rock
he is the sock that keeps our feet clean of sin
that is why on him, we depend
he is our foundation that keeps us from falling
please hear us, we are calling
he is the rock of our salvation
he is our light
he is the kite that soars above
we have bad behavior
that's why we depend on jesus our savior

Ethan Sims, Grade 7
The Education Center, MS

Life Is Not a Pleasant Ride

life is not a pleasant ride
without someone to lean on,
when you feel lost and cold.

life is kind of like
a laugh without a smile,
or a cry without a tear,
we all need someone.

a little child would never smile if
no one was there to comfort him,
we all keep waiting, waiting on the world to change.

while we look for someone to comfort us
the world changes,
and time keeps slipping away.

John Church, Grade 7
L E Gable Middle School, SC

Where I'm From

I'm from February 26, 1995; from Spartanburg, South Carolina where I got my name and shed my first tear.
I'm from waking up every weekday at 6:05 getting ready for school and to catch the bus.
I'm from getting out of school and going to football practice Monday-Thursday 3:30-5:30.
I'm from getting out of practice and going home to do my homework and getting something to eat.
I'm from making A's and B's on my report card every year and semester.
I'm from testing and downloading any new music from my favorite artist every time I hear a new song.
I'm from putting great music and pictures of me on my MP3 player almost every day.
I'm from going outside with my friends and cousins to play.
I'm from looking at BET and MTV2 every day and night.
But most of all I'm from getting in the bed every night and telling my mother goodnight.

Trayvond Davis, Grade 8
Sims Jr High School, SC

Fantasy

The world of powerful wizards and treasure hoarding dragons
Valiant knights in shining armor rescuing damsels in distress
Magic used for good and evil is weaved throughout these tales
Trolls capture children too careless to watch how far they walk
Elves practice their archery deep within their woodland realm
While greedy dwarves dig deep in their search for more and more gold
And the mighty wings of the griffins carry them to the limits of the sky
Kings of the old Golden Age where gods ruled the people
Along with monsters of unspeakable darkness where it was taboo just to say their names
Seers, the tellers of the past and future look to create prophecies of great importance
Great battles of courage, bravery, and grit fought over things that were righteous
Sly deceits to trick the trusting to their own impending doom
A giant spider with poor eyesight that falls asleep when you sing
Or a tiny mischievous leprechaun with that ever elusive pot of gold
Fantasy is anything and everything your imagination can think of

Michael Nelson, Grade 8
Dillard Drive Middle School, NC

Sorry

Dear Santa Claus,

   Mr. Santa I have been very bad this year. But I still would like a surfboard. But I have been naughty so you could give me coal and a surfboard. Or coal, a surfboard, and a skateboard. I know I'm asking for a lot but you could give me coal, a surfboard, skateboard, and a salt water aquarium, with a nitro R/C truck. Also a new bike with nice rims. But I've been naughty not nice so how about a grill to cook all that coal.

   Sincerely, Patrick

Patrick Motosko, Grade 7
First Flight Middle School, NC

Snowflakes

Snowflakes fall as the first flurry of snow appears.
Each one different, yet the same.
At first, everything looks similar, each snowflake exactly like the other.
If closely looked at, each snowflake has its own individual, geometric design,
every one looking like a miniature sculpture.
Initially, snowflakes appear identical.
If closely looked at, each one is unique.
In one point of view, snowflakes can be ice crystals falling from the sky, but in another approach,
beautiful works of art with a one of a kind structure.

Stephanie McCabe, Grade 8
Mount Carmel Academy, LA

The Girl in the Mask

The mask that I wear, it helps me to hide
The fact that I'm broken and dying inside.
I hide from the world the torture and grief
It seems to be growing, to my disbelief.
Does it really seem fair that I should be judged?
People should learn to not hold a grudge.

The pain I endeavor gets buried away
Until there becomes a day
Where somebody will care to ask
What exactly I hide behind my mask.
A brave soul will find the key
To my heart and unlock the real me.
But as for now, I sit here and wait
For that special someone to come through my gate.

Amanda Vohringer, Grade 9
Scholar's Academy at CCU, SC

Take a Moment

Take a moment to really see our environment.
Take a moment to see that it needs help.
Global warming. Pollution.
Take a moment and realize that this was our doing.
Take a moment and try to help.
Do what you can and try your best.
Recycle. Compost.
Take a moment to share your knowledge.
Take a moment to influence people to follow your lead.
Help preserve our environment.
We only have one and there are no second chances.
Take a moment.

Alysha Colon, Grade 7
Carolina International School, NC

War

Marching, marching, practice makes perfect
Falling in step with your brothers and sisters to your goal
Training to be the end for your enemy
Well trained soon to be
Brothers won't die harmony
    Chaos, fire, is this "the end?"
Or is this how it began, with desert sand?
Man's conflict could decide
The fate of humanity itself
The best of the best, causing battlefield deicide
    Men die in wartime horror
Children idolizing simulated battlefield mutilation
Civilians veiled to this
Brothers mourn for their fallen and maimed
Born again from ashes, heart bleached in loss,
He is the end, that's what he is.

Derick Harjo, Grade 7
Haynes Academy for Advanced Studies, LA

Santa

One day on Christmas Eve
Santa Claus is making his good list,
For kids who've been good
Fewer kids make it every year
Therefore, Santa makes fewer toys,
That means Santa will no longer be,
People stop believing in Santa Claus
Therefore, there will be no more Santa

Rodney Clack, Grade 7
East Millbrook Magnet Middle School, NC

Already Autumn

Sitting here shiftless, staring intently
Out the foggy open window
Staring into the deep sky
With its fluorescent scarlet light on the horizon.
The leaves of trees turning various colors
Falling swiftly to the ground of the valley
The beautiful colors crunch beneath my feet
Kaleidoscopic colors drive my soul wild

A sensational breeze rushes through my hair,
Blowing the silk against my face.
The crisp, cool air fills the room with sweet pine
And spreads the scent of Mother's scrumptious pumpkin pie.
The cheerful children laugh and play
Playing games of hide-and-seek
Their overwhelming joy slices the silence
And fills my heart with a sensation of love.

The sun sets leaving a luxurious lunar light
Filling my thoughts with curiosity and awe
Remembering that a beautiful day lay ahead
I was taken over by anxiousness.
I could not believe it was already autumn.

C. Stephanie Magri, Grade 8
St John Neumann Regional Catholic School, GA

The Feast

Thanksgiving Day ready to play,
"O boy what a feast!"
Cooking with mom makes me happy,
"O boy what a feast!"
Going outside seeing the poor and the hungry
Saying fish and bread keeps the poor man fed,
"O boy what a feast!"
Ham, turkey, mac and cheese, rice, pies, potato salad,
Fried chicken, yams, collard greens, pork n beans,
Mashed potatoes and gravy, corn, chocolate cake
"O boy what a feast!"
All this adds up to the blessings that God gave
For us to see another day
All I can say is:
"HAVE A HAPPY THANKSGIVING DAY."

Ronald Paul Mitchell, Grade 7
Hubert Middle School, GA

I Look Up at the Sky

I look up at the sky
Only because I cry
I cry because I'm distressed
I cry because I'm depressed
So I look up at the sky

I used to wonder sometimes at night
If everything will be all right
And to see by my surprise
You were always by my side
Now I don't wonder at night

I sit next to a tree
And there is no one next to me
I look up at the sky
I just began to cry
Because nobody is next to me

I take a really big sigh
Wait until the late night
Now not worrying about a thing
I can tell when it's spring
When I look up at the sky

Megan Akins, Grade 9
McKee Jr High School, AL

Childhood Memory

It was time to go.
I took one last look
Around my home.

Rooms and halls
Were empty except for
Floors and walls.

The trucks were packed.
Boxes and bins
Were all neatly stacked.

All to do was to breathe,
Too speechless to speak.
It was time to leave.

Emily Sigler, Grade 8
Margaret Green Jr High School, MS

Spiders

Spiders, hiders definitely
Sneaking around in the dark
With no spark...
Where no one can see
But after the night
When it is bright
People might fright
When they are seen

Cody Marietti, Grade 7
St Andrews Middle School, SC

What Nature Means to Me

What nature means to me, it might not mean to you.
What I say about this here nature is coming from my heart and is very clearly true,
But this message nature sends me; it may sound very queer;
And in case you haven't noticed, what I am about to say is coming very, very near.
The message I hear from nature I see come and come again,
But it is very important, so I ask you listen here and maybe write this down with a pen.
I see that when it rains, our earth is getting a drink when the water starts to flow,
And that when it is sunshine, our flowers start to grow.
I notice that when it is cloudy and cold, everything seems to sleep, or go into a trance,
And when the wind is blowing, the trees begin to dance.
What is this I am saying?
Nothing at all — just that you should listen to the earth;
And think about this poem and remember it with worth.

Amanda Capritto, Grade 7
Boyet Jr High School, LA

How

How can you help it when people don't need you,
How can you help it when people don't believe you.
How can you help it when people always lie,
How can you help it when there is nothing to do but cry.

How can you help it when your life grows so cold,
How can you help it when your true story is never told.
How can you help it when your trust won't grow stronger,
How can you help it when your life won't last longer.

How can you help it when your heart is completely loveless,
How can you help it when the ones who were important live above us.
How can you help it when there is no one there,
How can you help it when life is supposed to be unfair.

How can you help it when your heart is full of hurt,
How can you help it when people treat you like dirt.
How can you help it when no one's left to care,
How can you help it when your parents were not the perfect pair.

How can you help it when help can't be bought,
How can you help it when freedom isn't what you really thought.
How can you help it when you thought you wrote the perfect poem,
How can you help it when you thought you had a family and didn't even know them.

Derrione Gates, Grade 9
Three Springs of Courtland School, AL

Letting You Go

Letting you go is very hard,
because I've always loved you from the start.
I intended on loving you until the end,
but the things you're doing have started to extend.
Letting you go feels like someone is throwing sticks and stones at my bones.
And I'll be so glad when you're gone.
Letting you go seems so wrong.
But letting you go will make me more strong.

Christina Gaddis, Grade 9
Kate Griffin Jr High School, MS

Oh, Sweet Summertime

All packed up,
And ready for the car ride
Can't wait for our feet to touch the sand
Tons of snacks and movies
To make the time go by
Inviting friends and family
Ready for a fun trip

Luggage carts and duffel bags
Smelling the sticky, summer air
Waiting for the elevator
We are almost there
Unpacking all of our things
Getting our beds ready
Eager to go to the beach

Bathing suits and sun tan lotion
Packing lunches and getting beach chairs
Ready to start the short walk to the beach
Toes in the hot sand
Waves crushing down the beach
We find an empty spot to settle down
Summer is finally here!

Leah Caffey, Grade 8
Westchester Country Day School, NC

Friendship

I'm sure we've all heard that friends come and go,
And when you can't find the word they'll always know.
If you live your life with happiness and friends,
Nothing else would suffice
Because they will be there until the end.

Macie Coker, Grade 7
Lake Castle Private School, LA

Pink

Pink is the rosy color on cheeks
The soft gentle touch of care
Pink over the horizon to brighten your day
The warmth, love, and care of pink

Kaitlin Nakincheng, Grade 7
L E Gable Middle School, SC

Thanksgiving Time

Thanksgiving is the time to feast.
With gravy, turkey, and even yeast.
We all get together and have a lot of fun,
Watching football and playing with toy guns.
Our bellies are full and there is corn in our teeth,
We feel the need to take a short sleep,
The children are happy and full of schemes,
Of Christmas time and holiday dreams.
At the end of the day and the cobbler is gone,
We give kisses and hugs and then go home.

Kaitlyn Wildman, Grade 7
Sylvania School, AL

Behind the Mask

Every day when I wake up,
I do my hair,
I do my make-up.
I feel a sense of security behind it
And I ask:
Who am I
Behind that mask?

I go to school,
I see a clique of girls
Their hair in place and make-up cool.
They must feel that security, too,
And I ask:
Who are they
Behind that mask?

When I go home
I glance at the mirror
And remove the make-up
I feel less protected, but better, more "normal"
And I answer:
The mask is gone,
And this is truly me.

Justine Ker, Grade 9
Cedar Creek School, LA

Words I'd Never Say

I'd never say there's a monster under my bed
But then again I've never got the courage to look
I've never said that I wouldn't steal from a cookie jar
Because I've tested that temptation too many times

I'd never say I still like stuffed animals
But then again Mr. Bunny would be embarrassed
I've never said that I don't have a southern accent
Because then that would make me a liar

I'd never say that I still play dress-up
But then again I have a great stride in high heels
I've never said that I wouldn't be a rock star
Because I would qualify all too well

I'd never say that I wear flip-flops year-round
But then again I don't own a pair of tennis shoes
I've never said that I don't like heights
Because I love airplanes

Words I'll never say
Things I'll never do
What's in store for the future?
I don't know, how about you?

Abby Johns, Grade 7
Lost Mountain Middle School, GA

Life

Saturday morning, the day begins
Hope is in the air
But others talk of other chores
Things just don't seem fair
Life pounds several troubles
Onto people's heads
Once they come about
People start to dread
But life is bound to trouble
Worry and disgrace
Everyone and everything
It's bound to be in your face
Life is like a person
She could smile and then be sad
For just to know the good times
She must also see the bad
What some people do not know
And what some never see
Is that life brings more happiness
All for you and me
Lindsay Kornick, Grade 9
Mount Carmel Academy, LA

President

Here I stand in front of my nation
Never thought it would be a vacation
I was just another resident
But now I am your president
Make decisions for our nation
Not always a cause for celebration
Half my life is a mystery
A famous man in history
Jackson Morris, Grade 8
Priceville Jr High School, AL

Geezer in the Freezer

There's a dead guy in the freezer
Yes, he is an old geezer
I don't know how he got there
He gave me quite a scare

He's next to the ice cream
And he made me scream
He smells really bad
And he makes me sad

Because he is dead
I put him to bed
I will bury him
Next to Tim

So now there's no geezer
In my cold freezer
Corey Ballard, Grade 7
First Flight Middle School, NC

I Like Dirt Bikes

They taste like mud.
They sound rowdy and loud.
I know the smell of a dirt bike —
smells like sweat and outdoors.
The exhaust pipe does not smell good.
The sight of a dirt bike is really cool
and it makes me feel tough every time
I get on it.
I love the feel of a dirt bike.
It's just great.
Johnathan Gault, Grade 7
L E Gable Middle School, SC

Twin Towers

I was just about seven,
When a lot of people went to heaven,
It was a bad day for America,
Because of the terrorist group Al-Qaeda,
Had just attacked the Twin Towers,
And within hours,
They were down,
To the ground,
I may have been young,
But it has still hung,
In my mind,
For some time.
Benjamin Pendleton, Grade 8
Albemarle School, NC

Gone Forever

I was a boy
my father passed
I couldn't go on
too much pain

like a knife
shoved into my heart
too deep
wouldn't come out

a huge mess
afraid to live
my father was
never to return

went to a camp
to get over death
some new friends
knew how I felt

tried to move on
still part of my life
gone forever
Bryant Weaver, Grade 9
North Wilkes High School, NC

Music

Music
Rolling like the river
Never commanded,
For eternity remaining
Serene voice of all
Brimming with joy
In me always,
Bringing me peace
Swelling, broadening,
Forever moving
Transcends all life
And turns it to
Light
Rita Meganck, Grade 8
Dillard Drive Middle School, NC

Goodbyes Are Forever

After a while
you learn
the difference between
holding a hand and
falling in love.
You begin to learn
kisses don't always
mean something,
promises can be broken
just as quickly
as they are made, and
goodbyes really
are forever.
Hayley Bradshaw, Grade 8
Yazoo County Jr High School, MS

Complete

Flowing, spilling over
Pencil moving across paper
Phrases exploding in my mind
Word tumbling over word
Paper quickly filling up
I am writing an image of colors,
My words all clicking into place to
Create a rainbow,
A rainbow where
All the colors
Mingle together, but
Each is separate,
Beautiful on its own
The circle of words
Is half done,
Almost done,
Done.
My poem is complete.
I am complete.
Maryam Ahmed, Grade 8
Dillard Drive Middle School, NC

High Merit Poems – Grades 7, 8 and 9

Me
I am the only one who is me,
The only what who can do it my way
If you try to do it like me,
You might as well hit the highway.

I can only talk like me
And like no one else
I am the only one with my personality
The only one like myself

I am the only one who can play guitar like me
But that's not necessarily the best way to play
I am the only one who can skate like me
Even though I usually leave my board behind

I'm the only one who can play hockey like me
Even though some are better
I'm the only one I know who spells their name like me
Even though there are probably more

So even though no one is like me,
And that includes you too
Only I am like me
And only you are like you
Jordin Kolman, Grade 8
Dillard Drive Middle School, NC

It's the Game
It's a game of collision.
It's a game of fierce rivalries.
It's a game of pinpoint precision.
It's a game of hatred and passion.
It's America's favorite game.

From quarterback to strong safety
From linebacker to pulling guard,
One thing you can count on is everyone's hitting hard.
Along with fall comes football,
The very best game of them all.

There is nothing quite like game day.
People pile into the stands like a great fleet.
Come kickoff time, all the seats are empty
Because everyone's on their feet.
The whole stadium is shaking with intensity.

Everyone loves football and how could you not?
From the roar of the band and the clash of the pads,
Oh and that one little cheap shot.
Football is a marvelous game.
It's a game of pride and sometimes shame.
Michael Sikorski, Grade 8
St John Neumann Regional Catholic School, GA

Our Wonderful World?
Just think how great the world would be
If people stopped saying it's all about me
When people feel down
There'd be someone around
To comfort, care,
And always be there
The sick would be healed
The poor could still live
Then why don't people give?
Our world has become twisted
Since it first existed
We didn't care what happened to others
If we get what we want we don't need one another
We see people hurt
We're not even alert
We don't stop and help,
Too busy with ourselves
Just look around
And maybe you'll see
Just how great the world would be
If people stopped saying it's all about me
Molly Gallagher, Grade 8
Dillard Drive Middle School, NC

My Love for Him
The way I love him he will never know
The way he is so nice
The way he makes me smile
The way he looks brightens my day
His smile is contagious and makes me smile
If only he knew how I felt
If only he felt the same way
If only he thought about me the way I feel for him
If only our love could be together
It would make me happier than ever
And love harder than ever
Hanna Honer, Grade 7
Carolina International School, NC

Every Moment Counts
Time is ticking
Every little moment counts
Why does it go by so quickly?
Why don't we seize the opportunities that come our way?
They might be the only opportunities that come our way
To make our life worthwhile
So that we don't have to think
About that ticking clock
That seems to just keep ticking on
We can't stop
We won't stop
Do you know why?
Time is ticking
Every moment counts…
Christen Killgore, Grade 8
First Flight Middle School, NC

Inside Hurricane Gustav

During Hurricane Gustav,
I stayed at my house.
A tree was about to fall
by my friend's house.
In the evening
the lights went out.
My dog started barking very loudly.
Inside my house
it was very hot.
It was raining very hard.
My cousin got scared
when the lights went out.
Lightning shook the house.
Clouds were all over the sky.
The rocks in my yard
were moving from the wind.

Kenry Tolliver, Grade 7
Leonville Elementary School, LA

The Tide Is Rolling Out

The tide is rolling out. Out to sea.
Where all the rest go
when it leaves the open shore
where I am.

The tide is rolling out.
Leaving me here, all alone, scared,
not knowing what to do.
Leaving me to fight my battles
all by myself without any help.

The tide is rolling out.
I needed it here to save me from
all the dangers that the world holds.
I needed it there to hold me
and love like nothing else could.

The tide is rolling out.
Going back forever.
For when it goes away,
the same one never comes back.
It goes away forever. Leaving me to die.
Dying not from common cause,
but from sorrow.

Kristin Huffman, Grade 9
Challenger High School, NC

Katrina

Katrina came like an ogre
Coming to annihilate the human race

It swung its winds whipping away homes
Leaving water in its place
Along with broken hearts and stolen lives

Bushra Ahmad, Grade 7
Lake Castle Private School, LA

Sweet Home Alabama All Summer Long

I love the Alabama Crimson Tide.
I love the plays that they do because they are like enjoying rides.
I also love to watch Julio Jones make spectacular catches in the air.
And there have never been better coaches than Nick Saban and Bear.
This year so far we are 6-0.
Can we finish off the year 14-0?
I think we can and we are going to prove it.
We are going to beat Auburn in just a little bit.

Cody Terry, Grade 9
Three Springs of Courtland School, AL

My Long Black with Yellow Flower Dress

My long black with yellow flower dress,
How I loved to wear my dress,
I wanted to wear my dress everywhere,
Out to grandma's we went,
I could not wait to show grandma my long dress,
Jumped out of the car in my long black with yellow flowered dress,
Just to notice my grandma's dress,
The same exact dress I was wearing,
Beside her I stood,
Our dresses the same,
How happy I was,
Our dresses so long,
Our dresses so black,
Shapes of flowers,
All yellow on black.

Essence Wagoner, Grade 9
North Wilkes High School, NC

My Life Is Ok

My life is ok but just too boring.
My life is ok my smile shows it.
You may not like me or my family, but I still stand bright and tall
Is it the clothes my mom works hard for, for me to wear.
Or is it my sassiness that phases you.

Well I really don't care.
Because my life is ok.
One day I would love to escape from the world.
The economy is low, no summer school, no jobs.

But I think my life will be ok.
I just want you to know that my life is ok.
I just wish that people would stop the violence in the world.
I just might be ok then.
But until then I'm going to be cool as the summer breeze.

Someday I would love to change the world.
President Barack Obama I'm coming in 4 years.
But I would need you to do your job.
Because my life is fine as a straight line.
It is ok because my life is ok…

Taliyah Campbell, Grade 8
Miller Core Knowledge Magnet Middle School, GA

So Much

So much depends on a good friend to love,
So many who pretend then push comes to shove,
Seem such a friendly sight at first,
Then you realize it was just an unending thirst.

Kendle Kelly, Grade 7
Lost Mountain Middle School, GA

Georgia in Seasons

Cherry blossoms and swaying trees,
Speckled meadows and soft grass,
Fluffy clouds and warm sun,
Slight breezes and rain sprinkles,
Georgia in spring.

Flowing streams and squishy swamps,
Sweet tea and iced lemonade,
Family outings and pretty parties,
Hot beaches and shopping galore,
Cool camping and far-out fishing,
Georgia in the summer.

Golden hay fields and burnt orange pumpkins,
Leaves fall and scarves come out,
Soft winds whisper and say, "Fall is here.",
Trees die and grass withers,
Georgia in the fall.

Puffy coats and hats, too,
Jack Frost kisses your nose and you say, "Shoo!",
White mountain tops and bare ground,
Hot chocolate and cozy fires,
Georgia in winter.

Brittany Collis, Grade 8
Fannin County Middle School, GA

Saying Goodbye Is Never Easy

I always took for granted
what I thought I'd never loose.
Because I never thought it would happen
until I heard the news.

They say you were chosen for his garden
his precious hand picked bouquet.
God really needed him that's why he couldn't stay.

Saying goodbye is never easy.
It's the hardest thing to do.
But what hurts the most,
is not getting the chance to say it to you.

So today, Jesus, as you are listening
in your home above,
would go and find my granddad
and give him all my love.

Austin Lichte, Grade 8
Yazoo County Jr High School, MS

Autumn's Call

With one quick and sudden puff,
It knocks summer off her feet.
Another breath brings the trees to their knees,
Leaves shaking and trembling with fright.

This is autumn's call
For frost and chill to join him.
In battle he will not lose,
To summer's fearful bite.

Summer it seems,
Is truly fighting her hardest.
Yet autumn has the swords of frostbite
And ice on his side.

A fallen warrior hits the ground.
The call of autumn has prevailed,
The enemies victorious rejoice.
Summer has again lost her fight.

However summer will return.
She will reclaim the throne,
Which for a time is hers.
Then autumn's call will echo again.

Julianna Werner, Grade 8
St John Neumann Regional Catholic School, GA

Haunting Halloween

As crimson leaves fall from the trees
It is clear that the time of year is near
The time for walking in the streets
Looking for succulent treats
And avoiding things that give you the creeps

Nonstop excitement all night long
Vivacious fellows running along
As you can see there is much to do
But don't be certain that nothing can scare you
A phantom of two might just say boo

Frivolous fellows fringe at their sight
Gaudy girls grasp in fright
They have an improbable impulse to inflate you with terror
But you shouldn't let them ruin your night to remember
Here are tricks to keep those phantoms out of your wits

Don't flinch, fling, flip, or flop
Stand up straight just like a rock
Be vigilant and vibrant
Not babyish and bashful
Do all these things and you will surely be successful.

Marie Porras, Grade 8
St John Neumann Regional Catholic School, GA

Love Birds

I'll take a stand on any issue, at any time, regardless of how fraught with controversy it is.
If you ask me how I feel about love; well love birds, here's how I stand.
If by love you mean the immature soul mate that makes fun of every little thing you do;
if by love you mean the men which we call pigs and have to wait on hand and foot;
if by love you mean the little children you make food for every night or else;
if by love you mean the king of the jungle who expects hot dogs and hamburgers
with ketchup, mustard, pickles and God forbid the world would end if they did not
have cheese for every football or baseball game or sporting event;
if by love you mean the sweaty animals we watch dirty up our clean everything;
and if by love you mean the little boy that demands dinner every night and a warm towel
on the toilet after every shower, then certainly I am against it with all my power.
But if by love you mean the heart warming arms you can fall into after a long hard day;
if by love you mean the brown eyes that give you butterflies when you gaze into them;
if by love you mean the companion you can share your deepest feelings and thoughts to;
if by love you mean the magical creature that gives you no words in your mouth every
time you think of him or stand near him;
if by love you mean breathtaking lips that kiss your forehead or cheek with compassion;
if by love you mean the addicting desire always to be with him and stand with him;
and if by love you mean the man you can never stop thinking about and want to spend the
rest of your life with, well then love birds, I am all for it and this is my stand.

Cailin McCarley, Grade 9
North Forsyth High School, GA

Gangs

I can't find rhyme in all my work every time I think about it it makes me jerk. See here's how it goes, there are gangs everywhere. Watch them ride by on the street always playing that beat they never stop doing what they're doing drive bys selling drugs going to jail for awhile oh and don't forget that if you're out you die.

Gangs are complicated I don't know why anyone would join. Think of it this way you're in a gang but a gang of one. If one person hurts you or attempted to hurt you don't you need 16 people backing you up if you do you're a wimp if not you're a soldier. Soldiers are supposed to keep their composure even though they hold the weight of the whole world on their shoulder. Soldiers are soldiers not the soldiers of gangs keep that in mind don't lose faith one day we might not have to worry about gangs.

Joseph Pollard, Grade 9
Three Springs of Courtland School, AL

Where I Am From

I am from a place who tries to make a difference to change the world by being part of each other to understand their feelings.
I am from a person who loves to play Nintendo such as Mario and Zelda.
I am from an artist who draws to make joy on all who wants to smile.
I am from a musician who plays music to entertain people and helps others enjoy the sound of music.
I am from a small town full with amazing and exciting things.
I am from a home which always keeps me warm and comfortable and in control of my feelings.
I am from my mom and dad and my brother who will always help me in times when I struggle and in pain.
Forever they will become my home, my place, where I am from.

Dylan Fallaw, Grade 8
Sims Jr High School, SC

Mothers

Mothers should treat their children with respect. They should listen and understand what their children are saying. They should participate in everything their children are into. They should take pride in what their children are doing. And be thankful for what their children have done. They should always stick by their children's side and never leave them. They should believe in them and cheer them on. They should be worried when they are not in sight. They should love them and never leave them there confused and worried about the answer to do you love them, or do you love them not. They should know it already. And not only you love, help them love themselves.

Lyric Narcisse, Grade 7
Saint James High School, LA

High Merit Poems – Grades 7, 8 and 9

The Winter Season
The cold winter air
Is something we just have to bear.

The sun never shines
Through these winter times.

Because it is here,
We have something to fear.

We love when it snows,
But hate when nothing will grow.

This always happens when winter appears.
It's just a portion of what has happened through the years.
Anna Caroline Sanford, Grade 7
Picayune Jr High School, MS

Storms Make Me Feel
Storms and hurricanes
make me feel scared.
Tornados make me anxious
as trees sway back and forth.
My heart beats faster and faster!
I glance at the flowers blowing,
hearing the whistle of the wind.
Possibilities roll through my mind
while listening to the sound of the thunder.
Rain pours down outside
feels so gloomy and dark
Bad weather makes me feel sad
Now I know that God is watching over me!
Lindsey Billeaudeau, Grade 7
Leonville Elementary School, LA

Who I Am
I am cold
I entice
Children to play
In my chariot of ice
I am made into balls and forts
Then people play an awesome sport
I come in fall
I leave in spring
I am a sign
Of a special time
I come in a season of important meaning
A time of giving and receiving
When Christ was born that Christmas night
I reflected that glorious light
Alas, my time has come to go
But I will come again, for I am snow.
Chris Graham, Grade 7
St Mary's School, SC

Me
I've been told you can see the hurt in my big brown eyes
and the pain in my smile
and if you want to know why then listen for a while
I've been through so much and I'm only fifteen
I've been hurt a lot in my life and I wish it was just a dream
I know I'm not perfect and you shouldn't expect me to be
but know the love in my heart is eternally
I care too much and that's never good
and I trust more people than I really should
I always get hurt and I don't know why
tears stream down my face because it hurts deep inside
I try to be strong and happy for my friends
but it all seems to fall apart in the end
If everyone loved and cared like I do
then everyone would see that my love is true
Angel Tolbert, Grade 9
Cullman Sr High School, AL

Nervous
I am jiggly
I am cold as the whispering winds
I am shaky like the branches of a tree
I am paranoid as if it were the first day of school
I am sweaty as if I just ran a mile
My heart is beating fast as a cheetah running after its prey
I am twitching as if someone scared me
I keep looking around as if someone is watching me
I want to hide like an ostrich sticking his head in a hole
I am NERVOUS
Christa Watson, Grade 9
Georgia Washington Jr High School, AL

Beyond Compare
When I was ten years I lost my father
My best friend even my role model
My life was going too fast at full throttle
Words I lost never to know again
I guess life sometimes isn't what you plan
I was too young then to understand
That when God is ready He spreads man
And takes them to an unknown land
I was indeed my father's child
Because my mother looks at me as wild
But my thoughts are mild
My heart is hard to receive
Some choose to contrive I can't believe
How my life has deceived me
I ask myself over and over how could this be
He was reaching out to me but I was too blind to see
I refuse to grieve but I live in grief
The way I acted was beyond my own beliefs
Sometimes my life is above my own two feet
I lost my father then I lost myself
Because I was him even in his death
Jonae Reynolds, Grade 9
McKee Jr High School, AL

Farm

Uncut hay, blowing in the wind
Apple trees blossoming
Cows mooing
Mist coming off the pond at day break
A fresh fig off the bush
Love this farm

Caitlin Conn, Grade 9
Warren Early College High School, NC

Mona'e Bryant

M ona'e is my name
O ctober is my favorite month of the year
N ever tasted a kiwi before
A dventurist
E LA my favorite school subject

B orn wise
R adiant and loves to write
Y ellow my favorite color
A te peaches before in my life
N ever be mean to my fellow classmates
T uesday my favorite day of the week.

Mona'e Bryant, Grade 7
Hubert Middle School, GA

Hate Is a Strong Word

Hate is a strong word
But there's no other to describe
The feeling inside of me
All the lies you told
My faith you broke
There's no need to hold on
So I'm letting go
Letting go of what I never had

Kristy Thomas, Grade 8
Dillard Drive Middle School, NC

The Lake

The lake is as peaceful
As the bright blue sky,
Then off in the distance
The sound of a baby bluebird cry.
The sun shines luminously
Over the warm wet sand.
The water seems to stir
With the touch of a hand.
The sun fades away,
Far below the trees.
The lake is flowing
To meet up with the seas.
As the dark sky drops,
The crickets begin to weep,
But on the tranquil lake,
Not a sound, not a peep.

Kristin Rockhold, Grade 8
Magnolia Springs Baptist Academy, AL

I'm Somebody

I'm somebody who can be what ever he wants to be in life,
I'm somebody who will do anything to be the best.
I'm a warrior who goes through the worst of anything to get on top,
I'm somebody who will make anyone proud of me.
I'm a go getter,
I'm going to get anything I want.
I'm somebody who doesn't take anything for granted.
I'm Fabeian Davis who is going to be the best if I put my mind to it.
I'm a soldier who will fight for his country.
I'm a star that shines in the black of night.
I'm going to be the most important person you will ever meet.
That's me, Fabeian Davis.

Fabeian Davis, Grade 8
Yazoo County Jr High School, MS

Dear Mom

Dear Mom,
In every average letter,
The first thing people like to say, is "Hey, how are you?"
But I'm just going to tell you that I'm okay.
I'm over here in Europe, just got drafted states,
In a country called Belgium, I'm hoping that's okay.
This war is full of tragic despair, in people's eyes there's fear,
I miss you so badly, but glad to say, I'm happy you're not here.
I'm a nurse at the hospital, over here at the base,
I try to cure the sick and wounded,
It's so hard to see their heartbroken faces.
I know you're glad to hear, that I'm not fighting in this war,
After these years of misery, I won't be here no more.
Though I've seen so many things I dread,
These past four years haven't been so bad,
But being away from the family is making me sad.
Mom I hope I'm making you proud, tell daddy that I'm sill his little girl,
And tell brother that I still look up to him,
And that he's the best big brother in the world.
I'm sorry, but I have to go now, some more soldiers just came in,
And duty calls, I love you all, and I'll see ya'll at the end.

Ali Rojas, Grade 9
Northgate High School, GA

Where I'm From

I am from cartoons; from Nickelodeon and long days watching.
I am from the lonely white house in the middle of town.
I am from the rose bush the whole side of the walkway covered in petals.
I am from church every Sunday and big dresses, pretty hair and smiling faces.
I am from the always talking and caring.
From I love you more than the world and always caring.
I am from Christianity; always be true to God.
I'm from Larners, South Carolina; sweet tea and apple pie.
From the cold nights listening to stories about past family members;
The fireflies all around, and the loud talks at Granddaddy David's.
I am from the back room with undiscovered treasures.
That's where I'm from.

Hayley Gibson, Grade 8
Sims Jr High School, SC

Soccer

This is the sport
This is the sport that I loved
The minute I got on the field
This is the sport that I loved
The minute I got on the field and scored a goal
This is the sport that I loved
The minute I got on the field, scored a goal
The coach screamed "way to go Jordan"
This is the sport that I loved
The minute I got on the field, scored a goal
The coach screamed "way to go Jordan"
I said "thank you" and kept playing
This is the sport that I loved
The minute I got on the field, scored a goal
The coach screamed "way to go Jordan"
I smiled and kept playing
Then I ran off to go steal the ball
This is the sport that started everything
And I am running as fast as I can
Trying to get the ball from the girl to score again!

Jordan Brady, Grade 7
L E Gable Middle School, SC

I Am a Deer

I am shy and quiet
I wonder why they take my family away
I hear a car horn
I see a bright light
I want to cross the road
I am shy and quiet

I pretend I can cross the street
I feel scared
I touch the hard pavement
I worry about the future
I cry when I see someone get run over
I am shy and quiet

I understand the consequences
I say I can make it across
I dream about crossing the street
I try to cross the street
I hope, I hope I can cross the street without getting hurt
I am shy and quiet

Daniella Aguirre, Grade 8
Dillard Drive Middle School, NC

Georgia

Living in Georgia's fine,
It is the greatest place to sink a line.
Bass, brim, and trout,
Sportsmen know what it's about.
Turkeys, bears, and deer
With all this, don't you wish you were here!

Zach Gibbs, Grade 8
Fannin County Middle School, GA

Thanksgiving

Love fills the room
You and your family gather for prayer
Turkey, stuffing, pie,
This is the day of giving thanks
You and your family gather for prayer
As soon as you say amen, you dig in
This is the day of giving thanks
For the laughs and memories
As soon as you say amen you dig in
You always eat too much and save no room for pie
For the laughs and memories
We cherish the good old times
You always eat too much and save no room for pie
Even if it's your favorite flavor
We cherish the good old times
They will never be forgotten
Even if it's your favorite flavor
Turkey, stuffing, pie
They will never be forgotten
Love fills the room
It's one of the best times of year

Megan Panzanella, Grade 9
Ardrey Kell High School, NC

God

He, whom I trust and believe in;
The One who is watching over me;
The One I can depend on to help me through hard times;
He, who loves me for who I am;
The One who forgives me for all my sins;
He, who helps me to never give up;
That person is God.

Mariah Sanders, Grade 8
St Anne Catholic School, SC

Raymond

Hair the color of the night
Eyes the color of a tree trunk
Friend since second grade when we first met
Big enough to stand up for his friends
Responsible enough to stay home alone for hours on end
Cool enough to just give me all his cards and ask for nothing
A twelve year old genius and a strategic game expert
A huge help in some subjects and a true friend in others
Can give you all the support you need
A lifesaver when you needed and a trumpet player
May not be the best but just keeps working at it
A positive influence on all who meet him
Has a very positive and awesome family member
Still wants to be a good friend no matter what
All in all a friend for life.

Vincent Barnett, Grade 7
Haynes Academy for Advanced Studies, LA

Auburn Blue
When temperatures cool,
And leaves turn brown,
In Alabama,
You can hear the sound.
Shouts of War Eagle!
And Roll Tide!
Fans getting ready
to take a side.
Crimson red or
Tiger blue,
To which team
Are you true?
I bleed Auburn Blue.

Josh Schultz, Grade 9
Sylvania School, AL

Thanksgiving
Thanksgiving is wonderful.
All of my friends and family
Come together to pray to the Lord
In perfect harmony.

The dinner is great.
Their love is good.
For all of this,
Thank the Lord I would.

Kendall Newberry, Grade 8
Magnolia Springs Baptist Academy, AL

What Will Happen?
What will happen?
Will we separate?
I can't lose you.
no matter what's at stake.
I love you truly!
Through every day.
You fill my heart
full of love!

We're two peas in a pod.
or two flying doves!
What will happen?
Will we separate?
If we do, it's my life you'll take.
I love you truly.
that's no mistake!
Then when I see you,
it's my life you make!

My eyes will glisten,
my heart will jump.
But without you,
it might not pump!!!

Bailey Blankenship, Grade 8
Priceville Jr High School, AL

The Terrible Storm
When Gustav arrived
I was angry.
Trees collapsed
onto telephone poles.
Television and electronics
were history.
Animals fled
into their safe places.
The rain poured harder
than flying rocks.
The sun slept
for three days.
Grass filled its belly
with rainwater.
Stones crumbled
as the debris flew.
Why does fall
have to be so cruel?
Prayers and God
kept us safe.

Sterling Richard, Grade 8
Leonville Elementary School, LA

Basketball
Basketball is a blast,
I've played it in the past.
The ball is big and round,
I bounce it against the ground.

It's hard to make a basket,
To dribble and to pass it.
It really is a lot of fun,
In the gym or in the sun.
One hundred percent is what I give,
And on the court is where I live.

Travis Poché, Grade 8
Lee Road Jr High School, LA

George Outdoors
I love the outdoors.
That's where I find peace.
My peace is here in Georgia!
If only I knew where.
It might be in the Smokeys.
It might be in the Appalachian.
It may be in the Blue Ridge Region.
It might be chilling at the coast.
It might be in the air.
The air I breathe.
My peace is here in Georgia.
I will find it someday.
It will never leave Georgia.
Georgia, is where it stays.

Chase O'Neal, Grade 8
Fannin County Middle School, GA

Storms
When storms come in
and out of my life
I think of my mom.
When the sun rises
in the summer
I think of my mom.
My mom has a kind heart.
Being outdoors with my mom
makes me feel good.
My mom likes
to watch the sunset.
My mom is as sweet
as a blackberry.
My mom believes in God.
And loves every child.
I can see my mom as an angel.

Brody Cason, Grade 8
Leonville Elementary School, LA

Shadow of Scars
Though wounds healed,
body or mind,
scars show history.
Leaving a trace,
the memory of its owner,
gains another past.
An illusion of what once was
The shadow that hides behind you,
forever.

Billy Tran, Grade 8
Mansfield Middle School, LA

Trust
Trust in me with all your heart and soul
Trust in me that I will never let you go
You held me down and lifted me up
Its not love we have it's trust
You hold my heart and kiss my face
When I think of you I forget this place
Knowing that you trust in me
Our love will always and forever be

Sterlin Melvin, Grade 9
Midwood High School, NC

Moon
The moon sits
Lonely in the sky.
The stars are
His only company.
He stares down
Upon the sleeping town.
He smiles
His job is done.

Haley McDonald, Grade 7
Margaret Green Jr High School, MS

I Look at the Sky at Night

I look at the sky at night
Wonder what could be outside
The layer that keeps us in
It is like invisible art that we can't see

I look at the sky at night
Wonder if we will ever leave
Go out side and play around in the giant playground
See the giant planets that are around us

I look at the sky at night
Wonder if any other life is out there
Think about what will happen if they come
If they will be friends or enemies
I look at the sky at night

Carlos Arrieta, Grade 9
Warren Early College High School, NC

Sickness

Sickness always fills my mind,
Will I get cancer or go blind?
Does it enjoy hurting us?
Does it feel it really must?

Why does it get her not me?
Why are some people so lucky?
Will it be here really soon?
Maybe on the next full moon.

Should we always live in fear?
For what may not happen for 20 years,
That's why we must live every day,
And cherish the fact that we can still play.

Kate Power, Grade 7
First Flight Middle School, NC

Glass

Oh no, there are chips in my glass!
The perfect facade comes crashing down.
Help me mend these cracks in my glass,
These chips, and nicks, and breaks in my glass,
So carefully laid to give an impression,
Backbreaking work, now torn and bleeding,
It's all falling down,
Coming down around me;
Getting cut and scraped and opening wounds,
Hurt and regretful, here I lie.
Won't someone help me mend this broken glass?
Won't you put your glass face aside and help me mend mine?
But as you take yours off and cry to me, I see something there
You have chips in your glass.

Cayla Schafer, Grade 9
Muscle Shoals High School, AL

Running from Rain

The hurricane was coming and everyone was running,
But not us; we stayed and prepared for the hurricane.
We got furniture, cats, and plants and put them in the garage.
I thought I was seeing a mirage
When all the plants were in the garage!
The cats were having a ball climbing the wall.
The hurricane came and was just a short rain.
I feel sorry for the people who left
For they ran away for just a short rain
Instead of a hurricane!

Charlotte Wade, Grade 7
Bishop Noland Episcopal Day School, LA

The Metal

The most brutal of all music,
Never stained with acoustic,
You cannot destroy us,
Don't even try, do not stress,
Metal is not popular but that's okay,
After hearing the lyrics, you're forced to obey,
The lord of all lyrics,
Infamous to critics,
We rule all and you know,
Soon it will show,
We do not understand the word defeat,
Our transformation will be soon complete,
All genres will be forced to bow down,
Today commences the countdown,
Stinging silence will never hit your ears,
Number one genre, Metal. Three cheers!
We need no luck, no four leaf clover,
This poem is like your attempts, over.

Cody McNutt, Grade 9
Northgate High School, GA

Me and My Best Friend

We messed up our mothers' trust
And we caused such a big fuss
We miss each other
Wish we could hang out further
We feel we should hang out, and that's a must

Flavia Gallegos, Grade 8
Armstrong Middle School, MS

Living a Life

Living a life of lies and hate
And nothing good becomes your faith
Days go fast as you're trying to get past
And maybe your first day may be your last

Living a life with Mom and Dad
Death is not the future but yet the past
So don't live your life in fear
Because even the baddest cry a tear

Rashaan Baxter, Grade 7
St George Middle School, SC

Cloudy Days

When storms come into my life
I feel scared
of so many horrible things
Winds blow hard.
Skies turn gray
like fresh fertile soil.
Trees stand bold and tall
Grass is so muddy
and all washed out.
We take cover for storms,
I always prepare
like it's a practiced drill.
They make us stronger.
Looking back on all of this
will make you laugh
Storms are to be fought off
and go away.
When it's over
the angels sing!

Annette Winbush, Grade 8
Leonville Elementary School, LA

For You

For you,
The rain is falling,
But the sun is shining.
The color on the wall is black,
But the color I see is white.
I want to run,
But I want to walk.
I don't have patience,
But I can wait forever,
For you.

Alexa Ciepierski, Grade 9
Northgate High School, GA

Storms

Storms make me feel horrible.
Our grass gets wet and muddy.
My dogs can't go out and play.
In the morning it rains,
at noon, and at night, it rains.
God protects
all his people the best He can.
Being inside is boring,
there's nothing to do.
The swing is wet and rotting.
Gray clouds move fast across the sky.
Air, fire, and water
do not work right.
Getting caught up in a storm
or bad weather is not good,
when one is coming
stay inside and pray.

Logan Donatto, Grade 7
Leonville Elementary School, LA

Happy Earth

Trees are wonderful green, yellow, red and now brown.
The leaves slide slowly from the trees end to the now browning grass.
The snow starts to fall and slowly covers the grass with a white blanket.
The trees are dead now.
The snow starts to melt making the grass the greenest grass around the town.
Trees bloom with rainbows red, blue, yellow, green, orange, purple, and pink.
The world is happy.

Milana Hendricks, Grade 7
Weldon Middle School, NC

Your Love

I loved you I loved being in your crew
I put up with all your pain without one complaint
You don't understand what you put me through and I didn't get even one "thank you"
You simply let me live a lie by not telling me "goodbye"
It would have been fine if you gave me more than a sign
When the day finally came I never ever felt the same
I knew that it was going to end but I still wanted to be your girlfriend
I miss all the time we spent how so quickly it came and went
You seemed so unaffected I felt rejected
I cried so much I missed your touch

I waited for the day when we would meet again when I saw you I blurted out "amen!"
You barely even noticed me despite my desperate plea
I calmly waited longer hoping that I'd grow stronger
I almost burst in tears for I was scared of my fears
I once again fell in love but you had a lack thereof
Even though we barely said a word, that was exactly what I had preferred

I then remembered all the hurt, how you were a piece of dirt
I began to fill with pride and my feelings for you began to subside
I finally found someone new someone who loved me too

Ashley Peterman, Grade 8
Freedom Middle School, GA

Missing You

We laughed and played every day —
Until I got that phone call saying you went away,
If only I could have asked for you to stay.
Most people say you're in a better place —
It's hard to let you go —
You had a personality that you always let show.
I miss the way you let your love for me glow,
It hurts to move on because you were like a brother
Even though we had different mothers.
I never thought that your last words to me would be
"Never give up always stay with your situation —
No matter how tough it may seem."
I appreciate all the dedication and motivation you gave to me —
You said, "School is hard, so do your best on every test."
I didn't believe, but now I see.
Missing you is something I just can't explain —
So again thanks for everything.

LeAndra Gray, Grade 8
Lake Middle School, MS

Night Life

The cool night air,
Stirred by the wind,
Rippling leaves,
As it passes by,

An owl hoots,
And little mice scurry,
To the safety,
Of their burrows,

Stars twinkle,
Making figures,
For small children,
To trace,

Moonlight filters,
Through the closed shades,
Of the window,
A peaceful ending to the day.

Jennifer Haines, Grade 7
East Millbrook Magnet Middle School, NC

Rain

Pitter, patter, pitter, patter,
The rain disperses on my roof.
It's drizzled all day and night upon these Georgian hills,
Gently rocking me to sleep.
I wish it would never stop,
But the rain needs sleep, too!

Hannah Garland, Grade 8
Fannin County Middle School, GA

Sitting

I sit.
Then I stand.
And then I sit again.
And when I'm bored, I walk around the room.
I walk to the corners and to the center
And when I'm tired,
I sit down.
I get bored
And upset
And my patience wears thin,
And I get frustrated
With myself,
With life.
And when I stand,
I easily get sore and tired.
So I sit.
It's hard to be brave.
So I watch my life flash by,
And I try to stand,
But I don't last for long,
So I sit.

Elizabeth Domzalski, Grade 9
Northgate High School, GA

Wings

In the night
Bright stars and purple skies
I grew wings
Silver mirrors of sky and sun.

And I would fly far away
From this sad and angry Earth,
'Cause I'm not fenced in by metal and concrete.
But I'm afraid of heights.

People are always hurrying
From gray building to gray building.
And they always stare down, but there's nothing there
Except their own busy feet, and lost dreams, and salty tears,
Staining the asphalt.
I would look up
'Cause up there there's golden sun,
Pearl-white clouds, and sapphire sky.

And I would fly far away
From this sad and angry Earth,
Till I reached beyond the heavens,
'Cause I'm not fenced in by metal and concrete.
But I'm afraid of heights.

Madeline Hollingsworth, Grade 7
The Franciscan School, NC

One Halloween Night

On a nippy gusty night
Boys and girls get ready for a fright.
All Hallow's Eve upon us looms.
A ghastly figure rides on a broom.
Haunted mansions are houses of doom.

Pink and orange hues light the evening sky.
Vestiges of daylight say good-bye.
Lunar fullness shines on an orb weaver's web.
Ghosts hang from the trees, made of sheets from my bed.
Jack-o'-lanterns are carved, flickering flames in their heads.

The eyes of an owl lurk in the dark,
While kids in gory costumes, romp through the park.
Knocking on doors, they yell "trick or treat"
Collecting scrumptious goodies later to eat.
Chocolate, tarts, candies and gum all taste so sweet.

Nebulous ice crystals encircle the moon,
Signal that winter is coming soon.
Clouds of our breath make a wispy vapor.
Children pass neighbors having decorations of paper,
Returning home tired from their Halloween caper.

Andrew Hinds, Grade 8
St John Neumann Regional Catholic School, GA

Wind, Rain, Snow, and Wonder

Let the wind wrap itself around you,
Let the wind billow out your clothes,
Let the wind rush through the lonely streets at night.

The wind blows leaves from trees,
The wind howls through the night,
The wind forces animals to retreat back to their homes.

Let the rain pour down on you with silver pellets,
Let the rain put you to sleep,
Let the rain scatter itself upon your roof.

The rain washes your heart free of longing,
The rain slashes patterns across your car window,
The rain is relaxing to those who sit back and listen.

Let the snow fall gently about you,
Let the snow form a blanket upon the ground,
Let the snow fulfill your every dream.

The snow brings delight to little children,
The snow fills you with wonder,
The snow fills everyone's heart with joy.

Rebecca Krueger, Grade 7
Haynes Academy for Advanced Studies, LA

The Accident

A lawnmower, a rock
And an eye make contact
The pain was horrible
It felt like my eye was gonna blow

When I got home with my parents
I had to wear an eye patch
It had to be over my good eye
There were so many problems with that

I ran into walls
My head hurt all the time
I couldn't see to eat
My parents had to feed me sometimes

There was one thing I hated the most
I couldn't see the TV
It was all blurry
I couldn't see the people either

So I took the patch off
I just stopped wearing it at all
The doctors said it would make my eye better
I regret my decision back then.

Katrina Seager, Grade 9
North Wilkes High School, NC

His Last Words

As he lay on his cold death bed,
Memories from his life fill his head.
His trouble from childhood,
To the day he was saved,
He will indeed carry these memories to his grave.

As he prays for angels;
Tears run from his eyes with happiness,
For his life in heaven will never end;
But the one on Earth will with very few sins.

As he talks to me for the last time,
His happiness most could never find;
His last words were, "Spread God's Word;
And in heaven your voice will be heard."

Michael Portner, Grade 8
Margaret Green Jr High School, MS

A Mystery

The future is a mystery.
Don't dwell in the past
Because you're afraid of what might happen.
You decide what happens,
And what decisions you make.
The choices are clear,
But what path will you take?
Right or left?
Which one is you?
Everyone will know whatever you do.
Right or wrong?
Make a choice.
Hurry up now,
You have a voice!

Hailey Jackson, Grade 8
Armstrong Middle School, MS

I Am

I am a martial artist
I wonder how I'm going to do
I hear the judges bow us into the fight
I see the confidence in my opponent
I feel ready

I pretend I am the best
I think I'm going to do great
I worry that I might get hurt
I dream of doing well

I hope that I will get clean points
I understand if I don't place because I know I did my best
I say good job to my opponents
I want to know how my kung-fu family did
I try my best
I am a martial artist

Casey White, Grade 7
H.E. McCracken Middle School, SC

Cheerleading

Arms go up,
Arms go down,
People are flying
All around.

Shout it loud,
Proud, and true,
The Haynes, yellow jackets,
Are coming for you.

Spirit and pride
They have it all
So energetic
Until they fall.

They are thrown, so high,
In the air
Doing things most people
Wouldn't dare.

Jessica Smith, Grade 8
Haynes Academy for Advanced Studies, LA

What If

What if my mom and dad were still together?
What if Ali and Tyson had faced each other?
What if 9/11/01 never happened?
What if Babe Ruth didn't play for the Yankees?
What if we didn't have technology?
What if the Holocaust never happened?
What if the Great Depression never happened?
What if I didn't move from Michigan?
What if there were no sports to play?
What if violence didn't exist on Earth?
What if the U.S. wasn't in debt?
What If

Tevin Gripper, Grade 9
Northgate High School, GA

Puppy

A puppy that watches but never yelps.
The puppy has two brothers,
oldest barks while leaving the other to whimper.
The puppy is sometimes thrown
and tossed by cats.
The cats wear fake diamond collars
and eat two week old shrimp for breakfast.
The puppy goes through tough times,
especially when a dog and a puppy are lost from the litter.
Although that happened to the puppy
he came through with only bumps and bruises.
Changing his life for the better.

Dorgan Peake, Grade 7
L E Gable Middle School, SC

The Hurricane Song

There once was a family, a set of eight,
Who had experienced an interesting fate.
Crammed in three cars, headed up north,
They were quarreling and fighting so on and so forth.
They landed in Toledo after an interesting ride;
Soon enough the water and land would collide.
They played poker and Scrabble and watched the trees sway,
But three people left the day yesterday.
Soon we had left in two cars that were there,
Heading back home to an unknown despair.

Grant Reddoch, Grade 8
Bishop Noland Episcopal Day School, LA

Misinformation

Misinformation, such a big word,
Just like interpretation.
They can both mess up realization,
Or by a miracle make a better creation.
We do not control misinformation,
We only control our interpretation.
Then comes realization.
Whether it destroys something big,
Or if misinformation wrecks the small,
Misinformation can mess with it all.
Yet we work through it,
Problems big and small,
We get through it all,
It proves one thing,
Misinformation doesn't beat realization.

Blake Manale, Grade 7
Haynes Academy for Advanced Studies, LA

Heroes

Who are the real heroes in life?
They can't be found in a comic book,
Or even a cartoon.
They are the people that risk their lives
Every day, fighting for our country.
Willingly giving their life every day,
Knowing that they could never come back.
They might not be known world round,
They might not be known by name,
But they are looked up to by many.
They might not be fighting a mad scientist,
Slaying a dragon, or driving around in a Bat mobile,
But they are fighting injustice,
And doing everything they can to better our country.
They might not get a fancy cape or sidekick,
But they are just as much heroes as Spiderman or Superman.
They do all they can to help others,
And never put themselves first.
Our real heroes are the ones who are fighting
For us this very minute.
The real heroes are our troops.

Elaine Damico, Grade 8
Mount Carmel Academy, LA

Eager for Winter

Down, down, down
Red, yellow, brown
Leaves here
Leaves there
I see leaves falling everywhere.
Birds chirping
And deer lurking
On this autumn day,
Can't wait for the winter
Just one step away.

Ben MacDougall, Grade 8
Dillard Drive Middle School, NC

Shadows

In the shadow of the night
My heart was full of fright
I saw a sight
That wasn't quite right.

I stood — uptight
In the whining air
To see a pair of glowing eyes
Staring there.

I tried to run and hide but couldn't
I tried to move my body but it wouldn't
I felt shell-shocked — legs locked
But it was only the air.

Nothing there.

Anthony Lee, Grade 7
Three Springs of Courtland School, AL

Storm

As the storm rumbles the sky darkens.
A storm is ragging.
The clouds are turning.
The thunders is a rolling.
Lightning is a burning.
The rain comes down as hard as stones.
A fog comes from the road.
A sudden hard wind blows.
It stops.
It's the middle of this treacherous storm.
Then it starts again.
The water is coming up.
The rain is coming down.
The storm still raging.
The clouds are turning.
The thunder is a rolling.
The lighting is a burning.
Slowly calming down.
This angry storm settles down.
And simply disappears.

Riley Frank, Grade 8
Lake Castle Private School, LA

Have You Ever Noticed

Have you ever noticed how the leaves turn orange in the fall?
Or how the green grass grows?
Have you ever noticed that each snowflake is not like the other?
Or how flowers lose their petals?
Have you ever noticed the pictures in the clouds?
Or how the raindrops fall in a steady rhythmic beat?
Have you ever noticed thunder as though someone was beating on drums?
Or how lightning lights up the night sky?
I never notice.
All I notice is you.

Valeriya Kozmenko, Grade 9
Haynes Academy for Advanced Studies, LA

Fantastic Football Fridays

Pitiless players walk on the field
The crowd roars in a thunderous voice
They hurriedly huddle up and hash out a plan
Action adds adrenaline to their arteries
The quarterback quickly calls hike

Coaches and players anticipate victory
Tactics and strategies are used to win the game
Sharp shrewd sounds of helmets hitting make the crowd cringe
The crowd is enlighten to see no one is hurt
Players are now ready for the rest of the game

After the hypnotizing half-time show
Passionate players come back on the field
Perfected plays are used until the end
The end draws near and the winning team runs the clock
Time runs down to zero and the celebration starts

Fantastic fireworks fly into the fall sky
Players parade proudly in front of their fans
Lethargic linebackers from losing team linger in the locker room
While charging cheerleaders chase the champions
Celebration ends and practice begins again.

Anthony Staffieri, Grade 8
St John Neumann Regional Catholic School, GA

Differences

How could they be friends?
I guess it is because they don't know what is going on.
All they see is a friend in front of them.
If both knew what background the other came from, they wouldn't be friends.
One wears striped pajamas, the other wears nice clothes.
One gets to eat, the other gets starved.
There are many differences, but none as strong as this one.
One is a Jew, the other is a Nazi commandant's son.
One more thing divides these two boys.
A fence.
A fence that divides them because they are different.

Anna Hines, Grade 7
North Iredell Middle School, NC

High Merit Poems – Grades 7, 8 and 9

Storms of My Life

When storms come my way
it makes me sad
Especially when family members who died
that I never met before
it just makes me feel down and sad.
It was a hot summer day.
Just sitting in a tree wondering why.
Why must this pain hurt so badly?
It's dark outside,
and I am still thinking and wondering.
While sitting in the tree
hoping I had a shiny star.
Or even if I had a diamond
to cure all of this pain.
Maybe a Yorkie to play with
just to ease my mind.
I just wish to have
all of my loved ones back.

Kheila Francis, Grade 8
Leonville Elementary School, LA

What a Night

Twas a quiet night
People flying colored kites
Lights out
Without a doubt
People fighting
Dogs biting
Kids on the swings
And all sorts of things
Girls lying
Boys fighting
Why o why
People throwing pie
I looked up in the sky
Oh no look a pie
FLASH!!
SPLASH!!
Right on his face
Oh my gosh he fell on a book case
"Why me, why me!!" he cried
"No it's not you it's me" he sighed
What a night, people flying colored kites.

Krystal Smith, Grade 7
East Millbrook Magnet Middle School, NC

I Wonder

What would it be like with peace?
Nobody would cry, nobody would die,
It'll be like when you see the sun on a cold winter day,
I wonder if there will be only happiness,
And no sadness,
If there was peace among the world,
I wonder what would it be like.

Michael LaLonde, Grade 7
North Iredell Middle School, NC

Brown Hands

Brown hands
The hands of the ancestors before me
The hands of the brave
The hands of the slave
Brown hands
The hands that fought for our rights
The hands that worked each day and every night
Brown hands
That were beaten, battered and bruised
Couldn't hold the fate of their future, couldn't choose
The course of their path
Which they died for to take
Wondering did I get here by fate or mistake
The suffering and pain that brown hands had to go through
Racism and all different kinds of subdue
These brown hands
That we remember with honor and respect,
As we use the future to plan, and past to reflect

Desirae Smith, Grade 9
Northampton High School East, NC

What Is Peace

What is peace is something nearly everyone asks
Themselves at least once in their lifetime
Is peace a world without war, struggle, or famine
Without hatred and pain
Or is it self awareness, self forgiveness, and happiness
Within yourself and everyone around you
Peace is both
Peace is the world and its people working together
To make everything better
Peace is solving problems and finding a better way
Peace is harmony, love, and tranquility
Between yourself and others
In order to find peace you must create an understanding
Of yourself and the world as it is today

Courtney Cox, Grade 7
North Iredell Middle School, NC

Art

As pencil touches paper, I begin to create.
Gentle strokes form a mountain lion.
Details fill in the scenery.

Pastels of colors come to the paper next.
Orange and red makes the sunset.
Green and brown makes shrubbery.

The picture must have one last finishing touch.
As the final mark is made.
The picture comes to life.

Krysten Miller, Grade 9
North Wilkes High School, NC

Waiting

Waiting to hear what is important to hear
Waiting to see what is spectacular to see
Waiting, waiting, waiting for a lot

Waiting to know what we wish to know
Waiting to say what we hope to say
Waiting, waiting, waiting for something

Waiting for him is maybe not worth it all
Waiting for love is probably pointless
Waiting, waiting, waiting for nothing

Jillian Schneider, Grade 8
Snellville Middle School, GA

Music

Music
Like vitamins for the body,
Like food for the hungry,
Like water for the plants,
Like chicken soup for the soul,
Like a medicine,
That helps cure a disease,
You know you need it,
Just like you need…
Music

Taylor Coley, Grade 7
Advent Episcopal Day School, AL

Apology

You leave and come back
You think I'm talking smack
I would never betray a friend
I got your back until the end

My best friend forever
Who is very clever
Love you like a sister
I couldn't live without your beauty

Hate to make you sad
Because then I'm just mad
Never want to be alone
That's why I call your phone

I am so sorry
Can you forgive me?

Tasha Lewis, Grade 8
Carolina International School, NC

Snow

Snow is pretty cool,
The way it comes down softly.
Snow is a wonder.

Naomi Pinkney, Grade 7
Opelousas Jr High School, LA

When It Rains

When it rains,
the raindrops fall
upon the earthen ground
The thunder crashes
the lightning flashes
across the cloudy sky

Tim Milowic, Grade 7
Cathedral School, NC

Horseback

Dodging trees, crossing streams.
Through the orchard
Under the stars, under the moon
My friends and I just trotting through.
The horses, fast, beautiful, and great.
Racing on straitaways, just for fun
Stop to give the horses an apple.
We snag one, too.
Lots of apples, lots of trees.
A quick breeze on our faces.
We get tired, as it gets later.
Put the horses up, good night!

Austin Chastain, Grade 8
Fannin County Middle School, GA

I Am

I am strong, wise, incredible
I am fast, short, intelligent
I am athletic, swift, fit
I am imaginative, different, creative
I am educated, short-tempered, a boy
I am…Christopher Davis

Christopher Davis, Grade 8
Dillard Drive Middle School, NC

Being Gray

Gray is the morning sky,
a fresh new slate.
Gray is when you wake up,
the morning you'll be late.

Gray is an empty room,
lost in the middle of nowhere.
Gray is the barren lot,
that once held a vibrant fair.

Gray would be a stagehand,
if all the world's a stage.
Gray is the peace keeper,
when others go into rage.

Gloomy, glossy, graceful gray,
here for yet another day.

Hannah Moyles, Grade 8
Zebulon GT Magnet Middle School, NC

Soccer

You run swift and tackle hard
Use your head or get a card
It is a game for everyone to play
Through the night and through the day
The ball is struck and you say
GOALLL!!!
Soccer is the game of champions

Adam Cushman, Grade 8
Wren Middle School, SC

Red

Red is like the tomato
Which is bright not like the potato

I see red leaves
Sometimes there in the trees

I see red roses in the grass
I like to smell them when I pass

I like the color red a lot
So I paint a little red pot.

Carrie Beth Wallace, Grade 7
L E Gable Middle School, SC

Heartbreak

When I think of heartbreak
I hear the sound
of angels fade away.
Mirrors crashing
Petal by petal
a rose dies.
Never ending weather
as bad as hurricanes
Time is paused.
Volcanoes burst in flames.
Our heats of gold
slowly melt.
As we say goodbye
you said it's because of you.
I just walk away.

Tiffany Angelle, Grade 8
Leonville Elementary School, LA

Guitar

It has a neck,
a body too.
It has strings,
and is painted blue.
The strings you strum,
make beautiful sounds.
I'm glad it doesn't sound
like dirty blood hounds.

Cody Maull, Grade 7
St Andrews Middle School, SC

So Many Things

There's so many things in my life
That I've done wrong
That I do regret
So many of those things
My family and friends look down on me for.
They judge me for things that
I cannot change and have
Absolutely no control over
But in the end
I'm not sure I would change them
Because those things
Make me who I am today and
Make me a better person.

Brittany Bradshaw, Grade 8
Yazoo County Jr High School, MS

Amazing Georgia

Georgia, Georgia, is how the song goes,
You feel the warm sand running through your toes.
The smell of the beautiful pine trees,
And the sight of blue rolling seas.
Leaves crunching under your feet,
Deer huddling together for heat,
Long green pastures full of cows,
Birds chirping over head at the sight of them.
Lay your head down and close your eyes,
Watch the stars in the beautiful night sky,
This is Georgia, oh this is Georgia.

Andrew Johnson, Grade 8
Fannin County Middle School, GA

My Storm

When storms come in my life,
I feel depressed.
Leaves falling from trees,
sadness appears on my face.
I try to put my feeling in the fire,
but they never seem to burn.
I sit upon a rock and think about
what is happening.
I see a comet in the sky
and wish upon it.
The crickets chirp in the evening,
telling me not to worry.
As I walk in the grass,
I hear a voice telling me to keep my head up.
I feel a slight wind chill down my arms.
My feelings will get better,
There's nothing to worry about.
God answers my prayers and send
angels down to watch over me.

Dorie Darbonne, Grade 8
Leonville Elementary School, LA

Waiting

When will the time come?
Waiting, waiting, waiting, for that day
There's no easy way, with our situation
All I want is everything
Need to find the way, the right way
Helpless but want to be independent, need
some guidance
Not giving up yet

Finally, so close I can feel it
Happy, anxious, excited on the outside
Inside I'm impatient, speechless but ready
Just a little bit longer

Everlasting joy
I've made it, I won
Supernatural, so unreal
Let the whole world know that there is victory

Irene Chinchilla, Grade 8
First Flight Middle School, NC

Holidays

New Year's Day celebrates
the beginning of each year,
fireworks resonate
inside everyone's ears

Halloween is spooky and fun
with tons of candy for everyone,
just be careful with how much you eat
after you go trick-or-treat

Thanksgiving brings friends and family together
to give thanks for all things
as they dine like kings

But out of all these
Christmas is the best,
many presents lie under the tree
making it hard to rest

Jordan Bryant, Grade 9
Sylvania School, AL

Preparing for the Fight

Preparing for a hurricane is never easy;
Fortifying houses and windows with wooden armor,
Witnessing the immense lines at the gas stations,
Leaving at the last minute trying to avoid traffic,
Evacuating mostly because my brother was so frantic,
Feeling what it's like to be in a ghost town,
Everyone's afraid because all you can see are frowns,
People keeping nervous eyes on the weather channel,
Many of us trying to break through blocked traffic lanes,
Now you know the burden of dealing with a hurricane.

Haider Mir, Grade 8
Bishop Noland Episcopal Day School, LA

Accepted

He has a place for me in his heart
Just as I am
Accepted,
Not denied,
Just accepted for being me
He's my world,
My everything,
As you may see.
With the face of an angel,
And a heart of gold
How could I resist
My one true partner.
Forever in love,
Careless,
And free,
He's the one for me.

Miranda Caraway, Grade 9
Escambia Academy, AL

The Fallen Soldier

Across the sea you died for me.
You shall not have died in vain — no —
But for honor.
The things you saw great and small,
You couldn't come back to share it all.
The things you shot,
The things you missed,
They've all gone away with the mist.
The one we loved the most
Is nothing but a ghost.
Across the sea you died for me.
But how can this be?
Thank you, fallen soldier.

William Morrison, Grade 8
Magnolia Springs Baptist Academy, AL

Pandas

Pandas are so cool
They eat a stick called bamboo
They live in the zoo

Thomas Ticossi, Grade 8
Dillard Drive Middle School, NC

LSU Tigers

L ose a few games
S till have great fans
U nderstand every play

T igers are their mascot
I like this team
G o for the touchdown
E very play counts
R ight plays win their games
S till have a great coach

Eric Roussel, Grade 7
St Thomas More Catholic School, LA

My Traditional Thanksgiving

When I walk in my grandma's house my nose and taste buds do back flips,
My stomach growls and a smile sits on my lips.
Bear hugs and warm kisses for everyone there,
It's like a big, huge family affair.

With such a big table crowded with food,
Everyone there is in such a jubilant mood.
Deciding between turkey or ham,
Does nothing but create a taste bud jam.

As we sit down to eat,
Everyone is excited for their big huge treat.
We pray to God for this food,
And thank him for being valued.

The food was so scrumptious,
It was better than our everyday lunches.
Family tradition requires looking in the newspaper for good deals,
An abundance of wish lists are revealed.

Leaving late into the night,
I'm sure Grandma's neighbors would have rather taken flight.
As we get in the car with full tummies and droopy eyes,
We smile and wave our goodbyes.

Alyssa Guigou, Grade 8
St John Neumann Regional Catholic School, GA

Pre-planned Goodbye

You wake me up every morning
and make me laugh and have a superpower
to comfort people in the most difficult times.
I can tell you anything — you've got a knack for keeping secrets.

But you scare me. No one's
ever seemed so caring without dropping me.
All good things come to an end —
I should know that by now.
But talking to you makes me feel like
nine in the afternoon — the impossible — maybe
this could last forever.

I have to remind myself not to get my hopes up
or to think too wishfully.
I have to know it's going to end
to appreciate the good times.
Time is ticking, and it will soon run out.

So this is my pre-planned goodbye.
Prepackaged, sealed with a kiss,
ready to hand over when you wave the last time.
This is to say thank you, and to tell you that when you leave,
you can always come back.

Emily Cutler, Grade 9
Indian Springs School, AL

Christmas Time

Christmas time is full of cheer
This holiday comes only once a year.

The houses are strung with lights that glow
And glisten in the new fallen snow.

Joyful dreams fill the children's heads
As they lie fast asleep in their beds.

On the door hangs a big red bow
And all around is mistletoe.

What a dream to ride in Santa's sleigh
That wish may come true on Christmas day!

Presents lay beneath the tree.
Here's one for you and one for me!

Claire White, Grade 8
Albemarle School, NC

Teen Issues

As a teen,
People start to say I'm getting mean,
We start to think we're falling in love,
But in the end it's just a big pile of mud,
We start to shop designers,
We also start to become whiners.

Things become our way,
Or no way at all,
Our grades slowly start to fall,
School gets tougher and tougher,
But when playing sports with boys it gets rougher and rougher.

We believe we start to get "cool,"
But all we look like is a fool,
Life as a teen,
Can sometimes be a drag.

Linh Tran, Grade 8
Carolina International School, NC

Sun, Moon, and Stars

Big, yellow, orange, in space
Gone for the night
The next day it shines bright
It gives us day and gives us night
We thank you sun for being our light
But when you're gone the moon comes out
To watch over us and the stars as its children
One for everyone and one for each building
They both work together to make us safe
And they do a fine job it's a piece of cake
Thanks again Sun, Moon, and Stars as you shine
So bright from afar.

Kyle Ryan, Grade 7
Cathedral School, NC

Love

Love is a four letter word with a special meaning
love for your friends, family, boyfriend,
girlfriend, or just an unconditional feeling
When you love someone, you know it is real,
you can feel it in your heart and soul
Sometimes it can tear you apart; other times
make you feel whole
Love makes you feel like you're flying through
the sky or floating in the clouds up above
But even when I feel down and sad, the one
thing that gets me through the day is LOVE

Calah Caballero, Grade 9
Mount Carmel Academy, LA

The Perfect Hockey Game

I see the puck coming
I see the assist
Soon enough
It'll meet with my stick.
I hear no sound
My wrist bends back
I hear the contact
With a resounding snap
The puck flies through the air
And into the net
Right past the goalie
As fast as a jet.
The siren sounds
And so does the crowd
The goalie moans
The fans are screaming
We won the game
I skate around the rink
The other team is in shame
But just when I thought I got enough
I saw the Jr. equivalent of the Stanley Cup.

Dane Peddicord, Grade 8
Dillard Drive Middle School, NC

Roses Are Red, Violets Are Blue

Roses are red, violets are blue
Love never crossed my mind until the day that I met you

Roses are red, violets are blue
When I'm with you my heart feels brand new.

Roses are red, violets are blue
At times when I'm blind I could only still see you.

Roses are red, violets are blue
When I have nothing else to look forward for I still have you.

Myron Perry, Grade 8
Seminole County Middle/High School, GA

New Examples

The joys of the adult world are gone.
Watching them, they find peace in the strangest things.
They lack the simple joy of a child on Christmas morning.
Or running onto the beach for the first time after a year of learning.
The explosion of laughter from a baby, or discovering something foreign and new.
Always on the go, and never stop to breathe.
And what about their children?
Are they so bold to have their children as sleepless and busy as they?
Turning down a family football game, or ignoring their kid to watch TV.
Why do they expect so much from their children if they're not willing to pay attention to them?
So adults, you are supposed to be an example for children,
But you, watch them, listen to them, for they are your example.

Tori Hines, Grade 8
Covenant Christian School, GA

Lofting Leaves

As fall begins the leaves change colors
From a great glossy green to a ravishing red
Then finally to a bold brown
Barely hanging onto the tree they stay there
Until the blustering breeze blows the leaves off so they gently loft onto the luscious lawn

On the luscious lawn they lay
They are just laying there doing nothing
Until a tall teenager comes to rake them up
He rapidly rakes repeatedly until he has a large pile
He then jumps into the pile causing the leaves to fly into the air and gently loft onto the lawn

Again nearby the trees lose their leaves
Some radiant ravishing red some beautiful brown
Then along comes a fellow dressing in yellow
He watches in amazement as the leaves fall off the tree
The wonderful myriad of colorful leaves lofting onto the luscious lawn

Here comes the leaves worst enemy the yard worker
In his hand he has a huge horrible leaf blower
He has come to ruin the beauty of fall
Quickly he blows the leaves into the street
Now they lay there being crushed by cars beautiful no longer

Matthew Panetta, Grade 8
St John Neumann Regional Catholic School, GA

A Breathtaking Fantasy

She is like a mystery hopefully one day she will become clear to me. I am in awe of her power. Her beauty is that of a flower. I have never been shy or a coward, but in her presence all that I am can be devoured. Every time I see her my love for her grows like a rose and when she is away I dread the day. When she is gone I hurt within because of the small chance that I may never see her again. While I am sad and her name gets mentioned its like a prescription and I get happy with out intention. It is clear to see I love her and she loves me, I love her three times more than any one loves her. My love hovers above her like a cover. Her smile astounds me I wish she could always be around me. When we get older I want to see her at the alter and when that's done I want us to have a daughter or son more than one. Her love is pure like a dove it seems as though it was sent from above. Our love is no stranger and if she was in trouble I would be her hero and save her from danger. I hope and pray that together we will stay, being with her has revealed to me why Shakespeare compared his love to a summer's day. She is always on my mind her love has made me blind. I hope she will be mine until the end of time.

Christian Goodly, Grade 8
St Margaret School, LA

Coincidences

Meeting and making an acquaintance,
Could not have been only a coincidence.

Every day I stride with you;
I am faithful and confide in you.
How could I ever deny you;
I am never shy about you.
Never cease believing in you;
I know you'd be hurt if I deceived you.
No matter what I may say to you,
I will turn and still cry for you.

As I gaze into the mirror, I see you;
Smiling back at me is my reflection,
Reminding me of you.
You've become a piece of me,
From which I cannot remove.
As I stare into the mirror, I see you;
Beaming back at me is my reflection,
Reminding me of you.

Finding and forging our friendship
Was not by chance, not even coincidence.

Alyssa Gebhardt, Grade 8
Haynes Academy for Advanced Studies, LA

Who Am I

Who are you,
Who am I,
What am I?
Maybe you would know,
If you would just stop,
And look.

But no,
All my life I've been rejected,
Stuck down and destroyed.
It's crazy to believe that someone is one thing,
But in the shadows of the night,
They are completely different.

This message is for the people of the world,
Who has nobody,
Who knows nobody.
There are people,
Who care for you and love you,
People like me.

I know how you feel,
I've been through it,
And I'm here to listen.

Eddie Jones, Grade 9
Lake City High School, SC

One Single Drop

When storms come into my life,
I feel so worried.
My imagination goes wild,
Dark clouds take over the sun.
Scent of rain is in the air.
Rocks roll from the harsh winds.
Buildings slowly fly away,
animals cry for help.
One single drop of rain
is just the beginning.
One single gust of wind
is just the beginning.
By the end, you will wish it was all a dream.

Kristen Mouton, Grade 8
Leonville Elementary School, LA

When Will This Nightmare End?

My head turns side to side
As my perfect worlds collide.
Sometimes I can't sleep
Knowing someone else's pain is deep.
No one can find
A peace of mind
I might as well get out with it
If I don't, I'll have a fit.
Some kids don't know their fathas.
Havin' to live with the babies' mamas.
Government says they're gonna do somethin'
Just like the weak in mind they do nothin'.
But still makin' over ninety grand.
Over time the idea of help gets lost in the sand.
The economy goes down day after day.
So many people don't get the pay
My country is tumblin'.
Like football too much fumblin'.
People still broken from 9/11.
When will this nightmare end?

Phoebe Burns, Grade 7
Monrovia Middle School, AL

Football

The people in the stands yelling your name.
Waiting for you to make it into the Hall of Fame.
The adrenaline pumping through your body.
Your heart is thumping thumping thumping.
You are running for the end zone.
Shifty like a mouse.
But they are trying to protect their house.
But you score and you win the game.
Leaving the other team nothing but shame.
You hold up the trophy for all to see.
Everyone was excited for you and for me.
That is the game that I love.
Football.

Braxton Chastang, Grade 9
Escambia Academy, AL

My Puppy
She is white and brown,
Never makes me frown,
But sometimes I wish
She would just settle down.
She is a tiny fluff ball,
Small and white,
And once she's potty-trained,
She'll sleep with me at night.
I love her, and she loves me,
How much more happy could I be?
Kendall Gaudin, Grade 7
St Thomas More Catholic School, LA

Christmas Cheer
It's that time of year.
The world is filled with Christmas cheer.
The decorations, the lights,
The candles in the night.
The presents like bears,
The combs for your hair.
The bells that ring,
The people that sing.
It's that time of year.
So fill the world with Christmas cheer!
Emily Canada, Grade 8
Mount Carmel Academy, LA

Flower
Flower
Colorful, peaceful
Sprouting, blooming, yawning
Paint dropped from heaven's throne
Rose
Katie Woods, Grade 7
Lost Mountain Middle School, GA

Ten Seconds
My life is the game
The crowd roars
10 seconds left
Down by 2 and tired
One more three-pointer

Exhaustion embraces
The players
Number 7 passes the ball
5 seconds left
Up to me to score
Shoot and the ball
Soars through the air
Nothing but net
Fans go crazy
Once again
Undefeated.
Justin Collins, Grade 9
North Wilkes High School, NC

If You Were a Flower
If you were a flower you'd come from a tiny seed
And someone would care for you and make sure there are no weeds
If you were a flower the butterflies and bees would come to you
Pleased with the attractive smell you give off yes it's true

If you were a flower you will see the trees,
The majestic birds and the quiet buzzing bumblebees
You'd hear the crickets chirping and doing their thing
O' that musical sound will make you want to sing

If you were a flower on a cold winter night
The harsh snow and winds will give you a fright
And on that dark, cold winter night
Your precious, delicate petals will be in spite

But, as the season spring comes around
You will be found,
As a sweet spring flower
And spring's misty rain will give you a shower
If only, if only you were a flower
Niiya Walker, Grade 7
Carolina International School, NC

Perfection
Creak.
It's impossible to be silent though you might try.
You see the white door and open it.
Inside is a bedroom stale in the river of time.
Untouched by outside forces.
No life exists in this room.
Just a few books and some photos untouched by different parts of time.
Just a room untouched by human hands yet ready for someone to move in.
It's as if its longing for a friend just like a dog in the pound.
It's as if it hasn't been with anyone for thousands of years yet everything is perfect.
You can feel its spirits and memories.
It will teach you some lessons you can't learn in life and maybe not even death.
Could it be that you could be so perfect if no one in the universe is with you?
Then who would want to be perfect right?
Yet it was such a perfect room…perfect everything.
But then my friend…they brought the TV in.
Laura Bratisax, Grade 8
Atlanta Academy, GA

Light
Light is enemy of darkness
It battle darkness in wars
When guns are shot and tanks are used
One army is light and one army is dark
When there is an eclipse they try to make peace but fail
When the moon comes out the night is getting ready for the moon
When the sun comes out day is getting ready for the sun
But when you turn off your light the darkness laughs
John Lopez, Grade 8
Leesville Road Middle School, NC

I Am

I am wonderful and unique,
I wonder what my purpose in this world is for being here today
I hear the stars calling out to me every night
I see many opportunities down the road ahead
I want a sunflower garden that surrounds a water fountain.
I am wonderful and unique.

I pretend the stars are the shiniest diamonds in the black sky
I feel a need for Russian down deep inside
I touch the bible that contains his words and pray
I worry that there will always be a missing part of me
I cry when I think about the ones that I have had to leave.
I am wonderful and unique.

I understand that life has its challenges
I say love, laugh, and live it up
I dream of meeting my true love one day
I try to believe everything will work out
I hope that people see good in me for…
I am wonderful and unique.

Vika Sondgeroth, Grade 9
Warren Early College High School, NC

Georgia on My Mind

That old song, "Georgia on my mind"
Describes my feelings perfectly
With the peaches, the apples
And, of course, the Southern Twang
All part of my heart
Growing up with State Fairs and Barbeques
Laying on the grassy banks of the river
Listening to the loud songs of the birds
With our Southern Belles and Country boys
It feels like my heart is bursting from pride and joy
Peach pies and apple dumplins'
Fills my stomach and dreams
Ah, Georgia

Sarah Allen, Grade 8
Fannin County Middle School, GA

A Day at Middle School

Rushing through the hallway trying to get to class,
I do this almost every day and every day I pass:
6th graders, 7th graders, 8th graders and more!
Teachers, staff, and faculty standing at their door
watching and observing us for appropriate behavior

Now my day begins like this:
First I have Language Arts my teacher is the best!
After that I have Algebra which is better than the rest.
After that it's Social Studies where I have so much work.
Then I have to go to lunch and struggle to eat with a spork!
After lunch it's Reading, that class goes by so fast!
Finally I have Science and that is my last class!

Alaina B. Tanis, Grade 7
H.E. McCracken Middle School, SC

Lonely Bridge, No More

As I walk the lonely bridge at night,
I need help from this walk of life.
As you lend me a helping hand,
You know I'm not the person people think I am.
A week has gone by
Still I cry down by the lonely bridge.
Although my loneliness blinded me.
I now see the bridge is no longer lonely,
It is filled with joy and happiness.
You lifted me up and filled my heart with joy.
Now I see the place you need to be,
You in me.

Valerie Little, Grade 7
Flat Rock School, AL

A Girl Called Nothing…

She kept to herself
Never hurt a single soul

She kept to herself
Never talked to anyone else

No one knew her name
No one ever felt her true pain

She stayed alone day in and day out
To never really see what the world was all about

She cried to herself in her world that was without
She was the girl called "Nothing"…

Phoenix Dean, Grade 8
Appling County Middle School, GA

Gustav

During the hurricane I felt nervous.
I was stuck behind closed windows
   but I could see everything.
The rocks were being washed away
   by every drop of rain.
It was like a nightmare.
Oh, how I wanted it to leave.
The sun was completely invisible.
There were no birds in the sky.
The sky shook in terror.
All the innocent people who had suffered
   Our trees swung back and forth
until I thought they were going to crack.
That afternoon brought massive flooding.
The tin flew and the wood banged for hours.
   But what can I say —
   it was hurricane season.

Wendy Charles, Grade 7
Leonville Elementary School, LA

Movie Life
My life is a movie.
There is a soft beginning,
With shallow actors.
There is a beautiful middle,
That seems to last forever.
And as usual, a fatal ending,
With a tear-jerking disaster.
Lisa Lambert, Grade 9
Lawrence County High School, MS

Kittens
Kittens are annoying,
like a little sibling.
They're as soft as
a child's blanket.
They're as precious
as a newborn baby.
They take cat naps
throughout the day.
They like to be snug in a blanket,
warm all the time.
Crying when
they're hungry,
just like babies would.
Hannah Shockey, Grade 7
L E Gable Middle School, SC

For on Cartermill
The wind, the air, the dark
in some strange way all perfect
I knew he would go quickly
so I took my chances

Go-carts go fast, I know
it swerved and swirled, we yelled
we screamed and laughed with joy
around the light pole, again

Then all of a sudden a horrifying shriek
I had leaned out too far
my side across the pavement
my foot captures in the wheel

Sprinting toward the house I cried
peroxide cleaning my open sore
the pain is too much
my foot doesn't hurt anymore

Twenty band-aids two months later
totally healed, the shape of Texas
no more overwhelming aches
I am now completely peaceful
Kayla Campbell, Grade 9
North Wilkes High School, NC

Love
When a man and woman meet
They don't really know
How things will turn out
Because their love doesn't show

But little by little
Day by day
Their hearts connect
In a special way

They're always together
Like a hand in a glove
After a while
They find out they're in love
Caleb Foster, Grade 7
Carolina International School, NC

The Cat
The evil cat
In the hat
Scared away
All the rats
The rats went away
To a field
Where hawks awaited
For their yield
Justin Carollo, Grade 8
Lake Castle Private School, LA

The Life of Hurricanes
Many people walk
through the high waters
screaming for help.
The city is a disaster!
We all pray to God
to make it through.
Dark clouds take over the sky
Trees fell like big scary creatures.
Morning comes and still no help is here
Dead animals and bodies float away.
When storms come in summer,
it always seems a disaster.
Everyone prays day by day.
Many homes damaged badly,
here lies damaged cities.
Kaylin Savoy, Grade 8
Leonville Elementary School, LA

Fall
Fall sneaks up on us
Decorating our yards
Changing our beautiful trees
Ashley Hrubala, Grade 7
L E Gable Middle School, SC

Woods
In the morning
over a green field
behind the blind
a hunter waits for a deer.
Brandon Rowe, Grade 7
Rock Mills Jr High School, AL

Trees
As the tallest and broadest of plants
Casts shadows on the elephants
Trees help everything grow
But lose their leaves in the snow
And make home for the littlest ants.

From oaks to maples and redwood
They do what no other seed could
Makes paper and waxes
So drop all of your axes
And let the trees grow as they should.
Nicholas Waked, Grade 8
Dillard Drive Middle School, NC

Bees
Bees, yellow and black
Do not bug them or they will
Sting and fly away
Donald Trahan, Grade 7
Opelousas Jr High School, LA

Gustav
During the storm Gustav
the wind was strong.
Trees swayed to and fro.
The sky had turned black fast
Trucks were swaying side to side.
Angels watched over us the whole time.
Houses shook and rattled.
Most storms occur during the summer.
Our dogs were going crazy.
It ended around noon
and I was worried but glad
that it was over!
Brennan Lafleur, Grade 7
Leonville Elementary School, LA

Meet Me on the Court
My favorite sport
Is played on a court
All you need is a net and ball
And a ref with a whistle to call
Crush your spike, ace your serve
Challenge me if you've got the nerve
Parker Harrell, Grade 7
St Thomas More Catholic School, LA

Fall Frenzy

The pale moon rises beyond the hills
Lighting the dry stubble in the field.
Yet it is not the sharp wind that chills,
But the spectral vision now revealed
As ghostly players emerge to play.

Some are chillingly gaunt and bony,
Others dreadfully depraved and dark.
Lining up towards their foes with glee
With a shrill screech or a snarling bark,
The game begins as a clashing fray.

Clamorously starts the ghastly game
Of kicks, snaps, runs, tackles, and passes.
Like the Four Horsemen of former fame.
Their frightening fury fired the masses
And swiftly sent the ball on its way.

Aggressively they fought each other
Up and down the field evenly matched.
Then falling one after another
Until none was left to be dispatched,
Concludes the game with the light of day.

Mark de Give, Grade 8
St John Neumann Regional Catholic School, GA

A Leaf's Lugubrious Lot

Yes, autumn is impeccable, yes, autumn is great
But for a frailty like my kind what is my fate
Will I stand here audacious and overconfidently?
Or will the angst of my jaundiced self get the best of me?

I look down beneath me and see my kaleidoscopic friends
And wait for winter to end this ludicrous trend
I oscillate in the wind watching the myriad of leaves
And wonder if anyone else sees what I see

They seemed to be having fun, simply carefree
Unconcerned, nonchalant, dancing effervescently
It didn't seem too tragic then, this falling to the ground
They laughed so ecstatically, though they didn't make a sound

The wind started picking up, all of a sudden
It was time for me to sail, just like Aladdin
The anticipation was over and it was done
Before I knew it the antic had begun

I slowly landed elegantly on the dirt
Back to the tree, I would never revert
I lay there speechless, filled with disbelief
But I assumed this was normal for a freshly fallen leaf!

Shannon Arputharaj, Grade 8
St John Neumann Regional Catholic School, GA

old smokey

old smokey loved to hunt,
he would run these hills pulling stunts,
although old smokey was not the runt,
he struck a track no dog could run,
he ran and ran like the end was none,
until he came upon his bear that weighed a ton,
the bear took his swipe,
there was no bark the rest of the night,
we tried to find him but there were no findings in sight,
finally we found him he laid there with no fright,
this was smokey's last night,
the night the bear took the swipe.

John Price Cancilla, Grade 8
Priceville Jr High School, AL

Tiny Places

Please don't put me in tiny spaces,
that will really scare me.
I can't even think about being in a locked case.
I just need to be let free.

I like to be in big crowds,
just the thought of being stuck,
I want to be in shrouds,
then I want to be in the muck.

I guess you can say it's not a big deal,
it's just MEER,
nothing to stress over a meal,
JUST A FEAR.

One time I was in a toy box,
playing hide and go seek.
I couldn't stand it like chicken pox,
I broke it, I had to peek.

So that's just how I am.
It's not so bad,
don't you see ma'm.
It's not that sad.

Murphy Grant, Grade 7
First Flight Middle School, NC

School

School is where we spend our day
And kids go to learn and play.
Teachers won't let us sit in the seat of our choice
So they tell us to use our inside voice.
Pencils and pens they let us use
We have to write so how do we refuse.
At the end of the day
Nobody wants to stay.
Then as the weekend comes we think
We will see each other at the skating rink.

Ciara Martin, Grade 7
Broadview Middle School, NC

Secret

Secrets
Trusting others
With something
So delicate
One small slip
And you lose the trust
Wanting to tell the world
Knowing you can't
Something wanting to burst inside
A slip to another person
The secret is out
Your trust is lost
Everything is gone
Faded away
Trusting others is so hard
The secret
Was told

Makaela Helton, Grade 8
William Lenoir Middle School, NC

Defender

I kick the ball
I ruin people's dreams of scoring.
They're angry,
When I kick the ball up the field.
I am shadowing their every move.
I am a DEFENDER.

Gabby Boniface, Grade 7
L E Gable Middle School, SC

Shadows

Shadows are the mysterious strangers.
The phantoms and ghosts
That make the world so eerie,
But yet mystically enhance
The beauty and fascination
Of everything in the universe.

Michael Eccles, Grade 8
St Margaret School, LA

Tragedy

A piece of my mind
And a piece of my heart
Lives taken in a storm
Flipped trailers
Smashed homes
Trees in the road
House damaged and more
Mosquitoes everywhere!
Plenty of rain
Cold weather, insane grass
Tears as diamonds
May God help us
Please hear our prayers.

LaShonta Levier, Grade 8
Leonville Elementary School, LA

Katrina

During Hurricane Katrina it was very sad.
Rain and winds destroyed New Orleans.
During the day and night cars and houses were floating.
People have lost everything including their lives.
I know in New Orleans people felt like the earth was turning.
Trees are breaking, falling and floating in water.
It was flooding so much that the water was picking up everything
In my mind I'm thinking about how sad it was for those people.
People were drowning trying to save their animals.
I pray that God bless those people with all the things they have lost.

Chad Noel Jr., Grade 7
Leonville Elementary School, LA

I Am

I am determined and focused
I wonder if my life will come out as I imagine it
I hear birds chirping and I feel the wind blowing
I see angels protecting me as I go through life
I want to become successful and wealthy
I am determined and focused

I pretend I am the sun in the sky
I feel encouraged when I think of hope
I touch clouds as I make my way to the top
I worry that I may not achieve my goals
I cry when I think of all the loved ones I've lost
I am determined and focused

I understand that life isn't going to be easy
I say I can, I will, and I am going to become successful
I dream that millions of people will admire and look up to me
I try to make a difference in not only my life, but other lives as well
I hope that my future life will be better than my past
I am determined and focused

Shirlecia Hunt, Grade 9
Warren Early College High School, NC

Love

At night when you're laying down and all that is on your mind is one special person
You fall asleep
Wake up and that person hasn't left yet
Then you know you've found love
You've found it
Keep it
Hold on tight
Don't let it wave you goodbye
Because love is something sacred
Love is something special
Love is all those wonderful things that make you feel good inside
But if you don't take a risk on love
You'll have a life full of regrets
The only thing you can regret are the risks you didn't take

Macoya Bryant, Grade 7
East Millbrook Magnet Middle School, NC

Flamingo

Oh flamingo flamingo down by the bay,
How I wish I could be with you and fly away,
Oh how I would soar to the heavens and far beyond that,
Just to be with you that is a fact,
Oh flamingo that sits by the bay,
I will watch you for just one more day.

Michael Slaten, Grade 8
Priceville Jr High School, AL

Just Fall

Standing still letting the crisp cold breeze
Blow along my face swiftly
Silence quickly creeps up on me the slightly shivering
I stare down into piles of scarlet, orange, and yellow
All around things are peaceful and mellow

Glaze up to the frothy frosted glass
The florescent sunburst has faded to soft and gentle pink
The leaves turn brilliant colors and sway in the strong wind
Bundled up cozy in a simple sweater
Always flawless for fall weather

Mystical creatures atop of many complexions
Gathering color candy or tart and chocolate flavors
The savory smells of turkey and ham
Family and friends all gather together
Creating many memories that will last forever

Children play outside while they laugh and bellow
Skipping or running through the trees
The jump and smash through piles of many leaves
The loveliest season is really just fall
Shining shimmering and better above all

Michelle White, Grade 8
St John Neumann Regional Catholic School, GA

Gustav

During Hurricane Gustav
I was frightened.
It was soon to be evening.
Summer was coming to its end.
Electric boxes were shot.
Immense trees sway and tumble.
The sky was filled with dark gray clouds.
Cats and dogs
ran frantically for shelter.
Trash cans, tree branches, and mailboxes
flew everywhere.
My family and I watch the terrors
from inside my house.
We pray to God to help us.
I then close my eyes
and listen to the noises
blending with the wind and rain.

Mary Papillion, Grade 7
Leonville Elementary School, LA

Airways Above a School

You can see thoughts floating
Off a school —
The thoughts of the world's future.
"What do I write?"
"When is it due?"
"I'm so bored!"
The thoughts are like mirrors
Reflecting the world's future.
"Give me your sandwich!"
"No!"
"Then I'll see you at 3:15 at the flagpole."
If the kids of today
Are the leaders of tomorrow
Then the thoughts of today
Are the predictions for tomorrow.
"Fight! Fight! Fight!"
Someone had better clean up
The airways above a school
Or the future
Won't ever be clean.

Clay Hamilton, Grade 7
L E Gable Middle School, SC

Destruction of Gustav

During Hurricane Gustav,
I went to my grandparent's house.
Trees are falling and are destroyed everywhere.
It was in August, two thousand eight.
Animals were safe and we were ok
Most houses were saved
but some where destroyed.
Weather was bad
and there were tornados everywhere.
It was during a really great summer too.
Tornados were big and they destroyed everything
Lights would flicker
in my grandparent's house.
Sun was one under thick clouds of rain.
Storm was gone and we were all fine!

Alex Bordelon, Grade 7
Leonville Elementary School, LA

Lost

My heart is torn,
I don't know what to say,
My mind,
My thoughts are getting in my way,
I look close and still am lost,
I hear something calling my name telling me to come closer,
I look around and there is no one to be seen,
I am lost in a forest and cannot be found.

Lauren Halperin, Grade 8
Carolina International School, NC

We'll Be Together Again

You were tired; I saw it in your face.
The end was coming at a fast pace.
But, how I wanted you to stay.
In time, I came to understand,
Your will was not my command.
Life just became too hard for you.
I didn't want to see…but I knew.
You had to be where you could fly.
Mom, it's so hard to say good-bye.
You were mine for all those years;
I'll miss you and cry my tears
But I also know, that's okay,
For we'll be together again some day.
Ashanti Harrison, Grade 9
Warren Early College High School, NC

What If?

What if we didn't have any friends?
What if we didn't have any music?
What if we didn't have technology?
What if we didn't have something to do?
What if we didn't have transportation?
What if we didn't have any animals?
What if we all had to be the same?
What if we have no personal places?
What if we had no nature?
I know what life will be boring.
Krissy Tripp, Grade 9
Southside High School, NC

Veronie

V aliant by all means
E nlightening and beautiful
R adience that gleams
O utgoing, so wonderful
N oble at all times
I ndependent and strong
E ncouraging, inspiring our dreams
Kendrick Moody, Grade 7
Lloyd-Kennedy Charter School, SC

Love

Love is not a game
Love is like life
You live it, love, and treat it right
And once you mistreat it
It'll deceive you and break your heart
Strike you like a knife
And watch you bleed
And it won't do you right
Love is like a two-sided figure
Good and bad side
Now that is love
A strike of wrong and right
Jia 'Vante Davis, Grade 9
Acadiana Prep High School, LA

Obviously Autumn

Towering trees are covered with lush leaves
Then the astounding autumn spreads her blanket over Earth
With her beautiful blue sky and crisp cool air
Yes, it's obviously autumn.

Autumn progresses before my eyes
While emerald, scarlet, and crimson colors fly
The blustering breeze billows as leaves land lightly along the lawn
Yes, it's obviously autumn.

Above, the grand geese travel swiftly south
The turbulent day seems to pull the beautiful birds along
They switch positions in their familiar formation
Yes, it's obviously autumn.

The blossoming young children play in the prominent piles of lovely leaves
They wear light jackets in the nippy air
With rosy cheeks they play till dusk
Yes, it's obviously autumn.

The leaves on the ground begin to turn brown
As brother winter embarks on his journey to take over
The nights grow longer as the sunlight shrinks
Yes, it's obviously autumn.
Elizabeth Pettit, Grade 8
St John Neumann Regional Catholic School, GA

The Beauty of Autumn

Sparkling sunlight strike my eyes
Kaleidoscopic leaves laying everywhere
Up on the treetop, birds hum enchanting songs of the fall
I walk on ahead, leaving it all behind

Crisp, gusty winds slap my face
Leaves leisurely drifting down one by one
So peaceful, so calm, so quiet
Still, I walk on ahead, leaving it all behind

Breeze hisses and howls in my ears
Glamorous trees of all sizes and shapes sway sluggishly
Nearby, the water surges serenely and steadily down the stream
I walk on ahead, leaving it all behind

Fresh, icy air occupies my lungs
Leaves smash underneath my shoes
Above squirrels leap from branch to branch, below ducks wade down the stream
Still, I walk on ahead knowing there's something even better out there waiting for me

I keep walking and walking, faster and faster
None of these things can withhold me or brace me back
Everything is so flawless and picture perfect
But still, I walk on ahead to my home sweet home full of laughter, full of love.
Truc My Dao, Grade 8
St John Neumann Regional Catholic School, GA

I'm Not Perfect

I'm not perfect in this world but I do my best
Even though it's hard when I go through tests
I call and depend on Jesus to do my best
Long as I depend on Jesus He'll help me.

I don't feel like I'm good enough to go on
I'm trying my best but it doesn't seem good enough
I know the Lord truly loves me
And all the people around me.

I just need someone to truly help me
Everyone falls but it's hard to get back up
But I get on my knees and pray and fight my way back up
It might seem hard at times but Jesus loves me.

DeAnna Walton, Grade 8
Mansfield Middle School, LA

Life

Life is like a car ride.
You look out the window
And watch everything fly by.

If you're not careful,
You might miss something.
And there isn't any pause or rewind button
To go back and catch what you missed.

Everyone's destination is different.
How long it will take you
To arrive at your destination is unknown.
Your ride might be a long one,
Or a short one.

Grab onto what you can,
Take in the scene flying by your window,
And watch out for all those other people
In their cars experiencing their own rides.

Rebecca Vorisek, Grade 8
Mount Carmel Academy, LA

My Haters

Don't hate me,
because I'm black.
Don't hate me,
because of my skin color.
Hate me
for my actions.
But don't hate me,
for the way I look.
Judge me for my disposition,
not for my complexion.

Shawki Jefferson, Grade 8
Seminole County Middle/High School, GA

Hurricane Gustav

During the Hurricane Gustav,
I was very scared.
It was very horrifying to see
what happened to my little city.
When Hurricane Gustav was passing
over us to go to another city,
the weather was really bad.
When we went outdoors there
were trees everywhere.
People's homes were destroyed.
All of the trees that were left in our town
were scattered everywhere.
I read the Bible the whole time I thought of the hurricane.
I imagined that the whole thing was over
but it wasn't over yet.
After it was over crickets started to make noise,
and the dogs started to bark loudly.
When it was over, my family was safe
and no one was hurt.

Jasmine Mayon, Grade 8
Leonville Elementary School, LA

Leaving, Coming

Gathering my bags, I looked back at my once home.
Memories of all of what had happened flashing back.
Snowball fights in the winter,
Stargazing in spring,
Splashing and dunking each other in summer,
Playing with the leaves in autumn.
Sighing I turned and walked, walked to my new family.
I paused, hearing something.
"Keina!" I turn my head, hearing my name.
Running, I see him running.
Dropping my bags, I ran
I ran to him.
Softly, he gripped my face
Softly, deeply our lips touched.
Letting go, he pulled me close.
"You're not taking her away from me."
I did not need to look behind to know that they are furious.
Closing my eyes, I heard the leaves swishing
They are gone.
Still holding me close, he gathered my bags.
We are going home.

Danielle Kendrick, Grade 9
Rowan County Early College School, NC

Blue Ridge and I

I've called you home for my thirteen years.
You know the reason for all my smiles and all my tears.
Together we've faced so much.
Natural disasters, attacks, and such.
Somehow we always come out on top.
Hopefully Blue Ridge and I will never drop.

Hayley Miller, Grade 8
Fannin County Middle School, GA

Autumn Leaves

Autumn leaves coming down.
Swirling, twirling to the ground.
See the colors all around.
Hear the crushing, crunching sound.
As the children jump abound.
And as the leaves scatter round.
Ethan Marlowe, Grade 7
North Iredell Middle School, NC

Water Lilies

Delicate fairy dresses
With bright yellow jewels
That glisten in the sun.

On a flat green bed
With the sheets parted
They rest on clear, flowing, liquid glass.
Marcela Caraveo, Grade 7
Poland Jr High School, LA

The White Beast

Flashing through the trees,
A hint of white upon the air,
Never has one seen a sight,
That gave such a scare.

The rabbits cower in fear;
The same do the deer.
They never know what's coming,
Until the beast appears.

With fangs like daggers,
He pounces upon his prey.
Such a vicious beast,
Ev'n though he sleeps all day.

The beast is a mighty hunter,
All the people say.
You had better watch out,
Or the beast will make you pay.
R. Mitchell Gunter, Grade 8
Wren Middle School, SC

Autumn

Leaves are falling
Birds are calling
It's starting to get cold
The year is getting old
The leaves are red
They make me turn my head
The temperature is hitting rock bottom
The season is autumn
Mitch Mallian, Grade 8
Dillard Drive Middle School, NC

Rose Petal*

Red,
As it falls to the grave,
A tear comes down,
With pain and memories,
For all the times we had together,
It was hard,
To see you die,
But yet,
I look to the sky,
Knowing you're watching,
Knowing you're here,
But it's not the same,
Not seeing you year after year,
Yes I will miss you,
Yes I will cry,
But I lay this rose petal here,
For all the good times.
Destiny Segars, Grade 9
Lumpkin County High School, GA
*Dedicated to: My Grandma

A Day in the Life of a Flower

Standing in the field, proud and tall
Surrounded by nature
Going through seasons
Spring, summer, winter and fall

Watching people, animals and more
Talking, walking, barking back and forth

Winter comes I wilt 'til spring
Spring comes, I bloom and sing

Standing up again happy and tall
Going through seasons again,
Spring, summer, winter and fall
Mackenzie Griggs, Grade 7
Carolina International School, NC

A Sight to See Georgia

Georgia, Georgia you will see
It is as pretty as it can be.
Georgia, Georgia day and night
it is such a beautiful sight!
See the state free, free
as free as can be
The gorgeous stars glisten,
while people listen,
to stories from generations past.
Oh, how they need to last.
Georgia, Georgia you will see
It is as pretty as it can be!
Jennifer Jarrett, Grade 8
Fannin County Middle School, GA

Animals

Animals in pain,
I can find a cure.
Animals in need,
I can be their shelter.

Animals approaching death,
I will make them calm.
Animals abused and neglected,
I will care for them.

Animals sick and wounded,
I can ease their pain.
Animals in need of a home,
I can put them up for adoption.

Animals that love,
I adore them back.
Animals unfriendly,
I will make them friendly.

Animals in need of urgent care,
I will nurse them back to health.
Animals suffering,
I can cure that suffering.
Courtney Houston, Grade 7
L E Gable Middle School, SC

Love and War

Let it be said — this is an epiphany
everyone deserves to be treated equally.
In this world nothing is fair
no one seems to care
Yet love is in the air
so get a fair share.
All this war needs to stop
this is coming from my heart.
My love for this world is very strong.
This war — so wrong.
Benji Thorpe, Grade 7
Three Springs of Courtland School, AL

Gumdrops

Gumdrops, gumdrops,
Chew, chew, chew,
Gumdrops, gumdrops,
For me and you.
When you're sad
They'll make you glad.
Gumdrops, gumdrops,
Chew, chew, chew,
Gumdrops, gumdrops,
For me and you.
Christian Saxon, Grade 7
St Andrews Middle School, SC

My Labrador's Love

My Labrador's love flows like a river;
Always gently flowing, never ending;
No request of mine is too much for her;
Eager to please treating me like a king.
Wherever I go, by my side always;
If I request, she will do any task;
Her eyes dance with joy, throughout all the days;
There is nothing that I cannot ask.
But, our days together here on this earth;
End as her heart no longer sings to me;
She floats through the clouds toward a new birth;
No pain holding her, as I set her free.
    Her endless love touched the heart of a girl;
    Some day we will meet in another world.

Melany Eicke, Grade 9
Mount Carmel Academy, LA

Don't Let Your Sister Hunt in Your Deer Stand

One year I let my sister hunt in my stand
big mistake, of course
an eight pointer walked out
and she was a good shot

I sat in that same stand the rest of the season
big mistake, I didn't see a single buck
but I refused to give up

My friends made fun of me
big mistake, one asked if I was crazy
I said no

In the end they will be sorry
they made a big mistake
because when I kill a big buck the war is on!

Michael Dean Church, Grade 9
North Wilkes High School, NC

My Father

My father is the clouds in the sky
My father is the birds that fly by
My father is always around
When I'm happy or feeling down
My father is the moon at night
I love it when he shines his light
My father is the season spring
He is the birds that come out to sing
He is the fish that swim in the sea
He is a dove watching over me
He is the Earth moving 'round and 'round
He is a flower blooming from the ground
My father is the ocean that flows
My father is the wind that blows
I will always love him so
For I know he is with me wherever I go

Angel Starks, Grade 9
McKee Jr High School, AL

Candy

Everywhere you turn it's there.
Its colors nowhere near rare.
Left, right there's nowhere to hide.
Candy will always be there.

Everywhere you turn it's there.
There's even commercials I swear.
Circles, squares it's even in bars.
It's just too good to withstand.

Everywhere you turn it's there.
Pulling you in with its stare.
Such vibrant colors make it so hard to pass by.
Candy will always be there.

Everywhere you turn its there.
In all different flavors and sorts.
Cherry, chocolate, sour, and sweet.
It's just too good to withstand.

Everywhere you turn it's there.
Tempting you just for one bite.
But once you start, you just can't stop.
Candy will always be there.

Brittany Marks, Grade 8
Priceville Jr High School, AL

Glory Through My Eyes

Some say my life is my glory,
others merely say my glory is my deeds,
I say my glory is both. My glory is
incomplete without one or the other.

Today I ask myself:
Can the pieces of my glory that I have
lost come back to me?
The answer I find is maybe.

Will people forgive me for the few wrong
things I have done, compared
to the many great things I have done.
If they tell me they have forgiven me,
how do I know that they really have?
Will my glory truly ever be returned?

My life is the glory that lets me live
for myself and others. When life leaves
my body all people will remember me
by: the way I lived, what I
contributed to the community, the way I
treated people. Simply one word "Glory."

Numera Sachwani, Grade 8
Fayette Middle School, GA

Hurricanes

Sky is getting darker;
Nobody is in town.
Trees gently swaying;
Windows boarded up.
Sun is going down.

Wind is getting stronger;
Hurricane is getting nearer.
Trees falling down
Making loud noises.
People are in fear.

Sarah Carpenter, Grade 7
Bishop Noland Episcopal Day School, LA

Storms in My Life

Storms in my life make me feel so sad.
When I lost my Nanny, I was upset
because I never got to say goodbye.
Just thinking of her makes me cry.
My nanny was special to me.
She always made me laugh.
She was always nice to me,
and she never made me sad.
I remember playing at her house with my cousin.
During the summer, I would always go to her house to visit.
On rainy days, we would watch
the vampire show, Buffy.
On sunny days, we would go play whiffle ball or football.
I feel sad when I'm walking in the hall
to go to my room after football practice in the evening
because I see her picture.
Not all the gold in the world
can ever replace my nanny.

Chase Theriot, Grade 7
Leonville Elementary School, LA

Monkeys

Monkeys, o monkeys, how I love thee,
Up in the sky, sitting in a tree.

Swinging through the jungle on a vine,
Looking for a banana on which to dine.

Hanging by your tail, jumping through the air,
Looking like nothing could give you a scare.

Screaming your howl to show your great might,
Showing you're strong by getting in a fight.

Gorillas, apes, chimpanzees and more!
Monkeys, monkeys, monkeys galore!

Matthew Polito, Grade 7
St Thomas More Catholic School, LA

Peace

War, fighting, violence
All happening in the world
But where is the peace?
Is it hidden?
Is there peace at all?
There is —
We just have to find it
Stop the war
The fighting, the violence
Start the silence;
The serenity.
Use armies:
But not for war.
This is what happened when they did:
Two armies once met
But not for war or to fight
They met and declared
Peace

Andrew Nguyen, Grade 7
Haynes Academy for Advanced Studies, LA

Inner Strength

You gotta find your inner strength.
If you can't then just throw life away.
Gotta learn to rely on you.
Beauty, strength, and wisdom too.
You're beautiful inside and out.
Lead a great life without a doubt.
Don't need a man to make things fair,
'Cause more than likely he won't be there.
Listen girl, gotta know it's true.
In the end all you've got is you.

Deidre Green, Grade 8
Bridgeport Middle School, AL

My Grandmother

My biggest fear in life is when I have to go to bed at night.
I hear all the animals, and it makes me feel so anxious.
The coyotes are howling, and I get the chills.
The leaves are blowing, and they hit my window.
I feel sad when I think about my grandmother.
She used to sit in a brown chair in the living room.
She would never stop talking.
When I go to bed at night, I see the moon
and think about my grandmother.
It reminds me to take out my rosary
and say my prayers.
I get on my knees and pray.
As I pray, I feel like God is talking to me.
The angels are always on the side of God.
When I am finished praying,
I go in my bed and fall asleep while looking at the stars.
It starts to rain, and the earth gets wet.
I feel sad when I think about my grandmother in heaven.

Adrienne Wheaton, Grade 7
Leonville Elementary School, LA

If Only She Could See

She carries the weight of the world on her shoulders
She wears her heart on her sleeve
The smile she paints on her face
Is becoming hard to believe
She fears being underestimated
Not realizing what she holds within
Disappointment highly anticipated
She gives up before she begins
If only she could see
What's so obvious to the world
Maybe then she would believe
That she is a beautiful girl

Casey Irby, Grade 9
S. S. Murphy High School, AL

A Bad Storm

One day was a bad day
We had a tornado warning that day
The tornado came in our neighborhood
And uprooted a tree and it landed on our house
We got in the hallway and stayed
There for about three minutes
We checked to see if everything was ok
Then we grabbed our flashlights and candles
And ate what my grandmother made.
Then we all calmed down and went to bed

Symphonia Harris, Grade 7
The Education Center, MS

Thunder at Night

In a night as dark as charred land
There is a light made from Zeus's hand
A crack and a bang heard far and wide
Wonders around yelling through the sky.
A screaming shriek breaks the beat
Of the pounding rain falling on your feet.
It races down to the whimpering ground
Hitting with a thud from the pound of the racing light
And they stay there crying from fright.
Fire pops and cracks lighting the night
Just to get put out by the sky's tears of might.
The flames go out left not a spark
And the thunder goes down to light up the lifeless dark
With a thud and a crash
The ground sets ablaze
And eventually stuns the ground with a forever daze.
As the thunder cracks and laughs
Moving away with a washing wind
The ground lays there, lifeless and still
Life blooms again just to get killed.
And start the cycle over again.

Matt Fisher, Grade 9
Ardrey Kell High School, NC

Death

The day will soon come in which no one is ready for,
The day in which the Reaper comes to visit,
The day you leave…forever,
The day you can't turn your back on.
The clock is slowly tick-tick-ticking away,
With every breath you take is the uncertainty of not knowing.
Then, one dark, stormy night, the alarm goes off,
The signal that called for Him to come,
You scream, you plead, for one more chance,
No, it's your time, take it and don't leave it.

Kaitlyn Forgione, Grade 9
Challenger High School, NC

Yazoo County Girl

Life as a Yazoo county girl,
sitting at home wondering about my life.
On the block hanging with a couple of homies.

Life as a Yazoo county girl,
If my life had no kind of rhyme,
where would I be?
On the corner selling drugs,
being a drug addict,
or shot dead in my casket.
But where will I go?
To heaven or to hell?
If I had a choice I would choose neither
because everyone deserves a second chance.

Life as a Yazoo county girl,
making last minute changes.
To what? My life,
my wardrobe,
my schools?

Life as a Yazoo county girl,
so much to think about,
so many decisions to make.

Shaquita Brown, Grade 8
Yazoo County Jr High School, MS

Autumn

I open the door and then I see,
Red, yellow, and orange leaves.
The leaves are falling to the ground,
And then they turn brown.
The jack-o'-lantern is on the porch,
It glows eerily.
It is like a glowing welcome into someone's home.
The children walk on the leaves they make a cracking noise,
The streets are filled with children,
They are dressed like cats, ghosts, and pirates.
Autumn is my favorite season,
And now you know why!

Anna Byrd, Grade 7
St Francis Xavier School, AL

Matt Schultz

M asculine
A funny person
T rustworthy
T ruthful

S illy
C heerful
H umongous
U nderstandable
L ovable
T he best
Z ealous

Matt Schultz, Grade 8
Dillard Drive Middle School, NC

Trees

Big or small in size
Leaves of so different colors
Bumpy bark appears

Grady Sweeney, Grade 8
Appling County Middle School, GA

Blue Ridge

There is lots to do in Blue Ridge,
Hunting, fishing, camping, it's all fun.
Don't you wish you could do it all?
When you hunt, it smells like trees.
When you fish, it smells like fish.
When you camp, it smells outdoorsy.
Living in Blue Ridge smells like nature.
When it rains the earth comes alive.
Blue Ridge is my favorite place.

Madison Mullins, Grade 8
Fannin County Middle School, GA

An Emotional Storm

Today I feel so gloomy
as the sun stays hidden behind clouds.
The earth is soggy and wet.
Gray skies open up
as rain pours out.
I hear the rain
hit my tin roof.
Days like these
remind me of my great grandma.
In my dreams
I see her smiling.
She reaches to me
from the heavens.
Her eyes,
sparkling like diamonds.
I know she's in a better place,
but, I still wish
she was here.

Samantha Abshire, Grade 7
Leonville Elementary School, LA

Haunted and Horrifying But Great Halloween

Peeking out the window into the ominous night
Vivifying my costume's colors to be just right
Making my last quick calls to all my friends
Into the twilight where the fun begins

Shouting and screaming as we walk door to door
Looking at all the bright candies but we wanted more
Staring at the sweet little colorful delights
But onto the next house before it gets too bright

Funny and scary, pretty and neat
What festivity while they yell trick or treat
The vaudevillian costumes bring the entertainment with all the frights
What a sensational way to spend the most auspicious of nights

Not tired not sleepy, but it's time to leave
The darkened black skies even alarmed the tall trees
Although we are back home on the couch where we sag
Mom says, "Look at all the scrumptious candies you have in your bag!"

Eating the tremendous treats as we got very sleepy
Oh how I love Halloween so very dearly!
Now off to bed where I can sleep and dream
Of getting ready for the next haunted and horrifying, but great Halloween!

Gabriel Tomala, Grade 8
St John Neumann Regional Catholic School, GA

My Mom Is Not a Super Hero

Some super heroes can melt steel with their laser beam eyes
but my mother can melt my heart with her warm hazel eyes.

Some super heroes have extreme strength
but when my mother hugs me it makes all my worries go away.

Some super heroes can fly
but when my mother smiles at me it lifts me up
and makes me feel like I have wings.

Some super heroes can put broken buildings back together
but my mother's touch can mend my broken heart.

Some super heroes are bullet proof
but my mother takes what life throws at her,
even though she may fall she gets right back up.

Some super heroes have a truth telling lasso
but my mother can make me tell the truth by the look in her eyes.

Sure all these things super heroes do are great,
but my mom is my hero just the way she is.
I would not trade her for anything in the world.
She is my hero.

Heather Adams, Grade 9
North Wilkes High School, NC

Look at the Weirdo
"Hey, it's that weird kid walkin' down the hall."
"Yeah, I saw him yesterday feeding a stray cat."
"How pathetic is that kid?
Who does things like that?"
"He held the door for me yesterday,
Like he was all sweet and nice."
"He spends all his time in his yard reading books."
"Yeah, I bet he has head lice."
"To top it off, he mows lawns for cash,
And he likes anime."
"He acts all smart when we're in class."
"Do you hear what people say?
They say he likes philosophy
And spends weekends reading and writing."
"He barely has any friends at all."
"Can you say 'weirdo sighting'!"
The students continued their rambling,
So rudely and so cruel.
Then the most impressive person they knew said,
"I think…he's kinda cool."

Gabriel Ingram, Grade 9
Leesville Road High School, NC

Stormy Weather
During Hurricane Gustav
I watched the trees break in half.
Saw my dogs hiding under the sofa.
Waiting for it to come in the morning.
My canopy got hit by a tornado.
Sun was nowhere to be found.
Felt like I was in my house for a week.
Grass was covered by flood water.
God made the hurricane go away.
Water was about three feet deep.
I thought the house was going to fly away.

Kaleb Speyrer, Grade 7
Leonville Elementary School, LA

Family
Family sticks together
They're tight like
The screws on a well fixed bike
Even though they fight
They will always be tight,

Family spends time together
They eat dinner and hang out
Even travel to visit other members
No matter how far NO one left out.

Family helps each other out
With paying the bills and buying a car
Even helps through hard times
So treat each other nice.

Jaylaan Dillard, Grade 7
East Millbrook Magnet Middle School, NC

Goodbye Class
Goodbye Class of 2009,
I won't forget all the good times.
All the laughs made me feel fine.
We've gone through so much,
But now it is time.

Although we will leave on our different paths,
We still have the memories of our class.
So even though we are done,
I will never forget all the fun.
Goodbye Class of 2009.

Brandon Butera, Grade 8
Lake Castle Private School, LA

How Fun It Was
Me and her
Her and me
We are best friends
You see
Screaming in a thunderstorm
In the movies throwing popcorn
Laughing 'till we pee
I thought that would be our story
Found out the terrible news
Now I'm feeling blue
Nothing's worse than not being able to see you
I hope you miss me too
I only cry in the rain
So my family and friends don't see my pain
Seeing you every May
Just isn't the same as seeing you every day
Yes, life moves on
But every time it rains I look onto my lawn
And remember how it used to be…
Me and her
Her and me

Kasté Greczynski, Grade 8
Dillard Drive Middle School, NC

Thank You
Thank you for abandoning me for most of my life.
Thank you for cutting me with your words like a knife.
'Cause these troubles made me who I am.
Thank you for bringing me pain.
Thank you for making my loss your gain.
'Cause these troubles will make me a woman.
Thank you for making me feel ashamed.
Thank you for manipulating me with your mind games.
'Cause you're nothing without me.
Thank you for bringing me down.
Because I'm the one who rose with a crown.

LaKeytra Fox, Grade 9
Lawrence County High School, MS

The Answer Untold

"What's up?"
I reciprocate a "nothing much"
but something buried beneath me wants to spill my heart out to you,
like when a child spills his milk and wants to cry,
but can't.
There are things hiding behind my smiles and giggles,
lurking, waiting to leap out at you at any given moment.
Then you insist on discovering my obstacles, my issues, my disputes,
my complications, my predicaments, and my troubles
but what do you know?
Do you expect me to make a list, like I'm running through my life on a speed dating show?
I'm not as shallow as some might presume, I toughen up and tear through it, that's all.
Now you try to tell me that you got it worse than I do,
that may be so, I wouldn't know since I don't live inside your head,
yet nothing can reverse the tears rolling down my cheeks like the rain on a window,
and nothing will ever mend my broken heart,
now my emotions are surfacing, but how do I know you won't cause drama?
And how do I know that it's not just another one of your juicy bits of gossip?
Except, now we're best friends, and we stand and cry united,
so what's up?
"well, nothing much."

Camilla Eriksson, Grade 8
Dillard Drive Middle School, NC

Lands of the Past

There was once a land, fair and true. The sky clear and a beautiful blue.
With rivers flowing day and night, it was always such a wonderful sight.
The waters are sweet, clean and soft, its cradling waves will hold you aloft.
Colorful birds fly all around, overwhelming your ears with melodious sounds.
Every mountain towering towards the sky, touching the clouds…up so high.
A rainbow shines in every corner, bringing in a neighboring foreigner.
Flowers bloom daily, yellow and pink, and many more colors than you can think.
Darkness does not dare to show, hiding from the sun's golden glow.
Deep, cool forests, lush and green, dew-covered leaves with a silvery sheen.
At night, all the stars are assigned to some part of this beautiful landscape, this fine work of art.
But this land has come and passed, the true beauty could not last.
If only we thought of what was once then, maybe we could see it once again.

Shilan Hameed, Grade 8
Alabama School of Fine Arts, AL

Gramps

As I sit on the beach and watch the sunset I start to think. I think about all the good times we had. I think about the beach, the golf, and the soccer we used to play. I think about when I used to sit on your lap out on the patio while you would read your book. As I sit on the beach and watch the sunset I realize I miss you.

Matthew Klein, Grade 7
Atlanta Academy, GA

Survival

Out of the darkness into the blackness. Revealing light all about us. Shining within shedding old skin like serpents. Reaching for the tree of knowledge. Praying that our brother Kane isn't lurking about some corner. Praying we're able to survive, to live, to be free, to dream. Knowledge is one big tree and our branches have to keep branching out. We have to have knowledge to know how to survive. After all survival is the way of life.

Jyi Nicholson, Grade 7
Saint James High School, LA

Georgia
From fishing to hunting to riding four wheelers,
that's what we do down in Georgia!
Oceans, lakes, streams, and rivers,
hearing them all makes you feel very cozy.
It feels like you can almost touch the ocean air,
moving up from the coast.
The late night stars shine so bright
as you sleep by the fire and watch shooting stars go by.
Smelling the trees and all the wildflowers,
makes you want to stay a few more hours.

Dylan Ray, Grade 8
Fannin County Middle School, GA

The Elements
A flame,
Orange and hot,
Crackles and expands
Obliviously.
Fire.

A wave,
Blue and wet,
Crashes and ebbs
Methodically.
Water

A breeze,
Cool and refreshing,
Blows and swirls
Gracefully.
Wind

Laura Deckelmann, Grade 7
Haynes Academy for Advanced Studies, LA

The Holiday Season
Winter is finally here
which means Christmas is near
Everybody putting up colored lights
that shine so brightly in the night
Soft snow beings to fall
while people hustle to the mall
Decorating a Christmas tree
always fills a child's face with glee
It is finally Christmas Eve
a day when everyone gives and receives
The day slowly turns to night
Everybody turns off their lights
High above, Santa rides his sleigh
busy giving presents away
The holiday season is always so much fun
It is sad to see when it is all done

Meghna Gopal, Grade 9
Mount Carmel Academy, LA

Wind
Wind comes rushing, blowing, calling, and telling.
Telling of all where it has been and heard.
It blows the chimes then the rain comes.
When it is over —
Silence.

Jacob Godbout, Grade 7
L E Gable Middle School, SC

The North Carolina Seasons
I don't think that anything could
Be "fina"
From living in the great state of
North Carolina
The winters are short and not very cold
You don't need a jacket if you want to be bold
Along comes the spring
And temperatures rise
But to the flowers and animals it's not a surprise
The long summers come
And air conditioners are on
The long summer days start at the crack of dawn
Then comes the fall
When there are plenty of leaves, acorns, and pumpkins
It gets too cold, we have to wear long sleeves
I sometimes stuff them with lots of leaves
Whichever the season
Whatever we do
There is one thing that is constant
The sky is CAROLINA BLUE!

Sam Jones, Grade 8
Dillard Drive Middle School, NC

Test of Power
A swarm of angry drones
tear at my skin,
trying to make a wound.
Trying to stop me from my goal.
I fight to get past
the wall of pain they set
as the obstacle to prevent me from getting what I want.
I am persistent and strong willed.
I am determined and nothing will stop me.
The drones see defeat
like many of time before
and they slowly crawl back to the ominous trench
full of poisonous gases and treacherous lava bursts.
I won this battle,
but they will be back
with different strategies of defeat.
They have done many things,
mainly persuasion and their new
favorite is pain and suffering.
Let them come,
for I will always be ready.

Calli Farrell, Grade 7
Haynes Academy for Advanced Studies, LA

Baseball

You smell the grass
You feel the leather
You hear the crowd
You smell the food
You feel the silk layer of dirt
You hear the spikes clicking
You hear the crack of the bat
You feel the rocking of the stadium
You see the ball
Go over the fence
The crowd roars
Ball game!

Matt McAlister, Grade 8
Dillard Drive Middle School, NC

I Miss You

Packing up, dreading to go
Wishing I didn't have to know
All the things
I'd leave behind
It makes me grieve to write this
'Cause I miss you

All the days we spent together
I will never find another —
I looked forward every day
To see that smiling face
And now I'm feeling blue
Because I miss you

Logan Reeder, Grade 7
Northwest Guilford Middle School, NC

A Good Day

A good day
is when your favorite meal
is what happens to be
for lunch that day
A good day
is when you get your math test back
from last week
and you get an A
A good day
is when you win
dodge ball or soccer in P.E. class
A good day is not running into any
red traffic lights
on the way home from school
A good day
is when you watch
your favorite sports team on TV
and they win
A good day is a day when everything
seems perfect
Nothing beats a good day

Robert Freese, Grade 8
Atlanta Academy, GA

I Am Snow

I am snow.
I am cold like doing something you regret.
I melt into water as I cry like I lost a friend.
I am soft like after realizing I can't win an argument.
I splat carelessly and coldly like I have broken something valuable.
I am wet and my frost spreads like a bad grade on a report card.
I fall everywhere, leaving winters frozen paths like an unresponsive friendship.
I am dull like a spiritless person looking for someone to talk to.
I am droopy like discovering they sold out of a concert
You have been dying to go to.
I am snow.

Annamarie Nesiba, Grade 9
Georgia Washington Jr High School, AL

Atlanta Braves

As I walk in, the large stadium comes into view
I can smell the salty peanuts; which arouse my senses
Cheers are heard throughout the stadium as Chipper comes to bat
The sun sets and the crowd goes silent waiting for their team
A home run! The Braves win a million to one!

Jimmy Lake, Grade 8
Fannin County Middle School, GA

Real Frustration

I sit in front of my computer and let out a long sigh of disappointment and frustration.
I can't pull my eyes from the blank white page stuck in front of me.
Nothing exists except for me and that luminous chunk of blankness.
Time goes by, but there is still nothing on the page.
Another sigh spills out.

It's not just the page, though.
The page has united with its one and only ally.
That blinking line that never rests, never sleeps, never tires.
That blinking line that taunts you with its monotonous repetition, over and over again.
It's always there, waiting for words that you can't give.
No wonder they call it a cursor.

Julia Falgoust, Grade 8
St Margaret School, LA

Heroes

The Jews they bled the tears they shed
From their families they're ripped to the death camps they're shipped
It even happened to the little children and the parents had no way to shield them
All struggled for life through all the hurt and the strife
They lived in the filth and the mud just to put up with Hitler's crud
They weren't given any slack he had no right to attack
So what did they live for? That I am not sure
No place to be free always being seen
They couldn't run and they couldn't hide the Jews just flinched at the Germans' sight
Six million in that awful time were slain just think of all the hurt and the pain
The embarrassment the shame and still heroes they became
So in spite of it all they were heroes that did not fall

Shelby McKinney, Grade 9
Avery County High School, NC

The Leaves Always Fall

You can't stop the leaves from falling,
It's not meant to be that way.
Of course the leaves will always die,
But to you they will always stay.
They'll stay in your mind, in your heart, in your soul.
They fill that void, that empty black hole.
So whether it's the dark grim shadow of death,
Or the bright vivid colors of fall,
Please cherish the ones that you love
And remember: the leaves always fall.

Hunter Seech, Grade 7
East Hoke Middle School, NC

I've Got Your Back

Two years when we met
You said I'll have your back
And even now you're always there
When I'm down you pull me back up
And when all hope fades…
You hug me tight and say It'll be ok

When you moved away all hope began to fade
This time you weren't there
And I felt broken and weak
But when you called
It felt all good

Even though you weren't there
I still felt safe
Because I know you're always there
Always have my back
And never look away

We text, call, and email
But somehow it's not the same
Until that last day you said
Always watch your front because I'll always have your back.

Faith Emmons, Grade 8
Lake Middle School, MS

Seagull

Quietly flies over the sea
Looking for food
The seagull, white of the clouds and
Black of the sea floor

Hover, flap, hover, flap
The wings move swiftly
To keep in the sky and
Look for food.

Diving down, down
Snap! The seagull
Grabs its food and eats it hungrily.

Ethan Schroeder, Grade 7
Lloyd-Kennedy Charter School, SC

Death

It's bad to see somebody dead
When they're laying in the casket
Or laying on the floor
Several people in my family have died over the years
My grandmother's son (my uncle)
He died after being shot
My mama and aunts continue to miss him
He was well-known around the neighborhood
He had lots of friends
His friends know me today
His friends still love my grandmother
If he was still living today it would be fun to see him
But, I won't be able to see him again!

Jamari Harris, Grade 7
Hubert Middle School, GA

Little Me

I soar above the crowd
It's little me
Across the sky and above the moon
It's little me
I look down on my peers and everyone else
It's little me
There's still some good left in the world
Inside every one of us
It's all because of little me

Andre Cutter, Grade 7
Hubert Middle School, GA

Storms and I

When I think of storms I think of spring and feel really scared.
Winds blowing through my hair, all around me,
trees come crashing down.
My house is as still as stone,
although it feels like it's shaking.
It is twilight, and I am soaked and wet and very cold.
Water fills the dark gloomy land.
God is looking down on me and everything around me.
My cell phone is ringing, but I ignore it.
My dog is barking loudly at me on the back porch.
The moon shines down on me like sparkling diamonds.
My parents are inside telling me to get inside,
but I don't dare listen.
It is so peaceful in its own little way
with the storm passing by.
I look up at the sky and see a dark cloud coming at me.
I fall down to the ground, it takes me,
but my soul wonders Earth.
I am like an angel flying through the land of the people
There I am safe, and there I am free
and there I am happy, there I am me.

Brittani Evans, Grade 8
Leonville Elementary School, LA

Childhood Memories
Oh childhood memories.
How much I miss you.
You were the only one I loved.
You had made happy on bad days.
Oh childhood memories,
How much I miss you.
Daniel Ford, Grade 8
St Andrews Middle School, SC

Golf Tees
Golf tees on my dresser
Golf tees in my bed
Golf tees in my closet
Falling from my pants
Just like army ants
Golf tees in the shed
Golf tees on my pillow
Where they poke my head
Pate Bishop, Grade 8
Hatley School, MS

My Life Is Filled with Happiness
My life is filled with
happiness
My world is big and
bright
Though I may not be
that tall
My heart makes up
the height
Michelle West, Grade 7
Lake Castle Private School, LA

Close to God
Brown eyes warm.
The warmth of the sun bathes
my mind or body,
I am not sure which.
Prayers
and dreams
flicker.
They are stars.
Remember those nights
when the sight of the
full moon
would never cease to awe?
Vast and vivid
as a child's
fantastic imagination?
And now I feel as I did then:
gazing at random comets,
beholding heaven.
Saraf Ahmed, Grade 9
Cedar Creek School, LA

Love
Love is like a trophy
When you win it, it's yours
But when it gets misplaced
All you do is cry
Love is like a battlefield
You go in, but you don't come out
But at times you may succeed
Like if you find the perfect match
You think you're on top of the world
And all your roller coasters are over
At least you think it is
You're floating in the air
And dancing in the clouds
Then the big day comes
When you're getting married
And you're as happy as can be
But years later you're divorced
Now you're back where you started
Single with a broken heart
And no one to say I love you
Ashunti Coleman, Grade 7
Magnate Academy School, LA

Dogs
They smell
They're lovable
They're soft
They're dirty
They're awesome
They come in different
Shapes and sizes
They have beautiful colors
And most of all
I love them all
Kristina Bailey, Grade 8
Schley County Middle/High School, GA

Stormy Island
I feel so out of order
when storms come into my life.
My stomach gets nervous
and I get hot like summer.
I feel like fire has been burning my skin.
Can I just be left alone
on some big rocky island?
It feels as if nobody would notice.
Nobody knows I'm even here!
The rain keeps falling down on me.
Many beautiful flowers bloom out
and they are extraordinary.
When the sun is coming back out,
I feel slightly better!
Amanda Fontenot, Grade 8
Leonville Elementary School, LA

A Daughter's Hope
They set out on a lover quest
She didn't even know his name
He found her and they made a nest
Their biddings were the same.

Did you know you were forming me?
Did you even stop to think!
Surely as the sun rose,
You left this vessel to sink.

You left my mother stranded and
You didn't even care.
Fifteen years have gone by
And you never once were there.

Even though I lack a father's love,
And big strong arms don't hold me,
Love me! I scream out,
But you don't know who to adore.
Search for me! I cry out,
But you don't know who to search for.
I'm hoping for a day
That you will be there to console me.
This one's for you Dad, I love you.
Jazmin Myers, Grade 8
Coffeeville High School, MS

A Cold Night Breeze
A cold night breeze
Shook a tree with delight, with —
Leaves falling from sight
Brooke Langford, Grade 8
Armstrong Middle School, MS

Make It Better
What do you feel inside your soul?
Hatred, sadness, love and more.

Please don't hide while time goes by.
Tell someone who makes you smile.

I will be here to make you glad,
When you're happy or when you're sad.

Stand up now let's take control,
You'll feel better once you've told.

Now it's time for the day to end.
Let's make sure that you're tucked in.

Close your eyes and make a grin,
You'll feel better once you did.
Katrina Griffin, Grade 9
North Wilkes High School, NC

Swimming

You're at the meet and your heart starts pounding
You listen closely to the sounding
Of the shouts of all the fans
You go up and clasp your hands
Over your head as you step up to the board.
You look down at the lanes and the long, colored cord
You hear them say, "Ready, set, start!"
As you hit the water it makes a part,
Your legs are kicking and you go faster
You look at the girl beside you and start to go past her
You see the end and tell yourself, don't stop!
You swim even harder while your ears begin to pop
You look up and see that you've won
You feel as if you've accomplished destroying the sun
Swimming is fun, but it's also tough.
You smile and laugh and reach for your stuff.

Jessica L. Carr, Grade 7
Mount Carmel Christian School, GA

Rough Days

Hurricanes make me sad.
It kills many people.
They are very dangerous —
trees break in half —
houses are knocked over.
Our dog got scared
and stayed in the house.
She was soaking wet and crying.
A hurricane can be at any time of the day
Trash and dirt are flying around.
The basketball goal might get knocked over.
Our sun is not showing —
God is looking down on us
and watching over us.
We are going to have a rough day.

Kyle Carriere, Grade 7
Leonville Elementary School, LA

The Ruby Fire

Look at it;
It burns so bright
Even deep into the night
Consuming everything it can reach out and touch.
And when I turn away
I think it wants me to stay.
It takes all and gives nothing back.
You act like you want me to play,
But when I get close you keep me away.
You're like a burning ghost in the middle of the forest
Till you destroy all
And cause all to fall.

Matthew Hamilton, Grade 8
Covenant Christian School, GA

Echoes

Echoes are as loud as a lost baby
Roaming along the wilderness without its family.
They can even be quiet and lonely
As the little door mouse scampering across the hallways.
They can be scary yet still joyful
Like the jolly green giant.
In the cave I hear a loud,
Yet still terrifying, frightening noise, getting louder
And louder...
Until finally I
Scream!
Then all of a sudden, I thought I was dead
Within my small little bed.
My screeching sister finally wakes,
When over the phone her beloved breaks...
Up with her.
With my depressed sister here making me feel
Safe in her arms.
In this soft cozy bed,
She calms me down
As she tells me it was only a scary dream.

Nia Jones, Grade 7
Carolina International School, NC

I Am Me and I Am Now

I wonder when life will come to an end
I hear the echoes of laughter
I see people, homeless people wanting more
I want nothing but the world to have peace
I am me and I am now

I pretend that I am giving the world the best of me
I feel a sense that I can do more
I touch the souls of people around me
I worry about the world ending
I cry when I see any blood or death
I am me and I am now

I understand that God put me here for a reason
I say that I am me and that's all I can be
I dream of having all the success that I deserve
I try my hardest every day
I hope for the best and for all people to have the best
I am me and I am now

Ashley Copeland, Grade 9
Warren Early College High School, NC

Basketball

Dribbling...ups and downs of life.
Throwing...risking all that you have.
Shooting...reaching your goals.
Passing...taking a chance to do the right thing.
Missing...so mad you give up everything.
Blocking...getting upset because time ran out.

James Welch, Grade 7
L E Gable Middle School, SC

Keeper of the Fire

Keeper of the fire
Let the flames rage higher.
The sky is turning red
Now all the animals fled.
Ashes cloud the sky,
And lots of people die.
Corpses high and low
Eaten by the crow.
Soon the animals return
To everything burned.
And all the people came back
To everything black…

Jack Nolen, Grade 8
Poland Jr High School, LA

In My Book

I went to tryouts
There were fourteen of us
Only six made it
I wasn't one of them
I tried my best
And I worked really hard
But I wasn't the biggest
I wasn't the fastest
I wasn't the strongest
And I didn't make the most shots
But I tried my best
And I worked really hard
So in my book
I made the team

Ben Ritchie, Grade 8
Dillard Drive Middle School, NC

Just Because

Just because I'm black
Doesn't mean I can't go to college
Doesn't mean I can't get a good job
And doesn't mean I'm racist

Just because I'm black
Doesn't mean I steal
Doesn't mean I do drugs
Doesn't mean I have aids

Just because I'm black
Doesn't mean I'm on welfare
Doesn't mean I don't work
Doesn't mean I'm a drop out

Just because I'm black
Why does it matter?
What's the difference?
Can't you like me for me?
Think what you want I don't care

Kiahra Bacon, Grade 9
Warlick School, NC

What Is Love

What is love that I would fight dragons to rescue you?
What is love that I would walk a million miles to be by your side?
What is love that I would steal the stars to make a sparkling ring for you?

What is LOVE?

I do not know what love is but this is for certain
I love you with all my heart and mind
I would not want to live a moment without you by my side.

Jade Dupree, Grade 8
Appling County Middle School, GA

The Soul in You

The soul in you seems so selfish…
Yet I admire it so much it makes me somewhat feverish
You make me so warm and with a slight of wish
I remember our first instant kiss

The soul in you connects me with high definition,
However, at the same time, you give me the attention…
You make the pain ease away should I mention

The soul in you gives me the strength to keep up this relationship,
For it was you that asked me out like an invitation slip
Allowing us to skip our powerful friendship

I trust you physically and mentally and beyond a dimension
Therefore, I never worry a lot because you gained my permission

Why should I ever have doubts if our love is true?
You do the sweetest yet wisest things
Maybe at the fact we do things equally not just few
I love how you changed everything for me, which gives me the flu
I say this because of the soul in you…

Jasmine Blacknall, Grade 9
Leesville Road High School, NC

Life

Life is like a roller coaster,
It has its ups and downs.
Friends are like balloons,
They are there if you hold on to them, but if you let go they'll drift away.
Love is like a wave,
Hold on tight because you never know when everything might come crashing down.
Family is like your own set of repairmen,
When something is wrong they are always there to fix it.
Hope is like a washing machine,
There to rinse out all the bad and look up to the good.
The future is like a lamp,
Shining on and on till the bulb dies and the light goes out leaving you in the dark.
Life is like a roller coaster,
It has its ups and downs.

Kayleigh Storey, Grade 8
Mount Carmel Academy, LA

Starlight Path

As we look up to the far away stars,
they look down with a glowing arm to shine a light on us.
Please guide me through the night,
to help me find the light.
For my spirit is frightened so,
help that not be by shining a path for me.
From your light to the ground we can see,
a spirit floating freely.
Up, up, up it goes, to the stars and the moon,
where we have not gone,
to be happy and free for eternity.

Amber Turner, Grade 8
Carolina International School, NC

Stormy Weather

When storms come into my life
I feel kind of worried and kind of happy.
Storms and hurricanes usually come
around the end of summer.
When the storms arrive
I get worried about the water level.
We try to use stones and rocks
to try and stop the water from flooding us.
I pray for people in danger areas.
The sun doesn't shine anymore.
The best place to be
in a time like this
is indoors…
After storms
we see animals up and about.
The weather is rainy
and lightning starts.
For times like this
all we can do is pray.

Courtney Collins, Grade 8
Leonville Elementary School, LA

Insanity At Its Finest

Screaming out
And breathing in;
Living a dream,
It is all within.
Forgery and theft,
You just cannot get enough.
Keeping up with the sane,
It is all just a bluff.
Not keeping your self safe;
Leaving friends in the closed.
You lie to yourself,
While breathing to the loathed.
Never weep,
And never fray,
Just stay a while.
It is all just the same.

Ryanne Autin, Grade 9
Haynes Academy for Advanced Studies, LA

Season Spirits

The seasons are my friends. I see them every day.
It takes a lot, as you may know, to see them straight away.

Spring is bright and cheery.
Her smile makes flowers grow.
From her golden curls, life just seems to flow.
Summer is a playful boy.
Who can't seem to stay still.
He'll race you through the meadow or half way up a hill.
Autumn is a quiet girl you rarely ever see.
But don't worry, don't fret.
Don't think she doesn't care.
The harvest moon almost glows as bright as her auburn hair.
Winter is a silent boy who's eyes are as blue as ice.
Don't be afraid, he won't hurt you.
I don't care what you are told!
There are none I've ever met to match his heart of gold.

There you are good people, the seasons as they are known.
They are quick and they are hidden.
For by you they might not want to be seen.
But this I will know forever…
They will always appear to me.

Emily Martinez, Grade 7
St Thomas More Catholic School, LA

The Seasons of Life

In the spring, bright flowers bloom,
A mother's joy, a baby born,
New born birds sing happy songs,
A cool breeze brings joy to new life.

Summer comes and the weather is hot,
That child has grown the past few years,
The plants beg for water in the dry soil,
The teenager grows each and every day,
It is becoming cooler as the season changes.

The leaves are changing as it becomes fall,
The teenager is now becoming an adult,
Plants get older and older
And the adult increases in age.

Branches on trees become bare,
Wrinkly skin appears as the adult ages,
Winter is here and the plants start to die,
Death of a loved one occurs because of old age,
Many years have gone by and the seasons always change.

The pattern of the seasons is like the pattern of life,
But life repeats as spring comes back around.

Emily Wehle, Grade 8
Mount Carmel Academy, LA

Georgia Rules

When you visit Georgia
you can enjoy the smell of wildflowers growing in a field.
You will hear birds chirping in tall trees.
At night when the moon comes out,
you sit back and stare at the stars,
relax and enjoy the cool night breeze.
When you wake up you will find many activities to enjoy with your family.
You will be having so much fun,
you will be asking your mom to bring you back again and begging her, "Please."
While you drive home,
you go through many cities.
You look at the scenery and at the people.
You realize that this is a peaceful place,
everyone looks happy and at ease.

Andrew Dills, Grade 8
Fannin County Middle School, GA

My Deep Optimism

I am scared but I will hide my fear, and hope that my locked door is enough
To keep the demons out of my dreams tonight.
Yes, that would be nice. A solid wall between innocence and evil. If innocence is real.
Maybe a wall is there. Maybe it's just so thin, so hidden.
I know though, that my chance at life is hanging on one thin strand of hope,
That if even a minuscule wall is not there, that it one day will be.
And that it could have the power to wash my heart of its blackening evil.
And turn it into innocence. And protect this small bit of innocence,
From the demons that pick the lock on the door
That has malfunctioned so many times before…
Yet still my optimism gets to me.
I wonder, if innocence does not exist, that if it could not be created,
In another world, another realm. Maybe, just maybe, where it could be hidden
From all demonic spirits. Could it not be sheltered by one power greater
Than the lock breaking thieves, that have empowered too many souls.
So is Satan too strong to be defeated? Are we really doomed in this? Couldn't there be a little, hope.
Couldn't there be a little freedom from the chains that grip at mankind's ankles?
Without hope, wouldn't we all shut down?
Is it just so hidden in plain sight, that its disguise looks so much like this world,
That I must agree is corrupt, and touched by even evil that I may have only created in my mind,
That we could never see the slightest bit of hope, of innocence that Satan has yet to kill?

Blair Gallon, Grade 8
Milton Elementary/Middle School, LA

Tennis

T earing across the court in my state of fury, as if I am in an eternal boxing match with the ball
E ven though the fans are screaming at me and telling me to go, I'm not distracted one bit because in my point of view,
    the only ones on the court are me and my opponent
N othing will stop me
N obody knows how long it's been, I feel like it's been an hour or two, but who knows, it could've been only a minute or so
I know the chances of the other player winning are slim to none and I ALMOST feel a little sorry for them
S uddenly, I'm in the air and I swing my arm harder than I've ever done so, the loudspeaker goes on and the words
    I remember so fondly to this day were, "You won"

Rachel Kahle, Grade 8
Dillard Drive Middle School, NC

The Ocean
The ocean is like an angry elephant,
Because it splashes angrily on the shore,
It likes to splash and rampage,
Like a hurt giant.

Every day, it crashes upon the shore,
Like a horrible monster,
Each time it hits the ground,
People roar in anger at its rudeness.

Both people and ocean,
Get along nicely,
Unless the weather is bad,
Then the ocean becomes mad, like wet cats.

Alex Kline, Grade 7
First Flight Middle School, NC

Politics
People in the crowd roar and scream,
The candidate gives a hollow speech.
The voters cast ballets to show appreciation,
To the candidate that best serves them.
Signs wave back and forth,
Everyone is waiting each day for the crucial happenings,
Televisions on continuously not to miss a vital moment.
Radio and talk show host stay up to date with news,
Giving the freedom of the nation to all,
For the nation has a right to stand out.
The populace gives time and donates.
How effective will it be?

Chekara Gayle, Grade 7
East Millbrook Magnet Middle School, NC

Nature
Nature is many colors
It has many leaves and is made of many trees.
Nature's the wind blowing
It is the land white from snowing.
Nature is endangered from being beaten,
Mistreated and abused
Nature is like an abandoned child
Lonely, sad, color and hungry for love.
Nature needs us, we need nature
Our relationship is one way, not two
We take, we brake, and we take more.
Our responsibility is to fix this problem.
To find a cure for selfishness
To replace what we have stolen
We need to parent the lonely child.
Nature is many colors
It has many leaves and is made of many trees.

Jessica Elliott, Grade 7
Palmetto Middle School, SC

My Sanctum
My home
My special place
So quiet
So peaceful
The sound of waves, crashing onto the shore at night
The mist walking on the water in the morning
The trees dancing in the wind
The grass whistling
The smell of clean air
The aroma of gasoline hovering in the air
The ducks moving swiftly but quietly
Everything at peace
My get away

Tyler McCormick, Grade 8
Atlanta Academy, GA

The New Orleans Saints
It's fourth down and one.
They can't make it.
The other team fumbles.
They don't take it.
They need a field goal to win.
It doesn't go in.

A winning season is rare.
They just don't compare
To the other teams that win games.
They drive me insane.

Who dat say they gonna beat dem Saints?
No one needs to; they beat demselves.

I really want them to win,
I'm tired of making complaints.
But if winning is really a sin,
Then I guess they are the Saints.

Norwood Hingle, Grade 9
Haynes Academy for Advanced Studies, LA

Sway
Soft and gentle the breeze flows within me
The air is so crisp and light
It shuffles leaves
And disrupts oceans until they are distraught;
Blows away children's toys
And soothes the mind
It brushes over sand
Smoothing over footprints
Deep and gentle
Pure and lovely
The dainty breeze softly blows
I adore the wind
As it softly
Embraces my life

Megan Reynolds, Grade 9
Mount Carmel Academy, LA

The River

Flowing down the river
I see fish a swimming
Flowing down the river
I see birds of beauty
Flowing down the river
I see reflections of trees
Flowing down the river
I see glimmers of sunlight
Flowing down the river
I see my destiny going
Flowing down the river
Is a heavenly feeling.

Ashley Adams, Grade 8
Hatley School, MS

Soccer Is:

Dedication — pain — love — work
— drive — adrenaline
The way you feel running down the field
with the ball you kick for a goal
the goalie jumps to block
you stand you wait Goal
the first point of the game
you feel the sleet on your face
feels like a million needles
stinging at your nerves
as you run for the ball you slide you miss
as you get up soaked with muddy legs
and covered in bloody scrapes
a minute-forty eight
you're winning let the time run out
five seconds left
   you won!!!

Erika Miles, Grade 9
North Wilkes High School, NC

Memories

They come and go
You keep them still
Close to your heart
Locked away

Good and bad
Happy and sad
Part of who you are
There like a scar

You learn from them
You cherish them
Kept forever
Or thrown away

Always will be
Your memories

Jenna Freeman, Grade 8
Trickum Middle School, GA

I Cry

He was something new; something older
Our relationship was heating up, but I was getting colder
He was changing deep inside, but I liked him like he was
I just don't like the things he does
I wonder if he saw the pain in my eyes
I wonder if he ever saw me cry
I know that he's almost a man now and I'm just his girl
But I wonder how he didn't see that my life was in a total whirl
The days were getting colder
There was still a chip on my shoulder
It was time for me to say good-bye
Once again I cry

Danielle Busby, Grade 8
Clara Jr High School, MS

The Adventure of Cats

Cats sneak out from their houses like shadows
They do whatever they please
Prowling in the night
Pouncing and climbing all night long
They meet with others in a certain place
Yowling, calling for friends to join a wandering crew
Friends come crawling through the mazes of fences and houses
Stopping at nothing, as they grip their mate's scent
They join their mate and begin the adventure
As the sun rises through the sky
Sunrise is near
It is time to depart
The cats purr and lick each other to say good bye
They go home to meet their owners and give them a meow
Soon they fall asleep, awaiting for night to fall

Caroline Zheng, Grade 7
Haynes Academy for Advanced Studies, LA

Is Heaven for Real

Is heaven for real
that is an answer I need to know.
I sit in church Sunday after Sunday
listening to the preacher preach
talking about streets made of gold and wearing white robes.

They say, "If you don't sin you will go to heaven,"
but people sin every day.
Sometimes I sit and think and wonder
what have I done today?
Have I sinned?

They say, "All pain and anger will be washed away."
And so I say, "Is heaven for real." And sometime they will try to trick you,
but hold on and stay strong.
because if you believe that Jesus died for you on Calvary,
then you my friend will go to heaven.

Aaron Hudson, Grade 8
Yazoo County Jr High School, MS

Piece of Nature or Nature's Peace?

It is tethered to the ground,
Yet it can be pulled free.
It lives off the soil,
But can also be cared for by humans.
It grows from a small seed
And becomes humongous by comparison.
Some may have just beauty;
Others may do good things for us.
Under the guise of a flower,
Some plants maliciously take what flowers need.
After appearing on a tree,
It can bear fruit.
Nature's beauty —
A delicate object.
The wondrous flower.

Eric Le, Grade 8
Haynes Academy for Advanced Studies, LA

War

The merciless heat, the harsh beating of sun.
There is nobody left, but me, I am the only one.
I can hear them coming, the pitter-patter in the mud
They feed off hate, fear and blood.

I have been consumed by war, I cannot turn back
I was told to defend, kill and attack
They are closer now and gaining fast
There is no future for me, only a past
War is a never-ending maze with no exit path
It consumes its victims, its terrible wrath

They are close on me, I am frozen with fear
To think of the terror that is drawing so near
What am I doing, I have a wife and kids!
If they find me dead, O God forbid!

I must survive, but it's much too late
I am a U.S. soldier and this is my fate.

Harrison Payne, Grade 8
Mount Carmel Christian School, GA

Basketball

Big orange balls bouncing on the floor
Flying through the air trying to make a score
Players running, coaches shouting
Fans crying defense! Defense! Defense!
Bodies colliding, grunting in pain
Sweat on the floor, the players slipping and sliding
The ball flies through the air and through the basket
The crowd cheers for their favorite team
Boos echo through the gym after a bad call
Showing their passion the players go at it
All the way until the buzzer sounds
Now they can rest in peace.

Tyler Smith, Grade 7
North Iredell Middle School, NC

Everything's Okay

Everything's okay.
It seems that I've forgotten
The events of that day
And the horrors it held,
But in all honesty, I haven't,
And I never will.
Hey you, are you listening?
It's your fault I must pretend that I'm okay,
When I'm not!
You're why I don't remember
All the things that I should,
And I hate you, because…
I don't remember
A time without a tear,
A night without a nightmare,
A day with out the drama,
But I want to, with all my heart,
And you don't even care.

Kimberly Williams, Grade 9
Providence High School, NC

A Ticking Bomb

She is very angry at all times.
She has no self control.
She is red and bursting with flames.
She exceeds beyond her friends.
She is a fireball of passion.
She is always going off like an
Alarm clock that is spastic.
She is always downbeat
She is the flicker from a campfire,
going in no particular direction.
She is in a constant war zone
She is the grenade that has just hit the ground
She is angry at the world.

Keianna Carr, Grade 9
Georgia Washington Jr High School, AL

Blue Days

When storms come into my life,
I feel lonely,
While watching the trees blow away,
all I do is stay inside and watch the news.
The clouds turn a darkish blue.
While I sit and think
of dreams fading away,
I watch my mom
sit and think of her master plan,
Fall time isn't great.
Birds fly so far away.
The sun seems to never shine.

Marcretia Carriere, Grade 8
Leonville Elementary School, LA

Goodbye Adam

To a boy I will never forget
The moment you died I'll regret
To the football player you wanted to be
And a friend I'll later see.

You were such a clown
At our school in downtown.
A Michigan fan are you,
A team that is yellow and blue.

You were always true to your team
No matter how bad they seem
I'll miss you Adam, you friend of mine
Someone who will shine.

Until now is goodbye
But later is a sigh
Goodbye until we meet again
Eventually in heaven.

Cam Linh Nguyen, Grade 8
St Mary's School, SC

Dallas

D aring
A thletic
L ikes to play video games
L oves to play the baritone
A girl's dream
S mooth

Dallas Martin, Grade 7
L E Gable Middle School, SC

When I Look at You

When I look at you,
The only thing I can see
Is a heavenly angel
Staring back at me.

And when I look into
Your eyes, I see lots of love
And deep compassion,
Of which there is no form or fashion.

But, when I look upon your face,
I see my brother Jesus in its place,
And that face cannot compare with
Any other in the human race.

In all of these things that I can see,
There is one answer to this you see;
A faithful Christian living in you, and
To be one your whole life through.

Emily Hall, Grade 8
Hatley School, MS

The Ticking Clock

The clock that's round
　I hear its sound
"Tick, Tick, Tick,"
Its lovely music
　more than joy
It clicks at night
　and times just right
The small and large hands
　its handy helpers
Prompts me
　where to be
Yet the face's pace
　at merry haste
Is still ticking…

Luke Lepak, Grade 7
St Mary's School, SC

Spring

It's when the flowers grow,
　and the lilies bloom.
　They put on a show,
　that lights up the room.

It's when the Easter Bunny comes,
　and turns up smiles,
　that goes and goes and,
　always lasts for miles.

It's when our Savior rose from the grave,
　and defeated sin,
　so that we could be saved,
　and one day He is coming again.

Leanna Grantland, Grade 8
Priceville Jr High School, AL

Wind

Wind comes and goes,
　love comes and goes,
　and life comes and goes
　everything is like the wind
A lot of things in this world are simple,
　But one day it will all end…

Francisco Gaitan Diaz, Grade 8
Dillard Drive Middle School, NC

Outside

Outside is a desert
Nothing out there but sand and heat.
Wondering when the water will run out.
Why is it so hot?
Why no rain?
Please, make it rain.

Cole Daniels, Grade 7
L E Gable Middle School, SC

Orange

My mind is orange
No one feels like I do
Orange is different
It rhymes with nothing

My spirit is orange
No one is like me
Orange is different
Nothing can compare

My body is orange
Like no one else's
Orange is different
It is all too unique

I live life orange
No one could understand
I am different
And that's how I have always been

Dustin Soutendijk, Grade 9
Leesville Road High School, NC

October

O ctober
C alling my friends
T elling them to come over
O utside jumping in the leaves
B eside the tree talking
E ating some of our favorite foods
R emembering old times

Brittany Cook, Grade 7
Rock Mills Jr High School, AL

Dream

This place was so beautiful and clean,
With waters of the purest blue and green,
Nothing to worry about,
Just things to be happy about,
Until I woke to find it was just a dream.

Just a dream,
I thought to myself,
How could this be it seemed so real,
It was too real,
I guess that's why it's called a dream.

This place was so beautiful and clean,
With waters of the purest blue and green,
Nothing to worry about,
Just things to be happy about,
Until I woke to find it was just a dream,
Ahh reality…

Megan Moore, Grade 8
Carolina International School, NC

How Does Life Work?

I can't explain it
but this good feeling is filling my heart
everyone's together having fun
listening to music and just chilling
That's not how life works!
The feeling of love in those three days
filled the area like fog
everyone was there aunts and uncles, and cousins too.
in each place for three days for the family reunion
all filled with love
That's not how life works!
The screaming of kids playing
everyone eating their lives away
no drama during those days
only the drips of happiness from everyone's smiles
That's not how life works!
Life…Full of disappointments
the killing, shooting, murdering, and dying
life is what it wants to be
whatever emotion on whatever day
NOW THAT'S HOW LIFE WORKS!

Essence Daley, Grade 8
Charleston Charter School for Math & Science, SC

Hurricane Gustav

A dangerous mix of power,
Bringing indescribable misery to New Orleans,
Shaking the trees like an earthquake,
Flooding the neighborhoods of life,
Forcing humans into exile,
Halting the light of protection,
Strengthened by the waters of warmth,
Destroying nature's shield,
Weakened by its furious counterattack,
Only to die from its illness.

Gurnoor Benipal, Grade 8
Bishop Noland Episcopal Day School, LA

Love

You are gonna do wrong and mess up your life with him.
I'm not you I'm not gonna make the same dumb mistakes.
You need to think about your career and your school.
You're too afraid I'll ruin my life with this boy.
You're so obsessed with him you cannot live without him.
You have no idea I'm not obsessed I'm in love.
You don't know what love is you're way to young.
I do know, I just wish you'd remember.
Remember what? I know what I know is best.
Remember when you were young, in love with a boy.
Life is too hard to live in any ways!
Life is too hard to live in any ways!

Hannah Adams, Grade 9
North Wilkes High School, NC

Anger

Deep down,
I am growling
My mind is pacing:
A trapped tiger.
Need and wanting bubbling, hot in my blood
To scream
Go crazy
Hit someone, something
But I can't
Anger bottled up inside
Pounding to come out
My fury swells, ready to burst
But I mustn't let it out; I have to stay strong.

Andrea Velosa, Grade 7
The Franciscan School, NC

Be

People always say "I am me."
But what does that mean?
To call yourself by your name?
How can that be with a million Johns and Emilys?
To be you by your name.
It's your actions that matter.
And the words that you speak.
Treating others with kindness
And using your own style.
I am me, and you are you
But what matters is how we are
To make who we are.
And not just be you,
But be.

Meara McNitt, Grade 8
Boyet Jr High School, LA

I Am

I am brave and strong.
I wonder why so much crime is committed
I hear the world crying
I see the world drowning
I want happiness,
I am brave and strong.

I pretend I'm ok
I feel crumbled up
I touch sadness
I worry about the world,
I am brave and strong.

I understand anything can happen
I say "don't give up"
I dream for happiness
I try to aim for happiness
I hope my dream comes true,
I am brave and strong.

Kemberly Martinez, Grade 9
Warren Early College High School, NC

Matthew

My brother
My friend
Sticking together is what we do best
He's the center of my complaints
We constantly bicker and fight
Yet we secretly get along
In the chance that someone might see us together
Late nights bring us apart
But we'll always be close deep in my heart

Emily Delmestri, Grade 7
Westchester Country Day School, NC

My Pebble

Thousand upon thousands of years
Is how old you are
Yet you show no wrinkles,
No crows feet, and no weak bones
A little piece of your shining armor is missing
For you have been dropped several times
When you were young
You have seen things that
No one can explain today
Dirt makes homes in your crevasses
White paint floods out on to your
Smooth cold back
You have battle wounds
For you have fought with
Mother nature several times
You hide under leaves
And dig deep into the earth
The pebble I hold in my hands
Is a pebble that is a warrior
A warrior against the elements
You are my pebble my warrior

Erin Weatherly, Grade 7
Atlanta Academy, GA

Love Struck

I was always so scared to love,
I would rather yank a tiger's tail.
But when I stared love straight in the eye,
I completely let my guard down.
I thought, this isn't so bad after all.
I got over all my fears;
I never wanted to be scared of love again.
But instead of love, loving me back,
It just played with my mind and crushed my heart.
My mistake of falling in love so hard nearly killed me.
I gave everything to love,
But all love returned was heartache and confusion.
This is what I call Love Struck.

Lakisha Smith, Grade 9
Atlanta School, LA

Grandpa

Gone forever never seen again was a hard worker
Cared about his family died of cancer
He was like a father to me
Taught me how to work in the fields
Always made me happy
Always told me to follow my dreams
Moved to the U.S.A.
Still kept in touch with him
Made it to the fifth grade
My aunt's told me he was sick
I prayed and had faith that he was going to make it
Month's later I heard he was dead I couldn't believe it
I realize this was reality
I just couldn't hold the tears
I never saw his funeral or him again
But I know he's in a better place
Grandpa, I miss you so much
You helped me out so much in life
I will love you forever Grandpa.
All I'm sayin' is I miss you Grandpa

Johnny Ixcot, Grade 8
Schley County Middle/High School, GA

Halloween Night

Critters and creatures roam about.
It's Halloween night everyone shout!
Lock all your doors stay inside.
A spook is coming so you better hide!
No one is leaving their home tonight.
For the witches and ghosts have given us fright.
The dead awakens finally free,
They head off to capture you and me.
Keep everyone near for the daylight is here.
All creatures are fleeing no more need to fear.
Everyone comes out to see what was done,
All thankful that the new day has come.
But no one knows that they are waiting,
For next year to come to spook more places.

Brittany Lowe, Grade 9
Weddington High School, NC

Some Times

Some times in my mind
It feels like I'm getting left behind
Sometimes my rhymes want shine like a dime
Sometimes I feel like a fool when my mode isn't cool.
To think about what is going on in the world
Like fighting and writing about one another
Sometimes my brain sounds like rain.
When it's filled with pain, but I can't complain
About those things.
Sometimes I feel like I'm way too cool to act up in school.
It's all right to change your mind sometimes
Just let me find mine so that I could shine.

Wesley Wadley, Grade 7
Hubert Middle School, GA

Just Me

Right and wrong is how you have been taught
Don't do this
Don't do that
You've learned responsibility
You have fidelity in those around you
You are off on your own
Now live your life the way you want

Kelsey Cooley, Grade 8
Alexandria Middle Magnet School, LA

Healing

My heart fills with sadness
whenever I am sitting at home
wanting to do something that I know I can't do.
The sun shines brightly.
It's a beautiful day, but I still can't do anything.
I pray to God that I can heal quickly
so that I can have fun.
The earth moves in a circle,
and the next day, God answers my prayers.
I am all healed up!
The sun shines brightly
and the squirrels climb in the trees
and jump from branch to branch.
The oak tree's leaves move
from the animals in it that are jumping around.
I sit on the boulder beneath the tree
that lies like a bump on a log
and enjoy the sunshine as it shines down on me.

Andy Meche, Grade 7
Leonville Elementary School, LA

Storms

When Gustav hit I felt so miserable.
It was so hot
They had about twenty people in one room.
Many candles made it hotter.
I don't think a cactus
could survive in this heat.
There were leaves everywhere
branches all over the ground.
You could not sleep a wink
they just had too many people
and it just wasn't comfortable.
It was just too hot
I feel like I was sleeping
right next to the sun.
When the morning comes
there was nothing to eat or drink.
All you did was sleep all day
I felt like a rock every single day.
I did nothing all day
I could not go anywhere because of the rain.
I kept dreaming that the electricity would come back on.

Kylen Guilbeaux, Grade 8
Leonville Elementary School, LA

Our Home

Way back here in the Blue Ridge Region.
Where we all learn to do stuff.
Such as fishing, you can hear crickets chirping,
See the water ripple down the rocks.
You can touch the water and feel the clearness.
It's like water on a hot day that evaporates.
When the sun peaks over the trees to warm the cold earth.
The forest it rains, it snows, everything blows.
The rain falls like little drops of silver on this Georgia land.
The wind blows like groups of wolves howling mad.
You can smell the dew off the grass in the mornings,
you can hear the roosters crowing to wake you up,
You can close your eyes and feel the peace in the air.
You can do anything and know your home here,
Our home back in the mountains.

Courtney Harvey, Grade 8
Fannin County Middle School, GA

Let My Music Soar

There is a song in my soul
Gently tapping in rhythm
To each beat of my heart.
Let my words fly free
Into the night sky
Like a swan gliding on a lake
Softly and smoothly.
Allow the sound flowing inside my veins
To burst forth filling the atmosphere with
Every single emotion venturing throughout my nerves.
Let me aspire to my dreams
Because somebody inspired it
Let me give it my all
Let my music soar.

Emily Barrett, Grade 9
Mount Carmel Academy, LA

Just Be You

There's something I need to tell you
More than words could ever say
Every time I talk, you turn and walk away
Somehow I would never tell you if you'd stay

Go, run along
Why stand here like a sad song?
Even if I had something to say
Just be you and slowly drift away

Something that I don't know about you
There seems to be something crazy in everything you do
Why be silly in what you do?
Just be normal and act like you.

Euneeka Dudley, Grade 9
Southside High School, NC

Friends 'Til the End

We always stick together,
In thick or in thin.
We always know better,
Now and then.

You are my bestest friend,
No matter what.
You're there 'til the end,
Even though you can be a pain in the butt.

We always think of each other,
You are my buddy.
Even if we're with another,
We still can't resist getting muddy.

No matter what
We must rearrange,
Or the fights we will bring,
Our friendship will never change.

We stick together,
In thick or in thin,
We should always know better,
We're the best of friends.

Stephanie Thompson, Grade 8
First Flight Middle School, NC

Farms

The break of dawn starts to show
The red wood starts to glow

I see the mist in the air
Here the air is not clear

There's an animal in the pasture
Watch while it gets faster

Listening to this soothing hymn
Listen to it as it dims

The fields move just as a wave
The sight is meant to save

A whisper of wind shivers down my back
Listen to the leaves go crack…crack…crack

Where's this place I have found
With animals all around

It is so beautiful as if it's drawn
I shall say it is a farm

Morgan Stanford, Grade 7
St Francis Xavier School, AL

Friends

Friends are like family
They always have your back
They do everything with you
They give you advice
When you need it
Tell you what's
Good and bad
Give you money
When you need it
Give you a hand
When you're in trouble
Give you answers
When you don't
Even know the question
Give you a ride
When you want
To go somewhere
Skip class with you
When you don't
Want to be in there!!!

Alejandra Chegue, Grade 7
East Millbrook Magnet Middle School, NC

Index

Abercrombie, Meredith .... .28
Abshire, Kristen .... .26
Abshire, Samantha .... .180
Acosta, Brennen .... .107
Adams, Ashley .... .192
Adams, Hannah .... .195
Adams, Heather .... .180
Aguirre, Daniella .... .153
Ahmad, Bushra .... .148
Ahmed, Maryam .... .146
Ahmed, Saraf .... .186
Aiello, Chris .... .112
Airey, Kimmi .... .32
Akins, Megan .... .144
Al-Ghandour, Deema .... .51
Alexander, Deven .... .51
Alexander, Kayla .... .48
Alikhani, Matthew .... .43
Allen, Faith .... .100
Allen, Jonathan .... .95
Allen, Sarah .... .169
Anadi, Adora .... .121
Anderson, Alison .... .25
Anderson, Dalton .... .114
Anderson, Ryan .... .32
Andrus, Brittany .... .104
Angelle, Tiffany .... .162
Anthony, Nia .... .94
Aquilo, Katelyn .... .79
Archer, Benjamin .... .90
Armstrong, Blakeney .... .66
Arnaud, Ricky .... .90
Arputharaj, Shannon .... .171
Arrieta, Carlos .... .155
Arrington, Brittany .... .90
Artigue, Brooke .... .66
Ashenfelter, Jennifer .... .133
Ashton, Alexis .... .96
Autin, Ryanne .... .189
Babb, Chelsea .... .72
Bacharach, Eddie .... .96
Bacon, Kiahra .... .188
Bailey, Joy .... .49
Bailey, Kristina .... .186
Bailey, Nick .... .90
Ballard, Corey .... .146
Ballou, Gabriel .... .54
Barber, AnnaMae .... .140
Barker, Grayson .... .35
Barnaba, Jaleesa .... .20
Barnett, Vincent .... .153

Barrett, Emily .... .197
Barriault, McKayla .... .71
Barron, Brianna .... .92
Bass, Shekinah .... .105
Baugh, Kaitlynn .... .50
Baxter, Rashaan .... .155
Bazzell, Megan .... .68
Beadle, Jennifer .... .61
Beckwith, Michael .... .77
Beetles, John T. .... .28
Bellamy, Emily .... .102
Bellard, Zakayle' .... .47
Belleau, Peter .... .99
Bellard, Zakayle' .... .47
Belleau, Peter .... .99
Benipal, Gurnoor .... .195
Benjamin, Abby .... .56
Bennett, Armanni .... .101
Bennett, Regan .... .138
Bennie, Miranda .... .60
Benoit, Brittany .... .71
Bergeron, Emily .... .105
Bernard, Elizabeth .... .33
Berryhill, Carolina .... .134
Betbeze, Caitlyn .... .51
Billeaudeau, Lindsey .... .151
Billeaudeaux, Katie .... .105
Billings, Jacob .... .24
Billot, Braden .... .59
Binganisi, Susie .... .75
Birbiglia, Anna .... .37
Birchmore, Anna .... .50
Bishop, Pate .... .186
Bissell, Samantha .... .61
Blackmon, Matt .... .100
Blacknall, Jasmine .... .188
Blankenship, Bailey .... .154
Blanton, Meghan .... .130
Bligen, Dejan .... .66
Blomquist, Rachel .... .82
Bolter, Isabella .... .127
Boniface, Gabby .... .172
Booth, Sarah .... .118
Boothe, Corey .... .48
Bordelon, Alex .... .173
Bordelon, D.J. .... .41
Bordelon, Megan .... .98
Borough, Bianca .... .84
Bougére, Katie .... .43
Bourdier, Aimee .... .91
Bourgeois, Christian .... .57
Bourgeois, Sarah .... .47
Bowen, Christine .... .72

Bowers, Emily .... .104
Boyanton, Megan .... .125
Boyd, Anna .... .93
Boyer, Jack .... .87
Boyles, LeAnn .... .85
Bradley, TreAnna .... .10
Bradshaw, Brittany .... .163
Bradshaw, Hayley .... .146
Brady, Dakota .... .127
Brady, Jordan .... .153
Brady, Suzanne .... .115
Bran, Ashley .... .104
Bratisax, Laura .... .168
Brenen, Raina .... .119
Bridges, Evan .... .40
Broaden, Doriann .... .89
Broden, Tichina .... .78
Brooks, Evie .... .57
Brooks, Monique .... .83
Brown, Allen .... .91
Brown, Brendon .... .128
Brown, Douglas .... .23
Brown, Matthew .... .93
Brown, McKayla .... .50
Brown, Morgan .... .26
Brown, Shaquita .... .179
Brown, Sierra .... .71
Brown, Tatiana .... .133
Bryant, Heath .... .84
Bryant, Jordan .... .163
Bryant, Kristen .... .120
Bryant, Macoya .... .172
Bryant, Mona'e .... .152
Bryer, Joyce .... .109
Bui, Thomas .... .120
Burgess, MK .... .59
Burin, Andrew .... .27
Burns, Phoebe .... .167
Burton, Maribeth .... .82
Busby, Danielle .... .192
Butera, Brandon .... .181
Butler, Donyelle .... .94
Buxton, Zion .... .120
Byrd, Anna .... .179
Byrd, Kymie .... .139
Caballero, Calah .... .165
Caffey, Leah .... .145
Caffey, Megan .... .106
Cahill, Rayna .... .11
Calender, Ar'nekki .... .29
Callihan, Sean .... .80

Camel, Carey 21	Collins, Abigail 103	Dean, Phoenix 169
Cameron, Taylor 95	Collins, Courtney 189	Deckelmann, Laura 183
Campbell, Heather V. 64	Collins, Justin 168	Declouette, Ashley 25
Campbell, Kacy 112	Collis, Brittany 149	Deer, Jenna 114
Campbell, Kayla 170	Colon, Alysha 143	DeJesus, Natalie 109
Campbell, Taliyah 148	Compton, Breyia 73	Delmestri, Emily 196
Campoli, Brian 127	Conn, Caitlin 152	Delph, Maisha 59
Canada, Emily 168	Cook, Aquira 100	Dempsey, Brittany 55
Cancilla, John Price 171	Cook, Brittany 194	Denny, Stephanie 40
Capritto, Amanda 144	Cook, Sydney 132	deVeer, Nick 79
Caraveo, Marcela 176	Cooley, Kelsey 197	Dezern, Jordan 103
Caraway, Miranda 164	Cooper, Julianne 90	Dhanani, Danish 113
Carollo, Justin 170	Copeland, Ashley 187	Dickens, Kaitlyn 60
Carpenter, Sarah 178	Costley, Akasia 82	Diffey, John Marshall 129
Carr, Jessica L. 187	Courtney, Emily 55	Dillard, Jaylaan 181
Carr, Keianna 193	Covington, Brittanie 123	Dillard, Lauren 131
Carriere, Kyle 187	Cox, Carlie 115	Dillard, Madison 85
Carriere, Marcretia 193	Cox, Courtney 161	Dills, Andrew 190
Carter, Ashley 74	Cozart, Mackenzie 101	Disotell, Kelly 84
Carter, Shakia 61	Craft, LeAnté 114	Dittman, Mikayla 88
Casey, Destin 81	Crawford, Danesha 124	Doddridge, Christopher 106
Cason, Brody 154	Credeur, Katy 135	Dodson, Heather 88
Castello, Kayla 124	Crocker, Kathleen 78	Dokken, Emily 77
Castillo, Diego 59	Cromer, Cheyenne 108	Dolniak, Carly 77
Castro, Phoebe 85	Crumpler, April 92	Domzalski, Elizabeth 157
Celaya, Osmar 65	Cruz, Kenia L. 136	Donatto, Logan 156
Cervantes, Walter 67	Curry, Marissa 26	Dong, Brittany 23
Chalk, Cody 134	Cushman, Adam 162	Donohue, Connor 44
Chanson, Erling 90	Cutler, Emily 164	Dorsey, Kristi 52
Chappel, Lydia 140	Cutter, Andre 185	Duckworth, Destinie 126
Charles, Wendy 169	Dabhi, Krupa 77	Dudley, Euneeka 197
Chastain, Austin 162	Dadgar, Sorena 57	Dugas, Hanna 79
Chastain, Kristina 100	Daley, Essence 195	Dugger, Rebecca 54
Chastain, Morgan 79	Dalfrey, Taylor 51	Duncan, Justin Scott 111
Chastang, Braxton 167	Damico, Elaine 159	Dunham, Bradlie 38
Chawla, Sameer 80	Damron, Joseph 28	Duong, Tunhi 68
Chegue, Alejandra 198	Dance, Jamaal 82	Dupree, Jade 188
Cherry, Angela 113	Daney, Aliayah 118	Dyer, Jimmy 104
Chinchilla, Irene 163	Daniels, Cole 194	Dykes, Sherika 38
Chowdhury, Alisha 129	Dantzler, Darian 135	Eanes, Taylor 137
Christian, Gabriela 137	Dao, Truc My 174	Early, D'shon 84
Church, John 141	Darbonne, Dorie 163	Easterlin, Kylie 130
Church, Michael Dean 177	Darby, April 141	Eccles, Michael 172
Ciepierski, Alexa 156	Darby, Jenna 32	Edwards, Akeena 96
Clack, Rodney 143	Davis, Blaine 49	Edwards, Kasey 40
Clarida, Doug 53	Davis, Christopher 162	Egerton, Jhone 71
Clark, Zack 74	Davis, Fabeian 152	Eichman, Bailey 129
Coats, Brittan 20	Davis, Gabby 110	Eicke, Melany 177
Cobb, Brittany 84	Davis, Hannah 41	Eiserloh, Malerie 51
Coffman, Keith 91	Davis, Jia 'Vante 174	Elliott, Ethan 117
Coggins, Madyson 90	Davis, Makia 45	Elliott, Jessica 191
Coker, Macie 145	Davis, Marcus 124	Elsea, Ginger 24
Coleman, Ashunti 186	Davis, Trayvond 142	Emmons, Faith 185
Coleman, Crimson 95	Davis, Y'Nicha 58	Endress, Ashley 98
Coleman, John 54	Dazzio, Anna Katherine 122	Eriksson, Camilla 182
Coley, Taylor 162	de Give, Mark 171	Ernst, Katie 21
Collier, Nathan 33	de Pedro, Ana 53	Estrada, Cody Ian 66

Index

Evans, Brittani 185	Gallegos, Flavia 155	Grimmett, Chase 85
Evans, Erika 89	Gallon, Blair 190	Grindle, Whitley 114
Evans, Martwan 92	Galloway, Fame 99	Gripper, Tevin 159
Evans, Sha'Myia 30	Garcia, Rafael 85	Guerra, Cristina 50
Fagan, Brieun 123	Gardin, CJ 86	Guidroz, Shelbie 56
Falgoust, Julia 184	Garland, Hannah 157	Guigou, Alyssa 164
Fallaw, Dylan 150	Garrett, Whitney 105	Guilbeaux, Kylen 197
Farrar, Sarah 61	Gates, Derrione 144	Guillory, Dustin 129
Farrell, Calli 183	Gaudin, Kendall 168	Gunter, R. Mitchell 176
Favrot, Susan 73	Gault, Johnathan 146	Guo, Matthew 49
Feldman, Rachel 38	Gauthier, Morgan 104	Gurney, Erin 88
Fentiman, Mary 93	Gavigan, Bobbie Jean 137	Gurtner, Emily 119
Ferguson, Matt 31	Gayle, Chekara 191	Gutierrez, Daisy 138
Ferguson, Taylor 104	Gebhardt, Alyssa 167	Haas, Gage 121
Ferrell, September 122	Georgiou, Chrysoula 33	Haines, Jennifer 157
Ferriss, Nicole 113	Giardina, Ryley 42	Hall, Brailey 82
Fikse, Alayna 38	Gibbons, Gabby 103	Hall, Emily 194
Finley, Mikie 65	Gibbs, Zach 153	Hall, Sade 29
Fisher, Matt 179	Gibson, Haven 83	Hall, Sydnei 88
Fitch, Forrest 38	Gibson, Hayley 152	Halperin, Lauren 173
Fogarty, Lauren 136	Gibson, Ian 63	Hamack, Bridgette 120
Fontenot, Amanda 186	Giddens, Alex 76	Hameed, Shilan 182
Fontenot, Kristy 111	Gilbertson, Stephanie 60	Hamilton, Clay 173
Fontenot, Madison 114	Gill, Danielle 21	Hamilton, Matthew 187
Ford, Alexis 53	Gill, Mallory K. 103	Hammond, Tyler 137
Ford, Daniel 186	Gilleo, Caleb 50	Hampton, Patrick 136
Forest, Katelyn 29	Gilley, Amberlyne 119	Handy, Raven 130
Forgione, Kaitlyn 179	Gilliland, Amber 95	Hanna, Ashley 140
Forrister, Victoria 118	Gilreath, Ander 79	Harjo, Derick 143
Fortenberry, Stacy 81	Gingerich, Bethany 114	Harless, Garrett 107
Fortier, Paul 35	Giraldo, Paul 64	Harrell, Parker 170
Foster, Caleb 170	Gladwell, Kaitlyn 108	Harrell, Samantha 47
Foster, Daniel 30	Godbout, Jacob 183	Harris, Erika 132
Foster, Tashia 24	Goins, Brandi 68	Harris, Jamari 185
Fox, LaKeytra 181	Gomes, Emily 122	Harris, Jessica 117
Fox, Leah Marie 74	Gonzalez, Natalia 116	Harris, Keon 98
Francis, Courtney 21	Goodly, Christian 166	Harris, Sharlaina 58
Francis, Kheila 161	Goodly, Cullin 91	Harris, Symphonia 179
Frank, Riley 160	Goodman, Moriah Rae 136	Harrison, Ashanti 174
Franke, Jade 56	Gopal, Akshay 101	Harrison, Shernell 97
Frederick, Kaisy 32	Gopal, Meghna 183	Hart, Thomas 109
Fredricks, Rachel 33	Graham, Chris 151	Harvey, Courtney 197
Freeman, Jenna 192	Gramke, Margaret 36	Hayes, Coriana 138
Freese, Robert 184	Grant, Kamau A. 80	Haymore, Damesha 22
Frei, Aneicia 44	Grant, Murphy 171	Haywood, Deja 132
Freund, Daniel 66	Grantland, Leanna 194	Hearn, Logan 136
Froelich, Emily 125	Gray, LeAndra 156	Hedrick, Alex 112
Frye, Jared 135	Gray, M'Kenya 75	Helton, Makaela 172
Fryson, Terrance 50	Greczynski, Kasté 181	Henderson, Jessica 96
Fuller, Chance 58	Green, Deidre 178	Hendricks, Milana 156
Fuller, Jarvaris 48	Green, Emily 73	Hendrix, Teyairra 34
Furman, Diamond 31	Green, JJ 105	Herring, Laura 48
Fuselier, Stephen 25	Greenlief, Briana 37	Hill, Azia .54
Gaddis, Christina 144	Griffin, Alix 133	Hill, Brittany 103
Gaitan Diaz, Francisco 194	Griffin, Brandi Renee 92	Hill, Taylor 136
Gallagher, Conner 116	Griffin, Katrina 186	Hilton, Kaylee 41
Gallagher, Molly 147	Griggs, Mackenzie 176	Hindi, Doha 66

Hinds, Andrew 157	Jennings, Zachary DeShawn 96	Laethem, Maddie 53
Hines, Anna 160	Jobe, Austin 63	Lafleur, Brennan 170
Hines, Tori 166	Johns, Abby 145	LaFrance, Ashley 54
Hingle, Norwood 191	Johnson, Amelia-Kate 43	Lake, Jimmy 184
Hlebak, Nicole 106	Johnson, Andrew 163	LaLonde, Michael 161
Hollier, Brandon 59	Johnson, Dalaina 135	Lambert, Lisa 170
Hollingsworth, Lori 121	Johnson, Dalvin 58	Lambert, Tori 124
Hollingsworth, Madeline 157	Johnson, Jazzmyne 111	Lambert, Virginia 122
Holloway, Dannica 131	Johnson, Shawn 27	Lanclos, Destiny 42
Holloway, Kaila 98	Johnson, Stevon 22	Lanclos, Megan 128
Holm, Dustin 32	Johnson, Tyler 54	Landry, Gabrielle 122
Holmes, Hailey 53	Johnson, Zachary 26	Landry, Jacqueline 101
Holt, Travis 95	Jones, Arronice 111	Landry, Leslie 76
Honer, Hanna 147	Jones, Eddie 167	Langford, Brooke 186
Hooks, Chuck 76	Jones, Emily 132	Lapat, Laarni 83
Horne, Hykeen 64	Jones, Nia 187	Lasley, Joshua 94
Horton, Danielle 24	Jones, Salathiel 113	Latiolais, Shane 38
Hotard, Hannah 74	Jones, Sam 183	Lawrence, DeAnte 119
Hotard, Monica 66	Jones, Sekiyah 91	Lazare, Meleigha 80
Hotfelter, Ashley 110	Joseph, Chailin 86	Le, Eric 193
Houston, Courtney 176	Joudeh, Manar 90	Leach, Carley 141
Howard, Rachael 96	Kahle, Rachel 190	Leamy, Emily Merrin 140
Howard, Sherrece 76	Katz, Shelby 58	LeBlanc, Jordan 66
Hrubala, Ashley 170	Kearney, Kenneth 74	Ledbetter, Kayla 43
Hudson, Aaron 192	Kelly, Kendle 149	Lee, Anthony 160
Huffman, Kristin 148	Kendall, Shelby 23	Lee, JaJuan 67
Huffman, Zeke 25	Kendrick, Danielle 175	Leger, Derek 69
Hulsey, Anthony 35	Kennedy, Ashley-Olivia 48	Leger, Tristan 64
Hunnicutt, Laurin 60	Kennedy, Jennifer 71	Lehman, Katherine 12
Hunt, Shirlecia 172	Ker, Justine 145	Leistman, Lauren 45
Hunter, Kaitlyn 26	Kesler, Libby 74	LeMaire, Phillip 102
Hutchinson, Christopher 84	Khan, Shaheryar 55	LeMaster, Blake 101
Hutchison, Aba 81	Killgore, Christen 147	Lepak, Luke 194
Impastato, Chris 42	King, Ashley 54	Lester, Jeremy 126
Ingram, Gabriel 181	King, Bailey 62	Lester, Tiffany 70
Ingram, Kenya 40	King, Joseph 72	Levier, LaShonta 172
Ingram, Stephanie 28	King, Sarah 141	Lewis, Carol 82
Irby, Casey 179	King, Zachary 39	Lewis, Tasha 162
Isbell, Amber 26	Kirn, Jeb 127	Li, Joyce .67
Israel, Zachary 129	Klein, Matthew 182	Lichte, Austin 149
Ixcot, Johnny 196	Kline, Alex 191	Lista, Abigayle 53
Jackson, Femaria 24	Klingenberg, Anna 83	Little, Valerie 169
Jackson, Hailey 158	Klumpp, Walter 109	Lloyd, Caleb 122
Jackson, JeBresha 48	Knepper, Daniel 97	Lockett, Brandi 26
Jackson, Khilar 125	Knieper, Caleb 46	Lopez, John 168
Jackson, Lyman 85	Knox, Robert 68	Lorance, Dustin 44
Jacob, Daniel 102	Kober, Marc 56	Lowe, Brittany 196
Jacobs, Chasity 81	Koehler, Emily 89	Lund, Gretchen 100
James, Lauren 76	Kolman, Jordin 147	Lund, Hannah 113
James, Terrence 97	Konsouh, Khadiga 47	Lunstead, Jordan 119
Jamison, Shanquea 108	Koochekpour, Molly 83	Luscy, Conner 93
Jarrett, Jennifer 176	Kopti, Catherine 26	Luttrell, Eric 92
Jefferson, DeQuadrick 90	Kornick, Lindsay 146	Lux, Alexx 33
Jefferson, Jade 74	Kozee, Barbara Anne 70	MacDougall, Ben 160
Jefferson, Myleka 20	Kozmenko, Valeriya 160	Maddie, Antonio 97
Jefferson, Shawki 175	Krueger, Rebecca 158	Madho, Nirvana 90
Jeganathan, Gavin 86	Lackey, Kori 52	Magri, C. Stephanie 143

Index

Maiga, Drissa 76	Melton, Evan 33	Navarro, Hialeah 136
Mallian, Mitch 176	Melvin, Sterlin 154	Neal, Ashley 123
Maloney, Scott 80	Mercer, Laycee 132	Nelson, Matthew 69
Maltba, Anyssa 114	Merritt, Lindsay 41	Nelson, Michael 142
Manale, Blake 159	Messina, L. Brennan 137	Nesiba, Annamarie 184
Manning, Courtney 26	Meyers, Kathryn 130	Newberry, Kendall 154
Marcangeli, Amber 63	Miles, Erika 192	Nezat, Taylor 131
Marie-Smith, Tesia 34	Milks, Cameron 102	Nguyen, Andrew 178
Marietti, Cody 144	Miller, Hayley 175	Nguyen, Anthony 87
Markbreiter, Brandon 31	Miller, Krysten 161	Nguyen, Cam Linh 194
Marks, Brittany 177	Miller, Marquis 73	Nguyen, Sophie 131
Marks, Natalie 58	Miller, Paige 25	Nicholson, Jyi 182
Marlowe, Ethan 176	Milowic, Sarah 100	Niedrich, Nicole 107
Martin, Ciara 171	Milowic, Tim 162	Noblet, Elisabeth 127
Martin, Dallas 194	Mir, Haider 163	Noel Jr., Chad 172
Martinez, Emily 189	Mise, Jaymi 44	Nolen, Jack 188
Martinez, Kemberly 195	Mistrot, Seth 50	O'Donnell, Ashleigh 75
Martinez, Sadie 35	Mitchell, Asher 20	O'Neal, Chase 154
Massey, Raven 34	Mitchell, Ashleigh 91	Obregon, Yazmin 117
Matassino, Kara 131	Mitchell, Devin 140	Olwine, Maria 67
Mathews, Christina 82	Mitchell, Heather 64	Ortego, Addison 99
Mathus, Nichole 128	Mitchell, Jared 123	Osborn, Narisa 39
Matsey, Carol 69	Mitchell, Ronald Paul 143	Ott, Madison 78
Matutina, Nicko 20	Mobley, Imani 46	Otwell, Rebecca 125
Mauldin, Kristen 54	Moffett, Kendall 27	Owen, Collin 82
Maull, Cody 162	Mohr, George Robert 125	Pacheco, Stephanie 15
Maxson, Taylor 102	Monazah, Daniel 123	Pack, Chalice 128
Maxwell, Graham 42	Moncrief, Hannah 102	Pagan, Elisabeth 130
Mayberry, Katelyn 94	Monk, Eric 124	Panetta, Matthew 166
Maynard, Jessica 43	Montgomery, Jailyn 112	Panzanella, Megan 153
Mayon, Jasmine 175	Moody, Kendrick 174	Papillion, Mary 173
McAlister, Matt 184	Moon, Elysia 103	Pardue, Harley 23
McAlpine, Grayson 31	Moore, Ashley 34	Park, Rosa 43
McCabe, Stephanie 142	Moore, Cameron 69	Parker, Mary 80
McCarley, Cailin 150	Moore, Jalil 78	Paul, Kayra 116
McClendon, Kardarius 74	Moore, Megan 194	Pavelka, Meghan 50
McCormick, Amber 114	Moraes, Anthony 60	Payne, Harrison 193
McCormick, Tyler 191	Moran, Ian 130	Paynter, Cristina 30
McCoy, Taylor 124	Morgan, Courtney 76	Peake, Dorgan 159
McDonald, Haley 154	Morgan, Kasey 60	Pearson, Zamion 77
McElhenney, Dylan 23	Morgan, Maribeth 49	Peddicord, Dane 165
McGaha, Paul 77	Morise, Cecelia 104	Pedroza, Marta 81
McKinney, Dallas 104	Morley, Samantha 35	Pehling, Melissa 122
McKinney, Madison 107	Morris, Jackson 146	Pendleton, Benjamin 146
McKinney, Shelby 184	Morrison, Kendall 120	Perez, Ali 65
McLean, Michael 96	Morrison, William 164	Perry, Myron 165
McMicken, Sawyer 52	Motosko, Patrick 142	Peterman, Ashley 156
McNair, Justin 89	Mouton, Kristen 167	Petersen, Morgan 55
McNitt, Meara 195	Moyles, Hannah 162	Peterson, Abbey 87
McNutt, Christopher 13	Mullins, Madison 180	Pettit, Elizabeth 174
McNutt, Cody 155	Munson, Megan 136	Petty, Kayla 30
McZeal, Raven Nycole 101	Myers, Jazmin 186	Phetsynorraj, Bobby 102
Meche, Andy 197	Myers, Katie 133	Piacun, Maria 47
Meganck, Rita 146	Myers, Phillip 37	Pierre-Louis, Falisha 107
Meinert, Allison 14	Nakincheng, Kaitlin 145	Piersanti, Emilee 130
Melancon, Meagan 91	Narcisse, Darius 55	Pinkney, Naomi 162
Melancon, Melanie 34	Narcisse, Lyric 150	Pittman, Ashantia 129

Pittman, Austin 93	Rowley, Karlie 98	Smith, Daniel 135
Plato, Haley 40	Royal, Dustin 130	Smith, Desirae 161
Poché, Travis 154	Royal, Faye L. 63	Smith, Devin 44
Polito, Matthew 178	Rucker, Michelle 128	Smith, Jessica 159
Pollard, Joseph 150	Russotto, Adam 138	Smith, Katelyn 24
Ponce, Kimberly 137	Ryan, Kyle 165	Smith, Kirra 99
Porras, Marie 149	Sachwani, Numera 177	Smith, Krystal 161
Portner, Michael 158	Saladino, Christie 27	Smith, Lakisha 196
Potter, Candace 34	Salas, Tony 117	Smith, Ra'Lisa 42
Power, Kate 155	Salazar, Alexia 35	Smith, Tyler 193
Prentice, Hayden 136	Sanders, Mariah 153	Smith, Zach 108
Primes, Betsy 56	Sanford, Anna Caroline 151	Smith-Brown, Brendan 42
Prioleau, Mikayla 118	Sanford, Jay 72	Snavely, Michaela 119
Pruitt, Aynsley 45	Sanner, DeLashay 126	Soe, Mabel 135
Puri, Pranati 46	Satterfield, Alex 61	Solomon, Sharice 36
Quern, Kelly 115	Saunee, Jacquelyn 115	Sondgeroth, Vika 169
Quiel, Samantha 73	Savoy, Kaylin 170	Soutendijk, Dustin 194
Raleigh, Mikayla 89	Saxon, Christian 176	Spann, Courtney 87
Ramey, Lindsey 24	Schafer, Cayla 155	Spedale, Christopher 50
Ramirez, Ashley 130	Schenck, Joseph 108	Speegle, Lauren 57
Ray, Cassidy 74	Schexnayder, Lindsey 74	Speyrer, Kaleb 181
Ray, Dylan 183	Schmidt, Sonya 21	Spivey, Carson 68
Ray, Jessie 30	Schmitt, Thomas 116	Spohn, Richard 115
Reddaway, Michael 67	Schmitz, Jonathan 78	Spry, Bre 122
Reddoch, Grant 159	Schneider, Emilie 110	Staffieri, Anthony 160
Reed, Cheyenne 69	Schneider, Jillian 162	Stamey, Alicia 36
Reed, Jason 45	Schrieffer, Stewart 71	Stanford, Ansli 96
Reeder, Logan 184	Schroeder, Ethan 185	Stanford, Morgan 198
Reviere, Zoie 27	Schultz, Josh 154	Starks, Angel 177
Reynolds, Jonae 151	Schultz, Matt 180	Stelly, April 105
Reynolds, Megan 191	Scott, Carlos 31	Stelly, Laura 140
Rhodes, Kacey 20	Scurria, Alyssa 139	Stelly, Megan 37
Richard, Sterling 154	Scutt, Colleen 39	Stevens, Jaymarlon 120
Rick, Hunter 116	Seager, Katrina 158	Stevens IV, Lehrue 101
Rieger, Justina 29	Searcy, Briana 117	Stewart, Kierra 63
Riley, Nick 130	Seech, Hunter 185	Stone, Kaitlyn 72
Ritchie, Ben 188	Seelinger, Patrick 111	Storey, Kayleigh 188
Ritter, Jeremy 64	Segars, Destiny 176	Stout, Carole 52
Rizzo, Alexis 138	Shaikh, Yassara 88	Stuteville, Anna 82
Robert, Kolin 122	Sharp, Layla 34	Suber, Asia 127
Roberts, Tamarra 20	Sheehy, Trevor 96	Sumrall, Dillon 104
Robin, Emily 112	Shetley, Brandon 86	Sweeney, Grady 180
Robles, Megan 45	Shockey, Hannah 170	Tahir, Hiba 139
Rockhold, Kristin 152	Sigler, Emily 144	Tanas, Jacob 40
Roditti, Niccolo 49	Sikorski, Michael 147	Tanghal, Daniel 75
Rodriguez, Olivia 132	Simon, Lariel 125	Tanis, Alaina B. 169
Roe, Gabrielle 49	Sims, Ethan 141	Tankersley, Kaylan 87
Rogers, Caitlin 52	Sinha, Akanksha 87	Tankersley, Robert Austin 89
Rogers, Hunter 107	Sizemore, Josh 42	Taylor, Brittney 68
Rojas, Ali 152	Skeen, McKinnon 52	Taylor, Janay 48
Ross, Kelly 92	Skinner, Jordan 131	Taylor, Kyle 69
Ross, Miranda 116	Slaten, Michael 173	Taylor, Nikki 39
Ross, Morgan 109	Slimming, Jonathan 25	Tellez, Maria 16
Roussel, Eric 164	Smith, Adam 82	Terry, Cody 148
Roussell, Renata 59	Smith, Amber 68	Thacker, Diedra 40
Rowe, Brandon 170	Smith, Arman 79	Thao, Barbara 74
Rowe, Somer 65	Smith, Bobbie Jo 61	Theriot, Chase 178

Index

Thibodeaux, Tevin 75
Thomas, Kristy 152
Thomassee, Lane 82
Thompson, Dylan 54
Thompson, Jovon Denzel 88
Thompson, Stephanie 198
Thornton, Josette 28
Thorpe, Benji 176
Thorpe, Grace 42
Ticossi, Thomas 164
Tilque, Nathaniel 128
Titus, PiaMonae 93
Tolbert, Angel 151
Tolliver, Kenry 148
Tomala, Gabriel 180
Torbert, Zontavious 33
Touchet, Tabby 37
Towler, Cody 56
Trahan, Chris 42
Trahan, Donald 170
Trammell, Conley 62
Tran, Billy 154
Tran, Linh 165
Tran, Sophia 111
Travers, Sydney 139
Tripp, Krissy 174
Trippi, Kailei 126
Troutman, Stacy 78
Trulin, Devin 117
Tucker, McKenna 86
Tujague, Amanda 45
Tumbleson, Montiah 36
Tune, Destiny 87
Turberville, Joey 132
Turner, Amber 189
Underwood, Heather 17
Upton, Rachel 62
Uribe, Alejandro 81
Urrea, Carisa 34
Valino, Mariel 138
Van Norden, Charly 90
Vang, Ellen 121
Varden, Dana 134
Vazquez, Cecilia 34
Veillon, Mason 128
Velani, Zeshan 51
Velosa, Andrea 195
Villacis, Natalie 118
Vogel, Ross 23
Vohringer, Amanda 143
Vorisek, Rebecca 175
Wade, Charlotte 155
Wadley, Wesley 196
Wadsworth, Shianne 121
Wagoner, Essence 148
Wagoner, Jessica 65
Waguespack, Taylor 55
Waked, Nicholas 170
Walker, Brooke 88
Walker, Elizabeth 31
Walker, Jesse 104
Walker, Lindsy 47
Walker, Niiya 168
Walker, Quinn 57
Walker, Victoria 27
Wallace, Carrie Beth 162
Walleser, Karli 36
Walls, Summer 104
Walton, DeAnna 175
Ward, Alex 95
Ward, Cody 139
Ward, Heather 42
Ward, Tyrielle 122
Warner, Ji'Savorya 29
Washington, DaKayla 132
Washington, Jacquaniese 98
Watson, Auston 28
Watson, Christa 151
Watts, Zachary 121
Weatherly, Erin 196
Weaver, Brenna 18
Weaver, Bryant 146
Wehle, Emily 189
Welch, James 187
Wellington, Savannah 104
Wells, Heather 83
Wells, Patterson 39
Werner, Julianna 149
West, Austin 32
West, Michelle 186
Westra, Ben 39
Wheaton, Adrienne 178
Whichard, Dontè 83
White, Casey 158
White, Claire 165
White, Evan 57
White, Jessica 46
White, Michelle 173
Whitley, Colby 133
Whitt, Kirsten 22
Whittaker, Chassidy Cherie 70
Whitworth, Zachary 26
Wicke, Devin Denison 97
Widas, Jordan 109
Wiggins, Nebraska 97
Wildman, Kaitlyn 145
Wilkerson, Brittney 41
Wilkerson, Chance 36
Williams, Alexis 141
Williams, Annchester 74
Williams, Austin 99
Williams, Bailey 113
Williams, Benjamin 114
Williams, Emily 75
Williams, Katie 44
Williams, Kimberly 193
Williamson, Amelia 72
Willis, Ellen 99
Wilson, Kathleen 50
Winbush, Annette 156
Winkles, Prestin 63
Womack, Rachel 66
Woods, Elijah 32
Woods, Katie 168
Wootten, Sarah 110
Wray, Jessica 37
Wray, Thomas 21
Wright, JeVonda 112
Wright, Jordi 41
Wright, Thomas 106
Wyble, Mallory 66
Xaikhamharn, Xayasith 123
Yang, Christopher 41
Yarde, Tattianna 73
Yestrumsky, Justin 19
Yi, Yan Yao 42
Young, Justin 108
Zendan, Gabrielle 29
Zheng, Caroline 192

Author Autograph Page

Author Autograph Page